THE CAMBRIDGE COMPANION TO
SENECA

The Roman statesman, philosopher, and playwright Lucius Annaeus Seneca dramatically influenced the progression of Western thought. His works have had an unparalleled impact on the development of ethical theory, shaping a code of behavior for dealing with tyranny in his own age that endures today. This companion thoroughly examines the complete Senecan corpus, with special emphasis on the aspects of his writings that have challenged interpretation. The authors place Seneca in the context of the ancient world and trace his impressive legacy in literature, art, religion, and politics from Neronian Rome to the early modern period. Through critical discussion of the recent proliferation of Senecan studies, this volume compellingly illustrates how the perception of Seneca and his particular type of Stoicism has evolved over time. It provides a comprehensive overview that will benefit students and scholars in classics, comparative literature, history, philosophy, and political theory, as well as general readers.

Shadi Bartsch is Helen A. Regenstein Distinguished Service Professor of Classics at the University of Chicago. She is the author of *Decoding the Ancient Novel: The Reader and the Role of Description in Heliodorus and Achilles Tatius* (1989); *Actors in the Audience: Theatricality and Doublespeak from Nero to Hadrian* (1994); *Ideology in Cold Blood: A Reading of Lucan's Civil War* (1998); *The Mirror of the Self: Sexuality, Self-Knowledge, and the Gaze in the Early Roman Empire* (2006); and *Persius: A Study in Food, Philosophy, and the Figural* (2015).

Alessandro Schiesaro is Professor of Latin Literature and Director of the School for Advanced Studies at Sapienza University of Rome. He is the author of *Simulacrum et Imago. Gli argomenti analogici nel De rerum natura* (1990) and *The Passions in Play: Thyestes and the Dynamics of Senecan Drama* (2003) and the coeditor, with Jenny Strauss Clay and Philip Mitsis, of *Mega Nepios: The Addressee in Didactic Epic* (1993) and, with Thomas Habinek, of *The Roman Cultural Revolution* (1997).

A complete list of books in the series is at the back of this book.

D1520919

THE CAMBRIDGE
COMPANION TO
SENECA

EDITED BY

SHADI BARTSCH
University of Chicago

ALESSANDRO SCHIESARO
Sapienza University of Rome

CAMBRIDGE
UNIVERSITY PRESS

CAMBRIDGE
UNIVERSITY PRESS

32 Avenue of the Americas, New York, NY 10013-2473, USA

Cambridge University Press is part of the University of Cambridge.

It furthers the University's mission by disseminating knowledge in the pursuit of education, learning, and research at the highest international levels of excellence.

www.cambridge.org
Information on this title: www.cambridge.org/9781107694217

© Cambridge University Press 2015

First published 2015

Printed in Great Britain by Clays Ltd, St Ives plc

A catalog record for this publication is available from the British Library.

Library of Congress Cataloging in Publication Data
The Cambridge companion to Seneca / edited by Shadi Bartsch, University of Chicago; Alessandro Schiesaro, Sapienza University of Rome.
pages   cm. – (Cambridge companions to literature)
Includes bibliographical references and index.
ISBN 978-1-107-03505-8 (hardback) – ISBN 978-1-107-69421-7 (paperback)
1. Seneca, Lucius Annaeus, approximately 4 B.C.–65 A.D. – History and criticism – Handbooks, manuals, etc.   I. Bartsch, Shadi, 1966– editor.
II. Schiesaro, Alessandro, 1963– editor.
PA6675.C36   2015
188–dc23   2014033239

ISBN 978-1-107-03505-8 Hardback
ISBN 978-1-107-69421-7 Paperback

CONTENTS

CONTENTS

CONTENTS

CONTRIBUTORS

MIREILLE ARMISEN-MARCHETTI, University of Toulouse-Mirail

ELIZABETH ASMIS, University of Chicago

SHADI BARTSCH, University of Chicago

FRANCESCA ROMANA BERNO, Sapienza University of Rome

SUSANNA BRAUND, University of British Columbia

FRANCESCO CITTI, University of Bologna

CATHARINE EDWARDS, Birkbeck, University of London

KIRK FREUDENBURG, Yale University

JAMES KER, University of Pennsylvania

DAVID KONSTAN, New York University

CEDRIC A. J. LITTLEWOOD, University of Victoria

ROLAND MAYER, King's College London

VICTORIA RIMELL, Sapienza University of Rome

MATTHEW ROLLER, Johns Hopkins University

ALESSANDRO SCHIESARO, Sapienza University of Rome

MALCOLM SCHOFIELD, University of Cambridge

CONTRIBUTORS

CAREY SEAL, University of California, Davis

ALDO SETAIOLI, University of Perugia

PETER STACEY, University of California, Los Angeles

CHIARA TORRE, State University of Milan

CHRISTOPHER TRINACTY, Oberlin College

GARETH WILLIAMS, Columbia University

DAVID WRAY, University of Chicago

SHADI BARTSCH AND ALESSANDRO SCHIESARO

Seneca: An Introduction

As an object of study, Seneca puzzles. No other philosopher has presented us with so stark a challenge to resolve a life lived under dubious moral conditions with the legacy of his surviving writings. In Seneca's case, of course, the difficulty is heightened by the ethical and didactic content of his Stoic essays and letters, which offer guidance precisely on how to live life both happily and morally and which even in Seneca's time seem to have raised some eyebrows among his peers. Even if we accept Seneca's stance on the philosophical irrelevance of his great wealth and the inevitably of weakness in a mere *proficiens* in Stoicism, there will never be a satisfactory answer to the old question of whether Seneca did more good than harm in taking on the role of tutor to the young Nero Claudius Caesar Augustus Germanicus – and that of his political advisor when Nero became emperor in 54 CE. Even the question of whether Seneca himself was consistently for or against political participation in such a regime is complicated by conflicting evidence. But if Seneca helped his fellow elite or even the people of Rome by exerting some restraining influence on the flamboyant emperor's acts and policies (as, for example, Tacitus would have us believe), in hindsight it seems to have been his own legacy for which he did no favors, tainting his *nachleben* with the smear of hypocrisy and leading later readers to concoct multiple Senecas to explain the range of his life and work. As such, he provides a noteworthy contrast to other, less fraught exemplars of Roman Stoic thought. Seneca's contemporaries C. Musonius Rufus and L. Annaeus Cornutus left behind little in writing; the political figures Helvidius Priscus and Thrasea Paetus come to us only through their unambiguous actions in the pages of history; the ex-slave Epictetus and the emperor Marcus Aurelius, both of whom wrote in Greek, either present less conflicted personae or never had the power to act hypocritically in the first place.

Fortunately for both Seneca and us, modern scholars have been more tolerant than his own peers in passing judgment on his wealth or his embroilment in the Neronian court. The result is surprisingly rewarding.

For one, as the essays in this volume illustrate, Seneca's corpus provides a rich point of entry into an impressively large collection of philosophical, political, psychological, and cultural conversations taking place in the first century CE – and beyond. After centuries in which his fortunes waxed and waned (on which see Part IV of this volume), Seneca's writings, both his prose and his dramas, have finally been recognized as complex and valuable works in their own right, texts that provide testimonia to Roman Stoic practice in the early empire, to Seneca's modifications of Hellenistic philosophy, and to contemporary cultural and literary concerns a far cry from those of the Athenian tragedians. What this volume ends up illustrating – perhaps despite its "companionesque" brief – is that Seneca is not who we once thought he was. He may be a Stoic, but he modifies Stoicism beyond its received Hellenistic form (see the essays of Konstan, Wray, Seal, and Asmis). He may be Nero's crony, but he is well aware that future generations will value signs of his independence, not his servility (Bartsch). He may be a master rhetorician (so talented, Tacitus says, that Caligula tried to kill him out of jealousy, and Nero had him write a speech exculpating matricide), but in his movement towards dialogic exchange, he at least partly models the practice of philosophical conversation (Edwards, Roller, this volume). Himself inevitably a performer, he appropriates the pervasive theatricality of the Neronian regime to suggest it can impact self-fashioning as well as provide a means of resistance to power (Littlewood, this volume) – as we might expect of a writer who suggests that "style is the man" (Williams, this volume).

Fellow Spaniard Quintilian branded Seneca the maverick voice of his generation, yet we are tempted to say that since the first century, Senecan "contemporariness," with its bias towards self-transformation, hybridity, and experimental poetics, has never been more in vogue. His philosophical works, in particular, written in vivid, epigrammatic Latin and dealing with timeless issues of the human condition, have enjoyed renewed appeal in recent decades as ancient forerunners of the ubiquitous self-help genre: anthologies of the dialogues are still bestsellers in Italy, under titles that promise guidance on the quandaries of the human condition. Our modern fixation on the miracle of celebrity self-branding and reinvention and our conceptualization of a self constituted by its internal conflicts or contradictions have framed new investigations into Seneca's career, ever in metamorphosis, and the understanding of what it is to be a person. Senecan metatheater, the self-consciousness of his tragic protagonists, and his own self-satirizing, self-policing eye often seem inseparable to us now from the experience of the postmodern, although Seneca himself would urge us to take a good, hard look in his many virtual mirrors and examine such an assumption. One upshot of (falsely or not) spying ourselves in the looking glass of Seneca's texts has been the relatively recent resurrection of the tragedies as emotionally and intellectually demanding dramas; their new (or renewed) representability is thanks in part to a cultural and intellectual climate that no longer perceives their quasi-Cubist choppiness, manipulation of linear time, and visceral violence as flaws that limit serious engagement. As this volume documents, evaluations of the literary, political, and philosophical texture of the plays have undergone a major overhaul: scholars have opened our eyes to the juxtaposition or intercontamination of multiple genres and registers that make these texts so vital and dialogic, as well as to the interconnectedness between Senecan tragedy and philosophy, which cannot easily be reduced to a series of flat contrasts or one-way critiques.

Similarly, recent focus on reexamining the question of how Senecan texts interrelate has also begun to alert us to the ways in which tragedy, pantomime, satire, and epic and elegiac poetry – together with their differing cultural perspectives and ontologies – are woven into philosophical works such as the *Epistles to Lucilius*. Several contributors (Freudenburg, Rimell, Ker, Schiesaro, Williams) also discuss the specific Senecan strategy of citation, whereby snippets of earlier texts are imported verbatim into the present – a feature and performance of Seneca's celebrated, razor-sharp sententiousness and of his didactic principle of shocking audiences into questioning received beliefs. Each citation can stop us short, forcing us to ask to what extent the past can be rewritten or must haunt us, how far we can separate out elements (ideas, emotions, reference points), and how we might cope with their tendency to merge. As many of the essays collected here acknowledge, citations can be approached as case studies in how we address the theme of time and timing across the corpus: despite the ideal of the wise man who is not constrained by time and can in a sense rise above it, Seneca's writings are deeply concerned with what it is to be an imperfect mortal in time and specifically in 60s CE Rome. Whether he chooses to elide coordinates in time and space (in the *Epistles* and *Natural Questions*, for example, written in parallel in the years of retirement leading up to forced suicide) or pins a work to a specific occasion (the *Consolations to Marcia and Polybius*, the *Apocolocyntosis*), Seneca's brisk, time-conscious style, which seems to "capture the moment" (Williams), constantly reminds readers of what is at stake in living through this particular period of Roman history and invites us to deliberate the compromises, repressions, and self-discipline required to get through it alive. The extent to which *how* Seneca shapes his texts is never separable from philosophical content is one of the volume's overarching concerns.

Part I of the volume surveys the whole of Seneca's surviving output and grapples with the key question of whether and how we might conceive the corpus as a coherent whole or, more specifically, what we are to make of the myriad potential connections and contrasts between individual works written at different times, in different genres, registers, and styles. Susanna Braund's essay, which serves as a second introduction to the companion as a whole, molds itself around Seneca's own uncanny time management and fascination with a future always already lived, retracing Seneca's career not from beginning to end but from end to beginning. Tacitus's account of Seneca's death, alongside that of fellow courtier and literary talent Petronius, is a brilliant, multilayered homage to a life spent regulating performance, rehearsing the inevitability of death in order to be free to live, and staging the socially engaged life of the Stoic through ebullient dialogue with friends, writers, predecessors, and their texts. As Braund shows, it is difficult not to see Seneca's career intensifying in the buildup to what looks like an inevitable last act: after his early ill health and unlikely survival under Caligula and Claudius, Seneca enjoyed immense wealth and power in the first eight years of Nero's reign but fell afoul of fate and was forced to withdraw in 62, apparently producing all his *Epistles* and the *Natural Questions* in the fervent three years before his suicide. Yet despite the temptation, fuelled by Tacitus, to imagine "Seneca" as a single narrative leading to a foreseeable finale, we are also reminded here of how fragmented a figure he has appeared in the Western tradition and of how traditional fault lines – between philosopher and politician, philosopher and tragedian, serious thinker and maverick hypocrite, Stoic and millionaire – continue to stimulate and frustrate.

Christopher Trinacty takes up several of these apparently awkward pairings in his review of the tragedies, suggesting ways in which the plays confront specific political issues (with clear, though ultimately not datable, contemporary relevance). What emerges here is a range of reframed answers to the question of *why tragedy?* Seneca is interested in tragedy, Trinacty suggests, as a medium for doing moral and political philosophy but also as an inherently dialectical and hybrid genre that allows him to intertwine and contrast voices, positions, and reactions and to put debate and interrogation on display. With this perspective comes a renewed emphasis on performativity, on the power of dramatic language to violently shape reality, and hence also on the potential (and point) of actually putting these self-consciously rhetorical, "written" texts on stage.

As Catharine Edwards emphasizes in her piece on the *Epistles*, Seneca is again interested here in the ideology and ontology of literary form. These conversational, daily letters to close friend, fellow poet, and younger "student" Lucilius enact Seneca's philosophical project as a daily praxis contingent on reaching out toward another from within an enclosed retreat that stands for Stoic self-sufficiency. The letter is itself a place of intimacy, allowing full immersion in the Stoic program, while the (non)paradox of the Stoic who cultivates psychic self-containment but who is also a social animal deeply connected to his fellow human beings is visualized in the evident absent-presence marking all epistolary writing of this kind. The letter writer conventionally fosters the desire for and illusion of his addressee's presence, a trope that nevertheless highlights distance and separation. Once more, dense allusivity (and the blending of prose with quotes from poetry) comes to be inseparable from the philosophical spur to extend oneself beyond one's immediate niche, to engage in dialogue and self-interrogation. Discussion of the *Epistles* thus leads us smoothly into the following essay on the *Dialogi* themselves, read here alongside the *De Clementia, De Beneficiis,* and *Naturales Quaestiones.* Matthew Roller explains why, despite their many differences, it makes sense to group these works together and builds a detailed picture of their *dialogic* character. Seneca's dialogues, he argues, teem with voices that are themselves dialogized and thereby implicated in the protreptic of each work. Yet as we might expect, this well-defined category creates its own pressure to expand and overflow, so that we are tempted to reread the *Epistles* themselves as an ambitious, overgrown collection of *dialogi.*

In the pattern of overlapping treatments of Seneca *multiplex,* Malcolm Schofield's essay on Seneca, which spotlights the "politician and political theorist who was also a philosopher" rather than the "philosopher who happened to be in politics," also tackles the *De Clementia,* alongside the *De Tranquillitate Animi* and the *De Otio.* The *De Clementia,* Schofield suggests, almost becomes an exercise in the political theory of kingship (despite ambiguity in Stoic suggestions that kingship was the best form of *res publica*). Indeed, there is much about this treatise, including the focus on mercy itself, that strikes us as rather un-Stoic, and here, as in the *De Tranquillitate Animi* and *De Otio,* where the issue is defending the apparent paradox of politically active retreat, we see Seneca shaping his own idiosyncratic Stoicism in the context of Roman political discourse.

A wave of editions, commentaries, and studies on the *Natural Questions* (*NQ*) have lately rescued this work from relative neglect. As Francesca Romana Berno shows in her chapter, the *NQ* pursue core Senecan topics and concerns through the detailed and rational effort to understand seemingly incomprehensible natural phenomena that as such confuse and terrify mankind. The *NQ* emerge as a text fully integrated in the corpus, including the tragedies: some of the most notorious examples of vices discussed in its prefaces and conclusions – the sections in which Seneca frames the technical treatment of the book with more general reflections – display the same perverse features of the most successful of Seneca's evildoers, such as Atreus or Medea.

Kirk Freudenburg's contribution confronts what on first impression has often looked like a monstrous anomaly in Seneca's *curriculum vitae*, unworthy of his authorship. Yet the *Apocolocyntosis* – its presumed, mysterious title a stodgy mouthful perhaps designed to make us stutter like Claudius – is tentatively resituated here at the center of the corpus. The satire puts characteristic Senecan dialogism and time sensitivity on hyperbolic display. More is at stake perhaps at this historical hinge between Claudius and Nero than at any other point in Seneca's career, and his dark, Saturnalian celebration of this anxious transition constitutes one of Seneca's most complex and fascinating meditations on time. Freudenburg focuses here on how the *Apocolocyntosis* summons the model of Lucilius's raging Republican satire and in particular the section of his first book titled *Concilium Deorum* ("Council of the Gods"), with its savage condemnation of corrupt politician Lucius Cornelius Lentulus Lupus. Seneca seizes on this moment, already loaded with satiric tensions, and imports it into a present on the verge of a bright, young future under Nero. The result is explosive and utterly Senecan.

Part II of this volume focuses on pinpointing how Seneca, in the shape of his texts, situated himself in the present as a powerfully modern, political interpreter (and remaker) of his past. The first two essays, by James Ker and Victoria Rimell, work chiastically to explore how Seneca fashions the meaning of "Augustus" and "Augustan Poetry" and, later, how multiple Augustuses help craft his specular and risky partnership with Nero. As he transforms and fragments the past, Ker emphasizes, Seneca engages with readers' poetic memories and historical awareness, which he filters through evocations of timely moments in Augustan poetry and specific uses of memory by Augustus and his family. In doing so, he tells a self-exposing, self-promoting story about his own astute, creative management of the "book-ends" of Julio-Claudian empire, from Augustus to Nero. Rimell touches on many similar points but hones in on the generational and philosophical tensions that structure Seneca's specular relationship with Nero from the *Apocolocyntosis* to the *Epistles*, where the necessity and problem of dialogue between two in an autocratic regime get remade anew. The dilemma of Nero's extreme youth when he came to power and Seneca's role as older father figure, guide, or even double for the new emperor comes to frame larger, career-long consideration of how modernity appeals to the authority of the past and how the philosopher should inhabit time.

The next essay, by Gareth Williams, begins by discussing the conversational *Epistles* as a showcase text in which Seneca fully activates his philosophical undertaking as always indivisible from his poetics (note the points of contact with Edwards, Roller, and Rimell in particular). Williams's investigation of style and form pays close attention to the ideas and even advice embedded in the anatomy of Senecan prose: in brisk, concise, informal, and chromatic writing, Seneca sculpts the urgency to get on and *do*, to enter into philosophy as process, as a way of living your life. Seneca's critiques of past and present writers continually emphasize writing as a performance of the self, yet his reviews of others necessarily turn the spotlight back onto the words – and man – we are reading now. Language becomes a fundamental tool of Senecan philosophy, and for the first time, perhaps, we encounter a philosopher who thinks in Latin, for whom philosophy is an urgent, profoundly political, and culturally specific *Roman* project. This point is also developed in Mireille Armisen-Marchetti's discussion of Seneca's use of metaphor, simile, and metonymy. The kinds of metaphors Seneca employs and theorizes are especially fascinating, not least because they are so often drawn from a Roman military context. Senecan stylistics seize on and dwell in real time, as Williams also suggests, but also – even in texts like the *Epistles* in which the city of Rome and the emperor are largely absent – the bustle, stress, and violence of the contemporary world are vividly brought to the fore.

The final two essays in Part II knit together multiple strands in their discussions of theater and theatricality (Littlewood) and emotions (Konstan). Cedric Littlewood begins by setting Senecan and Stoic self-fashioning in its immediate cultural and larger philosophical contexts. He then maps out Seneca's drive to philosophize the theatrical metaphor implicit in Roman self-construction alongside his detailed, allusive teaching on making subtle but crucial distinctions between positive and depraved acting: with stage-happy Nero shadowing every move, this is an interpretative tight-rope. In this and the following essay, Seneca emerges as a highly original thinker who constantly pushes us to refine and perceive (or sometimes just accept) the subtle contradictions in our perspectives. David Konstan suggests that Seneca's understanding and classification of emotions, which are not merely instinctive reflexes but cognitive processes in themselves, is more nuanced and philosophically challenging than we have often assumed. Seneca's Stoic sage is not icy hearted and emotionless, and his analysis, for example, of the need to replace pity not with lack of concern but with a serene benevolence cultivated inwardly but directed toward one's fellow human beings finds new resonance in light of our own unprecedented exposure to the pain and suffering of others in a globalized, twenty-first-century world.

Part III of the volume explores the most fraught areas of tension within Seneca's thought, illustrating in the process how the meeting places of contrasting points of view often offer insight into what is original *and* problematic about his combined literary and philosophical project. To think of Seneca as a site of tension is certainly not to innovate: the very different tone of Seneca's prose and his poetry led some readers, including the fifth-century churchman and orator Sidonius Apollinaris and after him an entire throng of distinguished readers, including Lipsius, Erasmus, Diderot, and Lessing, to speculate that there might have been two or even three Lucius Annaeus Senecas rather than one. But to see the man whole (as the title of the 2006 study edited by K. Volk and G. D. Williams would suggest) has always been something of a challenge – one that these essays take up and develop. In the first one, "Senecan Selves," Shadi Bartsch suggests that the gulf between the normal self and the idealized Stoic self that Seneca constantly stresses actually *constitutes* the primary characteristic of selfhood as Seneca experiences it: selfhood lies in this gap. Another gulf opens up within Seneca's frequent characterization of philosophical self-control as a form of acting: the self-control of the Stoic sage, who never bats an eyelid at fate's surprises, is curiously reminiscent of the experienced courtier, who knows better than to grimace at a ruler's shenanigans. Bartsch suggests that Seneca's character was defined by the tightrope act he performed between these two performances, one everyday, the other ideal – and that he very much preferred to leave his readers with the "imago" of his philosophical self rather than the courtier he had to play at court.

David Wray's discussion of shame in Seneca's writing reminds us that Stoicism is often thought to disallow consideration of factors that cause shame as mere "externals." Seneca's Stoicism, however, admits talk of shame that sounds (as Wray puts it) "a lot like ordinary Roman *pudor*-talk." How then are we to reconcile the fact that the author of the letters advocates shaming others into Stoic behavior, while the version of shame he enjoins (unlike the Greek Stoic treatment of *aidos*) runs counter to Stoic orthodoxy? One answer has been to suggest that Seneca cannot shed the language and mores of aristocratic privilege. As Wray points out, however, early modernity read Seneca's shamed dramatic protagonists differently, seeing them as models of heroism and freedom. Perhaps Seneca wants us to feel shame's sting as a marker of our blameworthy characters – and perhaps, in spurring us to suicide, it will provide us with the incentive to exit the arena of shame and rehabilitate our dispositions. Shame, then, would approach virtue "precisely to the degree that its constraints nudge the agent toward the choice a virtuous agent would have made in a given circumstance."

While this sounds like a drastic remodeling of standard Stoicism, Seneca has already shown he is willing to modify "theory" if he can make "practice" have the right orthodox response. Carey Seal's essay confronts precisely this issue: How does Seneca understand the relationship between "theory" and "practice" in philosophy? Physics and logic are subtly intertwined in Seneca's writing, as the theoretical drive for natural knowledge is repeatedly shown to serve a practical function by giving the agent the cosmic perspective he or she needs to live well and to obtain mental mastery over the chaotic jumble of appearances here on earth. Seal reminds us that Seneca's exercises in part derive their force from aspects of Roman social life that seem to have little to do with philosophical argument but may appeal to a the traditional values of a disempowered elite. Elsewhere, however, there is an obvious tension between the two sources of moral norms, orthodox Roman (the *mos maiorum*) and Hellenistic Stoic; for example, there are many junctures at which Seneca seems to be aiming to induce moral progress through emotional rather than a purely Stoic intellectual appeal. It is a testament to Seneca's ingenuity that he is able to defend his practice without retreating from the Socratic link between reason and action.

In the following essay, Elizabeth Asmis examines the interplay of received Stoic orthodoxy with Senecan innovation. Seneca's willingness to take what he needed from tradition but to combine these elements into a whole with new philosophical emphases defines his original project as a teacher of Stoicism; as he himself announces, he appropriates the materials he inherits by digesting them and making them into something new. Reducing the role that logic played in Hellenistic Stoicism but linking physics and cosmology to the development of the moral self, he further innovates in his description of the *hegemonikon*, adapting Stoic theory to a Platonic-Aristotelian framework. Above all, Asmis argues, while he stresses the importance of a moral guide, he also finds that force of external stimuli is not enough to make the student morally good. He thus offers us a new view of the role of volition; as Asmis puts it, "we must turn our inborn wanting into a deliberate wanting by overcoming the wrong kind of wanting."

While Stoics are the most often-mentioned school, Epicurus is referred to more often than Socrates, Cato, and Plato even as Seneca voices a doctrine that is largely incompatible, in fundamental respects, with Stoicism. As Alessandro Schiesaro argues, Seneca often privileges Epicurean *sententiae* disconnected from a larger argumentative framework, a strategy of appropriation that limits from the outset the scope for doctrinal contamination, especially as it chiefly focus on moral issues, such as the limitation of desire, the importance of friendship, and the importance of intellectual *otium* where the distance between different schools is in any case more limited. These differences emerge much more emphatically when Seneca turns his attention to physics and the natural world. Here no agreement is possible between a Stoic worldview that regards the wonders of nature as a reminder of divine providence and a system that denies the gods any active intervention in natural or human affairs. Similarities in style and occasionally in the explanatory techniques only serve to highlight a substantial chasm: both Seneca and the Epicurean Lucretius, for instance, rely on sublimity as a crucial cognitive tool, but in its Senecan incarnation, striving for the sublime is the ultimate form of admiration for divine agency rather than the means though which human beings can raise themselves to the same level of understanding as the immortal gods.

Seneca's *nachleben* waxed and waned according to the tastes of the cultures that followed him. In antiquity, his collusion with Nero and his wealth worked to undermine the moral slant of his writings; it was his contemporary Musonius Rufus who was identified as the Roman parallel to Socrates (Origen, *Contra Celsum* 3.6). Seneca himself was additionally tarred by the salacious brush of the historian Dio Cassius, who reported criticism of his ethics and divulged kinky sexual habits. But the first essay in Part IV of this volume, Setaioli's discussion in "Seneca and the Ancient World," makes it clear that there were positive treatments as well, not only in the idealizing *praetexta Octavia* but also in the more balanced assessments of Tacitus. As Aldo Setaioli suggests, it is possible that the lack of reference to Seneca's philosophizing was due to his aversion to abstraction, his choice of language, Latin, and to the fact that Stoicism had yielded in popularity to neo-Platonism by the third century CE. On the literary side, however, we have more clarity about his influence; for example, his nephew Lucan's *Civil War* presents a fascinating case study in its rejection of Seneca's worldview in the prose writings and its points of contact with Seneca's tragedies, which depict a world devoid of a *logos* guiding nature and man toward a rational goal. Most of all, Petronius's *Satyricon* is a parody that humorously desecrates either Seneca's edifying moral teaching or his most pathetic tragic scenes. Even before the early 60s CE, though, Seneca was in vogue – already by the reign of Caligula, as witnessed by Suetonius (*Calig.* 53). The same biographer, however, attests the first of a long series of severe criticisms of Seneca's style.

Chiara Torre's essay explores the reverberations of Seneca's heritage on Christian writers up to the sixth century CE. Starting with the pseudo-correspondence of Seneca and St. Paul, she cautions us against confusing Christian respect for the *figure* of Seneca with respect for his writing. Once we make this distinction, we can eschew the supposed relationship between the positive Christian reception of Seneca and the influence of Stoicism among the Fathers. As one example, philosophically speaking, Seneca excluded anger as a tyrannical passion from the realm of good government, in which it is *clementia* that plays a large role; in Lactantius, on the other hand, anger (as *iusta ira*, which instills man with healthy fear) is a necessity for proper sovereignty. The "Christian" Seneca also appears in Roland Mayer's study of Seneca's reception in the Middle Ages and Renaissance, a period during which the author moves from being a generalized moral authority to a specifically Stoic one. Seneca's reception during this time was also confused by the lack of a distinction between the Elder and the Younger Senecas and by the distorting influence of the many florilegia of his works. Thus "Super-Seneca" slimmed down as spurious texts were pruned from the tradition. The tragedies, on the other hand, were not added to his corpus until the eve of the Renaissance, when they spurred enthusiasm and imitation.. As Mayer shows, the establishment of a more authentic Seneca also led to a new interest in his style, which had previously been very much eclipsed by Cicero's star. Lipsius's espousal of Senecan Stoicism gave rise to the spread of neostoic thought among European thinkers.

Here Peter Stacey takes over from Mayer. As his essay illustrates, Seneca was a revered political authority from the medieval to the early modern era. Thanks in large part to his work as well as Cicero's, European political thought owed a pervasive debt to distinctively Roman forms of philosophical thought. Political arguments about the character of good government – and the importance of good *self*-government in its brief – were derived from two Senecan texts especially: *De clementia* and, to a lesser extent, *De ira*. The fact that Seneca conceived of reason as a form of natural law had repercussions in legal as well as moral arguments, and his focus on mercy shaped John of Salisbury's *Policraticus*. In particular, the idea of the *res publica* as a divine trust served absolutist thought; indeed, the most unsettling feature of Machiavelli's work was its rejection of the notion that a prince ruled over a *res publica*.

Francesco Citti too engages with the importance of Seneca's philosophical heritage, tracing an expanse of time beginning with Lipsius in the seventeenth century and ending with the present. As he argues, Lipsius's view of a Christian providence notably reconciled the determinism of the divine plan and the rationality of the individual, and if Seneca's star faded from view somewhat in the intervening centuries, in the twentieth, the philosophers Dietrich Bonhoeffer, Paul Tillich, and Jacques Maritain all attested to the influence of his thought; Maritain, like so many others before him, found in Seneca's moralizing "a kind of kinship with Christian themes." And of course there is Michel Foucault, whose fundamental studies on Stoicism and the *Care of the Self* perhaps did more to reawaken scholarly interest in this "derivative" thinker than did any other work. As to Seneca's dramatic output, its influence on Shakespearean plots is well known; Citti focuses on *Oedipus*, *Phaedra*, and the *Medea* to outline a host of other playwrights and poets who bear the imprint of Senecan theater, including Racine, Corneille, Anouilh, and Ted Hughes. And, of course, there is Seneca the character, appearing both in art (usually in the act of dying) and on stage. These many aspects of Seneca, philosopher, politician, playwright, and model – if fallible to the end – fill out the pages of the following book.[1]

---

[1] The editors would like to thank John Henderson for his thoughtful comments on the manuscript of this volume.

PART I

The Senecan Corpus

I

SUSANNA BRAUND

Seneca *Multiplex*: The Phases (and Phrases) of Seneca's Life and Works

A Famous Death (65 CE)

On an April evening in the year 65 CE, Lucius Annaeus Seneca was dining with his wife Paulina and two friends at one of his villas just outside Rome when he received from Nero a message commanding his death. This is memorialized by the second-century Roman historian Tacitus at *Annals* 15.60–4 as part of a relentless sequence of forced suicides;[1] we also have other, much briefer accounts by Tacitus' contemporary Suetonius and by the third-century Roman historian Dio Cassius, writing in Greek. The death scene played out by Seneca, protracted by the frailty of his elderly body and ascetic lifestyle, has been for many the most memorable aspect of his life.[2] I will start with his death and work backward from there.

The key phrase in Tacitus' account is "the image of his life" (*imago vitae suae*, *Ann.* 15.62).[3] Seneca takes control of his death by staying calm and attending to both immediate concerns and the longue durée. For him, his death is both a philosophical and a political act. He first attempts to change his will in favor of his friends, but this is not permitted, which meant that his legendary wealth was bequeathed to the emperor. Instead of material bene-factions, he offers his friends "the image of his life." He then tells his weeping companions that it is no surprise that Nero, after murdering his mother and his brother, would execute his tutor, too. Seneca had been Nero's tutor since his recall from exile in 49 CE, so their relationship had been long and intimate. Seneca's death is highly self-aware and performative, with an eye on several audiences: those present with him (his wife, friends, and the

---

[1] Ker (2009a, 59) discusses Roland Barthes' 1972 essay on "Tacitus and the Funerary Baroque."

[2] So Ker (2009a, 12): "The death narrative has been preferred as a way to tell the Seneca story."

[3] Griffin (1974) takes this phrase as the title of her excellent essay.

soldiers), those in the imperial court, especially Nero, who would hear about his death, and posterity.[4]

It was not an easy death: Dio uses the Greek word *dusthanatesas* and, in a detail that does not match Tacitus' more extensive account, says that his demise was assisted by soldiers (62.25.2). These days we tend to privilege Tacitus' account, which is the fullest, though its intent – praise or mockery – is contested.[5] Seneca starts by cutting his veins in what is clearly a suicide modelled on that of Cato the Younger, as memorialized by Seneca himself in *On Providence* 2.9–12, hence a Stoic suicide.[6] After Seneca and his young wife Paulina, who courageously insists on joining her husband in death (though Dio 62.25.1 has Seneca wishing to kill her, too), have cut their arms, Seneca also severed the veins in his leg and behind the knees, because his blood was flowing so slowly (*Annals* 15.63). Tacitus attributes this to his age and frugal lifestyle (*Annals* 15.45), which we learn about from Seneca himself in several of his letters (e.g., *Epistle* 83.5–6, *Epistle* 123.3).

What followed was tormenting pain, which led him to ask Paulina, who was subsequently saved through Nero's intervention, to remove herself lest his resolve waver in her presence. The pain did not, however, stop Seneca from dictating extensive thoughts to his secretaries, or, if we follow Dio, revising the book he was engaged in writing (62.25.2). Unfortunately, Tacitus refrains from relaying those thoughts, saying they have been published, so we do not have Seneca's last words.[7]

Seneca then asks his doctor to provide poison in the form of hemlock. This choice indicates beyond doubt that Seneca was modelling his death on that of Socrates, an interpretation confirmed in an early visual representation from the third century CE of a double herm depicting Socrates and Seneca back to back. But because of his physical state, the poison has no effect. His last resort is to enter a steam bath to speed the flow of blood. In a gesture borrowed from Plato's *Phaedo*, he makes an offering to Jupiter Liberator, then is suffocated by the steam. This third and finally efficacious mode of death was probably not what Seneca wanted to be

---

[4] Cf. Ker (2009a, 33) on "the teleological structure of a life spent anticipating death."
[5] Syme (1958, 582 with n. 2) remarks upon Tacitus' equity or sympathy towards Seneca; Dyson (1970) takes a different view. On the agendas of the three ancient accounts of Seneca's death, see Ker (2009a, 39).
[6] For discussion of suicide in general and Cato's suicide in particular, see Hill (2004, 179–80).
[7] The *Epitaphium* attributed to him seems unlikely to be genuine.

remembered by, since steam baths were redolent of the life of luxury from which Seneca had so markedly abstained, especially in his final years. We can view these three attempts at dying as Seneca's final proof of "his ability to divorce himself from the influence of externals" (Hill 2004, 182), "as a set of trials that Seneca endures through *constantia*" and "a tour de force in the rhetoric of deathways" (both quotations from Ker 2009a, 268), or as Tacitus' mockery of Seneca's death by this triptych of death modes with different associations (Dyson 1970). In any case, Ker is surely right in seeing the variety here as a demonstration of "the polygeneric aspect of Senecan agency in his defining moment" (Ker 2006, 24). This is *Seneca multiplex* in a nutshell.

Seneca wanted his legacy to be the *imago vitae suae* (*Ann.* 15.62). Ironically, perhaps, given the struggle it was for him to die, it was the *imago mortis suae* that resonated for later ages. The many representations of the death of Seneca are analyzed in an excellent study by James Ker. In a chapter devoted to the receptions of Seneca's death (chapter 7), Ker shows how Jerome, for example, aligns Seneca's Stoic death with Christian martyrdom (*On Famous Men* 12.3) while making no mention of the bath (Ker 2009a, 184–5). By contrast, the visual iconography of Seneca's death makes much of the bath: illuminated manuscripts from the thirteenth century onward show Seneca standing naked in a barrel bath with his arms stretched out while attendants cut the veins and Nero makes an imperious executionary gesture. A late fifteenth-century illumination for the *Roman de la Rose* has Nero peeking from behind a curtain at an effeminized and youthful Seneca standing in a bath while the attendant applies a scalpel in the form of a pen to his left arm. Another image from the same period, an illustration for the *Speculum historiale* by Vincent of Beauvais, juxtaposes Seneca in his bathtub with the gruesome physical examination of Agrippina's naked corpse. The first treatment of Seneca's death in drama is in the final act of Matthew Gwinne's extraordinarily long Latin play *Nero* (1603), in which Gwinne's character borrows from Seneca's tragic and philosophical discourse. There follow, among many items one could mention, paintings by Rubens (1614–15), Luca Giordano (around 1650–3 and around 1684–5), Jacques-Louis David (1773), and Joseph Noël Sylvestre (1875), plays by Friedrich von Creutz (*Der sterbende Seneca*, 1754) and Ewald Christian von Kleist (*Seneca*, prose draft 1758, versified in 1767), and Heiner Müller's poem *Senecas Tod* (1992). Each of these treatments has its own agenda and appropriates particular aspects of Seneca to remake him as a Stoic sage or a proto-Christian martyr or a hypocritical courtier or a student of death.

A Fall from Favor (62–65 CE)

Seneca had spent the three years prior to his death out of favor with Nero, and it is clear that he anticipated his demise for much of that time, and earlier too (Tac. *Ann.* 15.64). The immediate provocation for Nero's command was the suspicion of Seneca's involvement in the so-called Pisonian conspiracy, a planned coup d'état that would have replaced Nero with the aristocrat Gaius Calpurnius Piso.[8] The fact and the extent of Seneca's involvement with this conspiracy are not clear. Tacitus reports a rumor that some of the conspirators planned, "not without Seneca's knowledge," to depose Piso immediately after the coup and replace him with Seneca (*Ann.* 15.65). That said, only one conspirator implicates him (*Ann.* 15.56), possibly to ingratiate himself with Nero, "who, in his hatred of Seneca, grasped at all methods of suppressing him." Indeed, Tacitus introduces his elaborate account of Seneca's death by noting that the death delighted Nero, who was keen to proceed by assassination since poison had failed (*Ann.* 15.60). There can be little doubt, then, that Seneca's fate had been fixed for some while.

Seneca used the years of his de facto retirement from politics by devoting himself to philosophical and scientific writings. From these years, 62 to 65 CE, date his letters, of which we have 124, addressed to his slightly younger friend Lucilius Junior, but clearly to be read as Seneca's shaping of the *imago vitae suae*. The letters augment his earlier essays, the "Dialogues" (*Dialogi*), as an extensive articulation of Stoic thought. His intentions are clear from the beginning of *Epistle* 8, where he says that his object in shutting himself away is to benefit more rather than fewer people through his devoted hard work. "I have withdrawn not only from people but from business, especially my own. I am writing for future generations, writing down ideas that might be valuable to them" (*Epistle* 8.2). He also wrote the *Natural Questions* during his retirement. In this work he investigates the workings of Nature, a concept central to Stoicism. He investigates meteorological phenomena, the waters of the world including the Nile, the winds, and earthquakes, and his weighing of previous scientific ideas is interleaved with assertion of the moral improvement that derives from the study of nature.

It seems likely that he spent much of his time at his villa in Nomentum, ten miles outside Rome. This estate, rich in vineyards, he probably acquired just before his withdrawal from politics.[9] Seneca expresses his pleasure at

---

[8] For the plot and subsequent purge, see Tac. *Ann.* 15.48–71.
[9] On his acquisition of this estate, see Griffin (1976, 289–90).

returning to his villa in *Epistle* 104 and promotes the image of himself as a viticulturist in *Epistle* 112.2, where he draws an elaborate analogy between viticulture and morality.

Tacitus provides an extensive account of the infamous interview in 62 CE in which Seneca asks Nero for permission to retire (*Ann.* 14.53–6). The request is refused. One of the first events of that year recorded by Tacitus is the death of Sextus Afranius Burrus, who had been sole prefect of the praetorian guard since 51 CE and with whom Seneca had exercised power since the accession of Nero in 54 CE. As Tacitus succinctly puts it, *mors Burri infregit Senecae potentiam* ("The death of Burrus broke Seneca's power," *Ann.* 14.52). Aware of the chill emanating from the emperor, Seneca requests an audience during which he eloquently thanks Nero for his generosity and then asks to be relieved of the riches Nero has bestowed upon him now that he is "an old man unequal to the slightest of cares" (*Ann.* 14.53–4). Nero's reply, of equal length in Tacitus' rendition (*Ann.* 14.55–6), starts with a studied compliment to the tuition in eloquence he has received from Seneca and proceeds to argue that, with Seneca still of *valida aetas* ("an effective age") and Nero still in the first stage of his rule, Nero cannot afford to allow him to retire. As Ker astutely remarks, the interview in effect presents two Senecas arguing with each other, since Nero's debating skills were shaped by his tutor; Seneca faces his "rhetorical doppelgänger" (Ker, 2009a, 48). The audience ends with Nero embracing Seneca and Seneca thanking Nero, but from then on, says Tacitus, Seneca changed his habits, banishing visitors, avoiding company, and rarely coming into Rome "as if ill or detained at home by his studies" (*Ann.* 14.56).

A graphic illustration of Seneca's fading influence is provided by the scene between Nero and Seneca in *Octavia*, the historical play transmitted along with Seneca's tragedies in one strand of the manuscript tradition but almost certainly not authored by him. The play is set in 62 CE when Nero is contemplating divorcing and murdering his wife Octavia to clear the way to marrying his mistress Poppaea. In a rapid exchange, Seneca tries in vain to dissuade Nero by advocating *clementia*; this is a reprise of the treatise on this topic he addressed to the young emperor soon after his accession. Throughout the scene, Nero is rude to Seneca, calling him "a soft old man [who] should be teaching boys" (445). Eventually, Seneca pushes Nero beyond endurance by appealing to his obligations to behave morally. Nero's reply – "Enough, stop pressing the point! You are trying my patience now. Let me act in a way that Seneca disapproves" (588–9) – is the epitome of a young man's rebellion against his tutor. Monteverdi in his opera *L'Incoronazione di Poppea* (1643) reworks this scene with enthusiasm.

Fortune's Favor (54–62 CE)

In this exchange in *Octavia*, Seneca refers several times to Fortune – and his own life perhaps epitomizes the wheel of Fortune. In his interview with Nero, Tacitus has him utter the following reflection, which expresses surprise at his social advancement:

> He asks himself: Is it I, born in the station of a simple knight and a provincial, who am numbered with the magnates of the realm? Among these nobles, wearing their long-descended glories, has my novel name swum into ken? Where is that spirit which found contentment in mediocrity? Building these terraced gardens? Pacing these suburban mansions? Luxuriating in these broad acres, these world-wide investments? (*Ann.* 14.53)

This passage, beautifully constructed to echo the astonished self-reflection put into Nero's mouth by Seneca at the start of his *On Clemency* (1.1.2–4), succinctly articulates Seneca's rise to great riches and power from a provincial beginning.

Seneca was at his zenith during most or all of the years 54 to 62. This period falls into two sections. The first five years of Nero's reign, the so-called *quinquennium Neronis*,[10] had seen a power struggle between Seneca and Burrus on the one hand and Nero's mother Agrippina on the other.[11] She was first isolated and then, in 59 CE, murdered, on Nero's orders and with the complicity of Seneca and Burrus (Tac. *Ann.* 14.7; Dio 62.12.1). The speech Nero delivered after Agrippina's death outlining the threat posed by his mother drew a hostile reception for its author, Seneca, in that he had in effect put a confession of murder into Nero's mouth (Tac. *Ann.* 14.11).

The years between Agrippina's death and the death of Burrus in 62 CE saw another power struggle, this time between the emperor and his two advisers. Tacitus marks this clearly by choosing as the first episode after Agrippina's death the concession by Seneca and Burrus to Nero's long-held desire to drive a chariot (*Ann.* 14.14). This was selected as the lesser of two evils, the greater being Nero's desire to perform on stage, an activity that would inevitably bring disgrace and literal degradation to any Roman noble. Their efforts were, however, in vain, given that as early as 59 CE, Nero built a personal theater for the Juvenalia (*Ann.* 14.15), a celebration he instituted to mark the first shaving of his beard, and by 64 CE, was indulging his passion for singing in public (*Ann.* 15.33). It may be significant that we hear nothing of Seneca from Tacitus in these years; it may indicate that, although

---

[10] Murray (1965, 41–61) offers a hypothesis for the origin of the phrase.

[11] The numismatic evidence from these years (discussed in my edition of *De Clementia*, Oxford University Press, 2011, Appendix 3), bears eloquent testimony to Agrippina's changing fortunes.

Seneca and Burrus had in the end acted against their sponsor Agrippina, their fates were actually bound up with hers. From 59 CE onward, Nero, by now twenty-one years old, was flexing his independence.

The allegations against Seneca made by Publius Suillius in 58 CE (Tac. *Ann.* 13.42) are worth examination, not least because they anticipate criticisms of Seneca repeated through the centuries. Suillius' position was highly partisan: he had been a favorite of Claudius. He calls Seneca "the embittered enemy of the friends of Claudius, under whom he had suffered a highly justified exile." He mocks Seneca for his narrow life experience and devotion to books, in contrast with his own unsophisticated pragmatism. He contrasts his own position as Germanicus' quaestor with that of Seneca, "the palace adulterer" (referring to the accusation that brought about his exile). He asks "by what branch of wisdom, by what precepts of philosophy, had he acquired three hundred million sesterces within four years of royal favor?" He alleges that in Rome, Seneca's nets were spread to catch the legacies of the childless and that "Italy and the provinces were being drained by his limitless usury." This last scenario is supported by a detail in Dio that one cause of the uprising in Britain in 61 CE was Seneca's handling of enormous loans he had imposed there (62.2.1). These are strong claims and they met with a strong response: Suillius was duly tried, found guilty, and banished.

Suillius' criticisms focus on Seneca's extraordinary wealth. He undoubtedly was "extremely rich" (*praedives*, the term used by both Tacitus and Juvenal).[12] Nero enriched Seneca with fabulous gifts (Tac. *Ann.* 14.53–4), including gardens, capital, villas, and other real estate (Tac. *Ann.* 14.55). He had properties at Baiae and Nomentum (*Epistle* 51.1, 104.1, 110.1), an Alban villa (*Epistle* 123.1), and Egyptian estates (*Epistle* 77.3); we get an impression of some of the luxuries available to him in *On the happy life* (17.2). There is no doubt that Seneca put his wealth to the stand aristocratic use at that time, that is, he lent it out. According to Paul Veyne, Seneca, with his innate business sense, created what we might call "one of the most important investment banks of his time" (Veyne 2003, 11). He advanced substantial loans to major provincial leaders, which is the backdrop to his becoming Britain's major creditor. That said, Seneca pretty consistently describes riches as a burden (the exception is his self-justification in *On the happy life* 23.1), decries dependence on material things (*Consolation to Helvia* 5.4), and praises poverty (*Natural Questions* 1.17.9).

Wealth, influence, and power are never far apart. In Seneca's case, his power was mostly informal rather than formal. He did hold a suffect consulship

---

[12] *Ann.* 15.64, *Satires* 10.16; Griffin (1976, 286–314) devotes an entire chapter to his wealth.

(that is, a short-term appointment) during 56 CE, yet he preferred not to attend senatorial meetings but instead used his authority as one of the leading members of Nero's informal cabinet of advisers, the *amici principis* or *consilium principis*.[13] Seneca's relationship with Nero had begun soon after his recall from exile in 49 CE thanks to Nero's mother, Agrippina (Tac. *Ann.* 12.8). When Nero came to power in the autumn of 54 CE, aged sixteen, Seneca's influence was at its height. Along with Burrus, he held the reins of power during the golden period at the start of Nero's reign.

Manifestations of Seneca's influence are evident from the start. He composed the eulogy for Claudius that Nero delivered at the funeral (Tac. *Ann.* 13.3) and Nero's accession speeches to the praetorian guard and to the Senate (Dio 61.3.1), in the latter of which he pledged to restore proper legal procedure and the Senate's authority (Tac. *Ann.* 13.4). Burrus and Seneca together exercised enormous influence over the young emperor, restraining an initial inclination towards slaughter (Tac. *Ann.* 13.2). He averted a diplomatic incident by preventing Agrippina from mounting the daïs to greet ambassadors from Armenia (Tac. *Ann.* 13.5). He also promoted Nero's conspicuous display of leniency early in 55 CE and authored a series of speeches in which Nero committed himself to the exercise of clemency (Tac. *Ann.* 13.11).

Seneca's role is reflected clearly in his writings from this period. His satirical skit *Apocolocyntosis* dates from the early weeks of the new reign. In this short but savage satire, Seneca lampoons Claudius for his physical defects and murderous domestic policies, and he incorporates extravagant praise of the gorgeous new emperor, who resembles the god Apollo. Seneca's treatise on clemency also dates from early in the reign (late 55 or 56 CE, interestingly, after Nero's murder of Claudius' son Britannicus). *On Clemency* is a novel blend of kingship treatise, panegyrical oration, and philosophical treatise designed to foster restraint in Nero. It was clearly not efficacious in the long run. But it does show how Seneca believed a Stoic philosopher might engage in political life, by shaping his ruler's behavior.

Femmes Fatales: Favor (49–54 CE) and Catastrophe (41–49 CE)

At the start of 49, Seneca was chafing in exile on Corsica, while his writings enjoyed great popularity (Tac. *Ann.* 12.8). Then he was recalled to Rome through the influence of Agrippina the Younger, new wife to her uncle Claudius. Agrippina gained the praetorship for Seneca and appointed him tutor to her son, Lucius Domitius Ahenobarbus, the future emperor Nero,

---

[13] See Crook (1955, 45–7) on Nero's advisers.

with a brief to instruct him in rhetoric, a category that included morals and political theory (Tac. *Ann.* 12.8), though not philosophy, according to Suetonius (*Nero* 52). This commission Seneca was not in a position to refuse, even if his heart's desire was to go to Athens.[14] Agrippina's marked favor is probably the source of allegations that Seneca was intimate with her (Dio 61.10.1). That said, there is a strand in Seneca's biography that portrays him as attractive to the imperial princesses.[15] From this point on, Seneca flourished in the imperial court, and he formed a lasting alliance with Burrus, another appointee of Agrippina's, who was prefect of the praetorian guard from 51 CE. It is not absurd to see power increasingly concentrated in the hands of this triumvirate. Though Seneca was not explicitly involved in Claudius' death, which was allegedly perpetrated by Agrippina through an agent, he stood to benefit hugely from it, both personally and politically.

Seneca's personal investment in the death of Claudius can be imagined to be vengeance satisfied. Back in 41 CE, possibly at the instigation of Claudius's wife Messalina (Dio 60.8.5), Seneca had been sentenced to exile on Corsica on a charge of adultery with Julia Livilla, sister to Gaius and Agrippina. Seneca spent eight years there, acutely missing Rome and all that Rome had to offer. The way Tacitus tells it, Seneca's exile was one of the first acts of Claudius' reign, but we learn from Seneca himself that Claudius commuted the Senate's death sentence to exile (*Consolation to Polybius* 13.2).

Seneca's *relegatio* (the less severe form of exile) entailed confiscation of half of his property, which was probably restored to him on his recall in 49 CE. We learn about the conditions of Seneca's exile from his *Consolation to Helvia*, his mother. Here he adapts the consolation format, designed to soothe a bereaved person, to his mother's situation of mourning the loss of a son still living, which he represents as a worse calamity than the death of his son, who died in Helvia's arms (*Helv.* 2.5.) only a couple of weeks before the news of Seneca's exile. Seneca does not dwell on his son's death and makes no mention of it elsewhere, nor of the boy's mother, who is evidently not the Paulina present at his death. His consolation to his mother consists of taking an upbeat approach to his experience of exile, presenting it as simply a change of place (*Helv.* 6–8), which is (or should be) insignificant for a Stoic citizen of the world (*Helv.* 8.5). Another work dating from his exile is the *Consolation to Polybius*, which is generally reviled for its fulsome flattery of Polybius and Claudius. Seneca takes the opportunity of the death of the brother of Polybius, one of Claudius' freedmen, to praise Claudius and express the hope that the emperor will recall him from exile (*Polyb.* 13.3).

---

[14] Thus the scholiast to Juvenal 5.109; it seems that Seneca never did go to Greece.
[15] See Syme (1958), *Tacitus*, p. 536.

According to Dio (61.10.2), Seneca also wrote a request to Messalina to help end his exile but later suppressed it.

The catastrophe of his exile came just when Seneca had achieved promotion to the rank of senator. This was a notable achievement for a man of an equestrian family from the provinces. We know that he was aged around 40 at this point and that his aunt, who was well connected through her marriage to a high imperial official, Galerius (governor of Egypt from 16 to 31 CE), acted as his patron. At around the same time, his oratory and literary works were attracting attention. The *novus homo* from Spain seemed to have it made. Then came the allegation. It is hard to assess its veracity; the charge of adultery with a princess of the ruling house had long since become a standard way of removing rivals and inconveniences.

Formative Years and Family Fortunes (Birth–41 CE)

We know little about Seneca's life prior to his arrival in the public eye. It is significant that both his brothers enjoyed prominent and powerful careers. Seneca was the middle of three sons of Seneca the Elder, who wrote his reminiscences of declamatory displays (called *controversiae* and *suasoriae*) as oratorical and cultural training for his sons, as well as a history of Rome that does not survive. His oldest son was Marcus Annaeus Novatus, who, following Roman custom, was adopted and renamed Lucius Junius Annaeus Gallio. He became a senator and was governor of Greece when the Apostle Paul of Tarsus appeared before his tribunal in 51–2 CE (Acts 18.12–17). He served as suffect consul in 55 CE and committed suicide a year after Seneca (Tac. *Ann.* 15.73). The youngest was Marcus Annaeus Mela, father of the epic poet Lucan, who was also implicated in the Pisonian conspiracy and committed suicide soon after Seneca (Tac. *Ann.* 15.70). Annaeus Mela chose not to become a senator, although he met the property qualification, but instead was an *eques* of senatorial rank, a *laticlavius* who by the emperor's permission wore the broad purple stripe that was the mark of a senator; he preferred the influence afforded by working for the imperial administration. He too was forced to commit suicide in the aftermath of the Pisonian conspiracy (Tac. *Ann.* 16.17).

We do know that by 39 CE, Seneca was a senator, thanks to a story according to which the emperor Gaius was so offended by his oratorical success in the Senate that he ordered him to commit suicide. He only survived because Gaius was told he was fatally ill and would die soon anyway (Dio 59.19). His popularity as a speaker is confirmed by Suetonius (*Gaius* 53). At *Epistle* 49.2, Seneca mentions his time as an advocate in the courts, and at *Controversiae* 2 preface 4, written soon after Tiberius' death in 37

CE, his father describes Seneca and his elder brother as preparing to enter public life. That could indicate that they were preparing to stand for the quaestorship (which granted entry to the Senate) or for the higher office of aedile.[16] The earliest work that we can date is his *Consolation to Marcia*, which dates from the reign of Gaius (37–41 CE), addressing an aristocratic woman on the death of her son.

Seneca talks about his early passion for philosophy in *Epistle* 108. His enthusiasm for Pythagoreanism under his teacher Sotion led him into a phase of vegetarianism that he only gave up when implored by his father (*Epistle* 108.17–22). Sotion and another of Seneca's teachers, Papirius Fabianus, were both followers of Sextius, the first and only founder of a Roman philosophical sect. The writings of Sextius continued to inspire Seneca throughout his life (*Epistle* 64.2–5), not least for his asceticism and interest in the natural world. It was from Sextius that Seneca learned the habit of the nightly unflinching scrutiny of his soul that he describes so vividly in *On Anger* 3.36. His education in Stoicism came from attending the lectures of another inspiring teacher, the Greek Attalus (*Epistle* 108.13–14).

What little we know of Seneca's youth depicts him as suffering from ill health. He at first ignored chronic catarrh until he became so emaciated that he became bedridden, possibly with consumption (*Epistle* 78.1; Griffin (1976, 42)). He was perhaps also depressed, because he contemplated suicide, deterred only by the grief this would cause his father (*Epistle* 78.2). Looking back on this period from the end of his life, he asserts that it was through the assiduous visits of his friends and his study of philosophy that he regained his strength (*Epistle* 78.3–4). Seneca seems to have been particularly devoted to his aunt, who nursed him back to health from a protracted illness (*Consolation to Helvia* 19.2) and may have taken him to Egypt for convalescence.

Seneca's family wealth and connections provided a fertile foundation for the talents he later developed. His wealthy family met the equestrian property qualification and probably far exceeded it. Though born in Córdoba, Seneca was raised in Rome from a young age, and it is hard to know exactly how much he felt himself a provincial; much more pertinent was his "newness." His father was a member of the municipal elite of Córdoba, capital of Baetica. His mother Helvia was from a distinguished local family. We do not know if this rich Andalusian family was descended from native Spaniards or from Italian settlers,[17] but since the area had been colonized much earlier (in the early second century BCE) and the native elite Romanized, the point

---

[16] See Griffin (1976, 43–5).
[17] Veyne (2003), *Seneca. The Life of a Stoic*, p.173 n. 3 outlines the many possibilities.

may be moot. Strangely, we do not actually know Seneca's date of birth. Scholars usually settle for the period between 4 BCE and 1 CE.[18]

Seneca *Multiplex*: A Fragmented Figure

We know so much (admittedly, much from Seneca himself), yet – how to pin Seneca down? Apart from a maverick view that fused Seneca the Elder and Seneca the Younger to form an image of a "single super-Seneca" (Hinds 2004, 162), the prevailing tendency has been to divide our Seneca into several Senecas. Several factors sustain this. For a start, his life spans the five Julio-Claudian emperors, Augustus, Tiberius, Gaius (Caligula), Claudius, and Nero. Moreover, the phases of his adult life can be linked with the fluctuating fortunes of the most influential individuals in the imperial court, Claudius' wives and Nero's praetorian prefects: his banishment represents the period of Messalina's power, and his recall marks the moment when Agrippina's star rose; his eminence is coextensive with that of Nero's praetorian prefect Burrus, and the collapse of his power comes when Tigellinus replaces Burrus. He can be seen as a philosopher in politics[19] or as a politician who also happened to be a philosopher. He might be seen as a provincial upstart who rose through patronage and literary celebrity or as a *novus homo* who unusually did not make his way through the all-too-normal flattery or informing on his peers.[20] Many have seen him as "the immoral moralist" (Rudich 1997, 27); maybe he was the original champagne socialist. For some, he has been a proto- or covert Christian and was long considered the author of a celebrated correspondence (actually a forgery) with Paul of Tarsus. Quintilian, the professor of oratory constructing an ideal syllabus for students a generation after Seneca's death, in a dedicated discussion of the multigenre Seneca (*Training of the Orator* 10.1.125–31), concedes that he is an author popular with younger readers at times almost to the exclusion of others – and this seems to be confirmed by the epigraphic evidence, which shows that Senecan prose and verse "permeated the Roman popular imagination" (Ker 2006, 23).[21] Quintilian's final verdict is that Seneca is a writer with an inadequate grasp of philosophy and a seductive stylistic decadence marred by an excess of *sententiae*; he cannot recommend him to students except those of maturity and discrimination.

---

[18] Setaioli (2000) pushes it a little earlier to 5 BCE.

[19] The title of Griffin's 1976 study. Cf. Sørensen's 1984 study, *Seneca, the Humanist at the Court of Nero*.

[20] Veyne (2003, 6); also Syme (1958, 581), contrasting Seneca with other contemporary orators active under Tiberius.

[21] For the adventures of the works in transmission, see Mayer in this volume.

Seneca's surviving literary output is enormous, and we know of other works that have not survived. He wrote in a wide range of genres, though not the most prestigious, epic and historiography. His poetry includes tragedies (eight plays survive), epigrams (including homoerotic poems[22]), and other poetry. Although it has often been assumed that the tragedies must date from the leisure of his exile, Fitch's magisterial work on dating[23] puts *Thyestes* and *Phoenissae* in the Neronian period, while *Hercules Furens* needs to be earlier than *Apocolocyntosis*, which parodies it.

His surviving prose works include three consolations; his satirical skit against Claudius; a three-book treatise on anger and another on clemency (incomplete); short essays discussing calmness, the happy life, leisure, providence, the shortness of life, and the wise man's powers of endurance; a seven-book discussion of gift giving and obligation; a disquisition on the workings of Nature in eight books; and letters to Lucilius. The dating of very few of these works is certain. We know that he also wrote speeches, a biography of his father, ethical essays including one on marriage, geographical treatises on Egypt and India, specific essays about the natural world including an early work on earthquakes (*Natural Questions* 6.4.2), and may have authored the *On remedies for chance events* (*De remediis fortuitorum*).[24]

Readers of Seneca since antiquity have had trouble seeing Seneca whole.[25] The fault line has several different configurations. There is the accusation of hypocrisy that dates from Seneca's own lifetime. Augustine likewise laments the contradictions between Seneca's moral writings and his lived life (*City of God* 6.10). Then there is the split that separates Seneca the philosopher from Seneca the tragedian, for example, in Sidonius Apollinaris in the fifth century (*Poems* 9.232–8): many have felt that the author of the tragedies could not possibly be the same man as the philosopher. This view had significant purchase in the Italian Renaissance, in the eyes of Petrarch and Boccaccio, with the latter assigning some of Seneca's tragedies to a son, "Marcus" (Panizza 1984).

Seneca's Stoic concerns may be perceived more or less strongly in all of these works. His extensive corpus of writing provides important evidence for the development of Stoic ideas under the Roman empire. His tragedies exercised an extraordinary (and underestimated) influence on European drama. Whether or not these dramas are recuperated as Stoic or Stoicizing texts,[26]

---

[22] See Sørensen, (1984, 129–30).

[23] Fitch (1981), corroborated through historical criteria by Nisbet (1990).

[24] Thus Ker (2006, 19–20).

[25] On exceptions in recent scholarship, see Ker (2009a, 11 n. 6).

[26] See Wray in this volume on Seneca's *Phaedra*.

and whether or not they are regarded as stageable or as Rezitationsdrama,[27] they provided a rich source of ghosts and tyrants and the "Tragedy of Blood"[28] for Italian, French, and English dramatists including Marlowe, Shakespeare, and Ben Jonson.[29] There is no era in which readers and scholars have agreed about *Seneca multiplex*.

Further Reading

Accounts of Seneca's life and works abound, for example, in the introductions to editions of his writings and as overviews in volumes of essays, for example, Ferguson (1972). The work of M. T. Griffin has long been central to any serious study of Seneca; her 1976 study, *Seneca: A Philosopher in Politics*, must form the starting point. She provides an incisive overview in her 1974 essay "*Imago Vitae Suae*" (1974). And of course any insight from Syme is crucial: see his *Tacitus*. Since Griffin, valuable studies by V. Sørensen and P. Veyne have broadened our perspectives. Ker's analysis of later receptions and recuperations of Seneca, especially those focused upon his death, offers much rich material for thought.

---

[27] Zwierlein (1966) is the classic argument for recitation; on the possibility or actuality of staged performances, see Sutton (1986), Kragelund (1999), Harrison (2000). Trinacty in this volume also touches on the matter.

[28] Eliot (1986, 78).

[29] See Braund (2013).

2

CHRISTOPHER TRINACTY

Senecan Tragedy

Seneca's tragedies, like Seneca the man, have often provoked strong reactions. If the *Octavia* and *Hercules Oetaeus* are any indication, dramatic writers in the generation after Seneca were noticeably inspired by his dramaturgy and poetics. Poets from Statius to Juvenal echo his mannerist tendencies and appropriate his language for their own purposes. Likewise, Renaissance playwrights and Shakespeare revisit Senecan *sententiae*, themes, and tragic devices (e.g., the ghosts that haunt Kyd's *The Spanish Tragedy* and Shakespeare's *Hamlet*). Senecan tragedy did not always suit the fashion and tastes of the time, its reputation reaching its nadir in the nineteenth and early twentieth centuries. In spite of Artaud's belief that Seneca's tragedies most closely approached the ideal of his theater of cruelty,[1] Eliot found "the drama is all in the word, and the word has no further reality behind it," and E. P. Barker, writing in the "objective" *Oxford Classical Dictionary*, felt they revealed "the erratic ability and the limitations which are common stigmata of paranoiac abnormality." For most critics, the shadow of the Greek tragedians of the fifth century was too overwhelming, and his works were often criticized as poor facsimiles of his Greek predecessors. His tragedies started to receive renewed attention after perceptive essays by Regenbogen and Herington underscored their strong dramatic power, nightmarish details, historical relevance, and psychological complexity.[2] Their importance as Silver Age poetry of the highest order is now generally acknowledged. Seneca finds in the Greek myths the raw material for his tragic universe, but the universe itself is of his own creation, motivated by the interests that shaped his life: philosophy, literature, politics, and rhetoric.

---

[1] Puchner (2006, 203–4).
[2] Regenbogen (1927–8), Herington (1966).

Why Tragedy?

From its inception, tragedy as a genre reflected and questioned its contemporary world. The underlying themes and motifs of Greek tragedy
reflected the ideology of the *polis*; ethics, politics, sophistry, rhetoric, and
literature itself influenced tragedy, and, in turn, were influenced by tragedy.
Griffith notes the varying interpretations of Sophocles' *Antigone*, a play
that "may seem to switch back and forth between being a piece of moral
or political philosophy, a religious rite, a sociological treatise, an imaginative poem, a stage drama, a political rally, a psychotherapy session…"[3]
Seneca's concerns were not those of the Greek *polis*, but he does display a
comparable finesse in blending the ethical, psychological, rhetorical, and
political interests of his day in the heightened poetry expected of tragedy.
If one follows Fitch's relative dating of Seneca's tragedies,[4] Seneca was
writing these plays primarily during the reigns of Claudius and Nero, and
characteristics of the tragedies undoubtedly touch upon the political and
social world in which Seneca himself was a major player. How much these
tragedies were meant to openly criticize or comment on the emperors or
the principate as an institution is a vexed question. To divorce Seneca from
his time period, however, is to lose some tangible connection to that era in
which he "lived through and witnessed, in his own person or in the persons
of those near him, almost every evil and horror that is the theme of his
writings, prose or verse."[5] His tragedies provide a lens through which one
can observe actions and speeches that resonate with his historical period,
even if one should not assume that behind characters such as Atreus or
Eteocles lurk a veiled allusion to Nero or that the portrayal of *extispicium*
in *Oedipus* derives from Claudius' interest in Etruscan religion (let alone
that the incestuous, limping Oedipus acts as a surrogate for the incestuous,
limping Claudius). The broader issues of living under tyrannical rulers,
decision making under emotional distress, the position of the individual in
society, and the calamitous results of seemingly innocuous actions are writ
large in each of the plays.

Recent work has highlighted that Seneca's literary antecedents were primarily Roman and that the Greek works that did contribute to Seneca's concept
of tragedy were probably Hellenistic and not the tragedies of fifth-century
Athens.[6] Republican tragedies by Ennius and Accius were vital intermediar-
ies to Seneca's dramaturgy, as were his famous Augustan precursors: Ovid's

[3] Griffith (1999, 26).
[4] Fitch, J. G. (1981).
[5] Herington (1966, 430).
[6] See Tarrant (1978), Tarrant (1995), and Boyle (2006).

Medea and Varius' *Thyestes*. Seneca's *Medea* is more indebted to the various representations of Medea found in the works of Ovid than to Euripides' play, and his *Hercules Furens* can be seen as a response to the *Aeneid* rather than to Euripides' dramatization of the myth. The detailed commentaries to the plays, however, do indicate numerous potential intertexts to the Greek sources, and one should not put possible moments of *aemulatio* past Seneca.[7] For instance, Euripides clusters words utilizing the μηχ- root (μηχανή and μηχανάομαι) around his Medea, hinting at her intellectual powers and possibly foreshadowing her eventual escape on the μηχανή. Seneca evokes this wordplay when his Creon calls Medea *malorum* **machinatrix** *facinorum* (266), a word found only here in Latin.[8]

The dialectical nature of tragedy was also a key consideration for Seneca. It is not Seneca qua Seneca but his characters who provide their own necessarily focalized views of the dramatic action. This allows Seneca to investigate the dark themes and polyvalent language of his tragedies through diverse voices. In his prose works, he sometimes makes use of an imaginary interlocutor (e.g., *Ben.* 4.8.2, *De brev.* 1.1–17) or a previous missive of Lucilius (*Ep.* 24, 27, *passim*) in order to articulate opposing positions, whereas the tragedies are built for such exploration. The perspectives of the chorus and the characters are independent, which often leads to the characteristic tragic tension over language and ideas and forces the readers/audience to question their own interpretations.[9] Thus words and concepts are shown to mean different things to different characters: in *Oedipus*, the ghost of Laius sees Thebes' troubles to be the result of "not the gods' wrath, but [Oedipus'] crime" (*non ira deum, sed scelere*, 630–1), but the following chorus finds Oedipus innocent, blaming "the ancient wrath of the gods" (*veteres deum / irae*, 711–2). Whose view is correct? This is a play in which the very concepts of *ira* (with cognates repeated ten times) and *scelus* (sixteen times) are debated, and Oedipus will come to the false conclusion that his self-blindness, caused in part by his anger (*iratus*, 959), results in his pardon (*scelera donat*, 1001). Does Oedipus jump the gun in his castigation and punishment (as Ahl believes), or does the play point to the beneficence that this self-made scapegoat will bring to

---

[7] See Mayer (1990), which shows Seneca's recondite mythological knowledge. There are critical commentaries to each of the plays, which point out many of these *loci communes*.

[8] For further wordplay in the *Medea*, see Segal (1982) and Ahl (2000, 166–70).

[9] Cf. Vernant and Vidal-Naquet (1990, 43): "But the tragic message, when understood, is precisely that there are zones of opacity and incommunicability in the words that men exchange. Even as he sees the protagonists clinging exclusively to one meaning and, thus blinded, tearing themselves apart or destroying themselves, the spectator must understand that there are really two or more possible meanings."

Thebes for the future?[10] The subsequent history of Thebes, explored impressionistically in Seneca's later *Phoenissae*, certainly looks bleak.

Each of Seneca's plays exhibits this same dense intratextuality, resulting in "verbal paintings of almost static situations well known to the reader, but depicted in ever fuller detail as the work progresses."[11] Because it is in the nature of tragedy to be a mélange of different genres (lyric choral odes, "epic" messenger speeches, iambic dialogue), the tragic poets incorporated a variety of meters and literary sources in their works. Tragedy offered a challenging opportunity for Seneca to explore his major concerns in a variety of poetic registers. This intermixing of generic viewpoints permits Seneca to stage the various ways in which different types of poetry confront an issue or concept. One can see this at work in Seneca's *Phaedra*. Hippolytus' opening lyric song in anapests features hunting imagery that Phaedra then perverts to apply to her erotic "hunt" for Hippolytus;[12] Hippolytus, however, reclaims this imagery as a beneficial feature of his Golden Age before the chorus eroticizes his hunting prowess in Sapphic hendecasyllables, making it a feature of his irresistible beauty (795–819). Finally, Theseus begins another hunt with Hippolytus the prey, concluding in Hippolytus' grisly death. The continual interpretation and reinterpretation of this imagery reveals the play of the signifier within the generic confines of tragedy and how differing genres of poetry modify its interpretation (e.g., in the "epic" messenger speech, Hippolytus' hunting prowess is figured as the foundation of his *aristeia*). By such generic and intratextual interaction, Senecan tragedy interrogates the language of his day, pointing out the limited perspective of those in the throes of passion, power, or panic.

Performance and Rhetoric

Although Seneca's influence on later playwrights is undeniable, some have felt that his plays are too rhetorical, too bloody, and too awkward for a proper dramatic performance. This, in conjunction with the general diminution of civic theater during the principate, led to the hypothesis that the tragedies were primarily meant for recitation, in which the play (or selected scenes) would be recited to a small audience. In recent decades, however, reevaluations of Seneca's dramaturgy as well as a general shift

[10] Ahl (2008, 40–2) on the "Self-Destructive Hero" and 56–9 for the "crime-scene investigation" of Seneca's version.
[11] Mastronarde (2008, 221).
[12] It is possible that such a "reading" of hunting imagery was already present in Hippolytus' formulation, cf. Littlewood (2004, 259–301) for such deviant intertextuality and Kennedy (1993, 46–63) for hunting as one of "love's figures and tropes."

in taste have poked enough holes in the *Rezitationsdrama* theory that a
majority of scholars support the possibility of performance, even if there
is no firm evidence for ancient productions. Certain scenes cry out for performance: the stichomythic and antilabic exchange between Medea and her
Nurse (*Med.* 159–76), the violent struggle between Phaedra and Hippolytus
(*Phd.* 704–35), Atreus' revelation of the leftovers of Thyestes' children (*Thy.*
1004–6), and the laments sung antiphonally by Hecuba and the chorus
(*Tro.* 67–163). While the long messenger speeches and monologues have
often been faulted for inducing yawns among some audience members, they
often show Seneca at his most epic and were popular topics among poets
and declaimers alike.[13] Essentially, these long rhetorical descriptions and
ecphrases like the report of Hercules' attempt to fetch Cerberus (*Her. F.*
650–829) describe off-stage actions that are particularly pertinent to the
tragedy at hand. Seneca's Theseus creates a katabasis narrative to stress
Hercules' fleeting victory over death and to blur the worlds of the living
and the dead, thus foreshadowing the conclusion of the play and Hercules'
final death wish.[14] While the *extispicium* scene of *Oedipus* and the filicide of
Hercules Furens may put to the test the feasibility of on-stage action, critics
and producers have found ways to stage these scenes (and, in the case of
Oedipus, without harming any animals!).[15] Conventions that appear odd
and unnatural to the tragic stage, such as one actor describing the actions of
another, may have been inspired by pantomime, a genre that was extraordinarily popular during Seneca's time.[16]

By examining the dramaturgical nitty-gritty of certain scenes, one discovers nuances in the actions and the characters that shape the overall meaning
of the play. Boyle has pointed out that the actor portraying Oedipus would
find himself staging the three stations of the Sphinx's famous riddle by pray-
ing on his hands and knees, walking upright, and finally leaving the stage
with a cane.[17] *Phaedra*'s stress on Hippolytus' beauty and the fragility of that
"good" (*anceps forma bonum mortalibus*, 761) would only be further accen-
tuated by Theseus' lament over the bloodied bits of Hippolytus' corpse that
have to be assembled for burial (note the "ugly scrap lacking shape" [*forma*]
at 1265–6). Likewise, does Medea (and the audience) actually see the ghost

[13] The storm at sea is one culprit (*Ag.* 421–578), but this was not only a *topos* among
epic poets (Homer, Vergil, Ovid), but also a topic for declaimers (*Suas.* 1.15).
[14] Note that the chorus's subsequent song again describes the Underworld with
metatheatrical (*quantus incedit populus per urbes / ad novi ludos avidus theatri*,
838–9) and philosophical details (864–74).
[15] Cf. Ahl (2008, 119) for staging the *extispicium* scene "effectively and legally."
[16] Zimmerman (2008), Zanobi (2008) and (2014).
[17] Boyle (2011, *ad* 69–70): "Seneca has Oedipus go through the definition of man hidden
in the riddle of the Sphinx."

of her brother and the Furies (*Med.* 958–71), which leads to the murder/ sacrifice of her first son? The murder of this child is not signaled in the text clearly, and the performance of this action would help to guide interpretation of the scene. At the end of the play, she throws the bodies of both children at Jason's feet (imagine the sight and sound of their bodies hitting the stage *contra* Horace, *Ars* 185) and ascends in the *machina* away from the mortal world. Her final personal attachments to humanity are now gone and she has become both more isolated and more transcendent – Me*dea*. The repetition of the word for "gods" appears as the first and last word of the play, but it is Medea who is truly godlike in her control of the play's action and, ultimately, its meaning. If these plays were staged, then metatheatrical language would attain further edge. For example, when Medea leaves the stage, she asks Jason, "Do you recognize your wife? I am accustomed to flee in this way" (*coniugem agnoscis tuam? / sic fugere soleo.* 1020–1). Boyle comments on her mockery of the tragic *anagnorisis* and the attainment of her true character, "The metatheatrical sense (here unresistable) is that this is how Medea always leaves her play."[18] Characters such as Medea and Atreus act as producer, director, and dramaturge in their plays; events, on and off stage, happen in front of spectators, sometimes in settings directly resembling a theater (*theatri more, Tro.*1125), with characters evincing the paradigmatic reactions to tragedy (*mirantur ac miserantur, Tro.*1148). When Oedipus appears after blinding himself, he claims "this face befits Oedipus" (*vultus Oedipodam hic decet, Oed.* 1003), indicating a change in mask as well as the proper role he has assumed. While their pacing and style may diverge from the tragic form of Aeschylus, Sophocles, and Euripides, these tragedies can and should be performed. Performance criticism can still do more to understand and to appreciate the theatrical force these plays possess.

Seneca's tragedies, however, stress the importance of the language of the protagonists, even over their performed actions. In his 1996 article, Goldberg highlights the centrality of rhetoric for the understanding of Seneca's tragedies as well as the revolutionary change that Seneca made in creating this "drama of the word."[19] In essence, Goldberg reverses the valence of Leo's claim that Seneca's tragedies were nothing but *declamationes … in actus deductae* "declamations portioned into acts."[20] This turn towards rhetoric revivifies a genre that, by the time of Horace, seemed to be a vehicle for special effects, not literary expression (cf. *Ep.* 2.1.189–93). Seneca's writing and speaking style were criticized by Quintilian, but with the caveat that all his

---

[18] Boyle (1997, 132) and (2014, *ad* 1019–22).
[19] Goldberg (1996).
[20] Leo (1878, 158).

students "were *only* reading Seneca" (*tum autem solus hic fere in manibus adolescentium fuit*, I.O. 10.1.126). His striking *sententiae*, memorable wit, pointed turn of phrase, brevity, irony, *colores*, antitheses, erudition, allusive language, and crafty repetition of succinct phrases embody the rhetorical trends of the day.[21] It is language that demands a careful reader.

The declamatory style of the previous generation can best be seen in the work of *Controversiae* and *Suasoriae* that Seneca's father compiled. The impact of Seneca the Elder on the Younger's tragedies is prominent, even at those moments when the Younger appears to flout the advice given by his father. For instance, Seneca gives Hecuba a monologue in the *Troades* (955–68) that clearly responds to elements from Ovid's respective speech in the *Metamorphoses* (13.494–532).[22] Seneca the Elder had found Ovid's speech to be excessive, quoting sections of it as correlatives of the declamatory style of Montanus, who was also "unable to leave well enough alone" (*nescit quod bene cessit relinquere*, *Contr.* 9.5.17). The Younger, however, echoes these "Montanisms" in Hecuba's speech and places particular weight on the very lines that his father criticizes. So the focus on Achilles' ashes still fighting against Hecuba's family (*cinis ipse sepulti / in genus hoc pugnat*) is emphasized in this play where the word *cinis* is repeated an astonishing sixteen times (more than in all of the other tragedies combined!). In addition, the Ovidian phrase "even in the tomb we have perceived him as an enemy" (*tumulo quoque sensimus hostem*) is particularly important in Seneca's play – the tombs of Achilles and Hector are major landmarks and define the places where children are killed (Iphigenia on Achilles' tomb) or discovered (Astyanax hiding in Hector's tomb) and from where spectators observe actions (*tumulo ferus spectator Hectoreo sedet*, 1087).[23] By intratextually recalling these Ovidian "Montanisms," Seneca displays and underlines one of the defining qualities of his dramatic poetry – the integration of language from intertexts in the larger body of the play. By doing so, he calls attention both to Ovid and to this particular section of his father's *Controversiae*, a moment in which Montanus expresses a sentiment that is germane to the action of Seneca's own *Troades*, "That boy dies, if he is found" (*puer iste si invenitur peritur*, *Contr.* 9.5.16). Seneca often finds passages from his father's

[21] Summers (1910, xv–cxiv) and Canter (1925) are still very good. Morford (2002, 167) finds Seneca's prose style emblematic of his era: "The leisurely pace of Ciceronian prose, appropriate for the exposition of unchanging moral and political principles, was inappropriate for a world of moral and political ambiguity."

[22] Well explored in Fantham (1982, *ad loc.*) and Hinds (2011, 42–9), who adds echoes of Ovid's *Tristia* and *ex Ponto* to the mix. One can also find additional echoes of Montanus' poetry (especially the lines mentioned at *Ep.* 122.11–13) elsewhere in Seneca's tragedies.

[23] In a similarly striking pattern, the word *tumulus* appears twenty times in this play.

work that can apply to the larger dramatic context and, through this dual intertext to Ovid and Seneca the Elder, Seneca reveals the *contaminatio* of rhetorical and poetic sources that is a telling feature of his tragic poetics.

Philosophical Tragedy?

Because of Seneca's philosophical corpus, many have seen a Stoic message or critique in his tragedies.[24] There is a fundamental difference between the ethical prose treatises that celebrate living a philosophically meaningful life and tragic drama, but one can find connections between the two. Seneca's prose writings concentrate primarily on the internal makeup of the individual and the ethical problems that one faces in the turbulent political and social world of Rome. One can see how the tragedies, *mutatis mutandis*, do similar work. Rosenmeyer believes that Stoicism alone among the Hellenistic philosophical schools "offers a body of thought and a language that are temperamentally adequate to the demands of serious drama" and finds the tragedies are constructed with the Stoic concepts of *sympatheia*, *fortuna*, and *natura* in mind.[25] Treatises such as the *De ira* and the *De tranquillitate animi* provide valuable information on anger and poetics (respectively), which Schiesaro has employed in a sensitive examination of the connections between passion and poetry.[26]

The search for a Stoic hero in Seneca's tragedies has uncovered few candidates, in spite of speeches that may intimate Stoic ideals: Thyestes does not practice the moderation that he preaches (*Thy.* 403–545), Hippolytus' Golden Age reverie is tainted by misogyny (*Phd.* 483–563), and Hercules' final adherence to his father's pleas contrasts with his vehement desire for self-punishment (*Her. F.* 1321–41). The choral odes often applaud Stoic commonplaces, but these are usually revealed to be flimsy dreams in the dramatic context. Astyanax and Polyxena, minor characters of the *Troades*, do embody Stoic resolve in the face of death, and the crowd's response to their deaths mirrors Seneca's elevation of those who bravely meet death, from the slave (*Ep.* 70.25) to Cato (*Prov.* 2.10). Death is an important topic in Seneca's prose, and many of his differing perspectives on death are illustrated in the tragedies.[27] Moments of universalizing discourse in the tragedies are paralleled in works such as the *Natural Questions*: at *Nat.* 5.18.1–16, Seneca considers the double-edged results of harnessing the power of the

[24] See Ker (2009a, 128) for a quick overview of the theories. Marti (1945, 219) claims these are "philosophical propaganda plays."
[25] Rosenmeyer (1989, 39) and *passim*.
[26] Schiesaro (2003).
[27] See Busch (2009) and Ker (2009c, 113–38).

winds for navigation – products from exotic lands are shared, knowledge of the world is gained, Rome's might is expanded, but such voyages also cause incessant bloodshed (5.18.9), encourage greed (5.18.10), and serve vice (5.18.16). Mankind turns each natural boon into an evil (*omnes in aliquod nos malum ducunt*, 5.18.16). The Argonautic odes of Seneca's *Medea* offer a mythological variant of the destruction of the Golden Age and deliberate how "writing new laws for the winds" (*legesque novas scribere ventis*, 320) leads to an evil greater than the sea, namely Medea (*maiusque mari Medea malum*, 363). In each work, Stoic optimism is dampened by the reality of man's propensity for vice or Medea's murderous potential.

Seneca's strong interest in the psychological makeup of his characters and their propensity for self-analysis finds analogues in the philosophical works, where often role playing and self-apostrophe feature in the analysis of proper Stoic behavior.[28] In this, the metatheatrical touches of the plays mentioned earlier also assume philosophical significance, as Seneca often stresses the need to play one role in life (ideally that of a Stoic sage) while recognizing the difficulty of such an *askesis*. If one takes Seneca's advice to envision that Cato is observing one's every move (*Ep.* 11.8–10), how do the (stated) reactions of internal characters in the tragedies affect the (unstated) reactions of external spectators/readers? Nussbaum and Wray suggest that Seneca's plays encourage certain critical reactions from Stoic spectators/readers that will ultimately aid the Stoic *proficiens* in his or her progress.[29] Others are less sanguine about such a reading practice.[30] Many of Seneca's protagonists think that they must act according to their character (known from previous literature as much as any sense of a reified self): so Ulysses addresses his *animus* in an attempt to summon up his trickster nature in the *Troades* (*nunc advoca astus, anime, nunc fraudes, dolos, / nunc totum Ulixem*, 613–4) and Hercules regards living with his crime as his thirteenth labor (*Her. F.* 1316–7).[31] For some, the distance between their ideal and the reality is too much to bear – Phaedra's belief that her love for Hippolytus is destined in part because of her family's erotic history leads not only to heartbreak but also to their mutual destruction. Medea and Atreus seem to be in

---

[28] See Bartsch and Littlewood in this volume. Edwards (1997), Bartsch (2006), Bartsch and Wray (2009), and Star (2012) discuss Senecan self-scrutiny, concept of the self, and self-address. Boyle (1997, 15–31) focuses on the ability of Seneca's rhetoric "to *represent* and to cause 'shock,' and to do it, here and often elsewhere, through a self-dramatising rhetoric of cosmic and psychic violence, in which the speaker does not so much express as construct him-or-herself out of the very language used" (31).

[29] Nussbaum (1993), Wray (2009).

[30] See Schiesaro (2003) and Mowbray (2012).

[31] Note that these are the two mythological figures mentioned as Stoic "wise men," whom Seneca compares unfavorably to Cato at *De Const.* 2.1–2.

control of the advancement of their revenge plots, but even their self-control and rationality can be questioned if one pushes Atreus' *rapior et quo nescio, sed rapior* (261–2) as well as Medea's feverish address to her dead brother and the Furies (958–71). Can *ratio* and *furor* somehow work together?[32]

Stoic imperturbability is starkly put to the test as these characters are rent by their emotions and often descend into madness. Many of the plays feature scenes contrasting passion and reason, but again and again the characters' passions are unable to be quenched and sometimes even convert the restraining character to the other's side. Atreus' attendant provides the chilling confession that his *fides* will lead him to keep silent after learning Atreus' plans (*Thy.* 334–5); Phaedra's suicidal urges lead her Nurse to abandon any *remedia amoris* to cooperate in the pursuit of Hippolytus (*Phd.* 267–73). Moments in which characters repeat good Stoic *sententiae* are problematized. The Nurse's advice to Hippolytus to "follow nature as the guide of life" (*vitae sequere naturam ducem, Phd.* 481) echoes Stoic orthodoxy but is meant to spur Hippolytus into a love affair with his stepmother. Stoicism clearly influences much about the tragedies, but the tragedies stand apart generically from Seneca's prose writings and question the precepts and *exempla* representative of Stoicism. In *Phaedra*, Venus and *Natura* blur into one another with tragic results, and Hippolytus will drop many a Stoic buzzword in his response to the Nurse advice: "whether it is reason or nature or dire madness: it pleases me to hate women!" (*sit ratio, sit natura, sit dirus furor: / odisse placuit,* 567–8). In *Oedipus*, the final choral song on fate (*fatis agimur: cedite fatis,* 980) obscures as much as clarifies the workings of *fata* ("death," "destiny") and may hint at the literary straitjacket in which Oedipus is confined (*fata* in the sense of "what is said").[33] Stoicism is not the key by which one can unlock the single meaning of Seneca's tragedies but rather one of many keys that help us to uncover the myriad associations that these works suggest.

Poetry and Intertextuality

Good tragedy is good poetry. Seneca's tragedies feature lines of uncanny beauty (the "panning out" of the wedding song for Achilles, *Tro.* 199–202), touching charm (the souls of children are allowed to carry torches in the Underworld because they are afraid of the dark, *Herc. F.* 855–6), brute power (Medea's incantation foretelling the fiery death of Creusa, *Med.*

---

[32] Schiesaro (2009, 226) points out that "Atreus ... did follow his emotions, and was thus able to devise a plan whose success is now increasingly likely; yet Thyestes experiences a similar inner tension, but does not listen to his emotions, and thus faces a complete defeat."

[33] Cf. Boyle (2011, lxxiii–lxxvi and *ad loc.*).

837–9), and philosophical reflection (the perspective of the captive chorus, *Ag.* 604–10). Both Herington and Eliot believed that Senecan drama offered an expressive model of particularly "speakable" poetry, in which the various meters, recurrent words and syntax, varied sound patterns, and brilliant rhetoric simultaneously strike the ears and spark the mind. Open any page of Seneca's tragedies and one will find the alliteration, verbal play, erudition, declamatory elegance, and intense figurative language characteristic of the great poets of the Silver Age. Seneca knits tropes, figures of thought, and figures of expression with purposeful verve demonstrating "an absorption of the rhetorical mode in Seneca's mind so complete that it constitutes his linguistic psychology, not merely the achievement of effects but a way of thought."[34] It is not simply that he has created poetry about poetry but that he has created *dramatic* poetry, whose dialectic questions the very language that makes it up. The characters and action of the tragedies are bound by this heightened poetic language, which leads to the strong impression not only that all the events are tightly connected but also that this is a tragic world with its own conventions.

Seneca's *imitatio* and *aemulatio* strongly tie his tragedies to the Augustan poets. Two of his epistles (*Ep.* 79 and 84) stress that it is not an "anxiety of influence" (Bloom) that drives Seneca but rather an "ecstasy of influence" (Lethem) that blends the works of his literary predecessors into original and innovative poetry.[35] Seneca's integration and juxtaposition of Augustan material in his tragic worlds both appeals to his sophisticated readership and provides his own representative readings of this material. These plays expose Seneca's reception of the Augustan poets and underscore Seneca's sensitive and critical readings of that tradition. Seneca's incorporation of these texts in his tragic context either creates pessimistic connotations from the source material or teases out those connotations from ambiguous moments in the original. If Dido is first portrayed positively in the *Aeneid* as *dux femina facti* (*Aen.* 1.364), Seneca's Hippolytus makes woman "the leader of evils" (*dux malorum femina*, *Phd.* 559) even while Seneca employs Dido as an archetype for Phaedra's passion.[36] In addition, Seneca often boils down his source material so that the dramatic characters or situations attain seemingly universal significance. When the Fury mentions that the house of Tantalus is a place where "brother is terrified of brother, father of son, and son of father" (*fratrem expavescat frater et gnatum parens / gnatusque*

---

[34] Pratt (1983, 30).
[35] Bloom (1997), Lethem (2011, 93–120). For more on Seneca's relationship with Augustan poetry, see Ker in this volume.
[36] See Fantham (1975). Hippolytus' use of "evils" (*malorum*) is suggestive of Phaedra's passion, which is figured as an "evil" throughout the play (see 101, 113, 134, 637–8).

patrem, *Thy.* 40–1), Seneca knowingly intensifies Ovid's remarks about the sinful nature of the "Iron Age" (*Met.* 1.144–50) and places all its faults in this one family. Their actions and motivations thus become emblematic of the human condition. While Seneca looks back to Vergil and Ovid most often in his tragedies, as in his prose works, his choral songs carefully evoke the meters and themes of Horace's odes. For instance, the chorus believes Hippolytus shines "more brightly than Parian marble" (*Pario marmore clarius*, *Phd.* 797) in language that Horace exploited for his Glycera (*Pario marmore purius*, *C.* 1.19.6). The eroticism of the Horatian ode will prove problematic in *Phaedra* as forms of *clarus* soon describe the contrast between the living and dead Hippolytus (1111) and culminate in the "shrill laments" (*claris ... lamentis*, 1276) that conclude the play.

Conclusion

Seneca's tragedies illustrate the poetic fusion of the varied interests of Seneca the man. The passionate zeal that energizes the characters seems to spill over into the poetry itself, creating works of exceptional complexity. Seneca believed good poetry should strengthen and clarify the sentiments expressed therein as a horn amplifies a sound (*Ep.* 108.10), and his tragedies show how this maestro manages an orchestra of ideas and concerns in a poetic register both novel and forceful. The poetic fabric of the plays is lush and replete with information of interest to readers with varied concerns; what Seneca writes of Vergil's *Aeneid* could be accurately applied to his own tragedies:

> There is no reason for you to wonder that each man can pick up material suitable to his own interests from the same source; for in the same meadow the cow seeks grass, the dog seeks the rabbit and the stork seeks the lizard. (*Ep.* 108.29)

The topics discussed in this essay are merely a selection of prey that Senecan tragedy offers the hungry reader.

Further Reading

Harrison (2000) provides a number of essays that examine the question of performance, while Kohn (2012) discusses the dramaturgy of each play. On the importance of declamation for Silver Age poetry, see Bonner (1949, 149–67). For the question of Stoic interpretations of Senecan tragedy, see Hine (2004). For more on intertextuality in Seneca's tragedies, see Schiesaro (2003, especially 221–8), and Littlewood (2004, especially 259–301).

3

CATHARINE EDWARDS

Absent Presence in Seneca's *Epistles*: Philosophy and Friendship

Seneca's letters to Lucilius, the *Epistulae morales*, composed late in the author's life, are predicated on the extended separation of author and addressee.[1] At one point, Seneca recalls the last time he saw his friend:

> There are times when the sense of loss, hidden away in our hearts, is quickened by familiar places; it is not that they bring back memories that are gone but rather that they rouse them from dormancy, just as mourners' grief, though dulled by time, may be provoked by the sight of the dead person's young slave or his cloak or his house. So, yes, Campania and especially the sight of Naples and your Pompeii made my sense of your absence unbelievably fresh. There you are before my eyes. I am about to part from you. I see you choking down your tears and, despite your efforts to check them, not managing to hold back your emotions. I seem to have lost you just a moment ago. (*Ep.* 49.1–2)[2]

Seneca's longing for the absent Lucilius (away serving as procurator in Sicily) seems as acute as Cicero's for Atticus in the darkest times of his exile. Seneca conveys not just the pain of the moment of departure from Lucilius (would they ever see one another again?) but also the anguish of remembering his loss, his continued separation from his friend; it is a kind of bereavement. If Seneca sometimes appears unfeeling in his exhortations (your friend has died? Find another! exhorts *Ep.* 63), there are other moments when his humanity is most poignantly realized.

Seneca's *Epistulae morales* were often regarded by earlier readers as essays in epistolary guise. This is certainly the view of Francis Bacon, for instance, writing in the early seventeenth century, who invokes Seneca as a

---

[1] I am grateful to participants in the Durham "Letters" conference (July 2011) and in London ICS Latin Literature seminar (March 2012), particularly W. Fitzgerald, M. Schofield, and M. Trapp. I have also learnt much from M. Davies' commentary on Book IV of the letters (Auckland 2010).

[2] Text OCT; translations are my own unless otherwise indicated.

model for his own essays.[3] In recent years, however, the epistolary qualities of Seneca's letters have come to be particularly appreciated.[4] The issue for most scholars is no longer whether they constitute a genuine correspondence between Seneca and his addressee Lucilius (to whom, though he is not otherwise attested, *De providentia* and *NQ* are also dedicated).[5] That these letters were originally written only for Lucilius is implausible given their comprehensive philosophical agenda – and their self-conscious aspiration to a broad and enduring readership. Rather, the letters' epistolary qualities have received closer scrutiny in relation to their philosophical project. A series of letters offers a compelling and vivid framework for the delivery of a philosophical education, which stresses, among other things, the importance of particularity, of interaction, and of scrutinizing the details of one's day-to-day life (Schafer 2011). The philosopher Epicurus, often referred to in the earlier letters, is a significant precedent.[6]

The letters are organized in twenty books of varying length. One hundred twenty-four letters are extant, but more were known in antiquity (Aulus Gellius quotes from the now lost Book 22, *NA* 12.2.3). Though the book divisions are uncertain for letters 84 through 88, the articulation of individual books is clearly significant.[7] Earlier letters are, in general, shorter and simpler than those later in the collection, many of which (e.g., 94, 95) explore issues of greater philosophical complexity. While earlier letters often draw on the philosophy of Epicurus, those later in the collection are more exclusively Stoic.[8] Yet Seneca is perfectly capable of criticizing orthodox Stoic theory or practice on occasion, treating the syllogism, for instance, with particular disdain (82.9).

Some of the letters purport to have been written from Campania (e.g., 49, 56) or the suburbs of Rome (104, 110, 123). Most, we infer, were written from Rome itself, though the city is barely mentioned. Places, notably the villa of Scipio Africanus in *Ep.* 86, can be vividly evoked.[9] Yet the letters are often disconcertingly free of reference to specifics – and apparently personal anecdotes invariably have a philosophical payoff (e.g., 57, 108.22).

---

3   'For Seneca's Epistles to Lucilius, if one mark them well, are but Essays, that is dispersed Meditations, though conveyed in the form of Epistles' (draft dedication to Prince Henry, unprinted preface 1612). BL ms quoted in B. Vickers ed. OWC edn, 1996, 677.
4   Cancik (1967); Maurach (1970); Wilson (1987, 2001); Mazzoli (1989); Lana (1991); Henderson (2004, 2006); Inwood (2005, 2007a).
5   Griffin (1992, 416–9); Cugusi (1983, 195–206).
6   On Epicurus, see Armstrong (2011), Dolganov (forthcoming), and, in relation to Seneca, Griffin (1992, 3–4); Schiesaro in this volume.
7   Lana (1991, 292–302); Hachmann (1995); Henderson (2004, 28–52).
8   Inwood (2005, 2007a); Schafer (2011).
9   Henderson (2004, 93–170); Rimell (2013).

The letters visit and revisit a huge variety of topics, from how the would-be philosopher should conduct himself during the Saturnalia to the validity of forms of philosophical argument, including more conventional epistolary themes such as ill health (27, 54, 67) and consolation (63, 99). An especially prominent concern, however, is death, how it should be approached (30, 70, 82), whether it might with justification be self-inflicted (22, 77) – and its perpetual proximity (1, 12, 26,101).[10] The later books lost, we cannot know whether the collection was ever presented as complete. Nero, to whom Seneca had for many years been tutor, then advisor, is never referred to. But Seneca, out of favor with an emperor notorious for his readiness to condemn those once close to him, must have expected, at any time, Nero's fatal messenger (Tacitus recounts the circumstances of Seneca's death, *Ann.* 15.60–4).[11] Any of the letters, then, might turn out to be the last, giving a particular force to Seneca's insistent assertion (e.g., 12.9) that we should live each day as if it might be our final one.[12]

Some letters are very brief (e.g., 46), others immensely long (e.g., 90). Their style is sometimes (deceptively) simple, sometimes overtly complex.[13] Seneca mobilizes richly developed images with an idiosyncratic brilliance.[14] Deeply immersed in earlier literature, he invokes Livy, Vergil, Horace, and Ovid with great subtlety;[15] the poignant parting scene quoted earlier from *Ep.* 49, for instance, has been read as resonating with the explicitly fictional epistolary world of Ovid.[16] Satiric elements are to the fore in Seneca's vivid evocation of a noisy bathhouse (56) or a wealthy freedman (27).[17] Cicero's letters to Atticus (explicitly referred to only at 21.4, 97.3–4, and 118.1–3) are a particularly significant point of comparison.

According to the treatise on style attributed to Demetrius and composed (probably) in the first century BCE, a letter's chief purpose was to convey friendship. "The beauty of a letter lies in the feelings of warm friendship it conveys and the numerous proverbs it contains" (Demetrius 232).[18] Letters, especially in the geographically extended Roman empire, in which members of Rome's elite were frequently separated from those close to them for years

---

[10] Inwood (2005, 302–21); Edwards (2007); Armisen-Marchetti (2008); Ker (2009a); Braund in this volume.

[11] Griffin (1986); Hill (2004, 145–82); Edwards (2007, 86–112); Ker (2009a).

[12] Henderson (2004, 5); Ker (2009a).

[13] Summers (1910, xlii–xcv); Traina (1987); on "Seneca's epistolary poetics," Henderson (2004, 5); Williams in this volume.

[14] Armisen-Marchetti (1989); Bartsch (2009).

[15] Setaioli (2000); Henderson (2004); Berno (2006).

[16] Rimell (2013).

[17] Cf. Wilson (2001, 175–6).

[18] Trs. Trapp (2003).

at a time, served as a crucial mechanism to sustain, to enact, and also to represent friendship over great distances.

The paradoxically significant role of absence in the understanding, indeed the actualization, of friendship is also highlighted in Cicero's treatise *De amicitia* (written in 44 BCE), a work that is an important point of departure for Seneca. The friendship taken as emblematic in this treatise is that between Laelius, one of the speakers, and Scipio Aemilianus, dead by the time of the dialogue's dramatic date in 129 BCE (4). A true friend is a kind of image of oneself, *exemplar aliquid ... sui*, claims Laelius,[19] "so that friends though absent are here ... though dead, are living; so great is the esteem [*honos*] felt by their friends, the remembrance [*memoria*] and the longing [*desiderium*] still associated with them" (*De amic.* 23). It is, it seems, precisely the loss of his friend Scipio that prompts Laelius to articulate the distinctive nature of their friendship. And it is Laelius' mental work in recollecting his friend that serves to makes the loss bearable (104). Though Atticus is the addressee of the treatise (4), Cicero does not present their own relationship as parallel to the friendship of Laelius and Scipio (5).[20] The model set out by Laelius requires friends to be of equivalent standing and equal commitment to and involvement in public life; Atticus, it seems, never aspired even to enter the senate.[21] The ideal friendship in this text is intimately related to service to the state as a common project.[22]

For Seneca, by contrast, friendship's importance lies in its role in the pursuit of philosophy. The Peripatetics had stressed the importance of friendship to moral development (for instance, Aristotle's *Nicomachean Ethics* IX.1, 1169b), but this view was not universal.[23] In Letter 9, Seneca takes issue with those who hold that the philosopher has no need of friends (a claim attributed to Stilbo and, it seems, the Cynics). Because the wise man is self-sufficient, he has no interest in utilitarian friendships. He pursues true friendship as an object of intrinsic beauty (9.12) – though even between wise men, friendship gives scope to activate their virtues (9.7–8, cf. *Ep.* 109). It is natural prompting (*naturalis inritatio*) that draws him to friendship.[24] A more technical exploration of this idea is offered in Letter 48, where our feelings toward our friends both stand for and serve as the first stage of our connection to humanity more generally.[25] We should note that this

[19] Echoing Aristotle, *NE* 9.4, 1166a31–32.
[20] Leach (1993, 18).
[21] Ibid., 9–11.
[22] On Roman friendship in relation to politics, see Brunt (1965).
[23] Konstan (1997).
[24] Graver (2007, 182–5).
[25] Ibid. 175–7. Cf. Asmis' discussion of pedagogy in this volume.

philosophical discussion of the meaning of friendship (and its relation to the Stoic doctrine of *oikeiosis*) immediately precedes Letter 49's highly charged evocation of the pain of separation. Indeed, friendship is a particular concern of the sequence of Letters 49 through 64.

For Seneca, the title "friend" is not to be bestowed lightly. He opens Letter 3 with a remonstration: "You handed over letters to be passed on to me to one you refer to as a 'friend.' At once you warn me not to discuss with him all the matters that concern you, saying that even you yourself are not in the habit of doing this; thus, in the same letter, you have asserted and denied he is your friend." The letter continues: "Consider for a long time whether to admit a given person to your friendship; but when you have decided to admit him, welcome him with your whole heart. Speak with him as boldly as with yourself" (3.2). Letter 7 also dwells at length on the need for care in choosing one's associates. Here the advice is: accept someone as a friend, if he can improve you or you can improve him (7.8–9).

A later letter praises Lucilius' philosophical progress with the arresting (even disconcerting?) exclamation, "I claim you for myself; you are my handiwork!" – *adsero te mihi; meum opus es* (34.2). Lucilius, insofar as he has progressed as a *proficiens*, a would-be wise man, is Seneca's creation. We might also imagine him to be Seneca's creation as a friend (even if Seneca would never refer to himself as a *sapiens*). Letter 35, however, makes clear that, as Lucilius is still a work in progress, the term "friend" cannot yet be properly applied to him.

> When I exhort you to study, it is my own interest I am pursuing. I want you as my friend but that is not possible unless you carry on developing yourself [*excolere te*] in the manner in which you've started. For now you love me but you are not my friend. (35.1)

The term "friend" here has a significance still more circumscribed than in Letter 3, where Lucilius was reproved for referring to a somewhat untrustworthy courier as his "friend": "The sight of a man, his presence, communion with him bring something of true pleasure, so long as he is not only the person you want but the kind of person you want" (35.3). Thus Lucilius is advised to hurry, *festina*, to find Seneca – but more immediately to hurry to find himself. In Letter 35, direct personal connection is desired but deferred. In the meantime, Seneca's letters, insistent goads to self-improvement, offer a more focused medium of exchange. This is a rather unsettling moment in the letters.

Yet if Seneca presents Lucilius as under construction here, he often refers to himself in similar terms; at 6.1, for instance, he writes that he feels himself to be undergoing a transformation, *me ... transfigurari*. In similar vein, Letter

27 opens with the observation that Seneca's words of guidance are addressed as much to himself as to his correspondent. The letters' concern with self-scrutiny and self-transformation has attracted particular attention in recent years.[26] Long offers a lucid exposition of the relationship in Seneca between the occurrent self, the present self that is prone to a multitude of lapses, and the normative self, the self one aspires or should aspire to become.[27] Some letters stage conflicts between these two aspects of the self (e.g., 28. 10). Yet, as Seneca seems to shift in the letters from authoritative moral guide to vulnerable elderly invalid, from objective analyst of philosophical argument to affectionate friend, one may trace a plurality of selves.[28]

Still, the coolness in Letter 35 seems a far cry from the longing so vividly conveyed in the passage in Letter 49, with which we began (even if one motive Seneca offers for Lucilius to hurry is that he himself wishes to be the beneficiary of Lucilius' friendship – and he is already a an old man). To be sure, Cicero's letters to Atticus sometimes vary in the degree of warmth they convey. Yet the shifts between Seneca's letters appear more carefully calculated. The sense of longing, the *desiderium*, in Letter 49 both is and is not for the person who was last glimpsed choking back his tears as the two men parted.

Janet Altman's study of epistolarity famously sets out the letter's role in emphasizing either the distance or the bridge between sender and receiver, thereby highlighting or eliding the separation between them.[29] Cicero, particularly in his letters to Atticus, can be found celebrating the letter's power to connect. We might note, for instance, "I do, believe me, take a short break from these miseries when I am, as it were, talking to you [*quasi tecum loquor*], even more so when I am reading your letters" (*Ad Att.* 8.14.1 = SB 164).[30] But in more troubled moments, the letter becomes rather an emblem of separation. Cicero's letters from exile are stained with tears (*Ad fam.* 14.4 = SB 6). He worries about the accidents that may befall letters in transit: "it is thirty whole days since I last heard from you!" he laments to Atticus (*Ad Att.* 3.21 = SB 66).

Seneca, by contrast, rarely considers the letter as a physical artefact. Highly infrequent, for instance, are references to the length of time taken for a letter to travel from author to addressee.[31] There are no comments

---

[26] Hadot (1995); Veyne (2003).

[27] Long (2009).

[28] Edwards (1997); Veyne (2003); Bartsch (2006); Henderson (2006); Bartsch and Wray (2009); Bartsch in this volume.

[29] Altman (1982, 13).

[30] Cf. *Ad Att.* 9.4.1 = SB173.

[31] Though cf. 50 and, on not hurrying to collect letters, 71.1, 77.3.

about handwriting or sealing. Rather, the letter is a kind of live connection between the sender and receiver. He attributes to Lucilius a complaint about the informality of his letters:

> You complain that the letters you receive from me are not finely honed [*minus accuratas*]. Now who talks finely [*accurate*] unless he also wishes to talk affectedly [*putide*]? I want my letters to be just as my conversation [*sermo*] would be if you and I were sitting or having a stroll together – spontaneous and easy [*inlaboratus et facilis*]; for my letters have nothing labored or artificial [*fictum*] about them. (75.1)

This passage parades the potency of Seneca's prose to generate an immediate engagement (though there is surely an irony in *fictum* – it takes considerable skill to generate an effect that is so artless). Lucilius' letters are also said to work a similar magic on Seneca, who comments: "I never receive a letter from you without being at once in your company" (40.1), in a passage that vividly conveys both the pain of longing, *desiderium*, and the sweet power of the letter to alleviate that pain, transporting its author to its addressee, making their communication feel immediate.

For ancient commentators, it was almost a cliché to characterize letters as the literary counterpart to conversation.[32] Letter writers were frequently encouraged to strive for a conversational effect. C. Julius Victor, for instance, writing in the fourth century CE, advises: "It is elegant to address your correspondent as if he were physically present, as in 'hey, you!' and 'what's that you say?' and 'I see you scoff;' there are many expressions of this kind in Cicero."[33] Here as elsewhere, however, Seneca makes a familiar trope work harder. Comparing the exchange of letters with Lucilius to a conversation serves in part to occlude the absence of Lucilius' side of the exchange. We should note, though, that conversation itself has a particular philosophical role in the Stoic project:

> Rightly you insist that we exchange these letters more frequently. Talk [*sermo*] is most beneficial because it infiltrates the mind gradually [*minutatim irrepit animo*]; set piece lectures, prepared in advance and poured out in front of a crowd make more noise but have less intimacy [*minus familiaritatis*]. Philosophy is good advice [*bonum consilium*]; no one declaims advice. (38.1)

Seneca is dismissive of the power of lectures as a medium of instruction and stresses rather the superior value of cumulative conversations in introducing the lessons of philosophy into the spirit of the *proficiens*, the would-be

---

[32] Cf. Trapp (2003, 184–9); White (2010, 63).
[33] *Ars rhetorica* 27 trs. Trapp (2003).

wise-man.[34] A series of letters is thus particularly apt as a mode of philosophical instruction.[35]

The power of the letter to bridge, to elide distance, can under some circumstances be extended still further. The letter is a stimulus, which prompts the reader to understand he may have his friend with him not only when he reads his letters or writes to him but whenever he wishes. Letter 55 places Seneca in Campania (the native region of Lucilius, as 49 underlines), while Lucilius himself is still absent in Sicily. Seneca encourages his correspondent to imagine himself to be in Campania also:

> And so you should not think that you are less well off because you are not now in Campania. But why are you not there? You only have to direct your thoughts [*cogitationes tuas*], to be here also. It is permitted to converse [*conversari*] with friends who are absent, as often as you like indeed, and for as long as you like ... A friend should be held onto in the spirit [*amicus animo possidendus est*]; a friend of this kind can never be absent. He can see every day whoever he wishes to see. So study with me, dine with me, walk with me. We would be living in narrow constraints, if anything were shut off from our thoughts [*in angusto vivebamus, si quicquam esset cogitationibus clausum*]. I see you, my Lucilius, and I hear you most vividly. To such a degree am I with you that I'm wondering if I shouldn't start writing you notes [*codicillos*] rather than letters [*epistulas*]. (55.8–11)

The sequence of letters beginning with Letter 49 documents Seneca's extended tour of the area around the bay of Naples.[36] In 55, as in 49, Campania offers Seneca vivid reminders of Lucilius' absence, though in this case it is Lucilius' response to that absence that is his focus.

The power of the written word to connect the author with absent friends is a topic Seneca raises in other texts, too. A preface in his *Natural Questions* (also addressed to Lucilius) offers this work as a substitute for direct contact between author and addressee (4. *pr.* 20). This claim is by no means unique to Stoicism. Diogenes Laertius quotes a comment of Epicurus: "only the sage shall know how to be of value to friends both present and absent in equal measure" (10.118). In Letter 55, Seneca goes further, however, suggesting, strikingly, that we can enjoy friendship most, derive greatest benefit from it, precisely when we are apart from our friends. The specific techniques Seneca suggests for keeping one's friend in mind (*animus* is a key term) are important. This understanding of friendship gives a particular role to *cogitatio*, mental reflection (55.8–11). Present, we take our friends for granted.

---

[34] Cf. *Ep.* 6.5–7.
[35] Schafer (2011).
[36] Henderson (2006); Berno (2006, esp. 220–2).

Absence, insofar as it serves to prompt the right kind of reflection on friendship, hones that friendship into something truly valuable. The claim Seneca makes may be seen as a specific challenge to Aristotle's stress on the importance of proximity for friendship (*NE* 1157b), and this is almost certainly an idea Seneca explored at greater length in his now fragmentary treatise on friendship.[37]

When informed by *cogitatio*, one's engagement with an absent friend is more focused, more considered than the casual face-to-face encounters one has, even with those to whom one is most attached. For Seneca, there are important parallels between the relationship between absent friends on the one hand and, on the other, the relationship of the would-be philosopher to earlier thinkers and practitioners of philosophy. The letters contain much advice on how to get the most out of one's reading, as a key part of philosophical education. Seneca stresses, for instance, the importance of reading the whole text rather than gathering eye-catching *sententiae* (*Ep.* 33).[38] In Letter 2, the importance of choosing carefully whom one reads rather than sampling indiscriminately corresponds exactly with advice about choosing friends in the same letter.

The great philosophical figures of the past – Zeno, Epicurus, Socrates, Cato – repeatedly held up here as models to the would-be philosopher, can be encountered only through texts (Seneca groups together philosophers known for their own writings with those, such as Socrates, known only via that of others).[39] Yet Seneca's incantatory prose also works hard to summon up these men as individual presences, whose behavior, vividly described, can still be exemplary (in this sense they resemble the *maiores* of Roman aristocratic families whose physical images [*imagines*] were thought to inspire later generations to virtue of a more traditionally Roman kind).[40] This relationship is dialogic, for these figures themselves can also (at least in the correctly trained imagination) bear witness to the virtue of the would-be philosopher generations later. Letter 11 concludes with advice from Epicurus, a characteristic of many of the letters in the first three books:

> "We must cherish some good man, and hold him always before our eyes, so that we live as if he were watching us, and order all our actions as if he were seeing them" ... Happy is the man who can make others better, not only when he is in their company [*praesens*] but even when he is in their thoughts [*cogitatus*]! ... Choose then a Cato; or, if Cato seems to you too harsh a model,

---

[37] <Qu>omodo <amic>itia continenda sit (Vottero 1998), esp. frag. 59V.
[38] Cf. *Ep.* 39, 45.1.
[39] *Ep.* 6.5–7; 64.10; 104.21–2.
[40] Cf. *Ep.* 44 and Nussbaum (1994, 354–7).

choose some Laelius, a man of gentler character. Choose a guide whose life and manner of speech and wise countenance have satisfied you; picture him always to yourself as your overseer [*custodem*] or your model [*exemplum*]. (11.8–10)

The would-be philosopher, drawing on his reading (as well as remembering his own mentors) must choose a model that suits his own character and develop a mental image of this model, picturing him in his mind's eye and conjuring up his voice in his imagination.[41] Given the claim in Letter 55 that, with the right use of *cogitatio*, one can derive greatest *voluptas* (pleasure) from friends when one is separated from them, this is perhaps also true of one's relationship to philosophical exemplars.

In the *De amicitia*, Cicero's Laelius stressed the importance of memory in sustaining friendship after the death of a friend. The role played by *cogitatio* in Seneca's portrait of the best kind of friendship has an important precedent in the words of Cicero's Laelius, who, grieving for his dead friend, is made to comment that, rather than losing these recollections along with Scipio himself: *alunturque potius et auguntur cogitatione et memoria mea*, "they are nourished and enhanced by my reflection and memory" (104). The combination of *cogitatio* and *desiderium* is a potent one. Seneca, in Letter 63, addressing Lucilius' grief at the loss of his friend Flaccus, argues that the temporary separations from friends (occasioned by travel or other constraints) that one learns to tolerate in life may be seen as a kind of preparation for the permanent separation brought by death (63.8). This advice was, it seems, a staple of consolation literature and offers comfort even to those of limited philosophical attainment.[42] Yet the mental techniques enjoined in Letter 63 in relation to friends from whom one is separated have a close affinity with those advocated in Letter 11 in relation to earlier generations of philosophers. This affinity becomes especially visible in Letter 64.

While Letter 63 tackles bereavement, the opening of the following letter, 64, offers an arresting instance of separation overcome: *Fuisti here nobiscum*, "Yesterday you were with us," Seneca declares to Lucilius. Some friends had come round, a cosy fire was laid, the conversation ranged over many themes. "Then a book by the philosopher Quintus Sextius the Elder was read to the company." Lucilius could be considered present because he was in the minds of the assembled friends. But Quintus Sextius is also a presence. Seneca describes the effect of Sextius' words: *quantus in illo, di boni, vigor est, quantum animi!* "Good god, how much potency there is in

[41] Cf., e.g., Demetrius the Cynic, *Ep.* 62.3.
[42] Summers (1910) *ad* 55.10. NB use of the term *cogitemus*. Cf. the arguments in *Ep.* 99, again dealing with consolation.

him, how much spirit!" The text and its author are strikingly elided. Hearing the words, Seneca exclaims at the great man: *vir magnus*. In this letter and through this letter, the absent Lucilius and the dead Sextius can participate in an ongoing philosophical conversation, that, implicitly, has the potential to continue beyond the lives of Seneca and his guests – and Lucilius – also.[43] Indeed, the letter goes on to comment:

> I revere the discoveries of philosophy and those who discover them ... but we should add to what we have inherited ... Even now much remains to do and much will always remain and one who is born a thousand ages from now will not be barred from the opportunity of contributing further. (64.6)

Seneca's own letters are addressed to future readers (cf. 8.2) – and he expects a response.

If Seneca's focus is more usually on the relationship between two individuals, this letter articulates most explicitly the Stoic notion of the community of the wise, a community that transcends both space and time.[44] There is a notable contrast here with Cicero's philosophical dialogues, which (though often involving distinguished individuals long deceased) imagine interlocutors engaged in conversation in the same physical place. Changing political conditions perhaps made such face-to-face encounters more difficult, reinforcing the need for a "countersociety of philosophers."[45] In Letter 44, Seneca, ostensibly addressing Lucilius' anxiety at his relatively lowly origins (equestrian rather than senatorial), highlights the status-conscious nature of Roman society and contrasts with it another and better one, a society "created by reason," one that includes the dead as well as the living.[46]

The virtual philosophical conversation is a key concern of the *Epistles* in book 7 (63–9). Letter 67 opens in a deceptively low-key manner. Seneca offers a self-consciously commonplace remark about the weather: "spring is gradually disclosing itself." Still, cold spells often confine the elderly Seneca to his bed.[47] He is, however, grateful to old age for enforcing this confinement:

> Most of my converse [*sermo*] is with books. Whenever your letters come along, I seem to be in your presence. Their effect on me is such that I seem to be not writing back to you but taking part in a conversation. And so as regards the subject you are asking about, as if I were chatting with you [*quasi conloquar tecum*] about its nature, let us investigate together. (67.2)

---

[43] Sextius is also a key authority in *De ira* 3.36.1–3. See Ker (2009b).
[44] Schofield (1999, 93–103); Graver (2007, 181–2).
[45] Williams (2003, 23).
[46] Nussbaum (1994, 354–7). Cf. *Brev.* 14.3–4.
[47] On Seneca as an invalid, see Edwards (2005).

It is no personal problem Lucilius is concerned about in this case but rather that key philosophical issue "whether every good is desirable." Yet the exchange of letters is here too lent the immediacy of conversation. In this passage, however, it is not only the exchange between Seneca and Lucilius that is termed *sermo* but also Seneca's engagement with his books.[48] The comparison serves to characterize his particular reading practice. What is modeled here is not passive reading but interaction, engagement with what one reads. At the same time, the analogy between epistolary engagement with one's friends, an engagement that can at times bear a high emotional charge, lends an urgency and emotional weight to our engagement with philosophers of the past – and potentially the future.

Cicero's Laelius could offer a model of virtuous friendship whose value reaches beyond the grave. It is, perhaps, no coincidence that Seneca invites us in Letter 11 to imagine Laelius himself as a friendly moral guide. Seneca extends Cicero's model of friendship to give a particularity, force, and personal investment to links with virtuous individuals not directly known to the would-be philosopher but fleshed out in his (or her) imagination. In Seneca's hands, the letter functions as a particularly privileged mode of connection, allowing us to transcend absence, to establish a kind of supercharged bridge not only between author and addressee but also between past and future generations of those aspiring to virtue. This image serves to implicate us, as readers, in the conversation. The act of reading the letters, it appears, can, if done in the right way, elide their textual nature completely, so that the reader is directly in contact with Seneca himself. Seneca makes clear that it is not good enough merely to overhear an exchange between himself and his correspondent Lucilius but that we too must actively engage in the conversation, transcending geographical and temporal distance. But if we too aspire to become Seneca's friends, then, like Lucilius, we must work hard to earn the title.

Further Reading

Until recently, scholars writing in Italian, French, and German offered the most thought-provoking modern discussions of the literary aspects of Seneca's *Epistulae morales* (e.g., Armisen-Marchetti 2008). The last few decades have seen a notable upsurge in interest in the letters (which in the Anglophone world at least were deemed overblown and self-indulgent for much of the nineteenth and twentieth centuries). Amongst the pioneers is Wilson, whose 1987 essay offers an excellent introduction to the letters.

---

[48] Cf. *Brev. vit.* 14.5 and Williams (2003) *ad loc.*

Seneca's treatment of the self has attracted particular attention (Edwards 1997; the collection edited by Bartsch and Wray 2009), as has his treatment of death (Edwards 2007; Ker 2009b). The richness and subtlety of his engagement with other literary texts is a key concern of Henderson's challenging but brilliant exploration of, particularly, Letters 12, 55, and 86 (2004). Seneca's letters as Stoic philosophy are perceptively analysed by Inwood (e.g., 2005), who is alert to their literary form and texture.

4

MATTHEW ROLLER

The Dialogue in Seneca's *Dialogues* (and Other Moral Essays)*

This chapter investigates the "dialogical" character of Seneca's *Dialogues* and other moral essays. It consequently focuses upon Seneca's philosophical works in prose other than the *Epistulae ad Lucilium*: namely, the ten works conventionally called the (Ambrosian) *Dialogi*, along with *De Clementia*, *De Beneficiis*, and *Naturales Quaestiones*. But as this description of the subject matter suggests ("Dialogues *and* other ...;" "works in prose *other than* ..."), these works pose generic and definitional conundrums. Labels commonly applied to some or all of these works include "dialogues," "essays," "moral essays," and "treatises" – a range reflecting scholars' perplexity in identifying candidate genres for these works and in assigning the works to these genres. I will argue that these works do form a coherent, definable genre and are therefore reasonably discussed together, and that Seneca himself, and subsequent writers who discuss his works, refer to this genre by the term *dialogi*, "dialogues." My discussion is divided into three sections. First, I further pursue these questions of name and genre in order to characterize these works more precisely. Second, and most importantly, I probe their "dialogical" character by investigating the various voices that speak in them. Finally, by way of conclusion, I revisit my initial division of subject matter and reflect on the similarities and differences between these works and the *Epistulae*.

Name and Genre

The works under discussion share an array of formal and stylistic features. All have explicit, named addressees. All display a general concern for the moral status of the named addressee and other implicit addressees, a concern couched explicitly or implicitly in terms of Stoic philosophy. All have

* I thank Shadi Bartsch, James Ker, Silvia Montiglio, and Gareth Williams for invaluable suggestions on earlier drafts.

a protreptic dimension, as Seneca seeks to persuade his addressees to adopt particular views or courses of action. And finally, all have a definite, unified theoretical or philosophical theme: these include consolation; virtues and vices (clemency, constancy, tranquility, anger); social practices, aspirations, and fears (benefits, leisure, the shortness of life, happiness); and the nature of the world (whether providence exists, the various natural phenomena investigated in the *Naturales Quaestiones*). These works broadly share the first three characteristics with the *Epistulae ad Lucilium*; the fourth, however – the unitary theme – is not a necessary feature of the letters (see the following).

The term "dialogue" (*dialogus*) was used in antiquity to label at least some of the works under discussion. A survey of this term's usages in the century preceding and following Seneca will help illuminate its implications. Throughout this period, *dialogus* can designate a literary genre with particular characteristics. It rarely designates real verbal exchange: more typically, it labels an invented exchange, presented in writing, between two or more interlocutors.[1] As a Greek loan word, it is fittingly used by some Roman writers to label the works of Plato.[2] Certain Ciceronian works are called *dialogi* by Cicero himself and later writers.[3] These works always involve several speakers and are theoretical in content, whether specifically philosophical (e.g., the *Academica*) or not (e.g., *De Oratore*). Furthermore, Cicero's *De Re Publica* and *De Legibus* are overtly indebted to Plato's *Republic* and *Laws* and thus reveal by their titles the generic and philosophical affiliation that Cicero intended for them.[4] Later writers, too, use the word *dialogi* to refer to invented conversations on theoretical or philosophical topics among two or more interlocutors.[5] That *dialogi* constitute a recognized Roman literary genre is clear from the fact that, in various authors, the term is listed alongside other terms designating genres, such as letters, history, oratory, satire, and poetry of various sorts.[6]

[1] Real exchange: Cic. *Att.* 5.5.2, 13.42.1. Invented, literary exchange: Cic. *Att.* 13.14/15.1, 13.19.3, *Fam.* 9.8.1; Quint. 5.14.27–8, 9.2.31; Suet. *Tib.* 42.2.
[2] Cic. *Or.* 151; Quint. 5.7.28; Fro. p. 230.17 VdH; Gel. 3.17.5; Apul. *Flor.* 20.9.
[3] *De Oratore*: Cic. *Fam.* 1.9.23, *Att.* 13.19.4, Ascon. 13C. *Academica*: Cic. *Fam.* 9.8.1, *Att.* 13.14/15.1, 13.19.3. *De Amicitia*: Gel. 17.5.1. *De Re Publica* and *De Finibus*: Cic. *Att.* 13.19.4.
[4] Schofield's analysis (2008, 63–70) assumes that Cicero's philosophical and rhetorical works are all properly designated "dialogues" (correctly, in my view) or "dialogue-treatises" (less correctly).
[5] Quint. 5.14.27; Tac. *Dial.*; Apul. *Flor.* 9.87, 18.130–40.
[6] Quint. 10.1.107, 129 (see the following), 10.5.15, 11.1.21; Suet. *Aug.* 89.3; Apul. *Flor.* 9.87, 20.12.

Now let us consider this word's association with certain works of Seneca. It is attached to ten Senecan prose works in the Codex Ambrosianus, an eleventh-century manuscript that is the most important surviving witness to these works, and in that manuscript's descendants.[7] These ten works are transmitted in twelve books, which are sometimes referred to as *Dialogi* books I through XII. The works themselves, however, also have individual titles and explicit addressees. The precise form of the titles varies among the manuscripts. As conventionally titled and in their manuscript order, these works are as follows: *De Providentia*, "On Providence;" *De Constantia Sapientis*, "On the Constancy of the Wise Man;" *De Ira*, "On Anger," in three books; *Ad Marciam de consolatione*, "To Marcia on Consolation;" *De Vita Beata*, "On the Happy Life;" *De Otio*, "On Leisure;" *De Tranquillitate Animi*, "On Tranquility of the Soul;" *De Brevitate Vitae*, "On the Shortness of Life;" *Ad Polybium de consolatione*, "To Polybius on Consolation;" and *Ad Helviam de consolatione*, "To Helvia on consolation." Whether these individual titles are attributable in some form to Seneca or were fabricated in the scribal tradition is uncertain.[8] When scholars speak of Seneca's *Dialogi*, then, they usually mean specifically this "Ambrosian" group of ten works.

Three other non-epistolary prose works by Seneca survive, transmitted in other manuscript traditions and nowhere directly associated with the term *dialogus*. These are *De Beneficiis*, "On Benefits," in seven books; *De Clementia*, "On Mercy," in two books; and *Naturales Quaestiones*, "Natural Questions," probably written in eight books but transmitted in a mutilated and disordered form in seven books. All, again, have explicit addressees.[9] These works represent the "other moral essays" mentioned in this chapter's title, to accompany the Ambrosian "dialogues" narrowly speaking. However, as noted earlier, these works exhibit many similarities in form, style, and content to the Ambrosian *dialogi*. Indeed, there is a compelling argument that *De Clementia*, which may have been planned for three books, was designed as a pendant to the three books of the earlier work *De Ira*. This suggests that Seneca, at least, regarded these two works (the latter expressly among the Ambrosian *dialogi*) as profoundly similar.[10] The term *dialogi* was also applied more broadly to Seneca's prose

---

[7] Manuscript tradition: Reynolds (1977, v–xx); Reynolds (1983, 366–9).

[8] Reynolds (1977, ix–x). Some manuscripts include the addressee's name in each title; others do not. The conventional titulature retains the addressee only for the three *consolationes*, to keep them distinct.

[9] Reynolds (1983, 363–5, 376–8) discusses the manuscript traditions. Again, the manuscripts vary regarding whether they give the addressee's name in the title.

[10] Mazzoli (2003, 133–8), citing earlier work by Bellincioni and Ramondetti; also Braund (2009, 70–3).

works, at least after his death. The grammarian Diomedes, writing in the fourth or fifth century CE, remarks that he found an unusual word usage "in Seneca, in the dialogue 'On Superstition.'" While only fragments of Seneca's *De Superstitione* survive, this citation shows that Diomedes knew the work under both a descriptive individual title and the overarching title or generic designation *dialogus*[11] – just as the Ambrosian works bear both individual titles and the overarching designation *dialogi*. Nor is this all. Quintilian, in his *Institutio Oratoria* ("Training for orators"), discusses Seneca's style and overall value as a model for aspiring orators. Quintilian writes, "[Seneca] handled almost every literary subject: for speeches, poems, epistles, and dialogues of his are in circulation."[12] The general congruence of this list with surviving or known works of Seneca – speeches are well attested, though now lost; poetry in the form of tragedies and epigrams survives; many (not all) *Epistulae ad Lucilium* survive, and other letters are attested – has long led scholars to suppose that, by *dialogi*, Quintilian meant prose works apart from the *Epistulae*, that is, the kinds of works that Diomedes and the Ambrosian manuscript also call *dialogi*. For otherwise this significant corpus of Senecan writing lacks a place in Quintilian's scheme. Moreover, the fact that Quintilian mentions *dialogi* along with speeches and letters (two prose genres) and poems (a metagenre) suggests that he understood *dialogus* as designating a prose genre. And while Quintilian's work postdates Seneca's death by a quarter century, the two men were contemporaries: Quintilian states elsewhere that as a youth he had witnessed Seneca's oratory and literary disputation.[13] It seems likely that Quintilian's terms for the genres of Senecan literary production are Seneca's own: for why would he use generic categories different from Seneca's when he had personally encountered him and knew his works intimately?[14]

Two passages from Seneca himself, containing the only occurrences of the word *dialogus* in his corpus, may confirm this interpretation. In *Ep.* 100.7, Seneca describes Livy's literary output: "He also wrote dialogues, which you could ascribe to history no less than to philosophy." This statement exposes the assumption that a "dialogue" should be philosophical, even if Livy's dialogues – oddly for the genre, yet fittingly for the author – were

---

[11] Diomedes, *GLK* 1.379.19 = F75 Vottero: *ut apud Senecam in dialogo de superstitione.* Fragments and testimonia: T64-F75 Vottero.

[12] Quint. 10.1.129: *tractavit etiam omnem fere studiorum materiam: nam et orationes eius et poemata et epistulae et dialogi feruntur.*

[13] Quint. 8.3.31, 12.10.11. Born in 35 CE in Calagurris, Quintilian spent his adolescence and young adulthood in Rome, returned to Calagurris ca. 60, and came back to Rome in 69. He must have encountered Seneca in the 50s during his oratorical apprenticeship.

[14] Vottero (1998, 9–10), stressing these authors' contemporaneity.

in equal part "historical." In the other passage, from *De Beneficiis* book 5 (18.1–19.7), Seneca stages a lively and contentious debate between the dominant, first-person voice ("Seneca") and an unnamed interlocutor. At a certain point (19.8), Seneca interrupts this exchange, saying, *sed ut dialogorum altercatione seposita tamquam iuris consultus respondeam....* The word *altercatio* refers to the contentious exchange of rejoinders immediately preceding, which Seneca says he is putting aside (*altercatione seposita*).[15] In contrast, *ut ... tamquam iuris consultus respondeam,* "to give a ruling like a legal expert," entails a monological reply to an inquiry, pronounced by the authority *ex cathedra*.[16] To my eyes, the word *dialogi* here carries its generic sense, and I would translate the ablative absolute thus: "breaking off the contentious exchange (that is characteristic) of *dialogi*, ..." For Seneca is announcing a change from alternating rejoinders to monologue and hence from the usual generic mode of *dialogus* (where one finds multiple speakers and rejoinders) to that of legal *responsum* (where one does not). This seems to imply that the work containing these words – *De Beneficiis* book 5 and presumably the rest of the work – falls into the generic category of *dialogus*.[17] Thus Seneca himself connects the term *dialogus* with philosophical content and interlocutors who argue, as instantiated in this work. And if *De Beneficiis* therefore counts as a "dialogue," then so should all other Senecan works displaying such features – not only the Ambrosian *Dialogi* but also *De Clementia*, the *Naturales Quaestiones*, and various lost works.[18] The present chapter, then, could have been titled "Dialogues" *tout court*, as *dialogus* is a correct ancient generic designation, and probably Seneca's own term, for all the prose works under consideration here. Dialogue was a productive literary form for Seneca, and he employed it throughout his writing career: the earliest, the *Consolatio ad Marciam*, is usually assigned to the late 30s CE, while the latest (probably), the *Naturales Quaestiones*, dates to 63–64, the last years of his life. When and why the particular dialogues found in the Ambrosianus were compiled and given their order, which has no evident chronological, thematic, or structural logic, is anyone's guess.[19]

---

[15] *Altercatio* in this sense: e.g., Livy 1.7.1–2; Cic. *Att.* 1.16.10, with the words of the exchange following.

[16] A legal *responsum* is indeed a reply to a question but need not recount the deliberations from which it emerged: e.g., *Ep.* 94.27 for *responsa* that do not provide their reasons. See Griffin (2013, 281).

[17] Mazzoli (1997, 344), *contra* Griffin (1976, 412n1) and others.

[18] So, e.g., Griffin (2013, 1n1), Vottero (1998, 9–10), Mazzoli (1997, 343), Mutschler (1995, 94–5), Abel (1991, 50–1, excluding *NQ*), Codoñer Merino (1983, 131–2). Cupaiuolo (1975, 60–1n2) surveys earlier scholarly opinion.

[19] Dates and chronology: Griffin (1976, 395–411), Abel (1967, 155–70). Regarding the structure of the Ambrosian collection, Schmidt (1961) discusses the problems and valiantly attempts an explanation.

The "Dialogical" Character of Seneca's Dialogues

I now examine how Seneca constructs the dialogue in his dialogues. I focus on the authorial voice, the addressees, and other voices or interlocutors that intervene in these works. As noted earlier, all of Seneca's dialogues have explicit addressees. Their names always appear in these works' prefaces (apart from those whose openings are lost) and sometimes elsewhere; in some manuscripts they appear in the works' titles as well. In naming addressees, Seneca follows a regular but not invariable Ciceronian practice; Platonic dialogues never have addressees. Sometimes the relevance of a dialogue's contents to its addressee is reasonably clear. Each of the three consolatory works – to Marcia, Polybius, and Helvia – focuses on its addressee's specific situation, as each grieves the loss of a family member. *De Clementia*, addressed to Nero, offers advice to the young emperor in the period immediately following his accession. And the addressee of *De Brevitate Vitae*, Seneca's father-in-law Paulinus, is apparently being encouraged to retire from his magistracy (18–19) and devote his remaining years to philosophy.[20] Two addressees appear to be chosen at least partly for the aptness of their names. Annaeus Serenus is addressed in three dialogues on calm and equable states of mind: *De Constantia Sapientis*, *De Tranquillitate Animi*, and (probably) *De Otio*.[21] Seneca describes Serenus as having a "fiery and bubbly spirit," and Serenus is made to complain of emotional disturbances he suffers. These works thus play on the addressee's supposed lack of serenity, while Senecan therapy holds out the promise of harmonizing Serenus' disposition with his name.[22] Meanwhile, *De Beneficiis*, a dialogue on social exchange and generosity, is addressed to the fittingly named Aebutius Liberalis. Liberalis is presented as already being a generous reckoner of obligations (*Ben.* 5.1), hence less in need of Senecan therapy than Serenus is. Nevertheless, we may suppose that reading this work will help him become more perfectly *liberalis*, that is, more perfectly "himself."[23] Sometimes, however, a dialogue's relevance to its addressee is opaque. *De Ira* and *De Vita Beata* are addressed to Seneca's brother Novatus (later, after

---

[20] Williams (2003, 19–20), with further bibliography.

[21] For *Ot.*, the dedicatee's name is missing from the Ambrosianus, but Serenus is generally accepted: Williams (2003, 12–3).

[22] For Serenus' disposition, *Const.* 3.1 (*animum tuum incensum et effervescentem*); *Tranq.* 1.1–17.

[23] Such play between a text's theme and its addressee's name is also found in letters of Cicero (*Att.* 1.13.5) and Pliny (Whitton 2010, 132n84); Seneca's practice is thus not unique. Liberalis (*PIR*[2] A111: Griffin 2013, 96–8, Ker 2006, 37) and Serenus (*PIR*[2] A618: Griffin 1976, 354–5, Williams 2003, 12–13, Lefèvre 2003) are, however, real people.

adoption into another family, known as Gallio), yet these dialogues contain no information about this brother's situation or temper to explain why this address is suitable. The two surviving dialogues addressed to Lucilius, *De Providentia* and the *Naturales Quaestiones*, likewise offer no handle for explaining the appropriateness of the address.[24]

All these works feature a dominant, authoritative, first-person voice, which for convenience we can call "Seneca." Seneca addresses the named addressee (and others) in a lively, engaging "I-you" style, employing frequent rhetorical questions and exclamations. He advocates a particular (generally Stoic) view on the topic of the dialogue and therefore cajoles, exhorts, and chides the addressee and other possible interlocutors, including the reader, to embrace this view. Yet, for all that the Senecan voice predominates, these works positively pulsate with further voices – voices that either break in upon Seneca or that Seneca himself introduces, via direct or reported speech, as supporting or challenging his position. Most characteristic, perhaps, is the (unnamed) voice that scholars sometimes call the "fictive adversary" but that I will call the "generalized interlocutor." Seneca sometimes introduces this voice – cues it to come on stage – with a phrase like *inquis, inquit, dicet aliquis, scio quid dicas* ("you say," "he says," "someone will say," "I know what you're saying"). Often, however, it breaks in without introduction. Typically it interposes an objection or request for clarification, and Seneca normally responds with a second-person address, as if in conversation with this interlocutor. Especially when cued with a phrase like *scio quid dicas*, this voice may appear, within the fiction of the dialogue, to be "imagined" by Seneca – that is, the authorial voice foresees an objection or nuance and preemptively gives it voice so as to circumvent it. But this voice can also be imagined as a "real" objector, another *persona* notionally independent of Seneca the authorial voice (although, of course, equally invented and constructed for the dialogue by Seneca the author). Seneca also proactively offers explanations or poses questions to an unspecified *tu* or *vos*, giving the impression of one or more "real" interlocutors (voices that are, within the fiction of the dialogue, independent of Seneca). Now, in its propensity to lodge "commonsense" objections or seek clarification, the generalized interlocutor is depicted as an "everyman" who is less well versed in Stoicism than Seneca, is not altogether comfortable with the paradoxology of Stoic argumentation, and hence makes a suitable (if sometimes resistant) object of Seneca's tutelage and guidance. As readers, we are sometimes tempted to

[24] Williams (2014), however, suggests that *NQ*, the *Epistulae*, and the (lost) *Libri moralis philosophiae*, all dedicated to Lucilius, are "related movements" in Seneca's communication with him.

identify this interlocutor with the dialogue's named addressee – especially when the interlocutor's rejoinders are introduced with the second-person singular form *inquis* and when *inquis* occurs in a passage in which the addressee also receives an explicit, second-person address. But the typicality of the situations and problems explored in these dialogues equally invites us to maintain a more general view of the interlocutor's identity – and the more so when Seneca uses the second-person plural or the third-person form *inquit*. Thus Seneca's slippery rhetoric of address conspires with the universality of the named addressees' situations (grieving, contemplating retirement, seeking serenity of mind) to make one person's problems or questions into everyone's. This "everyone" may include us readers, for we ourselves may find the dialogue's situation resonant.[25] Seneca's Stoic therapy then applies ecumenically to "you" in particular (the named addressee) and to "you" in general (the generalized interlocutor, the reader).[26]

Yet these voices – authorial voice, named addressee, generalized interlocutor – are by no means the whole story: a profusion of further, heterogeneous voices populates these works as well. Seneca frequently invokes the opinions of other philosophers, via direct or reported speech, and he regularly quotes edifying passages from poets, especially Vergil and Ovid. Exemplary figures drawn from the past or present, from Republican heroes and emperors to gladiators and slaves, may be given voice to externalize their moral states. The Stoic sage sometimes speaks or has his subjectivity described. The very topics of the dialogues can speak out, personified: in *De Providentia*, God (*providentia*) speaks at length (6.3–9), as do his alter ego *natura* (3.14) and his evil twin *fortuna* (3.3); and in *De Ira*, anger speaks (1.18.6). Furthermore, all such voices participate in an exchange of rejoinders. When citing philosophers or poets, Seneca regularly expresses approval or disapproval of their sentiments or propositions. He thereby either aligns these authorities with his own position or preemptively undercuts them as authorities to whom opponents might appeal. Simple approval for some saying of a famous philosopher is common (e.g., *Prov.* 1.3). More complex is Seneca's mocking of Chrysippus, early in *De Beneficiis* (1.3.8–4.6), for making impertinent statements about *charis* (gratitude). Not only does he undercut Chrysippus' authority in case opponents should invoke it, but he actively recruits the

---

[25] Efforts to distinguish *inquis* from *inquit* as indicating different speakers, or to distinguish voices that object from those seeking clarification, seem to me hypercritical (Codoñer Merino 1983, 135–9, citing earlier scholarship).

[26] That these interlocutors are not necessarily adversarial or fictive explains why I prefer "generalized interlocutor" to "fictive adversary." On this interlocutor's characteristics see, e.g., Gauly (2004, 78–85), Williams (2003, 27), Mazzoli (2000), Codoñer Merino (1983), and Pusch (1942, 28–45).

generalized interlocutor to his own side, requesting his support against anyone who might consider Seneca's criticism of Chrysippus out of order. Regarding poetry, an anonymous couplet quoted at *Ben.* 1.2 receives detailed exegesis, with the first verse criticized and the second approved. And in *De Providentia* 5.10–11, an extensive quotation of Sol's words from Ovid (*Met.* 2.63–81) is twice interrupted by (prose) responses from Phaethon, composed by Seneca – no such words are present in Ovid – to create a mini-dialogue on the subject of fortitude that supports Seneca's current exhortation.[27] Augustus' speech in *De Clementia* (1.9.4–11), interrupted by advice from Livia, replicates in microcosm the advice Seneca is offering Nero; likewise, in the *Consolatio ad Marciam*, the long consolatory speech addressed by the philosopher Areus to Livia (4–5) mirrors Seneca's overall advice to Marcia. God himself cannot escape the exchange of rejoinders: his long speech in *De Providentia* 6.3–9 is interrupted by an objection from the irrepressible inter-locutor (6.6), against which God must defend himself. A particularly strik-ing type of "further voice" is a speaker's own self, hypostasized to address him from a position of superior knowledge. Serenus, in his opening state-ment in *De Tranquillitate Animi*, describes his struggle to maintain an even moral keel and quotes the self-exhortations and Stoic precepts by which he seeks to corral his unruly states of mind. Thus a "better," more serene Serenus, presented as a separate and more philosophically advanced voice, chides the everyday, struggling Serenus for his moral inadequacy.[28] Such examples can be multiplied *ad libitum*. Seneca's dialogues, in short, teem with voices, all of which are "dialogized" – brought into the give and take of assertion, criticism, and defense and thereby implicated in the protreptic of each work. Giancarlo Mazzoli, a rare scholar who has attended seriously to these further voices, speaks of the "polyphonic play" of the *De Providentia*; this characterization is valid for all of Seneca's surviving dialogues.[29] Indeed, these voices and their characteristic interplay are often visible in fragments of lost works. This is consistent with the hypothesis that many lost works are also *dialogi*.[30]

---

[27] See Mazzoli (2000, 256–7) and Lanzarone (2008, 371–2), who shows how Seneca's additions change the moral valence of Ovid's text.

[28] *Tranq.* 1.11, 13; the phenomenon is widespread in Seneca. Bartsch (2006, 191–208, 230–43) and Long (2009, 26–36) discuss such dialogue between a philosophically superior, "normative" judging self and an imperfect, "occurrent" acting self; also Bartsch, this volume.

[29] Mazzoli (2000, esp. 256, "gioco polifonico"). This is not "polyphony" in the Bakhtinian sense of "equal rights" among voices: in Senecan dialogue, no other voice has "rights" equal to the dominant authorial voice. My phrase "further voices" is a nod to Lyne (1987), which first exposed me to some of these concepts.

[30] Vottero (1998, 9–10) considers eleven lost works to be *dialogi* (T19-F96).

This survey of the voices in Seneca's dialogues and the ways they respond to and anticipate one another allows us to revisit the definitional questions with which we opened. Scholars have long been perplexed by the differences in form, style, and content between Seneca's dialogues and their putative Ciceronian and Platonic models. Unlike these models, Seneca's dialogues are not typically framed by indications of time, place, and occasion; his speakers are not consistently identified, characterized, or given ongoing roles in the conversation; and very rarely does any Senecan speaker apart from the authorial voice expound theory or doctrine at length.[31] How, then, can Seneca's works reasonably be called "dialogues"? An old solution to this perceived problem was to classify Seneca's works as "diatribes," by which was meant a (sub)genre, or set of characteristic rhetorical moves, associated with "popular philosophy": a lively I-you style peppered with exclamations, rhetorical questions, and interjections by unnamed adversaries and a relatively unsystematic exposition of doctrine. This solution no longer commands acceptance, however, as no such genre or package of rhetorical moves is now thought to have been recognized in antiquity, under the name "diatribe" or any other.[32] An alternative solution, more recently favored, is to regard the word *dialogus* as a rhetorical term indicating a figure of thought: for Quintilian remarks (9.2.31) that the Greek word διάλογος can refer to what the Latins call *sermocinatio*, a subset of *prosopopoeia*. All these terms refer to the characterization of speakers in invented speech. On Quintilian's authority, then, scholars have suggested that Seneca's "dialogues" are so named not to indicate generic belonging but in honor of a rhetorical figure (διάλογος/*sermocinatio*) featured in them.[33] To me, however, this explanation seems unsatisfactory: as we have seen, *dialogus* (as a Latin word) can indicate a genre with the characteristics we find in Seneca's dialogues; and furthermore, Seneca's dialogues, thanks to the authorial voice's control over the presentation, contain significantly *less* in the way of invented speeches with multiple and extensive rejoinders, hence less opportunity for characterizing speakers via speech, than do the dialogues of Plato or Cicero. Seneca's dialogues thus offer less scope, not more, to take their name from this rhetorical figure.

---

[31] Pusch (1942, 8–10), Codoñer Merino (1983, 132), Mazzoli (2000, 249–50).

[32] Oltramare (1926, 252–95) expounds the "diatribe" thesis for Seneca; also Pusch (1942, 57–66). Modern critiques: Griffin (1976, 13–16, 411–15); Codoñer Merino (1983, 133–5); Powell (1988, 12–15); Williams (2003, 26). The implied charge of sloppiness in exposition has been met by detailed structural analyses: Abel (1991), Wright (1974), Grimal (1986 [1949]).

[33] Griffin (1976, 414), Williams (2003, 3–4), Ker (2006, 26), Lanzarone (2008, 13); but Pusch (1942, 16–20) already offers solid objections.

In my view, no solution is needed because there is no problem. First, crucial similarities between Senecan and Ciceronian dialogue have been overlooked. While many of Cicero's dialogues do feature careful scene setting and a set group of named interlocutors who take orderly turns exchanging rejoinders,[34] some do not. Two works in particular – De Officiis and Orator – closely resemble Senecan dialogues in key respects: they have named addressees; neither involves scene setting; and both feature a dominant, authorial voice that controls the exposition and introduces other voices as needed. Also like Seneca, Cicero in these dialogues regularly names, quotes, or paraphrases philosophers, poets, or exemplary figures from the past, with approval or disapproval; he sometimes employs rhetorical questions and exclamations;[35] and he sometimes introduces a generalized interlocutor, who may or may not be identifiable with the addressee, to pose objections or express a divergent opinion.[36] Thus no characteristic device of Senecan dialogue is without its Ciceronian precedent; the difference between these authors' practices is in degree, not in kind. Indeed, these differences might appear even less stark if dialogues by other authors, now lost, had survived – dialogues employing the "dominating authorial voice" model rather than the model of dramatic or narrated exchanges among several well-defined, turn-taking voices.[37]

These observations lead to a second, more fundamental point about the characteristics of "dialogue." In a contemporary critical environment that has absorbed the ideas of Bakhtin, Kristeva, and a bevy of narratologists, differences in the ways that literary works present speech and achieve focalization are now more readily perceived as variations of a single underlying phenomenon than as fundamentally different phenomena. For Bakhtin, at least in his later work, "dialogism" is a characteristic of language as such: every utterance is constructed in response to previous utterances and in anticipation of utterances that will respond to it in turn. Thus the words of others, real or imagined, saturate all speech. Indeed, "dialogue" narrowly speaking – a more or less formalized exchange of rejoinders among several speakers – is merely an interesting special case of the "dialogism" that

---

[34] De Or., Tusc., Fin., Acad., Div.

[35] Off. 1.112–4, 2.25; Or. 109–10.

[36] Off. 1.29, 74; 2.7; 3.76, 79, 100–110; Or. 36, 143–5.

[37] Cic. Att. 13.19.4 describes an "Aristotelian custom" of dialogue writing, in which a dominant voice introduces the speech of other voices. This well describes Off. and Or., and Seneca's practice. The total loss of Aristotle's dialogues, however, renders all such discussion speculative (Schofield 2008, 68–70, 75–6 discusses Cicero's Aristotelian dialogical praxis). Subsequent to Seneca, Tacitus' Dialogus involves careful scene setting and named speakers exchanging rejoinders, while Plutarch's Moralia exhibit both the orderly turn-taking model and the dominant authorial voice model.

characterizes all language.[38] On such an understanding, it seems hairsplitting to draw sharp distinctions between Seneca's form of "dialogue" and notional generic norms identified in Cicero and Plato. On the contrary, it seems natural and obvious to allow all works in which multiple voices discuss theoretical or philosophical problems to coexist under the same generic umbrella, regardless of variations in how exactly these voices are staged.

Why Seneca's Dialogues Are Not Epistles ... or Are They?

By way of conclusion, it seems worthwhile to explore one last scholarly conundrum: the relationship of Seneca's dialogues to his *Epistulae ad Lucilium*. There are striking similarities. As noted earlier, the dialogues and epistles both have explicit addressees, display a generally moral and Stoic philosophical orientation, and employ hortatory rhetoric. Now we may add that the *Epistulae* generally feature the same array of "further voices" as the dialogues do: other philosophers, poets, exemplary figures, and the addressee/generalized interlocutor, all choreographed by the dominant authorial voice of Seneca. Though on average much shorter than the dialogues, a few *Epistulae* are long enough to rival the shortest dialogues; and the dialogues themselves vary greatly in length.[39] Thus one may perceive a complementarity, where the epistolary form is perhaps deemed suitable for short to mid-length expositions and the dialogue form serves for mid-length to long expositions.

Yet there are also crucial differences between the Senecan epistle and dialogue, as recent work by Wilson, Lana, and Inwood has shown. First, there are formal distinctions: the *salutem* and *vale* formulae are inevitable at a letter's opening and closing but absent from the dialogues. Second, diverse topics may be treated within a single letter, whereas the dialogues are monothematic.[40] Third, the organizational scale of thematic discussions in the

---

[38] Particularly helpful for thinking about the ancient genre of dialogue is Bakhtin's late (1952–3) essay "The problem of Speech Genres": Bakhtin (1986, 60–102). My own language and thinking is indebted to the Bakhtinian formulation of "dialogism." Other scholars who discuss Seneca's dialogism in Bakhtinian terms are Gauly (2004, 74–7), Bartsch (2006, 240n13); similarly Meyer (2006), without invoking Bakhtin explicitly.

[39] The *Epistulae* range from 149 words (*Ep.* 62) to 4164 and 4106 words (*Ep.* 94 and 95). These longest letters just surpass the 4081 words of *Prov.*, the shortest complete Ambrosian dialogue. The longest Ambrosian dialogue, *De Ira* 3, is 9306 words, more than twice as long. Maurizio Lana (in Lana 1991, 290–305) provides word counts for the Ambrosian dialogues and *Epistulae*, but not for *Clem.*, *Ben.*, or *NQ*.

[40] Thus the (spurious) title/subject headings attached to each letter in the Loeb edition – as if each were a monothematic dialogue in miniature – are misleading and misrepresent the letters' character.

collection of *Epistulae* is both shorter and longer than in the dialogues. Within an individual letter, shorter length combined (sometimes) with diverse subject matter provides less scope for developing a given theme than the longer, monothematic dialogue form provides. But a given theme may be treated from diverse perspectives in many different letters, yielding a more sprawling, leisurely, contextualized exposition over the entire epistolary collection than could be achieved in a single, focused dialogue. Fourth, the collection of *Epistulae* displays an overall development – a "surreptitious narrative," in Wilson's words – that rewards reading the letters sequentially and penalizes reading them separately; the dialogues, conversely, seem to be autonomous works not intended to be read in any particular order.[41] Seneca surely had reasons to choose one genre or the other for a given purpose, and these scholars' helpful and subtle analyses give an inkling of what is at stake in this choice. But these scholars are also reproducing an ancient *topos*, which we see manifested in Demetrius' treatise *On Style* from the Hellenistic or early Imperial period. This work discusses at length (223–35) the similarities and differences in style, form, and content between letters and dialogues. Thus the debate about how and whether to pry these genres apart is itself two millennia old, a fact that constitutes the clearest possible proof of their close kinship and mutual entanglement – their tendency to gravitate together and, under certain conditions, meld. Indeed, James Ker has argued that Seneca's works in general resist being read in "monogeneric" ways; he examines generic blurring not only between dialogues and epistles but also elsewhere in the Senecan corpus.[42] Having opened this chapter by excluding the *Epistulae* from discussion, then, I close by bringing them back into the generic conversation as a kindred literary form that, in the end, can be distinguished from the *dialogi* only with care.[43]

Further Reading

The late nineteenth and early twentieth centuries witnessed much scholarly interest in whether "dialogue" is an ancient genre, what characteristics works called "dialogues" have, which of Seneca's prose works count as "dialogues," and how such works relate to their notional Ciceronian and Platonic models. Pusch's (1942) dissertation lucidly summarizes the

---

[41] Wilson (1987, 2001, 186 for quote); Lana (1991, 271–4); Inwood 2007a. Within multibook dialogues, however, individual books are clearly ordered; also, as noted earlier, *De Ira* and *De Clementia* may be paired.

[42] Ker (2006, esp. 31).

[43] In this spirit, I refer the reader to Catharine Edwards' chapter on the *Epistulae* in this volume.

evidence and arguments that characterized that discussion and provides all the earlier bibliography. More recently, with scholarly fashion favoring Seneca's *Epistulae* over his other prose works, the genre question has been discussed most fruitfully by scholars seeking to identify what is distinctive about the letters: for example, Wilson (1987 and 2001), Lana (1991), and Inwood (2007a); however, Ker (2006) offers a broader view. Furthermore, the rise of narratology and of Bakhtinian approaches to literature in the later decades of the twentieth century have decisively reframed discussions about "dialogue:" Bakhtin (1986 [1952]) is an accessible introduction to this critic's (late) thought about the "dialogicity" and polyvocal quality of certain kinds of literature. Scholarship on the diverse voices in Seneca's prose works – how they are presented, what authority they have, what their ideological effects are – is sparse, but Codoñer Merino (1983, e.g.) and especially Mazzoli (1997 and 2000, e.g.) have thoughtfully explored dimensions of this question.

5

MALCOLM SCHOFIELD

Seneca on Monarchy and the Political Life: *De Clementia, De Tranquillitate Animi, De Otio*

A Mirror for a Prince

Seneca's *On Mercy* (*de Clementia*) was one of his more dazzling literary performances and "a highly original work."[1] The very first sentence is designed to jolt the reader into rapt attention and expectation (*Clem.* 1.1.1): "Writing about mercy, Nero Caesar, is my undertaking: so as to act in a way as a mirror, and show you to yourself – as someone about to attain the greatest pleasure of all." This is to be an advice book for the young emperor, into only the second year of his reign, which will not, in the style that had been customary in such productions, specify a whole list of royal virtues to be demonstrated but instead announces an exclusive focus on just one: mercy. Nero is in effect being told – in no uncertain terms, and in a work presumably intended for general circulation – that he must make mercy his first and last priority. Seneca and his original envisaged readership alike would no doubt have had a strong suspicion that the emphasis would be one welcome to Nero. "*Clementia*," commented Miriam Griffin, "was part of the publicity of the new regime from the start,"[2] explicit in "frequent speeches" on *clementia* actually written for him by Seneca that the emperor delivered in 55 CE (Tac. *Ann.* 13.11.2). *On mercy* could have been construed by its addressee as further publicity, recording for posterity exactly the self-image he would have wished to be perpetuated. On the other hand, it could hardly fail to remind him just how much was accordingly expected of him after the cruelty and arbitrariness of Claudius. Seneca will shortly go on to say (*Clem.* 1.1.6):

> The burden you have taken upon yourself is huge.... That would have been difficult were that goodness of yours not something in your nature, but assumed

---

[1] Griffin (2003, 169).
[2] Griffin (1976, 135).

for the occasion. For no one can wear a mask (*persona*) for long: fictions quickly collapse into the individual's true nature.

No less arresting is the rhetorical device of the mirror that Seneca announces in his opening words and puts to work immediately – which ironically is precisely the creation of a *persona* for Nero, although one he is invited to see as what is to be his own true nature.[3] We do not know whether any Greek writer had resorted to such a device in addressing rulers or writing treatises on kingship. The most salient precedent in surviving Latin literature comes in Cicero's *De re publica*, where Scipio Aemilianus makes it the chief responsibility of a true statesman "never to cease educating and observing himself; to urge others to imitate himself; to present himself through the brilliance of the spectacle of his mind and his own life as a mirror to his fellow citizens" (*Rep.* 2.69). But that is a theoretical description expressed in the third person. Seneca invests the idea with audacious urgency by promising actually to show Nero "you to yourself" – and incidentally creating thereby a literary genre that was to become astonishingly popular much later, especially in the high Middle Ages.[4] As Quintilian would recommend to advocates, "a speech does not adequately fulfill its purpose or attain total domination if it exercises its force only so far as the ears, and the judge thinks he is merely being given an account of the matters he is determining, without their being brought out and shown to the eyes of the mind" (*Inst.* 8.3.62). The picture Seneca will paint is to be a mirror for Nero himself, not as in Cicero for the citizens to see the kind of life and character to which they should aspire (Nero is an autocrat). It is designed to give him pleasure: the pleasure of inspecting and examining his own good conscience – before looking away and contemplating the condition that will be the fate of the "enormous mass" (*multitudo*) of the populace, of how they would lurch into seditious chaos if they were to break "this yoke" (Seneca does not need to explain the yoke he refers to).[5]

The image of himself Nero will see when he looks in Seneca's mirror is therefore engaged in self-examination (*Clem.* 1.1.2): "Is it I of all mortals," the imaged Nero says, "who has found favour and been chosen to act on earth for the gods?" What then gets reviewed is Nero's absolute power of

---

[3] See Stacey (2007, 44–5).

[4] Petrarch stuck particularly closely to the Senecan model, not least in replicating its use of the mirror itself (Stacey 2007, 145–56). Others treated the prince as a model of virtue for the citizens to imitate (see, for example, Stacey 2007, 168–9), more in the mode recommended by Cicero (although Book 2 of *On the commonwealth*, rediscovered only in 1819, would have been unknown to them).

[5] For further exploration of the complexities of Seneca's use of the image motif, see section 2 of Rimell's essay in this volume.

life and death – or rather, killing (*necis*) – over the nations, and the calm judiciousness with which he wields it, even in the face of extreme provocation, with mercy "ready on standby." With the pleasure that, as promised, comes from scrutiny of a good conscience, he can then conclude (*Clem.* 1.1.4): "This very day, should the gods require me to account for myself, I am prepared to present for the reckoning the human race." Seneca's Nero is portrayed from the outset as an absolute monarch, made so by divine election. He holds that power as a trust (*fides*) and as guardianship (*tutela*) (*Clem.* 1.1.5): the concepts Cicero had invoked in explaining the duty of a statesman (*Rep.* 2.51, *Off.* 1.85) or a magistrate (*Off.* 1.124). But it is to the gods and only to the gods that he is responsible. Augustus's constitutional fiction (*Mon. Anc.* 34.2–3) that the emperor is no more than the *princeps*, the leading political figure in the *res publica*, a magistrate exceeding others only in his influence (*auctoritas*), is silently dismissed from view.

So if the reader is surprised when in chapter 3 Seneca writes "king or *princeps*" without differentiation (*Clem.* 1.3.3), it can only be because of the unpopular associations traditionally carried by the word *rex*,[6] not because room has been left for any doubt that monarchy is his subject. He will soon go out of his way to indicate that fussing over the precise choice of terminology would be wrong when he speaks of "*principes* and kings – and guardians of public well-being under whatever name they go" as being unsurprisingly the object of a love stronger even than that characteristic of private ties (*Clem.* 1.4.3). As Griffin points out,[7] this chimes with Seneca's disapproving review in *On benefits* of what might have prompted Marcus Brutus to the assassination of Julius Caesar. The first possible motive he ascribes to him is fear of the very word "king," although (he comments), "it is under a just king that there is the best condition of the *civitas* (citizen body)" (*Ben.* 2.20.2).

In the rest of *On mercy*, Seneca rings the changes between *princeps* and *rex*, sometimes within a single paragraph (*Clem.* 1.7.1, 1.16.1). He never addresses Nero directly as *rex*. And to begin with, he continues to locate the emperor's rule and its benefits within the framework of Roman republican discourse – *ius* (justice) prevails over every form of injustice, supreme liberty is in want of nothing except the license to destroy itself – and with an echo of Ciceronian talk of the best "configuration" (*forma*) of the *res publica* (*Clem.* 1.1.8; Cicero had in fact himself made Scipio propose the view that of the basic forms of political systems, kingship was by far the best, even if all of them are treated by him as deficient by comparison with an appropriate "mixed" constitution: e.g., *Rep.* 1.54, 69; 2.43). But in discussing

---

[6] See Griffin (1976, 142, 206–7).
[7] Griffin (1976, 147).

the nature of such rule – something that occupies much of Book 1 of the treatise – Seneca deploys many themes characteristic of the existing literature of advice to monarchs.[8] Particularly striking are two other elements: the sustained contrasting of kingship with tyranny that rounds off the first of the main sections of Book 1 (see especially *Clem.* 1.11.4–12.4) and the extended comparison of human kings with the king bee at the end of the second,[9] culminating in the epigram: "His one defense is the love of the citizens," which can be secured only by mercy (*Clem.* 1.19.2–6).

Kingship

At the beginning of chapter 3 (*Clem.* 1.3.1), Seneca announces his proposed organization of the whole work, which was apparently to occupy three books (only the first and the beginning of the second survive, if indeed the whole was ever completed). The information given there about the subject matter of Book 1 is lost, owing to corruption of the manuscript text. But there can be little doubt that the project was to be one of demonstrating that (as chapter 5 will put it) "mercy is something natural to humanity in general, but especially graces those who exercise *imperium*" ("rule": *imperatores* is the word Seneca uses here, but he is here just repeating something he claimed about "king or *princeps*" in chapter 3: *Clem.* 1.5.2, 1.3.2–3). That is why Book 1 of *On mercy* turns effectively into an exercise in the political theory of kingship. It is sometimes said of Seneca that he is no political theorist but always the moralist.[10] It is true that if Aristotle's *Politics* is taken as the paradigm, *On mercy* does not begin to look like political theorizing, whether in form or in content. But not much surviving Greek political theory much resembles the *Politics*. And in its own rhetorical mode and didactic register, *On mercy* certainly includes a great deal of theoretical exploration – a coherently interconnected set of ideas, vigorously argued through – of the fundamental basis of kingship, what it is to be a king, and how he must behave. In fact, it covers much the same kind of ground as Cicero's Scipio in his argument for kingship as the best political system (*laetissima forma rei publicae*, to quote Seneca himself again: *Clem.* 1.1.8) in *De re publica* (*Rep.* 1.56–63) – a work that does by common consent approximate the Aristotelian paradigm.[11]

---

[8] Aalders (1975) remains a useful guide to the surviving remains or traces of these works. See also Schofield (1999, 742–4), Hahm (2000, 457–64), and Murray (2007).

[9] Here Seneca draws on Vergil's celebrated treatment of bees in Book 4 of the *Georgics*, which, like all Greek and Latin writing, assumes that the queen bee is in fact male, rather than on kingship treatises (Braund 2009, 342–3; cf. 214).

[10] So, e.g., Cooper and Procopé (1995, xxv–xxvi).

[11] See also Griffin (1996, 281–2); cf. Rowe (2000).

Initially, kingship theorizing is acknowledged by Seneca to be something at least apparently digressive from his professed main theme. He insists that this is only an appearance (*Clem.* 1.5.1):

> My discourse seems to have retreated rather a long way from the topic. But my goodness, it presses hard upon the real issue. For if, as the argument goes thus far, you are the mind of your own[12] commonwealth (*res publica*), and it is your body, then you see, I think, how necessary is mercy. For you are sparing yourself when you appear to be sparing another.

Seneca has developed the argument, a monarchist adaptation of the already common metaphor of the body politic,[13] over the previous two chapters (*Clem.* 1.3.5–1.4.3), where he also makes the converse point that it is therefore "their own safety they love when for one human being they lead ten legions at a time into battle" and expose themselves to injury to defend the standard of their supreme commander (*imperator*). "For he," says Seneca, playing a similarly monarchist variation upon Cicero's theory of justice (*ius*) as what binds a people together in a true *res publica* (*Rep.* 1.42, 3.43), "is the bond that makes the commonwealth cohesive."

Thereafter no hint of apology is offered for the substantial installments of theorizing about kingship that occupy much of Book 1 of the treatise. One especially interesting discussion in its first section begins when Seneca has argued that those lower in the social order are freer to indulge in aggressive talk and behavior than is the king (*Clem.* 1.7.4). He makes Nero complain that this is "servitude, not *imperium* (rule)." "Yes," is the reply: "*Imperium* is for you a noble servitude"[14] (*Clem.* 1.8.1; the good king proves by his goodness that "the *res publica* does not belong to him" but "he belongs to the *res publica*": *Clem.* 1.19.8). Seneca then spells out various dimensions of restriction of activity involved in this subjection: the ruler's need to safeguard his reputation, his reliance on an armed guard when he ventures out in public,[15] the way giving vent to anger will actually – because of the hatred it provokes – make his position less secure (*Clem.* 1.8.1–7). That final point is

---

[12] Braund (2009: 102, 220), uniquely among editors, deletes *tuae* as "intrusive," to my mind on weak grounds.

[13] See, for example, Brock (2013, Ch. 5, Greece), Wiseman (2012, Cicero), and Béranger (1953: 218–52, the early empire).

[14] This translates *nobilem* (Wilamowitz) for MSS. *nobis*, which would give the sentence: "*Imperium* is for us, servitude for you." That yields a daringly striking and elegantly balanced epigram but contains no element preparing the reader for the preoccupation with virtue and reputation that immediately follows.

[15] Something traditionally associated with tyranny: e.g., Plato *Rep.* 8.566b–567e; but Seneca is careful to make the king's bodyguard more like Plato's guardians, protecting common safety: *Clem.* 1.13.1.

then developed at length through a treatment of the wisdom of the mildness Augustus displayed, at least in his latter years (*Clem.* 1.9.1–1.11.4).

The second main section of Book 1 poses the question (*Clem.* 1.14.1): "What then is the duty (*officium*) of the *princeps*?" For Isocrates in *To Nicocles*, this was in fact the first topic calling for investigation (*ad Nic.* 9): "First, then, we must consider what is the function of those who exercise kingship?" Seneca answers it in the first instance with the reply that it is the duty good parents have toward their children: a traditional analogy for kingship, now developed at length. But other analogies[16] are deployed in due course: the teacher, the military tribune or centurion, and then several more (*Clem.* 1.16.2–5), until a parallel with the doctor – again traditional and invoked already earlier (*Clem.* 1.2.1) – is explored in more detail, concluding with the maxim (*Clem.* 1.17.2): "The *princeps* should be attempting healing that does not just save the patient, but leaves a scar he can bear with honour." The last in the sequence is the model of the king bee, whose greatest mark of distinction is that for all his greater size and beauty, he has no sting (*Clem.* 1.19.2–3). The final section of the book (*Clem.* 1.20–6) deals with the attitude to judicial punishment that a *princeps* should adopt. Until Seneca's peroration on the evils of authoritarian cruelty (*Clem.* 1.25.1–1.26.5), reprising a prominent theme of the earlier *On anger* (see especially the contrast of king and tyrant at *Ira* 3.16–24), the discussion of punishment is organized and presented in a style much closer to an abstract philosophical essay than most of what has preceded it. This is where preoccupation with the emperor's judicial activity, noticed by the commentators as a particularly salient concern in *On mercy*, and no doubt reflecting disquiet with Claudius's conduct of affairs, naturally becomes most pronounced in Book 1. Following Seneca's initial declaration that "the greater part of humanity can be turned back to probity (*innocentia*)" (*Clem.* 1.2.1), he presents mercy, not severity (*severitas*), as the general policy to be followed in administering justice, seemingly going much further in this direction than he had in *On anger*. Here, as elsewhere, prudential considerations are accorded considerable weight (*Clem.* 1.23.2): "It is dangerous, believe me, to put a show before the citizen body of how big a majority there is of the wicked."

Mercy

So far this account of Seneca's project in Book 1 of *On mercy* has omitted any mention of Stoicism, although there is certainly something Stoic in its argumentative rhetoric. Thus, most notably, Seneca makes not inconsiderable

---

[16] Well discussed by Braund (2009, 57–61).

use of the Stoic notion of the *decorum* ("fitting") familiar from Cicero's *On duties* (e.g., 1.3.3, 1.5.2–7) in his account of what a king should be.[17] But the Stoic dimension should not be exaggerated. It was not Stoic doctrine that kingship was the best form of *res publica*:[18] debate in Aristotelian style on the comparative merits of different political systems is not attested for early Hellenistic Stoicism; the one mention of a preference for a mixed constitution (D.L. 7.131) is usually thought to represent the view of Panaetius.[19] Perhaps the inspecting and examining of Nero's own good conscience in the mirror Seneca invites him to contemplate is reminiscent of the practice of self-examination he recommends in other treatises and the letters. But what is promised to Nero here is very different from the focus on curing faults, resisting vicious tendencies, and being hard on oneself stressed elsewhere in Seneca.[20] The prospect held out to him is one of pleasure at the consciousness of his own virtue. As Shadi Bartsch comments, Seneca "has introduced the erotic pleasure of the mirror of vanity into the corrective usage of the mirror of self-improvement"[21] – in fact, there is not a word about self-improvement in Book 1 of the treatise.[22] The absence of much that is determinately Stoic in a kingship treatise by a Stoic should not surprise us. There is nothing uniquely or even distinctively Epicurean in what survives of Philodemus's treatise *On the good king according to Homer*.[23] From what we know of the genre, it does not appear to have been all that hospitable to the expression of doctrine characteristic of particular philosophical schools. What mattered was advising kings what their duties were and how they should practice the different virtues in fulfilling them, not explaining the deeper philosophical basis of duty or virtue.

---

[17] See Stacey (2014).

[18] See Brunt (1975), whose masterly treatment of Stoicism in political theory and practice under the empire has not been superseded.

[19] So, for example, Aalders (1975, 100–2).

[20] Braund (2009, 56–7) argues that various features of the work – notably its use of images and examples – are characteristic of "standard Stoic therapeutics." But they are not distinctively Stoic (see Brock 2013 on the accumulated Greek stock of political images), nor is Book I of *On mercy* conceived as therapy.

[21] Bartsch (2006, 185).

[22] The topic had been reserved for Book 3 (*Clem.* 1.3.1), although a mention of it is briefly slipped into a subordinate clause in the preface to Book 2: Nero's nature and impulse need to be converted into judgment (*Clem.* 2.2.2) – see Seal's comment on this topic in his contribution to this volume (pp.288–9).

[23] Which does not mean that the virtues of forbearance (*epieikeia*) and gentleness (*prâotês*, *hêmerotês*) that it dwells upon would not have been particularly valued by Epicureans: the political outlook of Roman Epicureans such as L. Calpurnius Piso, its dedicatee (and incidentally Julius Caesar's father-in-law), suggests that they were (see Benferhat 2005).

The treatise's focus on mercy was in fact decidedly unStoic. *Clementia* was an expression that had its home in Roman political discourse, which began to acquire prominence and vibrancy once Julius Caesar had become master of Rome after his victory in the civil war of 49–48 BCE:[24] the quality of mercy was what was to be hoped for in an absolute ruler, not something that would figure in lists of the virtues primarily expected of a statesman of the Republic.[25] There is no obvious Greek equivalent. What Greek Stoicism did talk about was pity (*eleos*), forgiveness (*sungnômê*), and forbearance (*epieikeia*; Stob. *Ecl.* 2.95.24–96.9; D.L. 7.123). Their view was that none of these dispositions was properly rational. All of them prompt remission of penalties prescribed by the rationality of the law, and the wise person will therefore not forgive or show pity or "be prone to ask for a reduction of the punishment that is due" (which is seen as characteristic of forbearance).

It is not until Book 2 that Seneca grapples with the problem this Stoic teaching presented for his advocacy of mercy.[26] He is fairly frank about it (*Clem.* 2.5.2):

> I know that among the ill informed the Stoic school has a bad reputation for being too hard and most unlikely to give good advice to *principes* and kings. It is objected that according to what they say, the wise person does not pity, does not forgive.

The definitions of *clementia* that he has already proposed (*Clem.* 2.3.1–2), very likely all of his own devising,[27] have not addressed the difficulty. His first couple of attempts look like general gestures in the direction of mercy: "Restraint of the mind when one has the power to take revenge" and "Mildness of a superior towards an inferior in determining punishments." He then offers a third that seems intended to get closer to the heart of the matter: "A tendency of the mind towards mildness in exacting punishment." This formulation may not literally conflict with Stoic doctrine, but it does not sound much like Stoicism. Finally, Seneca gives the definition he clearly finds most congenial: "Mercy is moderation which remits something of a deserved and due punishment." He prefaces it with an admission that it will encounter objections (he must mean: from the Stoics) "although it comes very close to the truth." This formula is in flat contradiction with Stoic teaching and particularly with its prohibition of forbearance: "the cry will

---

[24] See especially Griffin (2003).

[25] See, for example, Schofield (2009).

[26] Book 2 is written in a very different mode from Book 1 and indeed has occasionally (as notably by Erasmus) been thought to be the beginning of an alternative – and more scholastically philosophical – treatise on mercy: see further Griffin (1976, 131–3), and Braund (2009, 45–7).

[27] So Braund (2009, 66–8).

go up that no virtue ever gives anyone less than their due." Seneca responds by indicating that he is content to stick with the common understanding of mercy nonetheless: "Everyone understands that mercy turns aside short of what could deservedly be determined."

When he moves on to discuss pity and forgiveness, Seneca arguably has more success in squaring his position on mercy with Stoicism.[28] Stoics, he explains at some length, are thoroughly public spirited and philanthropic in their outlook and conduct. But that does not mean they give in to pity. Pity is a fault of minds unduly frightened by wretchedness (*Clem.* 2.6.4), whereas mercy is close to reason (*Clem.* 2.5.1). As for forgiveness, that is matter of not punishing someone you judge deserving of punishment, whereas (*Clem.* 2.7.3):

> Mercy has freedom of decision. It judges not by legal formula, but by what is fair (*aequum*) and good. It may acquit and assess damages at any level it likes. It does none of these things with the idea that is doing any less than justice – but rather that what it has determined is exactly where justice lies (*iustissimum*).

What Seneca says here could be read in two ways. It could be seen as implying a notion of equity of broadly Aristotelian cast: of a virtue enabling one to get the judgment in a particular case exactly right, in contrast to the inevitable roughness of the general rule encapsulated in the law of the land. Alternatively, it could be construed as capturing what it was that the Stoics meant all along when they talked of law as rationality, now in contrast with the inadequacies of human positive law – a view of Stoic theory of law and moral judgment that would be widely if not universally espoused by scholars of Hellenistic philosophy.[29] On either interpretation, Seneca is in truth now proposing yet a further way of understanding the notion of mercy, not as it stands compatible with the account he had favored earlier in chapter 3.[30]

His last word on the subject in *On mercy* (*Clem.* 2.7.4) is the characteristic remark that in his opinion, the controversy is a debate about a word but conceals agreement on the substance of the matter: presumably, whether

[28] For further comment on Seneca's treatment of these concepts here, see Konstan's remarks in his contribution to this volume.
[29] See, e.g., Inwood (1999a, Vogt (2008, Ch. 4).
[30] But implicit in "could deservedly be determined" (*Clem.* 2.3.2) may be the thought that common opinion would suppose there to be usually a range of alternative punishments that prima facie could appropriately be imposed, as in the imperial judicial process known as *cognitio* (Griffin 1976, 159–71; Griffin 2003, 169–77; Inwood 2005, Ch. 7). Perhaps we are to think that when at *Clem.* 2.7.3 Seneca treats justice as something that can be exactly determined (see what follows), the point would be that, in its mild treatment of human error, mercy (when exercised), on its more mature reflection, always gets things at just the right point on the scale.

you call what he is recommending as sound judicial practice the exercise of forgiveness or of mercy.[31] The manuscript text breaks off very soon after that.

The Choice of Lives

Nero, according to *On mercy*, is bound to his great position by divine election: that is his *fortuna*, his lot. He can no more abandon it than the gods can come down from heaven (*Clem.* 1.8.2–3). But for most humans, engagement in the public life of politics represents a choice. And the question of the right choice of life – should it be philosophy or politics (or indeed money or pleasure)? – had long been debated by Greek philosophers, from Plato (initially in the *Gorgias*) and Aristotle to the Stoics and Epicureans. Cicero returns to the issue frequently, for example, in the preface to *De re publica* and again in the discussion that concludes Book 1 of *De officiis*. The standard Stoic view is crisply summed up by Diogenes Laertius (D.L. 7.121):[32]

> They say that the wise person will take part in politics if nothing prevents it, as Chrysippus says in the first book of *On lives*. For he will restrain vice and encourage virtue. He will marry, as Zeno says in the *Republic*, and have children.

The decision between public occupations and *otium*, "leisure," "private life," representing withdrawal to pursue private concerns, is an issue regularly punctuating Seneca's *Epistles to Lucilius*, with Lucilius often being urged to abandon everything for philosophy,[33] as indeed is Paulinus in *On the shortness of life*. But it is in others of the moral essays that there is full-dress debate on the kinds of consideration to be weighed in answering a question that, in the dangerous world of politics under the empire, could well prove a matter of life or death. The topic must, of course, have been of pressing interest to Seneca himself, whose own life oscillated between *otium*, enforced or otherwise, and public activity, above all as Nero's principal adviser for the first eight years of his reign, until, as his influence ebbed away, he twice sought formal permission to withdraw, twice refused by the

---

[31] At this point, some commentators lose their patience with Seneca. The problem, however, is not that his argument is "feeble" (Braund 2009, 415) but that his comment on the controversy seems to imply that it does not in the end matter whether we suppose that mercy breaches justice or not. Perhaps behaving humanely was simply higher on his list of priorities.

[32] For discussion of this text, see Schofield (1991, 119–27).

[33] But despite "strong unqualified indictments of public life" in the Letters, we should note (Griffin 1976, 339): "At no point does Seneca's enthusiasm for philosophy and leisure blind him to the contrary claims of public life."

emperor. It might have been supposed that the differing emphases encountered in his discussions of the issues at stake could be correlated with his
own involvement or otherwise in politics as he was writing any particular
treatise or sequence of letters. Such correlations are difficult to make. For
one thing, few of Seneca's writings can be securely dated (*On mercy* is more
the exception than the rule, although there is agreement that the *Epistles*
must belong to his final years). And perhaps more importantly, the letters
and treatises are literary artifacts, designed to explore specific ethical problems in terms that are generally applicable (*On mercy* is again something of
the exception), even if sometimes with the needs or imagined needs of a particular addressee in mind. They cannot provide reliably transparent access
to Seneca's own current state of mind.[34] In the two works we now consider,
the opportunity to make a rhetorically compelling case for an interesting
point of view might well have been a prime consideration.[35]

Serenus, in *On tranquility of the soul* (*de Tranquillitate Animi*), is represented as complaining to Seneca that he is unsettled in mind, decidedly
querulous and fretful, neither sick nor well (*Tranq.* 1.2). A litany of unease
is then recited. We hear among other things how Serenus attempts to follow the advice of the Stoics and pursue a public career ("going into the
midst of *res publica*"), but how too whenever he encounters a setback
or something unexpected, he "turns back to *otium*" – but that does not
satisfy him either (*Tranq.* 1.10–12). Seneca offers him a diagnosis before
turning to provide "help" (*auxilium*). Or so he promises. The therapy is
deferred while Seneca takes time out to debate the choice of lives and to
engage with the views of Athenodorus of Tarsus, a Stoic who knew both
Cicero and Cato and became a trusted acolyte of the emperor Augustus.
Athenodorus distinguished between an ideal scenario and the course he
recommended for practical purposes. The best thing (Seneca agrees) is
involvement in public affairs and the duties of a citizen, assuming (as a
Stoic should) that one's aim is to "make oneself useful to citizens and mortals" (*Tranq.* 3.1). But it is a wicked world (Seneca now begins translation
or detailed paraphrase of an extended passage of Athenodorus). There will
always be more that hinders than supports virtue (an echo of Chrysippus's
caveat). So withdrawing from the forum and public life is the thing to do.
Yet – he adds immediately, expressing sentiments familiar from Cicero's
philosophical writings of 45 BCE – a private life gives a "great mind"

[34] See especially Griffin (1976, Ch. 10).
[35] For fuller discussion of *On tranquility of the soul* and *On leisure*, see Griffin (1976,
321–34). She suggests (ibid., 334) that the former is written with the ordinary person
in mind, while the latter offers a recipe for someone who has attained full rationality:
the wise (*sapiens*).

plenty of scope. In fact, one can do as much public good by study and by teaching the young and restraining them from headlong pursuit of wealth and luxury as the magistrate sitting in court to deliver the verdict of his legal advisor. A private life need not be merely private and is much more satisfactory if it is not (*Tranq.* 3.2–8).

While sticking to the letter of Chrysippus' position, Athenodorus evidently gave it a heavily revisionist reading. Political involvement is no longer the norm but an ideal never in practice realizable. Seneca disagrees with this rewriting of Stoic theory. Athenodorus "seems to have surrendered too much to the times, to have retreated too quickly" (*Tranq.* 4.1). He continues: "I would not deny that sometimes one must retire, but gradually, with flags flying and a soldier's honor intact." The theme of gradual but never full retreat is then given protracted rhetorical elaboration, concluded with the recommendation to combine *otium* with *res* whenever a life of fully active participation becomes impossible. It never gets to the point where honorable activity has no place (*Tranq.* 4.2–8). Here Seneca instances Socrates' resistance to the tyranny of the Thirty in Athens before allowing once more that there may be circumstances when one should claim "more" for *otium* and literature (*Tranq.* 5.1–5).

On leisure (*de Otio*) survives only in fragmentary form.[36] The manuscript text begins mid-sentence. It breaks off abruptly, at any rate if its author did actually deliver on his plan for an argument in two parts, the second establishing that someone who has spent his life in public service is now entitled to devote his mind to other activities in private[37] (*Ot.* 2.1–2: the text as we have it contains nothing of the sort).[38] The tone is one of much more wholehearted embrace of the private life than that conveyed in *On tranquility of the soul*.[39] In fact, Seneca early on imagines an objector exclaiming (*Ot.* 1.4): "What are you saying, Seneca? Are you deserting your side? ... Why are you, in Zeno's own headquarters, uttering precepts of Epicurus?" But as the most memorable passage of the essay indicates, his conception of the "quiet life" is very different from Epicurus'. He presents it as itself a form

[36] There is an edition of the Latin text with introduction and notes: Williams (2003).
[37] We might think of Seneca himself in CE 62, but it sounds like a standard topic of debate (cf. Cic. *Att.* 9.4).
[38] This is disputed by Williams (2003, 17–8), principally on the ground that the second part becomes redundant if (as he interprets) withdrawal to *otium* as the highest form of the active life turns out to be mandatory in all existing circumstances, given the argument of the final section of the surviving text. This is in my view an ingenious misinterpretation (see what follows).
[39] It has been suggested that "the more seriously Stoic teaching was accepted, the more ardent in some minds must have been the desire for retirement and mediation" (Brunt 1975, 19).

of active public service, albeit very different from what Athenodorus (or Cicero) envisaged (*Ot.* 4.1):

> Let us embrace with our minds two commonwealths (*res publicae*): one great and truly common – in which gods and humans are contained, in which we look not to this or that corner, but measure the bounds of our citizen body with the sun; the other to which the particular circumstances of birth have assigned us – this will be the commonwealth of the Athenians or the Carthaginians or some other city, which pertains not to all humans but a particular group of them. Some give service to both commonwealths at the same time – the greater and the lesser; some only to the lesser, some only to the greater.

The private life probably, says Seneca, gives better opportunities for serving the greater *res publica*[40] – service to God (*Ot.* 4.2: not, as Athenodorus had argued, to humanity).

There, then, is one difference from Athenodorus. The other is that Seneca means to argue only that Zeno's teaching allows settling for a private life from the outset (if, for example, the *res publica* is irredeemably corrupt, or one's health is poor), not that it makes it mandatory. It is true that the final section of the text as it is preserved finds Seneca putting the case that those enquiring "fussily" (*fastidiose*)[41] will not find any human *res publica* that a wise person could stomach (Athens, after all, sentenced Socrates to death). So they will find no ship they can actually sail in, even though putting to sea is for the Stoics the best option (*Ot.* 8.1–4). That might suggest that in practice, the quiet life is the only acceptable option. But Seneca's "fussily" suggests something less than wholehearted endorsement of the train of thought – which is in fact developed as support only for the proposition that the "law of Chrysippus" permits (*licet*) positive choice of such a life (*Ot.* 8.1).

Seneca's thoughts on monarchy and the quiet life come together at the beginning of *Letter* 73.[42] It is an error, he says, to suppose that philosophers are rebellious individuals who despise magistrates or kings or those by whom public affairs are managed. Not a bit of it. There is only gratitude to those who allow them to enjoy contented *otium*. Perhaps it is with these observations and their multiply ironic resonances that we may take our leave from Seneca's political theorizing.

---

[40] In other words, the cosmic city: see Schofield (1991, Ch. 3 and 4).

[41] This rendering and interpretation (see Griffin 1976, 332–3; cf. Cooper and Procopé 1995, 179 n.20) is disputed by Williams (2003, 113), but to my mind not convincingly.

[42] For intriguing if speculative commentary on this letter, which reads it as "an open letter intended for Nero," see Veyne (2003, 160–2).

Further Reading

The classic study of Seneca's political thought remains Griffin (1976; briefer accounts in Griffin 2000, 2002), which includes assessment of the previous major scholarly contributions. Mortureux (1989) supplies a useful survey of scholarship on *On mercy* up to that date. There is a fine critical edition of the text with prolegomena and commentary in Italian, Malaspina (2002), and a full edition with comprehensive introduction, text, English translation, and commentary: Braund (2009), which likewise provides ample information on previous work. Roller (2001, 239–47) offers a stimulating discussion of its notion of kingship; Stacey (2014) provides a helpful treatment of its exploitation of republican ideology. There is a valuable study of *On mercy*'s theory of monarchy and its exploitation in later medieval and early Renaissance political theory: Stacey (2007); see also his essay in the present volume.

6

FRANCESCA ROMANA BERNO

Exploring Appearances: Seneca's Scientific Works*

Scientific works made up a substantial portion of Seneca's *oeuvre*, which the vagaries of transmission have reduced, for us, to the *Naturales Quaestiones* (*NQ*). We learn from Pliny the Elder, Servius, Cassiodorus, and Seneca himself the titles or topics of some of these lost works. Pliny mentions among the sources he consulted both a *De piscium natura* and a *De lapidum natura,*[1] Cassiodorus a *De forma mundi,*[2] and Seneca recalls that as a younger man he had written on earthquakes.[3] The corpus also included two ethnographic books, one on India and one on Egypt, a region where Seneca had lived approximately from 19 to 31 CE.[4]

These titles alone testify to a breadth of interests that is uncommon in other Roman writers, even those, like Cicero, whose output is wide ranging. Unlike Manilius, or Stoic writers in general, however, Seneca does not favor cosmology and astrology, concentrating mostly on meteorological phenomena such as thunder, hailstorms, eclipses, and river surges, all of which, he argues, should not be regarded as terrifying supernatural events but as aspects of everyday experience that can be explained rationally. He does so, as in the case of thunderbolts, even when Stoic doctrine, which assigned them a divinatory function (*NQ* 2.32), would maintain otherwise. In this respect, Seneca is close to Lucretius' attitude, but he tends to avoid a direct competition with the Epicurean poet by focusing, rather than on rare if grandiose phenomena such as eruptions or the plague, on more familiar events.

* I am grateful to Silvia Ferrara and the editors for assistance with the English.

[1] Plin. *nat.* 1.9; 9.167; 1.26; Lausberg (1989, 1930–2); Vottero (1998, 87–92); T 100 a-b = F 7–8 H.; T 101 = F 6 H.; 358.
[2] Cassiod. *inst.* 2.6.4; Lausberg (1989, 1928–9); Vottero (1998, 33–5); T 56 = F 13 H.; 288.
[3] Sen. *nat.* 6.4.2; Lausberg (1989, 1926–7); Vottero (1998, 31–3); T 55 = F 5 H.; 288.
[4] Respectively mentioned at Plin. *nat.* 1.6; 6.60; Serv. *Aen.* 9. 30; *Aen.*6.154. Cf. Lausberg (1989, 1932–7); Vottero (1998, 19–22); T 19–20–21 = F 12; 9–11 H.; 233–7.

The overall objective of Seneca's scientific works is ethical. He investigates the causes of apparently inexplicable phenomena in order to show that they are natural rather than exceptional and should be regarded dispassionately, not in fear. The *NQ* promote the same kind of spiritual exercise we find in the *Dialogues* and the *Letters*, this time with the world of nature, rather than the self or society as its object, and in this respect they can be considered an integral part of Seneca's overall project to lead mankind to wisdom and serenity. His main effort is to unveil the real causes of phenomena whose seemingly inexplicable appearance produces confusion and fear.

Text

For a long time, the *NQ* was a victim of scholarly neglect, but in the wake of Hine's critical edition (1996), various other editions, and important monographs (most recently Williams 2012),[5] it has finally gained the attention it deserves. Unfortunately, the *NQ* are one of Seneca's worst-preserved texts.[6] The work has a bipartite structure (I–VII, or IVb–VII + I–IVa, variously numbered), and all manuscripts share a large lacuna at the end of book IVa and at the beginning of IVb. In the sixth century, John Lydus had access, perhaps indirectly, to a more complete text than the extant one, and editors from Gercke (Lipsiae 1907) onward have usually integrated the lacuna in book IVa with a passage from Lydus' *De mensibus* (4.107). Some uncertainty lingers as to the original order of the books,[7] which are conventionally numbered in accordance with the arrangement found in the *editio princeps*, whose unreliability in this respect was demonstrated almost two centuries ago.[8] Despite a lack of conclusive evidence, most modern scholars assume – on the basis of internal patterns and references – that the original structure of the book was III–VII, I–II.[9]

Thanks to specific historical references, for example to the great earthquake at Pompeii, *NQ* can be dated to the period following Seneca's retirement in 62 CE.[10] Seneca's addressee and occasional interlocutor is Lucilius Iunior, also known from the letters and *De Providentia*, a younger friend

---

[5] See also Hine's bibliography (2009) and (2010a).

[6] Hine (1980; 1992; 2009, 271–6).

[7] Hine (2010a, 28–31).

[8] Koeler (1819, 217–59).

[9] Codoñer (1979, 2–23); Hine (1996, XXII–V); Parroni (2002, XLVII–L); Bravo Díaz (2013, 22–30).

[10] Hine (2010b, 24–8). It is likely that the *NQ* was completed by 64, given the absence of references to natural events occurring that year, such as the appearance of a comet, which would have been mentioned in the list at 7.17.2.

from Campania of rather humble origins who is described at some length in the preface to book IVa. This passage provides useful information about Lucilius' job in Sicily and his philosophical and poetic interests (4.14; 4.1), as well as about his failed attempt to lure Seneca's brother Gallio into helping him in his political career. We also find in the *NQ* one of Lucilius' own verses (*FPL* 4, p. 314 Bl., in *nat.* 3.1.1), quoted alongside Vergil and Ovid, showing Seneca's appreciation of his friend's skills as a poet.

There is scant agreement over Seneca's sources, too.[11] He quotes several Greek philosophers, perhaps indirectly and possibly from memory, which would explain why some citations are inaccurate. All the authorities mentioned are criticized, including Stoic ones: Theophrastus is deemed reliable at 3.16.5 but not at 3.11.2–6, and Posidonius is even laughed at (4b.3.2). Seneca's interlocutors are often identified only by an indefinite pronoun (*quidam dicunt*): sometimes an imaginary Stoic (one of "ours," *nostri*) or an anonymous speaker is introduced (*inquit*). Opinions are either put forward as direct speech, which does not imply that we are dealing with quotations, or as paraphrase. Vottero's hypothesis that the doxographer Aetius may be the sole source has been definitively ruled out, and multiple sources are now deemed more likely.[12] Indeed, as Setaioli (1988) and Gross (1989) show, each possible source needs to be discussed in its context and on its own merits. The uncertainty over Seneca's sources in the *NQ* is unlikely to be resolved, given that almost all the texts in question have been lost. Of the few extant works, we should pay close attention to the role played by Aristotle's *Meteorologica*, which is mentioned several times, not least because of the thematic overlap between the two works. We can also find important links also Lucretius' sixth book, in particular in the passages dealing with thunder and earthquakes.[13]

NQ and the Senecan Corpus

Each book of the *NQ* deals with a specific topic: celestial fires (I), thunder and lightning (II), superficial waters (III), the Nile's flood (IVa), hail (IVb), winds (V), earthquakes (VI), and comets (VII). All the books broadly share the same structure, beginning with a preface that situates the topic in the wider philosophical context and ending in a conclusion that points out the

---

[11] Gross (1989); Setaioli (1988a, 375–452); Hine (2010b, 65–77).

[12] Vottero (1990, xxiv–xxxix); Parroni (2002, xxii–xvi); Williams (2012, 5–10); Bravo Díaz (2013, 66–81).

[13] Thunder and lightning: Lucr. 6.84–422 (*NQ* II); rain and hail: 6.495–534 (*NQ* IVb); earthquakes: 6.535–607 (*NQ* VI); Nile: 6.712–37 (*NQ* IVa); superficial waters: 6.840–905 (*NQ* III).

ethical consequences of a mistaken use of nature's gifts. Books are largely self-standing (hence the complexities arising in their arrangement): internal cross-referencing is rare, and topics are book specific, except in the case of book IVa, a thematic appendix to book III. The narrative follows a traditional rhetorical design, with the status of the *quaestio* followed by a doxographic list of the possible scientific explanations for a given phenomenon, each of which is discussed in turn. All the different arguments are weighed up until the most plausible explanation is selected. Seneca mentions several authors and theories, sometimes adding sarcastic remarks either directly or through a fictional interlocutor, and at the end of each discussion he expresses his approval for one of the authorities discussed; he seldom advances his own theory. A famous exception occurs in the debate about comets in book VII, where Seneca, in opposition to the teachings of his own school, maintains that comets are actual heavenly bodies and not volatile phenomena (7.22–9). With the main exception of book IVa, which is entirely devoted to the Nile, the discussion is generic, yet it is often interspersed with historical examples, such as the references to the earthquake at Pompeii (6.1–3) or to the comets in Imperial times (7.17.2),

The main goal of Seneca's argument, one he shares with Lucretius, is to give a rational aetiology of phenomena that appear extraordinary, such as the presence of rivers and fish under the earth, and/or terrifying (eclipses, comets, lightning, and hail), in order to eliminate human fear of them. Exceptional and dramatic events, Seneca reassures us, are only quantitatively different from ordinary ones. The most significant examples are floods (including the deluge: 3, 27–30), perhaps the most famous passage of the *NQ*, which – Seneca explains – are caused by a series of water surges and comply entirely with the laws of nature, just like any other natural phenomenon,[14] and earthquakes, which are akin to other natural events, only more destructive and larger in scale. The terror instilled in men by such disasters is thus revealed to derive from an incorrect evaluation.

The beginning of book II offers a classification of natural phenomena based on Aristotelian principles and deals with celestial, sublunar, and earthly phenomena (*caelestia, sublimia, terrena*). However, these factors are not sufficient to provide a coherent and uniform structure, as *terrena* should refer to waters (III–IVa) and *sublimia* to hail, winds, and thunder (IVb, V, I, II) but also earthquakes (VI), since they are generated by winds (2.1.3), and *caelestia* should include comets (VII).

The *NQ* share with Lucretius' *De rerum natura* their therapeutic goal, as well as comparable methods and rhetorical structures; occasionally, as in

14 Mazzoli (2005).

the case of earthquakes, topics overlap, too.[15] Seneca, however, never forgets his Stoic allegiances, and he takes pains to underline his distance from the rival school, especially on scientific issues. Epicurean science is based on the reliability of sense, especially sight (cf. frr. 36, 247, 251 Us.). In pointed contrast, Seneca repeatedly emphasizes the fallacy of sight, especially in the books dealing with phenomena whose dynamics cannot be verified by the naked eye, such the origin of lighting (II), hail (IVb), or the rainbow (I). The most important of the five senses, the very foundation of scientific knowledge, is subject to error and deception, both because of its intrinsic limitations and because of reflected and refracted images, optical illusions that, for instance, explain the rainbow (1.4.1). This fallacy of the senses must be redressed by reasoning and mental experiments, which, however, allow one to attain no more than a probable theory, since absolute certainty would only be guaranteed by direct experience.

Seneca's doxography is reasoned and thought through, in keeping with an epistemic model that mirrors his ethical outlook. The contrast between a changing and ephemeral appearance on the one hand and an immutable and certain reality on the other reality mirrors, here as elsewhere in the *Dialogues*, the opposition between fools, beset by vice, and the wise and virtuous man. Reason unmasks the superficially alluring appearances of vice as those of natural phenomena that had managed to seduce the senses and reveals their true nature. Senecan philosophy displays, here as elsewhere, its profound coherence.

Within the overall structure of each book, Seneca incidentally discusses several other topics, first of all ethical issues,[16] but also religion, politics, and human progress.[17] The treatment is limited in size but prominent, since it tends to occur in the prefaces and conclusions to each book, thus framing its scientific core with broader reflections about the philosophical underpinnings and the ultimate goal of scientific knowledge, moral improvement. An explicit discussion of moral issues can be found in the prefaces to books I, III, and IVa and in the final sections of I, IVb, II, III, VI, and VII. In books III and V, similar discussions are inserted within the main argument, although the transition is clearly marked.

The vices Seneca highlights are varied: *libido* (1.16: orgies and scopophilia; 7.30: decadence, effeminacy), *luxuria* linked to gluttony (3.17–18: fishes, in the book on superficial waters; iced drinks, in the book about

[15] See Schiesaro's essay in this volume.
[16] Berno (2003); Williams (2012, 54–92); *contra* Bravo Díaz (2013, 61–6).
[17] Hine (2010b, 77–91). Religion: Inwood (2005, 157–200). Platonic elements: Gauly (2004, 135–90). Politics: Gauly (2004, 207–18); Letta (1999); Berno (2003, 327–35); Hine (2006).

hail), *avaritia* (5.14: mines), *adulatio* (4a *praef.*: Lucilius' vice), *timor* (2.59: of lightning; 6.1–3; 6.32: of earthquakes, in the related books). *Timor* is the excessive form taken by a natural instinct, fear of death (*Ep.* 121.18), and should therefore be regarded not as a vice as such but only as an exaggerated emotion. This approach to fear invites comparison with Lucretius, especially the sixth book of *DRN*, where the poet explains that earthquakes are a natural phenomenon and a macroscopic intimation of mortality rather than a form of divine punishment. All the *mirabilia* listed at the beginning find a scientific explanation, while the book's frame focuses on its goal, which consists in eradicating human fears about this phenomenon in particular and mortality in general.

The other vices mentioned in *NQ* are more in tune with the Roman moralistic tradition, which had classified them according to *luxuria*, *avaritia*, and *ambitio*, than with Stoic categorization, according to which they would fall into the category of "desires" (*SVF* 3.397).

The coexistence of science and moral discussion has often been interpreted as undermining the scientific rigor of the *NQ*, but it actually follows the Stoic position according to which both logic and physics are inextricably tied to morality (*SVF* 2.38), as well as the standard association, in Roman thought, between science and ethics. Ever since Sallust, Roman moralistic thought had classified vices around three poles, *luxuria*, a love of luxury and excess in all its forms (including *libido*), *avaritia*, and *ambitio*, which is also manifested through *adulatio*.

The association between scientific and moral goals is also clear in the thematic arrangement of the work. Seneca's opening or final "digressions" share key terms with the scientific discussions occupying the bulk of each book and can therefore be read as a more in-depth treatment of one of the topics with which the books itself is concerned. For instance, Hostius Quadra satisfies his peculiar *libido* (1.16) through the use of mirrors that deform reality, precisely as mirrors, book 1 goes on to explain, are used to reflect a rainbow. This and other anecdotes show a perverse twisting of the scientific method: in books VIb and VII, vicious men betray the same unfulfilled passion for research that should normally characterize the philosopher; greedy men mine the earth as though their purpose is to reveal nature's secrets (book V), and perverted men artfully use their *ingenium* in the service of their own pleasure (in books I and III).

Seneca offers a nuanced evaluation of human progress (*NQ.* 5.18; 7.25–32), as he alternates between an "enlightened" optimism for knowledge's endless evolution on the one hand and the acknowledgment of man's laziness in pursuing knowledge on the other: human beings often use the gifts of nature in a corrupt way and put the greatest effort only into perfecting their own vices. References to the divine principle ruling the world and the praise of contemplative life as opposed to the pettiness of human pursuits, both typical of scientific texts, are concentrated in the prefaces to books I and III; they have either been interpreted from a Platonic perspective or as a show of preference for an ascetic lifestyle at a remove from political life. The "view from above" that is introduced in the preface to book I recurs in several philosophical texts, not only those influenced by Plato, in order to underline the smallness of human fears (as in Lucr. 2.7–13), but in this context it also introduces the main topic of the book, celestial fires. Since these phenomena take place in the highest regions of the sky and their causes cannot be observed by the naked eye, such a view from above is needed, both because of their location and because they require an effort of mental abstraction. The preface to book III also deals with the importance of scientific pursuits and its moral usefulness, since unlike other occupations, it suggests clear boundaries to human desires and aspirations. Seneca's insistence on the unpredictable nature of destiny and the vanity of human ambitions paves the way for his treatment of earthly waters, a very unstable element, which will be rounded off by the grandiose final description of the deluge. Again, rather than the reception of ultimately Platonic themes, we deal here with Seneca's own take on traditional themes in the light of the book's structure and arguments.

Politics is never discussed overtly, but interesting indications can be gleaned indirectly. The overall silence on Nero, only interrupted by very infrequent adulatory gestures, has been taken as evidence of Seneca's refusal to fight against tyranny but also as confirmation of indirect criticism of the regime, mediated by references to Alexander the Great (5.18. 10; 6. 23.2–3). The preface to IVa is particularly interesting in this connection. Seneca offers here a list of Julio-Claudian personalities whose political success was cut short by a disastrous fall from fortune: these are not remote or mythical examples but recent, in some cases raw cases that are well known to the readers of NQ and to the writer himself. The list introduces both Seneca's justification of his decision to pursue scientific investigations and his words of consolation to Lucilius, whose career has not taken off. Passages such as this preface can be read as an attempt on Seneca's part to explain his retreat from politics; rather than a surrender to Nero in the form of a total withdrawal to private life, however, they testify to the viability of a different form of political engagement: it is still possible to occupy public offices for the good of the State, provided they are not too close to the seat of power (Lucilius will find both satisfaction and serenity as *procurator* in Sicily), a compromise Tacitus will embrace in *Agricola*; if, however, the only option available is that of devoting oneself to philosophical investigation, it is important to pay attention to its ethical implications – the vices targeted in the *NQ* are, as we know from Suetonius, exactly those of Nero in the last part of his life.

The variety of themes highlighted suggests several thematic connections with other Senecan texts, especially with the *Epistles* (Williams 2014), which were written in the same period and to the same addressee. Both texts share an interest in general topics such as the fear of death or the importance of friendship, and specific issues, such as the anecdote about Nile's waterfall (4a.2.5 and *Ep.* 56.3) or the struggle (*rixa*) between different vices in our soul (4a *praef.* 2 and *Ep.* 56.5). Stylistic similarities are also evident. The links are especially significant between letters 55 and 56 and book IVa, and we might even suppose that Seneca composed them simultaneously. The *NQ* share with several other Senecan prose works an overall argument for the moral struggle against vice, but it is significant that in the *NQ*, as in the *Epistles*, there are no references to *ira*, on which a younger Seneca wrote a three-volume work. The retired philosopher, facing the implosion of Nero's regime, may have found it harder to criticize the most paradigmatic vice of tyrants.

On the connection between scientific investigation and *otium*, significant affinities emerge between the prefaces of book I and III and *On leisure* 5, while the detailed discussion about time in book VI (1–3 and 32) recalls similar arguments in *On the shortness of life*. *NQ* also shares some topics with tragedies: the debauched types we find in its moralistic digressions show the same ambitions to overturn human nature and to ascend to ever greater heights of evil as the vicious protagonists of Senecan dramas. Hostius Quadra is a *monstrum* (1.16.6) who, just like Medea (*Med.* 161) or Oedipus (l. 641), refuses to sin *ad naturae modum* (1.16.8) and, like Atreus (*Thy.* 893–5) and Medea (992–3), loves to exhibit his vice (1.16.3; 1.3.6).[18] Some descriptions in the *NQ*, such as that of the landscape under the Earth (*nat.* 3.16.4–5 and 19.1–2; 5.15), the flood (*nat.* 3.27–30), or the earthquake (6. 1–4; 6. 32), seem to evoke tragic *loci horridi*.[19] Eclipses and other phenomena are also described in similar terms. These points of contact show that the *NQ* are intimately connected with the rest of Seneca's works, especially the later ones, and point to a coherent vision of human beings, especially that of men in the thrall of passions.

[18] Also the anonymous figure of book III is dominated by *furor* (3.18.3), just as tragic characters (e.g., *Med.* 52; *Phaedr.* 184) embody a *luxuria* that conquers nature (3.17.2: cf. the *libido victrix* of *Thy.* 46), and has the power to invert land and the sea (3.17.1–3, cf. *Med.* 301–79). See Berno (2003, 55–61; 102–4).

[19] There are precise verbal parallels between the description of Hades by Theseus at *HF* 660–686 and of the underworld at *nat.* 3.16.4–5 and 19.1–2, cf. *nat.* 5. 15. The description of the flood as a macro-*adynaton*, with the confusion of all four elements in a primordial *confusio*, recalls in its very structure the *adynata* of Seneca's tragedies (e.g., the collapse of the world into chaos). See Berno (2003, 104–8; 203–6).

Style

The style of the *NQ* is varied: slim and cursory doxographic lists alternate with the rhetorical exuberance of the prefaces and digressions, and quasipoetic passages such as the description of the flood (3.27–30) almost blur the boundaries between verse and prose.[20] However, the consistent way in which arguments unfold, regardless of the topic at hand, provides a degree of uniformity. Analogy,[21] whereby something unknown is explained by comparing it to something known (using the usual *sicut* formula or variations thereof), is much in use, as are introductory formulas dear to Lucretius such as *quid mirum est?* This didactic format also recurs when Seneca discusses exceptional phenomena, the flood being a case in point. His technical jargon is also particularly interesting, as it often aims to translate technical Greek terms into Latin.[22] Citations from poetry, and the interlocutor's interventions, which are also present in other prose works, play a distinctive role here.[23] Such citations are mostly concentrated in the prefaces or at the beginning of books (see 3.1.1 and 4a *praef.* 19), but their distribution is not uniform, ranging from two in book II to fourteen in book III. Vergil's *Aeneid* and *Georgics*, together with Ovid's *Metamorphoses*, take pride of place, but several other authors, including Nero,[24] are mentioned. Seneca usually quotes these authors as authorities to be addressed in relation to a specific scientific matter. At times, this technique functions as a subtle *aemulatio*: for instance, in book III, Ovid is criticized for his superficiality in the description of the flood (*Met.* 1.285ff., in Sen. *NQ.* 3.27.13–14),[25] but Ovid's *Metamorphoses* XV is used as a reliable source for the several extraordinary phenomena that Seneca describes in his narrative (*NQ.* 3.20; 3.25), whereas the Pythagorean precepts detailed there provide a theoretical foundation for Seneca's description of the end of the world (*NQ.* 3.27–30).[26] Seneca uses interventions from interlocutors, either in the second (*inquis*) or third person (*inquit*), both in order to lighten the scientific weight of his exposition and also to highlight or clarify certain themes or to raise specific objections.[27] While the third person usually introduces scientific observations and objections stemming from

---

[20] Mazzoli (1970, 86). Stylistic features in general: Bravo Díaz (2013, 81–93).
[21] Armisen-Marchetti (1989, 283–311).
[22] Bravo Díaz (1991) and (1995).
[23] Mazzoli (1970, 215–47; 255–8); De Vivo (1992, Book VI); Hine (2009, 313–23). On Greek poets: Setaioli (1988, 47–90).
[24] *FPL* 2 p. 329 Bl., in *nat.* 1. 5. 6.
[25] Cf. esp. Degl'Innocenti Pierini (1990); Morgan (2003).
[26] Berno (2012).
[27] Gauly (2004, 82–5). See also Roller's essay in this volume.

the theories mentioned, the second person, which implies a reference to the addressee Lucilius, generally raises objections going beyond the scientific issue at hand and leading to moral significance of the discussion itself (e.g. 2.59.1; 4b. 13.1–2). The interlocutor, in other words, is double: on the one hand, he draws his inspiration from scientific and technical sources, whether anonymous authors or not, who are quoted by Seneca in either a subdued tone or with an overtly disparaging attitude; on the other, he uses a more intimate and familiar "you," whose function is primarily ethical. The latter kind of intervention is often the trigger for longer moralistic digressions. The varied style of the NQ parallels the variety of its contents, which combine sober technical discussions with impassioned ethical outbursts.

The very reason NQ was regarded as a minor work in the past – its admixture of science, philosophy, and ethics – is what makes it really interesting today. Its chapters exceed the limits of their literary genre both in contents and in style and establish important links with the whole of Seneca's corpus. As a later work, the NQ encapsulate a lifetime of study and philosophical reflection. Their perspective is on the whole wider than that of their most famous contemporary work by the same author, *Epistulae morales*, because moral issues are treated in the context of an overall study of nature, where Seneca finds a wealth of compelling arguments in his attempt to steer his readers toward serenity. The enduring appeal of the works lies in the constant tension between the grandiose descriptions of natural phenomena and the attempt to interpret them in the light of reason, a tension that mirrors the underlying contrast between appearance and reality. Appearances cause fear and vice; an understanding of reality paves the way to serenity and virtue.

Further Reading

Seneca's lost scientific works did not receive much scholarly attention until Lausberg's essay (1989) and Vottero's edition (1998). The critical editions of NQ by Hine (1996) and Parroni (2002) mark a great progress in the establishment of the text, and their proposal about the problem of the book order (III-IVa-V-VI-VII-I-II) is now commonly accepted. There is no consensus, however, about Seneca's scientific sources, except on the fact that there must have been more than one. Questions regarding contents, structure, and philosophical implications are discussed by Berno (2003) and, from a different perspective, Gauly (2004) and especially Williams (2012). More work on the scientific background is still warranted. Rhetorical aspects of NQ are particularly interesting, given the peculiarity of its literary genre and the plethora of associations not only with the contemporary *Epistulae morales* but also with the tragedies. The studies quoted offer relevant considerations of this topic, with special regard to the fictitious speaker, poetic quotations, and moralistic digressions. Less attention has been devoted to technical terms (for some specific examples, see Bravo Díaz 1991, 1995). In recent years, much work has focused on the reception of this work: Stok (2000), Berno (2010), Nanni and Pellacani (2012).

7

KIRK FREUDENBURG

Seneca's *Apocolocyntosis*: Censors in the Afterworld

Title: *Caue Monstrum*

Dio tells us that Claudius's death elicited from his murderers, Agrippina and Nero, outpourings of feigned grief that "hoisted to heaven" the man whom they had "hauled out on a stretcher" (ἔς τε τὸν οὐρανὸν ἀνήγαγον ὃν ἐκ τοῦ συμποσίου φοράδην ἐξενηνόχεσαν), a devilish play on words for which Dio gives no source.[1] He goes on to relate several other jokes that were told at the dead emperor's expense, including one by Nero who said that mushrooms should be considered food of the gods because Claudius had been made a god by eating one. Seneca's brother Gallio told a memorable joke as well, and Seneca himself, the very man who had written the *laudatio funebris* that Nero delivered to launch his deceased "father" to the skies, wrote a countervailing mock apotheosis of the emperor to which he gave the title *Apocolocyntosis*.[2] Dio explains that the word is formed on analogy with Greek ἀθανάτισις ("immortalization"), and if nothing else, this helpful gloss lets us know that at least some of Dio's readers would have found the title perplexing: its morphology is not immediately obvious, nor is there any discernible tradition in Greek that finds "dunderheads" being mocked as "gourds." For that, one needs a Latin *cucurbita* ("dolt" *OLD* s.v. 3). Most scholars now take *apocolocyntosis* to be a hybrid of *apotheosis* ("transformation into a god") and *kolokynt(h)e* ("gourd"), but it is far from obvious what that might mean. Perhaps still the one most certain thing to be said about the title is that it is a comical monstrosity, so funny in its outlandishness that, as Dio's gloss shows, it has never not needed to be explained.

---

[1] Dio 61.35.2.

[2] For Seneca as the author behind the *laudatio funebris* delivered by Nero, see Tac. *Ann.* 13.3. For the *Apocol.* as counterbalancing and ironizing the praise of Seneca's obligatory *laudatio funebris*, see Russo 1965, 7–10. As a negation of Seneca's earlier praise of Claudius in the *Consolatio ad Polybium*, see Degl'Innocenti Pierini (1981).

At least three basic problems come with taking the work mentioned by Dio to be the Menippean satire that begins *quid actum sit in caelo* and that we now generally know as the *Apocolocyntosis* of Seneca: (1) the principal manuscripts name no author for the work;[3] (2) the manuscripts give mundane but usefully descriptive titles (*Divi Claudii apotheosis per saturam* in S and *Ludus de morte Claudi* in V, with a slight variation in L), but never *Apocolocyntosis*;[4] and (3) there is no obvious or easy sense to be made of the title either literally (Claudius is not turned into a gourd) or metaphorically: he cannot be turned into a "dunderhead" because that is what he has been all along.[5] With no gourds in the satire to help make sense of the title, scholars have been left to explore whatever further connotations any given Greco-Roman "gourd" might offer up. Numerous solutions have been tested, morphological, metaphorical, pharmacological, anal-punitive, emendational, eco-historical, and otherwise, but none has proved decisive in setting the matter straight.[6] Still, the best sense to be made of *Apocolocyntosis*, if this is the right title, is to take it as Russo suggested: not as Claudius' transformation into a gourd but "Gourd's apotheosis" or "Dunderhead goes to heaven."[7] A fool's apotheosis, in other words, a Menippean adventure so misguided and so outrageously bungled that Gourd finds himself hauled off to Hades to serve as a whipping-boy functionary in Caligula's entourage for all eternity. Hoyos has suggested that "Gourd" (*cucurbita*) was the unflattering nickname spoken behind the emperor's back by the disaffected senators and knights who are the presumptive audience of the satire.[8] An insiders' joke, in other words: as if to say "first we had *Caligula* ('Bootkin'), now we have *Cucurbita* ('Bumpkin')," wryly jangling the rhythmic and assonantal similarities between the two names? However the gourd joke came about, its having a caché among senatorial insiders would help explain the title's strange disappearance from the manuscript tradition.[9] But as yet unobserved by the commentators is one highly specific satirical point that comes from titling the work with such an unwieldy mouthful of sounds, that is,

---

[3] Only in the sixteenth century did Seneca's name come to be attached to the work; see Eden (1984, 1), and Roncali (1990, v).

[4] See esp. Lund (1994, 11–13), and Bruun (1990, 76–7).

[5] The objection was first raised by Weinreich (1923, 11–12).

[6] For a survey of recent proposals, see Roncali (2008, 319–22), and Eden (1984, 1–4).

[7] Russo 1965, 17; see also Conte (1994, 420): "The curious term should be understood not as 'transformation into a pumpkin' but 'transformation of a pumpkin.'"

[8] Hoyos (1991).

[9] Given a title so outlandish, it is hard to imagine how it could have dropped so completely from the manuscript tradition. The "insiders' joke" thesis of Hoyos (1991) offers one possible explanation. It is also possible that somewhere down the line, the title was taken to be obscene: numerous grotesque sexual and scatological possibilities have been tendered to explain it.

from the very fact of its being so terribly hard to get right in pronunciation. Even when gotten right (and this is never on the first try), the title forces one to stammer: *Apocolocyntosis*. Like the satirized emperor himself, the word is a lumbering hulk, a seven-syllable *monstrum*, alien and unsettling. The mouth-work is even more involved if one attempts to reproduce the same idea in (the original?) Latin: *con-cu-cur-bitatio, vel consecratio Divi Claudi*. In either case, whether in Greek or Latin, just to say the name of the work aloud finds one struggling with far too many syllables and mocking Claudius' signature impediment. And in the specific case of *concucurbitatio*, saying the title aloud finds one very nearly mouthing Claudius' last, stuttering words: not, this satirist would have us believe, anything as suitably self-ennobling as, for example, *consecraui me* ("I've made a god of myself"), but *con-ca-ca-ui me* ("I've shit myself!").[10] Here again, though the commentators make no point of it, the humor of these last words surely has as much to do with the Dunderhead's stuttering as it does with his diarrhea. Claudius' command over either orifice is comically sputtering and loose, exactly as was his ability to control his wives, his freedmen, and the state itself.[11]

Genre: *Ludus Per Saturam*

The *Apocolocyntosis* is saturated with the formal and thematic structures of drama, for example, the five-act structure of a comedy or tragedy, the dullard Hercules of a satyr play, an Old Comic underworld adventure, and the rushed ending of a mime.[12] Thus, as the manuscripts indicate, the work lends itself to being taken as a skit or "play" (*ludus*) in the form of a pro-simetric satire (*per saturam*).[13] The mode of performance was, presumably,

[10] For these lines as a "Parodie auf den Topos der *ultima verba*," see Vogel (2006, 139). In what I say in the preceding, I presume that Seneca's satiric *concacaui me* represents the parodically stuttered counterpart to some noble last words that Claudius is purported to have said – or perhaps tried to say but actually did stutter while trying to say them. A suitably ennobling counterpart to *concacaui me* would be *consecraui me* ("I am become a god"), words that, if stammered, are easily played upon as a scatological pun; cf. the purported last words of Vespasian (Suet. *Vesp.* 23): *uae, puto deus fio* ("oh, I think I'm becoming a god"). Vespasian's last words are funny, but they feature an emperor solidly in control of his own joke. One should also note the sonic repetition in *uae me* and *-ui me* at the beginning and end of Claudius's satiric *ultima verba*, thus expanding the stuttering to the entire phrase.
[11] Such egregious failures of bodily comportment and control were commonly taken to symbolize larger ethical and political failings, such as a tyrant's innate *saeuitia* and lack of self-control; see Braund and James (1998), and Osgood (2007).
[12] On the five-act structure of the *Apocolocyntosis*, see Korzeniewski (1982). An excellent study of the work's multiple generic poses, with a view toward positing a (Kristevan) recalibration of genre, is Blänsdorf (1986).
[13] On *per saturam* meaning "in a mixture of prose and verse," see Reeve (1984).

a particularly exuberant "Saturnalian," perhaps semidramatic, recitation (see what follows). In other words, this is a Menippean satire that could be "played up," and probably was. And this is true of many of Varro's satires as well.[14] As a comical fantasy that both mixes and mocks a variety of prose and verse forms, mostly in Latin but with a generous smattering of Greek, the work belongs solidly to the Varronian or Menippean branch of Roman satire's twin *genera*.[15] In fact, it is the only such satire in Latin to survive in near complete form from antiquity.[16] With a bumbling scholar in the star role, the work has much in common with many a Varronian and (later) Lucianic satire, following precedents in Old Comedy, in Varro, and in Menippus himself, all of whom feature protagonists who ascend to heaven to see things from on high or descend to Hades to consult with the dead.[17] But these are mere generic housekeeping observations that, however useful and necessary they may be, fail to capture just how radically different the *Apocolocyntosis* is as a satire of the Varonnian/Menippean type. For the bumbling scholar sent up by Seneca is no ragged philosopher or mathematician, he is none other than the deceased emperor himself, a Dunderhead lifted to heaven not on the back of a dung beetle but by a decree of the senate, sent soaring on wings of praise sewn by Seneca himself. Though unnamed, the principal members of the satire's audience are easy to discern: not workaday Marcuses but political insiders who were themselves deeply implicated in Dunderhead's foibles and crimes and for whom the wounds he inflicted (whether with their active help, their grim resignation, or a tacit nod) were still quite fresh.

Most scholars date the satire's publication to mere weeks after the death of Claudius on October 13, 54 CE, with a plausible case to be made for the heavy-drinking Saturnalia celebrations of late December in the same year, when the "enslaved" of the city could be expected to find their satiric voices and celebrate the happy demise of the old man along with that of the old year.[18] For those who are invited to laugh along with this satire (try saying

---

[14] On the theatrical aspects of Varro's satires, including a theory of staged performance, see Wiseman (2009, 137–43); see also Freudenburg (2013, 324–36).

[15] On the interplay between Roman satire's twin *genera*, see Freudenburg (2013).

[16] There is a significant lacuna separating the end of Claudius' speech (7.5) and his entrance into the heavenly *concilium* (8.1). See Weinreich (1923, 80–4) and Eden (1984, 98–9).

[17] For Claudius as a Menippean "universal observer," unique among the genre's adventurers for travelling to heaven and to Hades in the same satire, see Relihan (1993). For the "schau von oben" motif in Varro's satires, see Krenkel (2002), vol. 1, 205.

[18] The theory that the *Apocolocyntosis* was recited during the Saturnalia of CE 54 goes back to Furneaux; see Eden (1984, 5 n.11). For recent support, see Versnel (1993) and Graf (2005, 204).

Apocolocyntosis while drunk!), the pain is very real and the Saturnalian revenge sweet. Both for its principal audience, for whom the satire draws an oversimplified picture of "us" versus "him," and for its author, this satire engages in serious political work.[19] The prevailing view holds that, without naming her, the satire pokes fun at Agrippina for sponsoring Claudius' deification and for taking on the role of head priestess of his cult (*flamonium Claudiale*).[20] The satire attacks several of her favorites, such as Narcissus, and it makes mocking reference to Claudius' god-like "incest" with his niece. And yet it says nothing about her poisoning the old man.[21] Josiah Osgood has recently argued that in the immediate aftermath of Claudius's death, Seneca needed to mix the messages he sent and to offset them: before the world at large, he needed to be seen performing his devotion to Claudius. But within the tighter confines of a nervous and largely disaffected senate, a body to which Seneca himself belonged as a long-time member and an alien "palace insider," he needed to be seen setting a clear distance between himself and the emperor who had rescued his political career and who, at Agrippina's urging, had elevated him to a position of high authority within the imperial household.[22] Seen for the particular kind of political work this satire does, the case for Senecan authorship is not perfect, but strong. To the senate, Seneca sends the message that, with the accession of Nero, a new day has arrived for that woefully abused body: Claudius's senatorial purges, his corrupt manipulations of the senate, his filling its ranks with unworthy members, and his many usurpations of senatorial privilege, all are part of a savage and darkly comical past. These senatorial abuses are the main accusations that the Deified Augustus hurls against Claudius in the *Apocolocyntosis* to sink his case for admittance to the senate house of heaven. No senator had spoken up like that while Claudius was alive. But in the *post mortem* fantasy of the *Apocolocyntosis*, there is one grand old senator who rises to the moral challenge and puts Claudius in his place. Claudius bribes, threatens, and cajoles. He very nearly gets his way. But then

[19] For an excellent summary of political readings, see Eden (1984, 8–12). On Seneca's personal investment in the death of Claudius, see Braund in this volume.
[20] Agrippina's model was Livia, who became *flaminica Diui Augusti* after her husband's death and consecration; Vell. 2.75.3, and Dio 56.46.1. Suspicious of his mother's growing powers, Tiberius denied her the right to be accompanied by even one lictor; Tac. *Ann.* 1.14.3. In contrast, Agrippina was granted an honor guard of two lictors: *decreti et a senatu duo lictores, flamonium Claudiale, simul Claudio censorium funus et mox consecratio*, Tac. *Ann.* 13.2.6.
[21] The *locus classicus* of the anti-Agrippina thesis is Kraft (1966), developed further by Horstkotte (1985).
[22] On Seneca's "golden predicament" after the death of Claudius, see Osgood (2011, 242–59) and Braund in this volume. Further on the political rhetoric of the work, see Leach (1989).

the emperor god, to whose memory Claudius had claimed such an abiding devotion, stands up and says no: he is not about to let the cruel and manipulative interloper barge into the senate and have his way with them yet again. For many in Seneca's audience, it is a wonderful fantasy.

Genre and Politics Reconsidered: Lucilius, Lupus, and *Claudius Censor*

The formal and thematic structures of the *Apocolocyntosis* are those of a Menippean satire, but the searingly live political focus of the satire is not. For that, one has to look to a different model in the so-called *inuentor* of Roman verse satire, Gaius Lucilius, whose late-second-century *Saturae* came to symbolize lost ways of *libertas* and uncompromised speech. One highly specific memory of Lucilius is cued in the course of the satire's heavenly trial when Diespiter, having been bribed by Hercules, gives his opinion that Claudius should be allowed to "wolf down steaming turnips" with Romulus (*feruentia rapa uorare*). The phrase scans as the second half of a hexameter line, and it has been credibly established that it is a direct quote from Lucilius' first satire, where the full (reconstructed) line once read: *Romulus in caelo feruentia rapa uorare*.[23] The quote is far from casual, for book 1 of Lucilius' satires features the famous heavenly *concilium* that judges the case of Lucius Cornelius Lentulus Lupus, consul in 156 BCE, then a censor and *princeps senatus*, an office he held until shortly before his death in 125 or 124 BCE. It is from this specific satire that Seneca takes the central conceit of the *Apocolocyntosis* by staging a *post mortem* trial in heaven. The influence that runs from the earlier verse-satire to its Menippean counterpart is clear enough, and many have noted it in passing.[24] Both works develop the same fantastical theme, but the influence runs much deeper, to points of contact that are actually quite detailed, especially in the further hidden connections that link Claudius to Lupus.[25]

Lupus was a highly controversial historical figure, for upon returning from his consular governorship in the east, he was tried on an extortion charge and soundly convicted of criminal activity. Sources put the date of his conviction in 154 BCE, which is odd because it is five years before the

---

[23] See Skutsch (1985) on *Annales* fr. 110 and Connors (2005, 126).
[24] See, e.g., Eden (1984, 16–17).
[25] Weinreich (1923, 94) goes farther than most in seeing at play in both works a humorous opposition between old Roman gods and *Graeculi*, with Seneca's Augustus matching Lucilius' Romulus as the chief spokesman for Rome's noble old ways. On Juvenal's fourth satire as a further adaption Lucilius' first satire (literalizing the Lucilian "Lupus as Big Fish" pun) by way of both Seneca's *Apocolocyntosis* and the divine council of Statius' *de Bello Germanico* (the parodic butt of the joke), see Connors (2005, 141–4) and Freudenburg (2001, 258–64).

Lex Calpurnia de repetundis was passed to establish a *quaestio perpetua* to try such cases. Some scholars therefore put the trial in 148 BCE to make it one of the first cases tried by the new law.[26] In either case, the scandal for which Lupus was tried and convicted does not appear to have damaged his political career to any significant degree, for shortly thereafter, in 147 BCE, he was elected censor. For Lucilius, a close friend of Lupus' bitterest enemy, Scipio Aemilianus, that is what makes his case so notorious and worth satirizing. For in this Lupus, the "Wolf," we have a case of a convicted criminal not just being given a chance to rescue something of his old career but of his being put in charge of the moral health of the Roman state as censor, which was perhaps the most revered office in the Roman state. His election to the office comes just one year after the death of one of his most outspoken critics, the Elder Cato (d. 149 BCE), who was also the most severe and combative censor ever to hold the office. Writing more than three centuries after Cato's death, Aulus Gellius (5.13.2) cites one of the censor's well-known maxims that, he says, Cato had used "in a speech that he delivered against Lentulus in a hearing before the censors" (*in oratione quam dixit apud censores in Lentulum*).[27] The story of Lupus' career can hardly be taken as a secret "exposed" by Lucilius. It was, rather, a scandal, and the basic details were a matter of public record.

When Valerius Maximus tells the story of Lupus more than a century after Lucilius' death, he catalogs it under the larger heading *de mutatione fortunae* and then under the smaller heading *de varietate casuum* (Val. Max. 6.9.10):

> Lucius Lentulus (Lupus), a consular senator, after he had been ruined by a charge of corruption under the Caecilian Law, was made censor along with Lucius Censorinus. Fortune wound him this way and that, among honors and disgraces, by following up his consulship with a (legal) conviction, and his conviction with the censorship, and by allowing him neither to enjoy uninterrupted good nor to groan under ceaseless ill.

For Valerius Maximus, the life of Lupus holds a stunning set of reversals, with good fortune followed by disgrace, then followed again by a marvelous recovery. But it is to the question of what happens after he dies, in the senate-house of heaven, that Lucilius turns in his first satire, in a mock-epic debasing of a famous scene in Ennius, the heavenly council that deliberates on the apotheosis of Romulus in book one of *Annales* (frs. 51–5 Skutsch).[28]

---

[26] On the trial, see Bauman (1983, 205–6).

[27] *Or. Rom.*² fr. 200 Malcovati.

[28] On the Ennian parody of Lucilius' first satire, see Gratwick (1982, 169–71). For a likely reconstruction of the satire's contents, see Krenkel (1970 vol. 1, 63–4).

In Lucilius' send-up of that patriotic tale, Jupiter seems to have caught sight of Rome in an agitated state, with crowds bustling and loudly wailing as Lupus is carried off in an especially lavish funeral. As in the first lines of Homer's *Odyssey*, Jupiter calls a *concilium* of the gods to discuss the sorry state of humankind. And as in this satire's *re-translatio* back into epic in the *concilium deorum* of *Aeneid* 10,[29] the protocols described are those not of Homer's Olympus but of the Roman senate on a particularly fractious day, with two gods stepping forward to dominate the debate.[30] The satire's fragmentary state leaves much in doubt, but it seems that one of the gods featured in the debate was a transparent stand-in for Appius Claudius Pulcher (suffect consul in 130 BCE), an effete and luxury-indulging philhellene who, under the guise of Apollo, speaks in Lupus' defense. And the other was Romulus, a déclassé outsider new to the assembly (i.e., the new god as senatorial *nouus homo*), who plays the rustic bumpkin by wolfing down hot turnips and ranting loudly against the soft ways of modern Romans of Lupus' ilk.[31] Taking issue with Apollo, whom Romulus mocks as a pretty boy (*pulcher*) with a fondness for effete dance, Romulus rants against foreign luxuries, pointing an accusing finger at Hellenized Romans who dine on expensive imported fish and sleep on silken sheets and who sprinkle their Latin with a mishmash of affected Greek.

Taken together, the set of characteristics that Lucilius has used to construct his heavenly Romulus strongly suggests that he is not to be taken as just any old Roman crank but a very particular one: he is the Elder Cato right down to his telltale turnips.[32] And thus we have in Lucilius' first satire one dead censor, an especially severe and iconic one, dressed in the guise of the divine Romulus, comically sputtering against and berating the new dead censor, his old enemy, the "Wolf," who had so famously corrupted the office that Cato had once held. The scenario has a precise analogue in the *Apocolocyntosis*, where Augustus, Rome's last censor before Claudius, plays

---

[29] Servius *ad Aen.* 10.104 comments on the book's divine council: *totus hic locus de primo Lucilii translatus est, ubi inducuntur dii habere concilium et agere primo de interitu Lupi cuiusdam ducis in republica, postea sententias dicere* ("this entire locus is taken over [adapted] from the first book of Lucilius, where the gods are represented holding a council, first conducting a hearing over the death of a certain Lupus, a leader in the state, and thereafter they pass sentence").

[30] On Lucilius' parody of senatorial protocols, see Marx (1904–5, vol. 2, 3–5) and Haß (2007, 72–3).

[31] On Apollo's decidedly "Claudian" coloration in Lucilius' first satire, see Marx (1904–5, vol. 2, 13–14), and Haß (2007, 72).

[32] Cato is reputed to have developed his love of turnips in imitation of the farmer-general Manius Curius; Plut. *Cat. Mai.* 2.2. He is said to have praised them as "the sweetest of delicacies" and to have taken pride in cooking them himself while his wife kneaded the bread; Plut. *Arist. et Cat. Mai.*, syncrisis 4.5.

the role of the divine senate's morally outraged new arrival. Like Lupus, Claudius was himself a censor whose censorship was fraught with scandal. And like Augustus (and presumably Lupus as well), Claudius was sent off to the next world celebrated as a censor, both having received the honor of a lavish *censorium funus*.[33] To mark a new beginning for Rome on the eight hundredth anniversary of the city's founding by Romulus, Claudius revived the office of censor in the years 47 and 48, and with Vitellius as co-censor, he used his office to undertake numerous reforms. As if to match the achievements of his blind ancestor, Appius Claudius Caecus (himself a highly controversial censor in 312 BCE and more recently brought back from the dead as the scolding censor of Cicero's *Pro Caelio*), Claudius undertook to build new aqueducts and to reform the Roman alphabet. He presided over a *lectio senatus* that saw the introduction of the *Aedui*, a favored Gallic tribe, into the senate, scary long hair and all. In addition, he set out to purge the senate of some of its less savory members by way of an innovative "volunteer" self-removal initiative, and he passed strict decrees against heckling noblemen who appeared as minstrels on stage.

In the two places where Tacitus steps back to summarize Claudius' achievements as censor, Tacitus fades either into or out of a jarring scene of Messalina's sexual misconduct, as if to suggest that the doddering Claudius, like his famous old ancestor, is blind. At *Annales* 11.12, the first days of Messalina's affair with Gaius Silius are described, figured as a daily licentious parade that passed between two houses. As such, the affair was much too flamboyant to escape anyone's notice (*serui liberti paratus principis apud adulterum uisebantur*), and yet, says Tacitus, Claudius was completely without a clue. "Oblivious to his marital situation, Claudius was busy with his duties as censor." The transition is abrupt and wonderfully jarring, taking us from a celebration of banned behaviors parading in the streets of Rome to the scholar-emperor huddled in among his books and taking a hard line against the immoral double-dipping of certain letters of the Latin alphabet. In the second and larger summation of Claudius' censorial achievements in 48 (Tac. *Ann.* 11.25), we have the same cinematography in reverse, with the censor's achievements put hard up against the sexual misconduct of Messalina, whose "bizarre sexual practices" had by this point become

---

[33] See Tac. *Ann.* 13.2.6 (above n.20). Price (1987, 64): "A seemingly traditional name, *funus censorium*, was often used for imperial funerals, though it is first attested for Augustus and its precise significance is obscure. It might allude to the grand funeral of a *censor*, a highly respected office which Augustus had himself held, or it may just be the equivalent of a 'public funeral,' originally authorized by the *censor*." Further on the problematic term, see Arce (2010, 322).

so outrageous that even Claudius had to take notice. Not that he actually managed to do that. Not on his own, anyway.

In a temporal sleight of hand that adds tremendous punch to his transition, Tacitus is quick to add that "at almost the same time" that the dullard-censor learned of his wife's misdeeds (*haud multo post flagitia uxoris noscere*), Claudius contracted a burning desire to marry his own niece (*deinde ardesceret in nuptias incestas*).[34] Tacitus then goes on to describe Messalina's demise and the happy effusions of the senate at her demise, and from there he moves immediately into a mock *concilium deorum* in the first pages of book 12, with the chief rulers of the city, which is to say the emperor's freed slaves, Pallas, Callistus, and Narcissus, gathering on high to deliberate over a matter of deepest import (*discordantis in consilium uocat ac promere sententiam et adicere rationes iubet*). The question is, whom will the emperor marry next? Agrippina wins this beauty contest (a judgment-of-Paris parody), and that means that Lucius Silanus, who was slated to marry Octavia, will have to be eliminated.[35] The way Tacitus tells it (and here again there is some artful manipulation of the sequencing to produce a jarring effect), Vitellius, who was Claudius' co-censor for the years 47–8, struck Silanus from the senatorial roles on the last day of his magistracy, December 31, 48 CE, and this despite the fact that the census purification had already been concluded some time before in the same year. The charge against Silanus was incest: sleeping with his own sister. Then, says Tacitus, in the consulship of Gaius Pompeius and Quintus Veranius, the marriage pact between Claudius and Agrippina began to take solid shape (*pactum .... matrimonium .... firmabatur*).[36] The entire account is structured in such a way as to suggest that the first act of the emperor on his first day as a non-censor (January 1, 49 CE) was to legitimize an incestuous relationship with his niece and to have that particular achievement among his *res gestae* validated by a complacent and willfully oblivious senate.

Returning to Seneca, we see that the condemnation of Silanus is the marquee example featured in the *Apocolocyntosis* of Claudius' abuse of his legal authority. For there we see that the gods deliberating in Seneca's heaven have nothing particular to say about the other thirty-four senators that Claudius put to death over the course of his long career, beyond naming them. But they have much to say about this case in particular.[37] And I think

---

[34] Tac. *Ann.* 11.25.

[35] Osgood (2011, 214): "His council scene is surely an invention, so obviously does it parody the mythical tale of the judgment of Paris."

[36] Tac. *Ann.* 12.5.

[37] The forced suicide of his "son-in-law" is used against Claudius by his accusers at 8.2, 10.4, and 11.2, and Silanus is on hand to welcome Claudius to the underworld at 13.5.

the reason for this is a good Lucilian reason: as censor, Claudius condemned his would-be son-in-law. That is bad enough. But even worse, he went after Silanus on a charge of incest at the very time that he himself was (or so the historians claim) sleeping with his own niece, Agrippina. The magnificent irony and hypocrisy of this is not lost on Seneca's gods. And thus, in one final and long overdue turn, justice is served, at least within the fiction of Seneca's satirical heaven: thanks to the intervention of a heavenly censor, the deified Augustus, Claudius is refused admittance to the senate and condemned to serve Caligula for all eternity as his whipping boy.

We do not know how Lucilius resolved the heavenly council of book 1 in the case of his own hypocritical censor, Lupus. But we can suspect that some kind of comic justice was meted out: fragments 41 through 47 suggest that Jupiter may have wanted to inflict a huge storm at sea, a standard expression of divine anger in epic, to sink the ships that glided on the Emathian winds to bring luxury goods from Greece to Italy.[38] We cannot be sure. But what we can say with some certainty is that with the mock-epic *concilium deorum* that judges and presumably condemns the misbehavior of Lupus, Lucilius is filling in for something necessary to but missing from the public record: he is providing a quasi-senatorial condemnation of senatorial misbehavior, an act of self-regulation that the actual senate in Rome never undertook. In the end, Lucilius' satire is as much about the senate and its failure to regulate itself as it is about Lupus, who was simply the latest poster boy of senatorial corruption. He was, after all, the *princeps senatus* for much of the last part of his life and thus the elected favorite of the senate. Given all of this, there can be little doubt that, upon his death, the real senate did not just fail to condemn their former *princeps*, but that they praised him to the heavens, as they were wont to do (and as certainly happened in the later case of Claudius), making all the obligatory decrees. Moreover, with all of the poem's talk about political corruption and the importation of Greek habits and luxury goods, as well as the outlandish expenses and pretensions of the Wolf's famous dinner parties – in fact, a good number of the poem's fragments concern these issues – the satire's criticism is best heard not as an expression of general moral disgust but as an assessment specific to a censor and delivered by a censor of a particularly stern, Greek-hating type (Romulus as Cato). That is, it takes a censor's eye view toward corruption by detailing the abuses of an actual censor who could not censor himself, let alone the state, on issues that were traditionally in the censor's purview. For, as this poem has it, Lupus was far more concerned with his bedsheets and what sauce to serve with his favorite fish, the Lupus ("bass" but literally

[38] See Lucilius fr. 41–47K = 39–45W.

the "wolf," his namesake) than he was with enforcing the laws (*iura*, also the standard Latin word for "sauces") of the Roman state.[39] This idea of conflating the victim of the satire with a fish, however momentary that metaphor may have been in Lucilius' first book, is an idea exploited to the full by Juvenal in his fourth satire, a poem that also features a mock-epic *concilium*, with the deliberative body no longer structured along senatorial lines but as a *consilium principis* consisting of Domitian and eleven prominent advisors (thus an Olympian dozen), most of whom are servile and depraved. Thus as we move from Lucilius to Seneca to Juvenal, we mark the transition from corrupt senate to browbeaten and fawning senate to no senate at all.

Perhaps the signature moment of Claudius' awkward browbeating of the senate during his censorship came when he argued his case for the inclusion of the *Aedui* into their ranks, a Gallic people especially close to his heart because they came from the region of Gaul where he himself was born.[40] In the fantasy of the *Apolocyntosis*, the story of their inclusion is parodied and given a new ending, as the home-bred Gaul, Claudius, a *Gallus Germanus* and an alien *monstrum* unlike any Hercules had ever seen, is refused admittance to the senate, sent packing by the very censor whom Claudius had striven so hard to emulate. As in Lucilius' first satire (and it seems that many of Varro's satires may have done this as well), the *Apocolocyntosis* has us imagine a real censor filling in for a fake or missing one, censoring the man who faked being him by finally saying what needed to be said but never was.[41] By recalling Lucilius' first satire as powerfully as it does, Seneca's *Apocolocyntosis* takes hold of a specific, anxiety-filled moment in time, one that was awash in obligatory hypocrisies – the loud, overdone formalities that transformed an uncharismatic and awkward old man into a god after he was gone, and made a savior "Apollo" of a musically gifted sixteen-year-old upon his succession[42] – and it lays claim to that moment as

---

[39] Just as Claudius is done in by a kangaroo court of his own design in the *Apocolocyntosis*, Lupus is apparently done in by the fishy laws that he had famously used against others: Lucil. fr.54M = 55K *occidunt, Lupe, saperdae te et iura siluri* "sauces/laws of (= 'conventions governing'/'rights of'?) smelt and herring (foreign small fry), Wolf/Bass, are bringing you to ruin." Further connecting Lentulus Lupus to Seneca's Claudius was the notorious reputation of the former as an especially cruel and unfair judge, see 1312–13M = 1228–30K and 784–90M = 789–95K.

[40] On Claudius' speech to the senate as 'hectoring' and offensive, see Osgood (2011, 165–7).

[41] On Varro's satires filling in for the missing censors of the 80s and 70s BCE, see Wiseman (2009, 148). Further on the "satirist as censor" analogy in both formal verse and prosimetric satire, see Freudenburg (2013, 313–7).

[42] The boy emperor's being heralded as a god upon his accession is surely just as ridiculous as the old one's being divinized *post mortem*. In both cases, Seneca sends up the rhetorical structures that were deemed necessary and that he himself must have had some public role in promoting to secure the transition of power from one emperor to the next. The success of this transition was by no means a foregone conclusion.

an occasion for a new kind of speech of a decidedly old (republican) kind. Seneca's adventurous and uniquely hybridized satire lets those who laugh along with it think that this time things will be different and that the hot turnips of Republican *libertas* are finally back on the menu.

Further Reading

The main further readings recommended here are in English. The notes that accompany the essay above provide a basic survey of recent studies of the *Apocolocyntosis* in various languages, with special emphasis on issues of genre and the work's political import. An impressively full recent bibliography, annotated in Italian, is Roncali (2008), the first pages of which reference earlier bibliographies. For significant recent additions, see Whitton (2013). The best general introductions to the *Apocolocyntosis* in English are to be found in the volume introductions to the editions and commentaries of Eden (1984) and Lund (1994), as well as the relevant chapters in Coffey (1976) and Relihan (1993). Along with Relihan, chapter 5 of Conte (1996), "The Quest for a Genre: Some Skeptical Thoughts on Menippean Satire," provides an outstanding introduction to Menippean satire in general. Freudenburg (2013) provides an introduction to Varro's satires, as well as his theory of satire. Wiseman (2009) connects Varro's satiric works to his person and to the politics of his day.

Whitton (2013) provides a fine analysis of recent political readings, as well as a balanced approach to the question of anti-Neronian subversion in the *laudes Neronis*. The most sensitive and thoroughgoing study of the politics of the *Apocolocyntosis* is Osgood (2011), especially the chapter on the "golden predicament" that Nero and Seneca faced in dealing with the memory of the deceased Claudius. To this should be added Leach (1989), who looks at the specific rhetoric of the work to see how the text engages the sympathies of its readers and directs their responses. Braund and James (1998) and Osgood (2007) treat the emperor's failures of bodily comportment as symbols of his ethical and political failings. Braund (1980) sees behind Claudius' failed entry into the senate of heaven his introduction of Gauls from Comata into the Senate in 48 CE. O'Gorman (2005) reads the *Apocolocyntosis* as a text that engages actively in the reception of classical literature through its habits of allusion, citation, and quotation.

8

JAMES KER

Seneca and Augustan Culture

The topic of this chapter most obviously invites us to think of Seneca's role in helping to shape Nero's early image as the new Augustus. In *Apocolocyntosis*, he envisages the deified Augustus fulminating at Claudius. In speeches written for Nero, he has the young emperor announce his plan to rule "following the model of Augustus" (Suet. *Nero* 10.1.2). And in *De Clementia*, he encourages Nero to surpass his ancestor. We may also think of the "Neronian classicism" (Mayer 1982) that accompanied this development – the varied emulation of Augustan poetry by Seneca and others, including Nero himself, who treated the Augustan canon as Rome's home-grown equivalent of the Greek classics.

Yet Seneca, in a life that extended through all the Julio-Claudian emperors,[1] had invoked the Augustan principate as a model before. Already in a work from the 40s, for example, he can be found wishing of Claudius, "Let him equal the accomplishments of the deified Augustus and surpass his years" (*Polyb.* 12.5). Nor can Seneca's engagement with the culture of the original principate be restricted to those gestures in which he sought to revive it in a given emperor's reign. Rather, he exploited myriad opportunities for bringing Augustan culture to bear on topics large and small throughout his varied writings.

In this chapter, we will first survey the main literary devices through which Seneca recalls Augustan culture in all its variety. Then we will conduct a case study comparing the uses he makes of one Augustan theme (concern with memory and dynastic succession) through all these devices. Seneca offers his Julio-Claudian readers his own selective and inventive reception of Augustan culture, often making multiple uses of single ideas.

---

[1] On Seneca's life, see Braund in this volume.

Three Devices

The Augustan moments in Seneca's writings are usually staged through example, intertextual allusion, or quotation – three of Roman literature's preferred devices for engaging with past history or literature. Let us consider these in turn.

Example

Of all the historical persons Seneca presents as examples in his prose writings, he relates the most detail about Augustus. With the conspicuous exception of *Epistulae Morales*, prominent examples involving Augustus are distributed across all the prose writings. A representative case comes in book 3 of *On Anger*, where Seneca shifts from examples of good behavior by Greek kings to mention how "the deified Augustus did and said many memorable things revealing that he was not governed by anger" and describes Augustus' cheerful tolerance of the insults made against him and his family by the Greek historian Timagenes (*Ira* 3.23.4–8; cf. *Ira* 3.40.2–4, *Ben.* 3.27). In addition, we see Augustus being mentioned favorably in connection with such topics as grief (*Marc.* 2–5, 15.2; *Polyb.* 15.3), resolution of legal disputes (*Clem.* 1.14–15; *NQ* 1.16.1), gift giving (*Ben.* 1.15.5, 2.25.1, 3.32.5), and clemency (*Clem.* 1.9–11, 1.14–15; *Ben.* 2.25.1; *NQ* 1.16.1). Although a few examples cast him in a somewhat less flattering light (*Brev.* 4; *Ben.* 6.32; *Clem.* 1.1.6), Augustus is almost always introduced by Seneca as "the deified Augustus" (*divus Augustus*), and there is overall such reverence for him that the negative cases come across as minor exceptions. Seneca himself can take some credit for shaping and sustaining Augustus' positive reputation.

Why illustrate with Augustus rather than someone else? In some cases, Augustus is the obvious person to mention, such as when Seneca is making a straightforwardly political point about the early history of the principate – as in *On Clemency*, where Seneca presents Augustus to Nero as "an example from your own home" (*exemplo domestico, Clem.* 1.9.1). Elsewhere, however, Augustus is relevant as an *a fortiori* example – "one blessed by the gods more than anyone else" yet still human (*Brev.* 4.2; cf. *Marc.* 15.1) – thereby universalizing an experience such as loss and grief. The *princeps'* political identity also provides a moral meta-language: anger did not "govern" (*imperasse*) Augustus (*Ira* 3.23.4), and he was a "conqueror" (*uictor*) of griefs no less than of nations (*Marc.* 15.3).

Seneca was the first imperial writer to recognize that the *princeps* was a monarch and the elite were effectively participants in a "court," where social etiquette and moral conduct were more in the spotlight. Augustus anecdotes thus gave him an opportunity to reanalyze in ethical terms some of the foundational dilemmas of the principate. He does not as a rule focus on contrasting good republic with bad principate: his examples that use Augustus frequently involve contrasts between positive and negative models *within* the principate. This often sets Augustus in opposition to the monstrous Caligula and Claudius. Just as often, however, the contrast is between Octavian and the deified Augustus – that is, between the younger man who (Seneca does not try to conceal it) "shed blood (*sanguinem fudit*) on land and sea" (*Brev.* 4.5) and the older and wiser *princeps* he was to become. This early bloodshed is the factor that allows Seneca, in *On Clemency*, to treat Augustus as a foil for the young Nero (cf. *Clem.* 11.2). Seneca essentially reanalyzes the mature Augustan principate as the result of a moral conversion.

The narrative process of many Augustan examples is a conspicuously deliberative process, as the *princeps* is confronted with competing paths and the former tyrant or potential tyrant becomes a king (a process that would be played in reverse in the anonymous Flavian play *Octavia*, lines 440–589, where Nero upholds the violent Octavian to refute Seneca's lessons). In this process, a pivotal role is often played by an intervening voice – that of Livia in *On Clemency* (*Clem.* 1.9.6), that of the house-philosopher Areus in *Consolation to Marcia* (*Marc.* 4.2–6.1) – and in some instances, Augustus fails to change because of the absence of an adviser (*Brev.* 4) or his failure to heed one (*Ben.* 6.32.1–4). In such cases the message is clear: the dilemmas of the principate, not only for the *princeps* but for the imperial elite, too, are best solved through the moral advice of a Seneca.

Intertextual Allusion

There is scarcely a passage anywhere in Senecan tragedy that does not allude to Augustan poetry, and this arguably does more to shape the tragedies than their debt to the original Athenian tragedies. The countless examples that have drawn recent scholarly attention include the fashioning of Seneca's tragic heroines after Dido in Vergil and Ovid and, more generally, Ovid's transformed or lamenting women in *Metamorphoses* and *Heroides*. Also, Seneca extracts the theme of Thracian cannibalism from Ovid's tale of Tereus and Procne in *Metamorphoses* book 6 to serve as a model and a foil for Atreus' contrivance of "something greater and grander than usual" (*nescioquid …. maius et solito amplius*) in *Thyestes* (*Thy.* 267).

As these selected examples already indicate, Augustan poetry serves as more than just a lexicon of words and themes. Seneca engages with his readers' poetic memory to create a self-conscious tragedy and, in the process, offers critical new readings of the Augustan poems themselves.[2] Here we can only summarize a few of the most salient literary effects (some of which are illustrated by our case study that follows). First, Seneca has the Greek mythic characters speaking in the heavily loaded language of Augustan poetry, putting the audience in a position to observe anticipatory ironies. Second, and conversely, he has characters speak with awareness of their post-Augustan position: they know they are repeating a role and they show a sophisticated reader's mastery of Augustan poetry as they compete with prior versions. Third, although some of Seneca's technique may come from the now lost works of Augustan *tragedy* (as his titles *Thyestes* and *Medea* surely do, echoing masterworks by Varius and Ovid, respectively), the surviving Augustan texts that we know he engages with are from elegy and hexameter poetry and (in the choral odes especially) Horatian lyric, making Senecan tragedy very much a polygeneric product. Fourth, by locating his plays as successors to the Augustan tradition, Seneca enters into a chain of authorial emulation and escalation that, in the case of the "something greater" motif of *Thyestes* and *Medea*, is closely tied to the intensification of the evil within the play. Fifth, Seneca's plays often have the appearance of having grown from a specific Augustan seed text or theme, something we see evidence of in the Dido and "something greater" motifs mentioned previously. An especially influential seed theme for Senecan tragedy has been traced by Putnam (1995), who notes that Seneca systematically amplifies and reiterates the same negative infernal forces and violent passions that in Vergil's *Aeneid* are relatively temporary and in the end are subordinated to the success of Aeneas' mission.

Virtually all of these effects were already in evidence prior to the end of the Augustan age, thanks to Ovid, whose literary career had been highly adaptive both in relation to the emergent Augustan corpus as a whole and internally in relation to his own prior works, not least in the play of genres. This is not to deny that Seneca develops his own form of tragedy but that much of what is characteristic about Senecan tragedy emerges from his interactions with "Ovidian loci" (Hinds 2011).

The origins of Seneca's intertextual practice may be better understood by considering Seneca the Elder's sketches of poetic emulation in the late-Augustan and Tiberian period, such as the instance in which Ovid, by subtracting words from a line of the republican poet Varro Atacinus, "found his own sense" (*suum sensum invenit, Contr.* 7.1.27) or the instance in which a literary critic who admired a specific sentence of Ovid (*Met.* 12.607–8) says that "it ought to be kept in one's memory when inventing similar sentences" (*Contr.* 10.4.25). And although up to this point I have discussed intertextual

---

[2] See the examples provided by Trinacty in this volume.

allusion as if it were restricted to the tragedies, Seneca's own discussion of "incorporative" writing in *Epistulae Morales* 84, a process compared to that of bees harvesting flowers and composing honey (*Ep.* 84.2–4), is conspicuous in addressing not poetry but philosophical prose.

Quotation

Throughout his prose works, Seneca directly quotes from poetry, often with explicit citation of the author. These quotations are sometimes ornamental, sometimes more central to the discussion and subjected to exegesis or critique in their own right. Philosophers, after all, do not have a monopoly on the truth (*Ep.* 8.8), and poets can often say it better (*Ep.* 108.10). As a rule, however, Seneca detaches quotations from their original context, and he often gives them "a philosophical, symbolical, or allegorical twist" (Maguiness 1956, 93), concentrating on one thing "while [the poet] is doing something else" (*dum aliud agit*) – such as when Vergil's description of a thoroughbred horse turns out to function as an ideal description of a great man (*Ep.* 95.67–9, quoting *Georg.* 3.75–85).

Seneca's quotations as a rule do not come from just *any* poetry. He quotes only very occasionally from republican poets, from Augustan elegiac, lyric, and tragic poetry, and from Horace's satires or letters, preferring Horatian allusions only. By contrast, he quotes frequently from the hexameter poems of Vergil and Ovid, treating them as an encyclopedic reservoir of phrases and scenarios already familiar to his readers. The majority of these quotations are in *Epistulae Morales*; quotation from literature was a standard element of ancient epistolary style.

Vergil is quoted most, and from virtually every book of *Eclogues*, *Georgics*, and *Aeneid*. The quotations vary in extent and motivation, with some adding mere color but others being substantial. Discussing kingship, Seneca quotes lines on bee monarchy from the *Georgics* (*Georg.* 4.212–13 quoted at *Clem.* 1.4.1 and *Ep.* 114.23); discussing the right attitude to have in death, he quotes Dido's last words, "I have lived and have completed the course that fortune gave" (*Aen.* 4.653, quoted at *VB* 19.1, *Ben.* 5.17.5, and *Ep.* 12.9). Seneca shows the same kind of reverence for Vergil as he shows for Augustus, calling him "our Vergil" (*Vergilius noster*) and treating him as Rome's national poet and "the greatest poet .... as if inspired by a divine voice" (*maximus uates .... uelut diuino ore instinctus*, *De brev.* 9.2). He contrasts his own philosophical approach to Vergil with the approaches of the grammarian or philologist, both of whom would waste time analyzing Vergil's language and style rather than his moral insights – as, for instance, in Vergil's comments in the *Georgics* on a topic dear to Seneca's heart, the fleetingness of time (*De brev.* 9.2–4 and *Ep.* 108.23–8, quoting *Georg.* 3.66–7).

The truth that Seneca discovers in Vergil's poetry is not philosophical as such: it is the kind of truth that emerges through the sublime poet's insights into specific kinds of human situations. There is a convenient affinity between the overall quest of Aeneas as a hero struggling to make progress in *Aeneid* and the progressing student of philosophy who is the main concern of *Epistulae Morales*. At the same time, however, after quoting the passage from *Aeneid* book 2 in which Aeneas describes a change in his state of mind, going from being a callous fighter unafraid to confront the Greeks in combat to being concerned for the family members he is shepherding (*Aen.* 2.726–9), Seneca surprisingly identifies the former as wise and the latter as foolish, since he is attached to external encumbrances (*Ep.* 56.12–14) – an *ad hoc* counterreading of the epic.

A few additional effects can be summarized here. First, seemingly illustrative quotations may smuggle in key heuristic devices or seed ideas, as is often the case with his frequent use of Ovid's *Metamorphoses* in *Natural Questions*. Second, Seneca sometimes incorporates more of the original context than is quoted explicitly, such that quotation is blended with intertextual allusion. Third, a quotation from one text may be accompanied by a separate allusion to another text altogether. Seneca's quotations are often the tips of icebergs.

Case Study: Memory and Dynastic Progress

The devices discussed above are in roughly complementary distribution across Seneca's oeuvre. But when Seneca happens to return to a given topic through all three devices, we can discern a subtle complexity. This is certainly the case for his treatment of the Augustan concern with how best to manage the continuation of the dynasty. As Seneca presents it, the shift of attention from one potential successor to another often hinged on a highly specific use of memory by Augustus and his family, and this has various lessons to offer Julio-Claudian readers.

At the beginning of his earliest surviving work, *Consolation to Marcia*, Seneca seeks to end Marcia's grief for her deceased adult son Metilius by having her choose between the models of maternal grieving seen in two women from the household of Augustus: Octavia, the emperor's sister, whose son Marcellus died in 23 BCE, and Livia, the emperor's wife, whose son Drusus died in 9 BCE. Seneca notes that each son prior to his death was being groomed to become the next princeps (*Marc.* 2.3). After Marcellus' death, Octavia spent the rest of her life "as if at a funeral": she "was unwilling to have any image (*imaginem*) of her dearest son" and "rejected the poems (*carmina*) composed to celebrate Marcellus' memory" (*Marc.* 2.4–5).

"Poems" no doubt alludes to such poems as Propertius 3.18 as well as Vergil's famous mention of the death of Marcellus in Anchises' pageant of Roman heroes in *Aeneid* book 6: "if somehow you can break harsh fate, / you will be Marcellus (*tu Marcellus eris*)" (*Aen.* 6.882–3); that passage, we learn elsewhere, caused Octavia to faint when she heard it recited (cf. Suet. *Verg.* 32). Livia, on the other hand, after Drusus' death, "did not cease from …. representing him to herself both privately and publicly"; she "lived with his memory" (*cum memoria illius uixit, Marc.* 3.2).

Beyond the emotional portraits, Seneca is at pains to draw out the political implications for Augustus as he sought to identify a successor: Octavia "raged especially against Livia, because she saw that the happiness promised to herself had passed to Livia's son" (2.5). Livia, by contrast, at least after receiving advice from the house-philosopher Areus, was able to transfer her ambitions to her other son, Tiberius. Seneca makes it clear that Livia's approach to grief and memory was an integral part of Augustus' accomplishment in overcoming the depletion of his household to ensure a successor by adoption (*Marc.* 15.2; cf. *Polyb.* 15.3). We may read this as a learning curve for Augustus and his household as a whole. Seneca has them proceed from an earlier practice of remembering the deceased successor only bitterly and regressively – especially in dwelling on his death – to a later practice of remembering the deceased in celebratory and progressive ways – the practice that proved so productive for the dynasty.

Yet Marcia's choice regarding how to end her grief is articulated not only through the example of Augustus' sister and wife but also through allusions to and quotations from Augustan poetry. The *Aeneid* is quoted and alluded to at numerous moments, such as when Seneca tells Marcia that her son "has arrived at the finishing post of the time granted him" (*metasque dati peruenit ad aeui; Marc.* 21.5, quoting *Aen.* 10.472), words of Jupiter as he consoles his son Hercules on the impending death of Pallas by pointing out that Turnus too will soon have to die. Such moments in the *Aeneid* are very much of a piece with the future death of Marcellus mentioned in book 6, and it is easy to see an overall affinity in *Consolation to Marcia* between these references to grieving within the *Aeneid* and the negative example of Octavia's grieving discussed earlier. Another work of Augustan literature is alluded to in the consolation's final line addressed to Marcia, where Seneca celebrates the fact that her son has joined his grandfather and the other "happy souls" (*felices animae*) in the heavens and learned about the regenerative cycle of the cosmos: "Happy your son who already knows these things!" (*felicem filium tuum qui ista iam novit, Marc.* 26.7). This alludes to a passage early in Ovid's calendar poem, *Fasti* – a text that scholars usually do not mention as familiar to Seneca – where Ovid uses the blessing "Happy the souls for whom it was a concern to know these things first (*felices animae, quibus haec cognoscere primis*) / and to ascend to a home above" (*Fast.* 1.297–8) to venerate the poets before him who have deciphered the cyclic motions of the heavenly bodies and have "thrust their heads up" (*exseruisse caput*) high above the human world (*Fast.* 1.300). Seneca, then, once again taps into an Augustan literary work that is dedicated to the persistence in time of Augustus and his household.

At this point it is necessary to return to the *Aeneid* and recognize the extent to which the schematic contrast Seneca sees between Octavia's melancholy and Livia's progressive memory is played out by Vergil in the tension between premature death and the telos of the poem in the foundation of Rome and the Julian family. Vergil's *Aeneid* spoke to concerns in the 20s BCE about Augustus' succession, and these concerns are explored most directly in passages that deal with Aeneas' son Ascanius/Iulus, "the dynastic name *par excellence*" (Hardie 1993, 91). One of the emblematic moments in the poem as regards Ascanius comes in the Buthrotum episode, where Andromache, living in her miniature replica of Troy and unable to relinquish her grief for her husband Hector and son Astyanax, farewells Aeneas and his party by saying to Ascanius (*Aen.* 3.489–91):

> O sole image I have of my Astyanax:
> thus did he bear his eyes, his hands, his mouth,
> and he would now have been maturing, of equal age with you
> *o mihi sola mei super Astyanactis imago.*
> *sic oculos, sic ille manus, sic ora ferebat;*
> *et nunc aequali tecum pubesceret aeuo.*

Vergil here has Andromache toy with the idea that Ascanius can essentially serve as a successor to Astyanax, whom the Greeks had sacrificed back at Troy. Ascanius will in an important sense turn out to be such a successor, though Andromache herself cannot move on. Of this episode, Hardie observes that "Andromache stands as a warning by the poet to himself of the danger of epic failure: .... Memory here is inert, limited to shadowy imitations that will never take on life and expand as the successful epic must" (Hardie 1993, 16–17).

I single out this moment in the *Aeneid* because Andromache's words are alluded to by Seneca in his tragedies and also directed quoted in his prose works – one of just a few opportunities that, as Trinacty (2014, ch. 1) shows, allow us to compare Seneca's varying approaches to a single idea. Comparing the relevant passages will give us an opportunity to observe two distinct paths of reception, each refracting for its own ends the *Aeneid's* thematization of the Augustan concern with succession. These two receptional paths also correspond in striking ways to Seneca's contrasting figures of Octavia and Livia discussed earlier.

The allusion to the Vergilian Andromache's words arises in Seneca's *Trojan Women*, in words spoken by Andromache. The difference is that in Seneca's play, Astyanax is still living, and Andromache tells Astyanax – not Ascanius – that he is the "sole hope for the Trojans" and "very like your father (*nimiumque patri similis*)" (*Tro.* 462–8):

> This face did
> my Hector have, thus was he in his walk
> and thus in his bearing, thus did he bear his strong hands,
> just so tall were his shoulders, just so threatening was he with fierce brow,
> tossing his hair over his neck.

Even as she utters these words, Andromache scarcely dares to hope that Astyanax will really avenge Troy, and within the play the comparison prepares for the brutal irony of an utterance she makes later. For when the messenger describes how Astyanax's body was shattered by its fall from the tower of Troy such that "the body lies formless" (*iacet / deforme corpus*), Andromache says: "Even so does he resemble his father" (*sic quoque est similis patri, Tro.* 1116–17). As scholars have noted, the resemblance goes back not simply to the mutilated corpse of Hector but to the dismembered corpse of the grandfather Priam (cf. *Aen.* 2.557–8), and "the threat that circularity and repression pose to the norms of continuity and linear progress is also played out in the spatial [viz. corporeal] dimension of the tragedy" (Schiesaro 2003, 201).

In *Trojan Women*, Seneca dramatizes a world of grief that, given his choice of genre and theme, has no Ascanius to whom it can transfer any hope of succession. It is also noteworthy that the Senecan Andromache's view of Astyanax as simply a path to further grief and lament over Hector and Priam bears some close similarities to the emotional world of Octavia in her grief over Marcellus. Indeed, the Senecan Andromache in vain exhorts Hector, "Break fate's constraints" (*rumpe fatorum moras, Tro.* 681), a clear allusion to the words of Anchises in *Aeneid* book 6, "if somehow you can break harsh fate (*si qua fata aspera rumpas*), / you will be Marcellus" (*Aen.* 6.882–3; cf. Boyle 1994, 194). To this extent, Seneca's tragedy draws attention not only to the fragility of the "bridge between the past and future" (Schiesaro 2003, 202) that Vergil's epic ostensibly sought to draw between the death of Astyanax and the mission of Ascanius but also to the corresponding risk that the household of Augustus ran if it grieved excessively for the loss of a groomed successor. *Trojan Women* makes an Octavia of Andromache, advertising how the epic teleology that had been available to make Ascanius the substitute of Astyanax can be turned on its head to exacerbate the sense that the Trojan line has been thoroughly extinguished with Astyanax.

The second of Seneca's receptions of the Vergilian Andromache's words comes in a fragment of his lost work *How to Maintain Friendship*, where he twice quotes one of Andromache's lines (F59.5–6 Vottero 1998):

> As our memory [of an absent friend] recedes let us call it back.... [W]e should use the swiftness of our mind and not allow any of our friends to be absent from us – let them return to our mind repeatedly. Let us keep the future present to us now, modeled on the past: "Thus did he move his hands and thus his lips" [*Aen.* 3.490]. Let an image (*imago*) be fashioned in our mind – a memorable one taken from the living person, not faint and mute: "Thus did he move his hands and thus his lips." Let us add to it the more relevant things: Thus did he speak, thus did he give encouragement, thus did he dissuade .... Let us survey his other virtues and occupy ourselves with how he used and managed them.

As we know to expect with Seneca, the direct quotation is not the whole of it: Seneca further incorporates a key term from the original content, *imago*. He also detaches the quotation to suit his own point, expanding the image into a full moral portrait. And in Seneca, the *imago* is just that, an *imago* in memory, rather than the living, breathing person (Ascanius) that it is in Vergil. At the same time, however, Seneca's characterization of the *imago* here as an image of the person that can be interacted with, rather than a dead and silent one, aligns the present discussion with a favorite opposition of Seneca's, ubiquitous in the prose works, between living persons and mere images (for example, *Ep.* 35.3) – except that in the present passage, he maintains that the image itself can be as animated as the living person, thanks to the mind's imaginative power. We may observe that this recollection of how the person was before we lost him is very much akin to the use of memory in *Consolation to Marcia* that Seneca ascribes to Livia in her celebratory memory of the deceased Drusus.

Even as he pursues his own ideas here, applying the Vergilian verses to new referents, Seneca in many ways still conveys the spirit of the original, especially in his emphasis on how this thought-exercise is intended to bridge between past and future. He arguably exploits the *Aeneid*'s teleological momentum (the momentum toward Rome) that is glimpsed in the Vergilian Andromache's fleeting perception of Ascanius as a new Astyanax to promote the potential for bridging the temporal and spatial divides that can separate one friend from another. Moreover, although Seneca's work on friendship is obviously not concerned with questions of how memory can aid in dynastic succession, the topic of maintaining friendship is not altogether removed from the concerns of living in the Julio-Claudian principate, since friendship (*amicitia*) was a primary bond both among elite Romans and between the *princeps* and the elite, especially any who (like Seneca) were known by the informal title "friend of the emperor" (*amicus principis*).[3] Seneca thus redirects the narrative energy that Vergil expends upon the foundation of the Julian family to serve instead as the moral and social energy that maintains the benefit of friendship even when threatened by rupture due to travel or – the implication is not hard to find – due to the exiles and murders frequently suffered by the Julio-Claudian elite.

Seneca, then, leverages Augustan discourse on memory and dynastic progress to facilitate some local transactions for himself and his readers – various forms of memory bridging and progressive projection, in contrast to the regressive memory that makes continuation impossible. But these are not the only transactions that Seneca conducts through selectively and creatively reproducing Augustan memory projections. Letter 21 is his most personal and direct analogization of Augustan culture to serve his authorial purposes. There he tells Lucilius that "a profound depth of time will come over us and few authors will thrust their heads up (*caput exerent*)," but he himself will survive and will take Lucilius with him (*Ep.* 21.5). As a comparison, he observes (*Ep.* 21.5):

> Our Vergil promised eternal memory to two [= Nisus and Euryalus] and he provides it:
>
> Fortunate pair! If my poetry has any power,
> no day will ever remove you from mindful eternity,
> so long as the household of Aeneas inhabits the immovable rock of the Capitol
> and the Roman father retains his imperial authority. [*Aen.* 9.446–9]

Here Seneca builds on Vergil's discourse of explicitly commemorating the ill-fated Nisus and Euryalus, in which Vergil first ties his subjects' future to his own future, then ties his own future to the longevity of the Julian family and Augustan principate. But we may further note how Seneca supplements the Vergil quotation with an allusion to the same passage of Ovid's *Fasti* book 1 discussed earlier in the image of the happy souls who have "kept their heads above" (*exseruisse caput*, *Fast.* 1.300). In the Ovidian passage, poets are immortalized through cosmic sublimation – an image that we may choose to see as simply reinforcing the Augustan calendar and the longevity of the principate – or as outlasting it. If the latter, then Seneca appropriates Augustan culture to build his own superior memory bridge into the future

---

[3] See Edwards' discussion of friendship in this volume.

for himself and Lucilius by relocating the guarantee of memorability from the rock of the Capitol to the sublime natural cosmos that is the object of philosophy.

Conclusion: A Successor to Maecenas

Each of the main devices Seneca uses for engaging with Augustan culture – example, intertextual allusion, and quotation – allows him to think about the Julio-Claudian present using a different aspect of Augustan culture. Yet we must not miss the opportunity to note the overall picture that emerges. As our case study in particular has shown, Seneca revisits the foundational narratives of the principate and asserts control over the moral and literary discourses by which the principate can be seen to have variously succeeded or failed. Seneca wants his readers to understand the respective moral conditions that can make or break the community of the principate, both in its original instantiation and in all its ongoing metamorphoses.

In his multifaceted engagement with Augustan culture, Seneca can usefully be compared to Maecenas, the famous "friend of the emperor," writer of poetry and prose, and influential patron of literature to whom virtually all the great Augustan poets were closely connected. Mayer has described Seneca as "the new Maecenas" of his age, pointing out that in addition to patronage, Seneca "had .... been as close to the *princeps*, but he could claim nicer morals and smarter prose: imitation became, as so often, emulation" (Mayer 1982, 315). By inserting himself into Maecenas' role as a superior successor, Seneca makes a bid to be the one who controls the potential for Augustan culture to inform future generations. As it happens, however, in several of the later works of his career, Seneca mentions Maecenas several times in a most negative light, criticizing him as an effeminate voluptuary whose moral depravity is evident even in his style of writing (*Prov.* 3.10–11; *Ben.* 6.32.2–4; *Ep.* 19.9, 92.35, 101.10–13, 114.4–8, 114.21–2; on *Ep.* 114, see further Williams and Schiesaro in this volume). In becoming the new Maecenas, Seneca evidently needed to kill off the old one.

Further Reading

On Seneca's use of Augustus as an example, see the survey article by Jal (1957) as well as Griffin (1976: 211–13); examples in individual texts are discussed by Braund (2009, *On Clemency*); Shelton (1995, *Consolation to Marcia*); Williams (2003, *On the Brevity of Life*). For Seneca and Julio-Claudian culture, see Gowing (2005, 67–81) and Roller (2001: 64–126). Further aspects of the Octavia-Livia example in *Consolation to Marcia* are discussed in Ker (2009a: 94–6). Seneca's intertextual allusions to Augustan poetry are discussed in a recent book-length study of the tragedies by Trinacty (2014); a foundational study for tracing the Augustan influence is Tarrant (1978). Specific aspects arise in virtually every study and commentary, including Fantham (1975, Dido); Schiesaro (2003, *Thyestes*); Putnam (1995, *Aeneid*); and Zissos (2008, on "shades of Vergil" in *Trojan Women*). For discussion of Seneca's quotations from Augustan poetry in the prose works, see the survey article by Maguiness (1956) and useful discussion by Tarrant (2006: 1–5); and the comprehensive treatment of poetics and individual poets by Mazzoli (1970). On specific authors, see Setaioli (1965, Vergil); Berthet (1979, Horace); Williams (2012, Ovid in *Natural Questions*). For text and commentary on Seneca's *How to Maintain Friendship*, see Vottero (1998); further aspects of fragment 59 are discussed by Ker (2009a: 281–3). Seneca's (mis)treatment of Maecenas is discussed by Byrne (1999) and Graver (1998).

9

VICTORIA RIMELL

Seneca and Neronian Rome: In the Mirror of Time

Seneca's career was a miracle of timing. His life spanned the reigns of the first five emperors (already an unlikely feat, given his proximity to government from the late 30s onward), and his forced suicide under Nero in 65 marked the beginning of the end of the entire Julio-Claudian dynasty. Indeed, it is Seneca's special relationship with Nero that has come to define his place in history as a writer, thinker, and political player. Nero was a new breed of emperor after the decrepit Claudius: a young, flamboyant, hellenophile poet and performer who ushered in both a new era of literary innovation and an intensified climate of artistic oppression and who came to embody (alongside Seneca and Petronius) the inseparability of artistic and political charisma in imperial court life.[1] A huge amount has been written on the extent to which Seneca "rivaled" Nero as both artist and leader, on how Seneca's polyglot self-reinvention, sparkling poetics, and fascination with the spec(tac)ular may be best understood against Nero's theatricalization of power.[2] While I will touch on all those aspects, my route into Neronian Seneca (and Seneca's relationship with Nero) will follow Seneca's career-long preoccupation with time – a topic that comes to be inseparable in many of his texts from the reality of living in this particular historical period and from an impulse to reassess Rome's repeated appeal to the authority of the past. Current critical opinion tends to see a gulf between the perverse distortion and uncanny foreknowledge of time's natural movement in Senecan tragedy on one hand and advice on the respectful acceptance and monitoring of time as care of the self in philosophical prose on the other.[3] However I will be pointing here to the provocative and intellectually challenging manipulation of time

---

[1] On Nero as a poet and actor, see Suet. *Ner.* 10.2, 20–2, 52, Tac. *Ann.* 13.3, 14.16, 15.49, Dio 62.29.2–4. For an overview of the climate of literary renaissance/oppression under Nero, see Fantham (1996, 153–62).

[2] On which see Littlewood in this volume.

[3] On distorted time and foreknowledge of a future that has "already happened" in the tragedies, see, e.g., Schiesaro (2003, 177–220); Seo (2013, 94–112).

that runs through the whole of Seneca's oeuvre and that seems to intensify alongside and in response to the regime change of 54.

Zeitgeists and Biological Clocks

The specular relationship between Seneca the pedagogue-advisor and his pupil-boss emperor is a ticking bomb bound to end in a crisis of succession. Like the all-knowing protagonists of Senecan tragedy, we read the *Apocolocyntosis* already biting our nails at the audacity of the exercise and at the unlikeliness of it being sustained for long. The critical point at the end of Nero's boyhood is dramatized by Tacitus in *Annals* 14.53–56: in Seneca's fourteenth year as guru (already equivalent to what would be the complete length of Nero's rule) and six years after Nero took the reins of power, the tutor's seniority is no longer required and his fortune and villas are now "vulnerable to accident" (*obnoxia casibus*, 14.55). Yet succession, generational tension, and the problem of dialogue between the two in an autocratic regime are themes constantly remapped in Seneca's work, starting with the *Apocolocyntosis* on the tricky, time-sensitive hand-over from Claudius to Nero and ending with the *Epistulae Morales*, where Seneca trains up the younger Lucilius to don the *toga virilis* of philosophy but jokes at letter 86 that he'll curtail his teaching, for fear that his pupil become his competitor (*adversarium*, 86.21). In the *De clementia* and in the notorious later mythologizations of Neronian tyranny (Tacitus' *Annals*, Suetonius' *Lives*, Cassius Dio's *Histories*), Nero and Seneca are both doubles and opposites at radically different life stages: the oxymoron of their partnership offers a significant frame in Seneca's texts for thinking through change over time, as well as for various nonlinear ways of conceiving time in an age we associate with fervent literary experimentation.

Nero was just seventeen when he came to power, not quite ripe for the role of *pater patriae*, and needing to be propped up by a behind-the-scenes father figure.[4] Seneca might have been middle aged (even his name seems to mark his status as always already a *senex*), but like stage-happy Nero, he was a populist and crowd pleaser, prized as the "voice of youth" and well placed to lend Nero a timely, modern wit that nevertheless harked back to the elegant oratory of Augustus. Managing the doubleness of this strategy seems to have been one of the key challenges of Seneca and Nero's "special relationship," its paradoxes frequently revisited in Seneca's surviving texts. Not only does Seneca adapt his performance expertly to circumstances; he also, apparently, pulls off an unlikely combination of experienced sobriety

---

[4] Suetonius *Ner.* 8.

and teen spirit. "At that time," Quintilian writes at the end of the first century, "Seneca's works were the only ones in the hands of young men" (10.1.126). Tacitus names Seneca and Burrus "guardians of the imperial youth," noting that Seneca's talents were so well suited to "the ears of the time" (*temporis ... auribus, Ann.* 13.3) – a testament to his evident ability to capture any zeitgeist, to surf what he refers to as the "torrent" of time, even (after Ovid) to make *tempora* his own.[5]

Other writers of the period, whose work in recent criticism has come to embody a particular "Neronian aesthetic" of boiled-down, bubbling intensity, project a brave new era that belongs to the (angry, pretentious, self-satirizing) young. The fleshily inventive *Satyricon* stars a reckless student protagonist next to the debauched freedman Trimalchio, who is counting the days till his funeral; the shepherds of Calpurnius Siculus' *Eclogues*, whether these poems were actually written under Nero or pretend to be, are in awe of the luminous young prince, and in the final poem, Lycotas envies Corydon for being young "in an age like this."[6] Earlier in the same poem, Corydon himself recounts how a man of advanced age confessed to being awestruck at the spectacles despite having grown old in the city: even the elderly are rejuvenated and pass negative judgment on their own youth in the light of such marvelous modernity. Meanwhile, Persius' satires are sickened by the necrophilia of tradition, by a culture that churns out prematurely old poets and is rotten to the core: the tight, six-poem book features a cast of adolescents, from the depressed philosophy major of *Sat.* 3 to the pretentious know-it-all noble of *Sat.* 4. As if poisoned by his own brew, the precocious Persius died in 62, aged twenty-seven, while Seneca's nephew Lucan packed in the mind-blowing epic *Bellum Civile* before going the way of his uncle in 65, aged just twenty-five, followed shortly by burnt-out, still-young Nero in 68. In the shadow of Nero's extreme youth, "Neronian literature" as we know it is preoccupied by (the political, aesthetic, and psychological consequences of) experiencing too much too soon.[7]

Facing Change

In his *De clementia* (dated to 55–56), Seneca addresses Nero and confronts his "youthful impulse" directly. In the opening lines, he announces that he

---

[5] *De brev.* 9.2. On Ovidian appropriation of Augustan *tempora*, see Hinds (1999). Studies of Senecan time include Motto and Clark (1987), Armisen-Marchetti (1995), Gagliardi (1998), Viparelli (2000), and Ker (2004, 219–25; 2009b, 147–76; 2009c, 184–5).

[6] Calp. 7.74–5.

[7] On which see Gowers (1994).

will perform the function of a mirror in order to guide the young emperor in the self-analysis and self-governance required of a great leader. In Seneca's hands, the mirror becomes not just a metaphor for self-examination but also the tool for a suspicious and ontologically probing reconceptualization of time and of conventional imperial history.[8] Now, that is, that we are in a position – under the youngest emperor ever (1.11.3) – to look back to the beginning, to see how Rome has begun to construct the narrative(s) of its emperors. In the first chapters of *De clementia* book 1, Seneca imagines the emperor addressing himself as if about to look back on his future reign and compose his own *Res Gestae*, echoing the older, not younger (that is, murderous) Augustus.[9] As the avuncular adviser holds up a post-Ovidian "mirror" to his transformable pupil, he has him recall instances of compassion as if reviewing the past: *alterius aetate prima motus sum, alterius ultima* ("I have been moved by the young age of one, and by the old age of another," 1.1.4). These opposite poles have their own distinct appeal and, above all, retrace the predicted comparison between mature Augustus and the adolescent prince: yet they are also inextricable and symbiotic in a text that preaches the point – equivalent to Narcissus' *heureka* moment – that other is in fact self and that merciful rule is actually *amor sui* ("self-love," 1.11.2). The more immediate paradigm for this principle is the partnership between (old) Seneca and (young) Nero, the former sticking his neck out for the latter, making himself indispensable, and entwining the fates of emperor and right-hand man. Of course, the scenes of father-figure lecturing young pupil (and soon to be Father) on self-love also looks like a updating of Sophocles' *Oedipus* for spectacle-hungry Neronian Rome: this kind of intimacy – as Seneca's own Oedipus has worked out from the start – is unlikely to end well.[10]

Less obviously, the *speculum* of the *De Clementia* sets up Seneca's argument for counterintuitive inversions of cause and effect: punishments result in or are followed by crimes, not vice versa ("the crime of parricide began with the law against it," 1.23.1). The mirror is a model for mercy as a virtue that can "turn back the clock" and return the guilty to innocence (1.2.1) and for poetic reversibility in general (actually, Seneca suggests, in some ways the emperor is a slave, and his subjects are sovereigns, 1.8.1). As an accessory that reflects, reproduces, repeats, the mirror also captures the problem of how Nero goes about defining himself within the exemplum-heavy history

---

[8] See Armisen-Marchetti (2006), Bartsch (2006, 183–229), and Ker (2009b, 264–5) on Seneca's use of the mirror.

[9] *De clem.* 1.9.1–4.

[10] On Seneca's all-knowing Oedipus, see Seo (2013, 94–121).

of Julio-Claudian empire. Seneca suggests that the conventional mirror of history is possibly, in this case, deceptive: Augustus was only "mild" as an older man (and perhaps because he "tired of cruelty"), having stained his hands with blood pre-Actium. According to Seneca, who apologizes for filling his volume with repetitions of Augustus' words (1.9.11), the first emperor found it difficult to look back at how he used to be in his difficult early years (1.11.1). Like Echo, who could only repeat *novissima verba*, Nero should aspire to mirroring only the *last part* of Augustan *fama*, though at the same time comparisons are out, and young Nero should be unblemished, "uncorrupted by the *exempla* of previous princes" (1.11.1–2).[11] He doesn't (or isn't) Echo, in other words, but instead his every pronouncement reverberates through the empire, and his emotional state ripples outward (*irasci non potes, nisi ut omnia tremant*, "You can't get angry without causing everything to tremble," 1.8.5). However, the image of Nero as blond *puer* with star quality on the cusp of manhood, destined to encounter a world that echoes *him*, places the emperor right back in Narcissus' ominously powerful shoes at the start of his Ovidian narrative.

Yet Seneca's point is that Nero must be a post-technological, self-aware mirror gazer from the outset, so that the patterns of history – and of Ovid's myths – may be rewritten. We are to understand that multiple mirrors are in operation here. Not least the one that figures the way Seneca sees himself in Ovid, as he makes the original move of applying the poetic-ontological template of the Narcissus-Echo tale to ethics and imperial history. But we may add to this Seneca's mirroring/echoing of Augustus or, more specifically, of Augustus' future mature self. In implicitly setting up the author of the *De clementia* as ideal or parallel emperor, the Seneca-Augustus pairing is an edgy one, for sure, especially when combined with the trope of reversibility. Seneca's use of the figurative mirror as a lens through which to view history differently is an impressive assertion of his own writerly-as-political power, but it also betrays an anxious (and again, post-Ovidian) awareness of how his "remedy" for Nero might well turn out to be a poison he cooks up for himself. The mirror of the *De Clementia* creates a chain of potential doubles – Seneca-Augustus, Nero-Augustus, Seneca-Nero – yet the lesson of Narcissus, as of Roman foundation myths, is that two must become one.

Forward Thinking

Under the star of the adolescent *princeps*, youth stands for revolution and new beginnings. But the discourse of age in the first and early second

[11] On Augustus as a foil to Nero in the *De Clementia*, also see Ker in this volume.

centuries is of course highly metaphorical, and to be young is also a state of mind, a way of being in time. To reach old age at the heart of empire – as Seneca did – is both to play an intelligent game and to embody the virtue of manly and philosophical resilience. It is to have remained constant in the face of change, to have grown healthily and steadily in an epoch of distorted or stunted growth.[12] Contrast the empty oratory of corrupt rhetorical schools, which "lacks the vigour" to "reach the grey hairs of old age" at Petronius, *Satyricon* 1–3; or alternatively, the god of perpetual youth (Bacchus) at Seneca, *Apocolocyntosis* 2.1.5–6, who is "ordered" to age in what is imagined to be a tyrannical cycle of time whereby each solar year begins and ends in *deformis Hiems* ("deformed Winter" 2.1.4); or the *occupati* of Seneca's *De brevitate vitae* who have frittered away their lives in the hectic metropolis and find themselves suddenly old, their bent bodies still harboring puerile and unevolved minds (*brev.* 9.4, cf. *Ep.* 4.2). Good kings grow old, Seneca reminds Nero at *De clementia* 1.11.4, but the reign of tyrants is short. At Tacitus *Annals* 14.57, when Sulla is speedily dispatched at his dinner table in Gaul (the assassins moving in faster than rumor) and his head carried back to Rome, Nero's delight at the sight of its "prematurely grey" hair pinpoints his disturbing interference in Roman time.[13] Implicitly Nero has caused Sulla to age ahead of time and now completes the intervention by whisking him ahead to an already classic "death at dinner." Both Neronian texts and later commentary on the period tell a story of time and space under pressure, of altering perceptions of the pace of life at a point where the "young" (as defined against *iuvenis* Nero) find themselves in unprecedentedly bitter conflict with the old guard and where the new elite is coming to terms with its vulnerability in the face of history.[14] Seneca participates in and even embodies this zeitgeist: but the aim of the *de Clementia*, we might say, is to integrate (or transform) perverse joinings of the aged and the youthful into an ambitious discourse of virtue in which the exemplary Nero may – by studying himself in the mirror of history – cheat time by fast-forwarding to *sapientia*.

Seneca is fascinated by the opportunity both to rethink being in time *now* and to redefine an earlier age under a new emperor who is immediately mythologized as a sun-god or the sun itself: Nero will symbolically regulate the light and dark of the era he governs, decide when countless lifespans are snipped off, and inherit a post-Augustan power to appropriate

---

[12] See Gowers (1994) on the juxtaposition of precocity and rot in Neronian literature.

[13] Cf. Suet. *Ner.* 11.1 on Nero's *Juvenales*, at which elderly aristocrats were forced to perform.

[14] Cf. Habinek (2000).

and manufacture time by rewriting the Roman calendar. As the historians tell us, the boy-king famously rebranded April, May, and June "Neroneus," "Claudius," and "Germanicus" after his three names, "leaping ahead" of Julius Caesar's and Octavian's July and August.[15] Tacitus quips in *Annals* 16.12 that according to the testimony of Cornelius Orfitus, the change to June was necessary because the month had been sullied by the execution of two Juniuses (the Torquati of *Ann.* 15.35 and 16.8), a double slaughter that had already turned part of the Roman year into dead bodies. In Seneca's hands, however, the prince's youth is made to stand for positive transformability, for the potential to reform or even save a man's life and thus alter his perspective on time: at *De clementia* 2.7.2, Seneca writes that the wise leader "will not inflict a punishment if he sees that the person's age will allow for reformation," a thought that – in the logic of this text – is easily turned back onto the "malleable" young emperor who finds himself under Seneca's gentle, statesmanly direction.

In the *Apocolocyntosis*, too, Nero's "positive" manipulation and appropriation of natural time is set against Claudius' soiling of Roman history. Fooling every good-news astrologer who made regular predictions of his demise, Claudius dragged out his life until the age of sixty-four, although as Mercury puts it, "nobody ever thought he was born" (*Apoc.* 3.2). In the Saturnalian world of this satire, Claudius' entire existence was an insult to civilized time; implicitly, he couldn't even choose a propitious time to die (Seneca has his characters make sly reference to the discrepancy between Claudius' actual time of death and the official version as overseen by Agrippina, who literally reset the imperial clock in order to facilitate the transfer of power to her son).[16] Nero, however, ushers in a new day, a bright spring in mid-autumn, at the end of a dark, metaphorical winter. He is both Lucifer (the morning star) and Hesperus (the evening star, 4.1.25–6), the pretty boy with ephebic, flowing hair (4.1.32) who will rule like Father Sun himself, venerable and gentle as he "tones down his brightness" to face his subjects (*fulgore remisso*, 4.1.31). But (whether or not we snigger) the message is that Nero belongs to the future: he is ahead of his years, a boy-father who will light up the sky both day and night.

Seneca's texts are invested not just in creative re-presentations of problematic Neronian youth but also in reconceiving the past for the present in a way that radically puts into question the possibility of return to a world of unsullied, "natural" time.[17] The *De brevitate vitae*, for example (probably

---

[15] Tac. *Ann.* 16.12.
[16] See *Apoc.* 1–3, Suet. *Ner.* 8, *Cl.* 44.3 and Tac. *Ann.* 12.68.3.
[17] Cf. Feeney (2007, 127–31).

written between 49 and 52, when Seneca was Nero's tutor), paints an Augustus tormented both by his inability to grasp time and by an idealized future that remains beyond his reach. This Augustus – in retrospect – epitomizes the powerful man who goes through life with a nagging *cupido temporis* ("desire for time" 4.3) and is only superficially happy, while inwardly "detesting every act of his years" (6.3). The first emperor longed for the future life of ethically coherent *otium* that Seneca himself will define and perform in detail in his *De otio* and *Epistulae ad Lucilium*. Seneca "quotes" a letter to the Senate in which Augustus communicated his desire for dignified leisure and explained that "since that joyful reality is still far distant," he would attempt to capture some of its "pleasure" with "the sweetness of words"(4.3). Unlike Seneca, this passage implies, Augustus was incapable of turning *verba* into *res* through the writing of letters: powerless to seize time, he fell into an endless battle with the "ulcers" of a diseased empire (4.5). Seneca suggests that Augustus' "Golden Age" is a paper-thin construction barely concealing violent angst, so that Neronian "cramming" *in artissimum* might be reconceived not as a moral flaw particular to *now* but as the unconcealment of a long-festering problem.[18] What's more, Seneca's mature philosophical advice here, in the time-pressured and vice-ridden years of Nero's boyhood, was just what Augustus *would have needed* to grasp his dreamed-of future.[19]

Later on in the *De brevitate vitae*, Seneca makes the point that only philosophers like himself have learned to manage time (and *otium*) correctly, with the result that they can "annex every age to their own" and "roam over" a "great stretch of time" (14.1–2). The philosopher "is not confined by the same bounds that imprison others," and no time can destroy or diminish his work (15.4–5). We might read this not so much as a bid to escape a plebeian experience of time as a laying claim to the kind of (supernatural) power over time that not even an emperor can achieve. Seneca's capacity to move freely backward and forward in time is epitomized by the text that accompanies Nero's stepping into power – the *Apocolocyntosis*: here, snippets of Augustan poetry mix with mock-Livian historiography, fragments of Euripidean tragedy, and lines from Homer, while in the underworld Claudius meets, among others, the eloquent Augustus and an archaic, Greek-speaking Hercules. Whereas Claudius cannot understand that he is being made to engage with the past (he mistakes ancient Hercules for a modern philologist), Seneca exerts his mastery of Rome's literary and political

---

[18] See *De brev.* 6.4.
[19] Cf. *Apoc.* 10.4 (Augustus bitterly reminds the council that Claudius killed his two great-granddaughters and one great-grandson).

history, prompting his readers to ask exactly what happens when the past is imported, piecemeal, into the present.

Living Backwards

When it comes to *cupido temporis*, Seneca never stops reminding us that by the time we get to Nero, we've seen it all before. Post-Augustus, writers are highly sensitive to the ways in which both poets and politicians represent and appropriate time, to the extent that time itself (messing with time, waxing lyrical about time) is now a corny, old-fashioned theme. The *locus classicus* for this idea is Seneca *Epistle* 122, a satirical piece on the current immoral vogue for rejecting natural temporal rhythms that has much in common with Persius 3 and Petronius' *Cena Trimalchionis*. It is now commonplace, Seneca remarks in this letter, to see *young* men living "contrary to nature" – banqueting in the dark (on birds fattened in the dark) and sleeping during the day (122.4). These adolescent rebels or ever-puerile grown men don't know *when* to live, let alone *how* to live (*Ep.* 122.3). They purport to exist differently in time, not just by swapping day for night but by doing things out of order – drinking before eating, eating before bathing. The topic of *lucifugae* or "light-dodgers" is a familiar one both in texts written under Nero and in later responses to the Neronian period. The historians report that Nero himself was fond of nighttime jaunts: he was the sun that never set, and his fancy for partying and making mischief into the early hours extended to lighting up the night artificially with the torched bodies of his victims (Tacitus' *Annals* 15.44).

Seneca's letter begins with a reference to the day's end (*detrimentum iam dies sensit*, "the day has already felt its lessening" 122.1), reminding readers that these epistles analyze, enact, and track the passing of each day in the would-be *sapiens*' life, where each day is a life in itself and each dusk a rehearsal for life's end.[20] From the start, the epistles have reiterated a critique of the night owl's bid to "extend life" (122.3) by carrying it over into the night while offering a transformative alternative to vice-ridden night lives in the scene of Seneca's own dedicated candle burning (see *Ep.* 8.1).[21] Here, toward the end of his collection and lifespan, sixty-something Seneca corrects the new generation's misperception of its place in time. Staying up all night does not lengthen life but rather anticipates death; inverting day and night is not the future-claiming novelty the young think it is but was already in vogue under Tiberius (122.10). Under Tiberius, witty men at court were

---

[20] Cf. Ker (2009a, 147–67).
[21] More in Ker (2004).

already mocking poets like Julius Montanus, who "used to insert a liberal dose of sunrises and sunsets into his poems"(122.11), prompting Varus to joke that the notorious nocturne Buta would know when to stay up and when to retire by the dusks and dawns punctuating Montanus' day-long recitations. The point is that Seneca is one of the few who can remember this, while the (Nero-inspired?) youth of today, implicitly, have little historical awareness and do not understand their situatedness in time.[22]

While letter 122 ends with Seneca's advice to Lucilius to stay on the straight and narrow of time's path and not to join those who row *contra aquam* (122.19), what he shows in this crepuscular epistle is something more nuanced. First, he puts dull parrotings of time's natural cycle on the same page as derivative and pathetic night lives, which should have died out a generation ago. Going with time's flow does not entail churning out verse punctuated by rosy-tinted dawns and homeward-bound shepherds (this is akin to being stuck in the past); it is about dedicated, daily (epistolary) praxis and embodiment. Second, Seneca pushes us to grasp the difference between wanting to dwell in past time by holding onto an artificial boyhood (made fashionable – again – under Nero) and immersing oneself in history and in the literary past in order to comment knowledgeably on the present. Letter 122 – like many others in the *Epistulae Morales* – is not only intensely aware of its place in diurnal and imperial time; it also presents itself as an interweaving of (informed references to) different moments from the Roman past. As an ingenious writer working and innovating within a tradition, Seneca understands and promotes his citation-peppered letters as hermeneutic sites in which multiple references – and times – converge and interact. In other words, the *Epistles* resist "being in time under Nero" as much as they instruct Lucilius in how to cope with the historically specific challenges of busy, urban life *now*: the would-be *sapiens* must take back the time stolen from him (*Ep.* 1.1). Seneca's choppy style and patchwork texts – speckled with allusions, quotations, and (in the case of the letters) imagined "future" interjections from Lucilius – are both dazzling performances of a world out of joint and the makings of a master class in historical awareness.[23] "Living backwards" is not the sin, exactly: having no clue this is what you are doing and lacking the philosophical art of self-inspection *is*.[24]

Elsewhere in the *Epistulae Morales*, Seneca comes closer to spelling out and satirizing the symbolic role of Nero himself both in revived attempts to light up the night and in rebellious reactions to the disciplinary force of

---

[22] Cf. *Apoc.* 2–3, with Robinson (2005) and commentary *ad loc.* in Eden (1984).
[23] See O'Gorman (2005) on citation in the *Apocolocyntosis*.
[24] *Ep.* 122.18: *retro vivunt*, "they live backwards."

normative, official time in empire – despite the fact that the letters, famously, never mention Nero. In letter 115, for example, Nero's new Golden Age, inaugurated in the *Apocolocytosis* and in the *De clementia*, is decried as a cultural cancer – not so much a nostalgic return to a simple, timeless, pre-technological era as a literal, voracious celebration of all things shiny and artificial. The "desire for gold," Seneca writes, has "settled deep in us and grows with us" (*Ep.* 115.11); we live in a "gold-plated" era, all too aware of its superficiality. Yet of course this kind of moralizing is also old hat and becomes the mechanism by which Seneca enacts – with casual irony – larger-scale imperial recyclings of Golden Age timelessness. Eons ago, Vergil drew attention to the uneasy proximity of literal to metaphorical gold, while Ovid played it up further, picturing half of Rome as superficially metamorphosed into glitz under Augustus' building program. One of the jokes of letter 115 is that its first nine chapters, culminating in the unacknowledged near-citation of Ovid's *Medicamina* (*scimus enim sub illo auro foeda ligna latitare*, "we know that beneath the gold hides ugly wood," cf. Ovid *Med.* 7–8), see Seneca in an anti-Ovidian pose, criticizing the young for their preening and *cultus* and recommending that Lucilius favor a simple, less-than-polished prose style. In other words he plays the greybeard traditionalist "correcting" (and then repeating) the youthful, long-dead Ovid.

Having reminded us indirectly of the Augustan poets' complex and satirical take on *their* Golden Age, Seneca turns at 115.12 to the popular contemporary use of Augustan poetry to "justify" the obligatory lust for wealth.[25] To illustrate this, he quotes four choice lines from the tale of Phaethon and Phoebus in *Metamorphoses* 2.1–2 and 2.107–8, describing the glorious palace of the Sun god and his extravagant gold chariot. Spelling it out, he adds, "And finally, when they want an epoch to look superior, they call it Golden" (115.13). Seneca seems to be alluding here to Nero's building projects (especially the *domus aurea*), as well as to his chariot racing and glorification of the sun.[26] But again, beneath the surface lurks a more intricate commentary on the distortions of time that are already beginning to define Neronian Rome. First of all, Seneca follows up this example by whizzing back in time to Euripides' lost *Danae*, quoting a translated chunk from the middle of the play where Bellerophon boasts about his love of money: unlike their Neronian counterparts, these theatergoers were disgusted by the character's greed and began to hiss him off stage. Euripides himself interjected and asked them to wait for the ending, when the protagonist would get his come-uppance. The moral of the story – Seneca writes – is that greed is punished

---

[25] On Seneca's reception of Augustan poetry see also Ker in this volume.
[26] Cf. *Apoc.* 4.28–9; Feeney (2007, 134).

in the end. But what this leap through time exposes is that extracting bits of old texts (exactly what Seneca himself does here and elsewhere) can be distorting and misleading without more detailed knowledge: what blind idiots people are if they think Ovid promoted an unthinking love of gold! How typical of grown-ups who behave like impatient, gullible children (115.8) to cut and paste the opening lines of *Metamorphoses* 2 without reading on to find out or remember that this is a story about childish impulsiveness and the tragic consequences of being dazzled by bling![27]

To conclude, then: Nero's better-than-ever Golden Age is not just a tired and morally bankrupt return to a return, Seneca implies. It is a pernicious antiphilosophical program that promotes destructive forgetting of what the literary past has to tell us about the consequences of disrespecting time. Throughout his career, and especially in the *Apocolocyntosis* and the later philosophical texts, Seneca vaunts his superhuman perspective on time, a vantage point set in further relief by his responsibility to the absurdly young, fashion-forward Nero. This paradoxical relationship, in which precocious "son" is always destined to outshine and destroy ingenious "father," infiltrates almost every aspect *both* of Seneca's youth-pleasing creative experimentation (with its hubristic time surfing and time warping) *and* of his philosophical meditations, which are so obsessed with breaking free from time's clutches, with – implicitly – finding a way to survive this particular cage of history. Tacitus understood this impossible game all too well when he wrote the drama of Seneca's final hours. In the account of *Annals* 15.64, he pictures our consummate actor, shapeshifter, and guru refusing to die on time, having already taken charge of his future. Blood flows too slowly in Seneca's senile (and highly trained) body, poison doesn't touch him, and so – after much suspense – he magicks himself away in a bath of steam. But not before producing his will, written years ago at the height of his wealth and power, almost in canny foreknowledge of this very moment.

Further Reading

Useful work on Neronian literary culture and Seneca's place in it includes Morford (1973), Sullivan (1985), Too (1994), Williams (1994), and Rudich (1997). Those interested in knowing more about time in Seneca should read Ker (2004) on nocturnal writers, Ker (2009c, 147–76) and Armisen-Marchetti (1995) on the *Epistles*, Robinson (2005) on the *Apocolocyntosis*, Schiesaro (2003, 177–220) on Senecan tragedy, and in Italian, Gagliardi

---

[27] Also see Zissos and Gildenhard (1999) on Ovid's enactment of Phaethon's messing up of natural time in *Met.* 2.

(1998) and Viparelli (2000) on time in Senecan philosophy. Find discussion of specular strategies in Seneca in Armisen-Marchetti (2006), Bartsch (2006), and Ker (2009b). Eden's (1984) commentary on the *Apocolocyntosis* and Braund's (2009) commentary on the *De clementia* are invaluable for anyone studying these texts in detail.

10

GARETH WILLIAMS

Style and Form in Seneca's Writing

You rightly urge that we increase the frequency of this exchange of letters between us. The greatest benefit is derived from conversation (*sermo*), because it creeps gradually into the soul. Lectures (*disputationes*) that are prepared in advance and are freely imparted before a throng have more noise but less intimacy. Philosophy is good counsel; no one gives counsel at the top of his lungs. Sometimes we must employ even these harangues, so to speak, when a doubter needs to be given a push ....; but when the task is to make a man learn, not to want to learn, we must resort to the more subdued tones of conversation. (*Ep.* 38.1)

A recurrent emphasis in Seneca's *Moral Epistles* is that the correspondence he shares with his addressee, Lucilius, is a conversation of sorts, an ongoing dialogue in which the cue for the next letter is so often supplied by the question or the provocation, the observation or the admission, that is allegedly contained in the (for us) invisible, Lucilian half of their exchanges. For present purposes, the problem of the relation of the *Epistles* to autobiographical fact[1] matters less than the effect that Seneca achieves through, or despite, the monologic form of his epistolary corpus: by creating the illusion of a dialogic relationship in-development between teacher and pupil or, perhaps more accurately, between fellow travelers on the same therapeutic path of self-improvement, Seneca fully *activates* his philosophical undertaking in the *Epistles*. The seemingly uncontrived nature of his correspondence – including the marked use of familiar, quotidian diction[2] and imagery, the unexpected twists and turns of setting and motivation from one letter to the next, and the absence of any clearly drawn master narrative to coordinate the 124 extant letters – suggestively evokes at a textual level the informality of spoken *sermo*.[3]

---

[1] Overview: Wilson (1987, 103 and 119 n. 3 = 2008, 61 and n. 3).

[2] Setaioli (1980, 1981).

[3] The letter as conversation: 67.2, 75.1.

By affecting an oral dimension in this way, the *Epistles* project, as Marcus Wilson well puts it, "a sense of the mind thinking rather than having thought,"[4] as if the correspondence unfolds in "real" time; and the oral aspect implicates Lucilius (and us) as active players in the therapeutic drama, as if licensed and encouraged to rise to the Senecan provocation. In this energized spirit, the Senecan persona frequently disparages the drier subtleties of Stoic dialectical argumentation on the one hand (e.g., *Ep.* 45.8–13, 48.4–12, 71.6, etc.), the rhetorical indulgence of words for words' sake on the other (e.g., *Ep.* 40.13, 75.7, 100.2, etc.): through such gestures Seneca continually reaffirms the need for philosophy to dig deep, to engage with substance (*res*) rather than just words (*uerba*), to form rather than merely inform.[5] The urgency of this Senecan calling is itself reflected in the conciseness and the quick tempo not just of the *Epistles* but of his prose style more generally. Whereas those who indulge in dialectical games (cf. *lusoria, Ep.* 48.8, 9) or rhetorical nicety rather than philosophical substance are akin to procrastinators who "do not live but are always postponing life" (*non ....uiuunt sed uicturi sunt, Ep.* 45.13), Seneca's lively mode of presentation catches the moment, as if its briskness counters the time pressure imposed by an insistent therapeutic need.

Basic to this vision of the *Moral Epistles* and of Seneca's prose writings as surveyed in this chapter is the proposition – for many scholars, the established fact – that style and form are inseparable from Senecan philosophical meaning; in a sense, they constitute that meaning. In the *Epistles*, his quasi-interactive engagement in practices of the self amounts to a textual version of lived experience; his therapeutic mode dynamically renders or recreates philosophy as "a way of life"[6] in this Senecan merging of medium and message. In and beyond the *Epistles*, however, verbal effect is philosophically meaningful for another reason. "The Stoic idea of learning," remarks Martha Nussbaum, "is an idea of increasing vigilance and wakefulness, as the mind, increasingly rapid and alive, learns to repossess its own experiences from the fog of habit, convention, and forgetfulness."[7] Seneca fully shares this preoccupation with wakefulness, an emphasis revealed not just through the substance of his written philosophy but also through its style of delivery: the dizzying array of stylistic tricks and techniques that give his writing such distinctive literary personality demands ceaseless vigilance in his audience.[8] By

---

[4] Wilson (1987, 108 = 2008, 69).
[5] Hadot (1995, 64).
[6] Hadot (1995).
[7] Nussbaum (1994, 340).
[8] Basic bibliography on those techniques: Merchant (1905); Summers (1910, xlii–xcv); Smiley (1919); Bourgery (1922) with Castiglioni (1924, 112–23); Norden (1958,

exercising our wakefulness in this way, the very experience of engaging with the Senecan text is one application or activation of the self-consciousness to which he consistently makes appeal in his works.

Our focus will turn in due course to the anatomy of Seneca's writing and to the strategies of style and argument by which he ceaselessly trains this vigilance. But certain sociocultural factors precondition his *modus scribendi*. These factors are briefly surveyed in the first sections that follow, providing necessary context for the portrait of Senecan practice that closes this essay.

The Influence of Declamation

Different is the purpose of speech-makers (*declamantibus*) who court the applause of their circle of listeners, and different is the goal of those who hold the ears of youths and idlers with multi-faceted and fluent argumentation. Philosophy teaches us to act, not to speak .... (*Ep.* 20.2)

Despite his rejection here of the rhetoric of pure display, Seneca's style, poetic as well as prosaic, is fully the child of an age in which oratory was no longer the living force in Roman political life that it had been in the Republic and in which the declamation of *controuersiae* (imaginary speeches for the defense or prosecution) or *suasoriae* (imaginary speeches of advice to mythical or historical figures who must make key decisions) had come to the fore in the schools as an increasingly elaborate form of exhibitionism in itself rather than a more grounded preparation for civic life.[9] Seneca's affective prose style is highly declamatory in its marshaling of sound effect to give resonance to his written word, in the shades of *controuersia*- and *suasoria*-like argumentation that he sometimes deploys[10] and in his general striving for impact at every turn. In the tragedies, the same tendencies are ubiquitous and unremitting, and it is largely due to them that the plays have too often drawn modern critical hostility for being excessively "rhetorical."[11]

A measure of Seneca's ancient celebrity as a "modern" stylist is Quintilian's extended treatment of his (de)merits at the end of his review, in the tenth

---

1.306–13); Leeman (1963, 1.264–83); Currie (1966); Kennedy (1972, 465–81); Wright (1974); Motto and Clark (1975); Setaioli (1980, 1981, 1985), all three of them now combined in 2000, 9–217); Traina (1987); von Albrecht (2000, 2004); Wilson (2001, and 1987 = 2008); and Richardson-Hay (2006: 75–126).

[9] Further, Bonner (1949, 71–83) with Fairweather (1981, 104–48). This is not to deny that "oratorical skill remained an avenue to wealth, influence, and prestige" (Mayer 2001, 15).

[10] See esp. Kennedy (1972, 468–9).

[11] On this point, Tarrant (1985, 22).

book of his treatise on oratory, of those Latin authors across the genres whom he commends to the aspiring orator:

> His works contain many excellent turns of thought (*sententiae*), and much that is worth reading for edification. But the very many corruptions of his style are exceedingly dangerous, because of the attractiveness of the vices with which it abounds. You could wish that he had spoken with his own talents but with another's judgment. For if he had rejected some things, if he had not been so passionately fond of the perverse,[12] if he had not had so much affection for all that was his own, and if he had not broken up the weightiness of his ideas through the utmost epigrammatic brevity, he would have won the approval of the learned rather than the enthusiasm of mere boys. (*Inst.* 10.1.129–30)[13]

Already, decades earlier, the emperor Gaius (Caligula) was allegedly "so contemptuous of a writing style that was too smooth and polished that he said that Seneca, then at the height of his influence, composed 'pure exercises' and that 'it was sand without lime'" (Suet *Cal.* 53.2) – *harenam* .... *sine calce* apparently in the sense that Seneca's prose lacks cohesion and sequence because he prioritizes the individual point and the brilliant moment. In turn, in his treatise of (probably) 94–5 CE, Seneca represents for Quintilian the corruption of all that Cicero stands for as "the master of Latin eloquence" (*Latinae eloquentiae princeps*, 6.3.1). While for certain modern readers Quintilian apparently treats Seneca with a judicious evenhandedness,[14] and while the two can even be seen to share certain common ground in their views on stylistic corruption, others find a critical harshness born of "a certain degree of prejudice,"[15] and even (W. H. Alexander) of malice[16] – a malevolence intensified yet further in what Alexander trenchantly characterizes as "the stupidities of Gellius and the positive indecencies of Fronto in their references to Seneca in the next generation."[17] Other factors may possibly influence Quintilian's judgment of Seneca, among them an antipathy to philosophers in general, Stoics in particular;[18] his Flavian predisposition to judge the Neronian régime harshly "for purposes of contrast"[19] arguably colors his view of Seneca, once that

---

[12] Reading G. C. Sarpe's *praua*: see Peterson (1891, 208).

[13] On this celebrated passage, Laureys (1991), Dominik (1997, 50–9), and now Taoka (2011).

[14] So, e.g., Laureys (1991, esp. 122–5).

[15] Peterson (1891, xxiv).

[16] Alexander (1935) – a remarkable essay.

[17] Alexander 1935, 244: Gell. *N.A.* 12.2, Fronto p. 153.8–154.2 van den Hout, with Henderson (1955).

[18] See Peterson (1891, xxv); Alexander (1935, 249–50); Austin (1948, xiv–xix, xiv: antipathy for philosophers, not philosophy *per se*); Dominik (1997, 53).

[19] Alexander (1935, 255).

power behind Nero's throne; and psychological interpretation has also been hazarded.[20] Beyond the seeming partisanship of Quintilian's critique, however, and beyond the role that Seneca plays as the symbolic antithesis of Ciceronian Classicism, the prominent length and placement of that critique merely underscore Seneca's standing in Quintilian's eyes as "the single most important exponent and chief source of the postclassical style"; "[t]hat a generation after the death of Seneca Quintilian feels compelled to deal at length with Seneca bears witness to the endurance of Seneca's influence."[21] At 10.2.1, moreover, Quintilian presents all the authors he has reviewed in 10.1 as "worth reading" (*lectione dignis auctoribus*): for all his criticisms, Quintilian hardly moves to exclude Seneca from his approved list – unless we strain to conclude that, by pitching his critique in the past tense, Quintilian in effect relegates his entire polemic against Seneca to the past, as if "[t]he confrontation is over," he has "succeeded in containing Seneca's influence," and it is therefore "now possible for him to evaluate Seneca more objectively and more honestly."[22]

Diatribe

While the declamatory accent privileges the individual moment over a steadier consistency, Seneca's looseness of form and argument is also characteristic of the mode of popular philosophical essay that is often termed "diatribe" in modern scholarship. The Hellenistic origins of this mode are conventionally associated with Bion of Borysthenes (*c.* 335 – *c.* 245 BCE); it broadly connotes a philosophical delivery inflected with elements of street harangue, colloquialism, colorful imagery, rhetorical questions and exclamation, interlocutory intervention and sharp rejoinder, rapid-fire imperatives, and sharp denunciations of vice.[23] Many of these features enliven Seneca's combative style, not least in his *Dialogi* – although suggestion that the term *dialogus* directly renders the Greek literary term or form of *diatribe* or *dialexis* has rightly won little favor.[24] Indeed, while many of Seneca's diatribic features existed in the Hellenistic popular philosophical tradition, and while they find rich parallels in that so called "prime example"[25] of the

[20] See for review Laureys (1991, 103) with Austin (1948, xxiii n. 1): "I sometimes wonder if Quintilian's distaste for Seneca was based on a kind of jealousy which he could not help."

[21] Dominik (1997, 53, 52).

[22] Laureys (1991, 123).

[23] Background : OCD³ 463–4 s.v. *diatribe*. For diatribic elements in Seneca, Weber (1895) and Oltramare (1926, esp. 254–95), and cf. Coleman (1974, 288–9).

[24] See Griffin (1976, 413–14).

[25] Long (2002, 49), albeit describing rather than endorsing a *status opinionis*.

genre of diatribe, Epictetus' *Discourses* (i.e., his oral teachings as recorded by his student Arrian), those features are hardly exclusive to the Hellenistic tradition. Seneca no more straightforwardly conforms to a simple generic prescription of "diatribe" than does Epictetus;[26] and the notion that "in some registers of ancient Greek the word διατριβή could denote a type of philosophical discourse or writing with definable characteristics" has itself been vehemently contested.[27] In this respect, the often-used term "Cynic-Stoic diatribe" (a modern invention) can too easily mislead when applied to Senecan discourse, giving too exact a designation to a wide and diverse stream of literary-philosophical influence.

The Stoics on Rhetorical/Literary Style

> You ask why, at certain periods, a degenerate style of speech comes to the fore, and how it is that abilities tend to deteriorate into certain vices .... This is what you usually hear commonly said, and what the Greeks have turned into a proverb: "As men live, so they speak" (*talis hominibus fuit oratio qualis uita*). Just as an individual's conduct resembles his speech, so a style of speaking sometimes reproduces the general character of the times. (*Ep.* 114.1–2)

In Letter 114, Seneca famously pursues the correlation posited here between speech and character by rounding on Maecenas in particular: "How Maecenas lived is too well known to need telling here, how he walked, how effeminate he was, how he wanted to display himself, and how reluctant he was for his vices to lie hidden. And so? Wasn't his speech as loose as he was in dress?" (114.4). The idea recurs in *Ep.* 115 ("Whenever you observe a style that is too anxious and polished, know that the mind, too, is no less absorbed in pettiness," 115.2) and frequently elsewhere in the collection[28] as a basic Senecan ethical principle in line with the Stoic ideal of living in harmony with nature. Since the Stoics held that "eloquence was a virtue and a form of wisdom" (cf. Cic. *On the orator* 3.65), and since only the *sapiens* commands virtue, he alone is the true *orator*;[29] the truest perfection of the art lies not in the acquisition and honing of technical skill but in the disposition of mind that lives in accordance with nature and cosmic reason. In consequence, embellishment and elaboration of the orator's task, all self-assertion and individual valorization, are irrelevant to the essence of his

---

[26] On Epictetus in this respect, Long (2002, 48–9).
[27] Jocelyn (1982, 3); cf. for lively debate Jocelyn (1983) and Gottschalk (1982, 1983), with Griffin (1976, 508–9 in 1992 postscript).
[28] Cf. 20.2, 40.2, 59.5, 75.4, 100.8.
[29] *SVF* 3.654–5 p. 164.17–26; Setaioli (1985, 831–2 = 2000: 181–2).

craft: adaptation to cosmic rationality overrides expression of self, and to speak well is to speak the plain truth.[30] Since the orator's duty is to teach, not to entertain, stylistic ornamentation that either clouds his hearers' judgment or aims to please is rejected, and the directness of natural simplicity is paramount; hence the chief virtues of the Stoic style (ἀρεταὶ λόγου) were defined as "pure Greek, lucidity, conciseness, appropriateness, distinction."[31]

Against this background, the compatibility drawn in *Ep.* 114 between Maecenas' oratorical/literary style and his character amounts to an unnatural reversal of the ideal Stoic correlation. Elsewhere, Seneca offers no formal manifesto of Stoic stylistic principles, and his purely theoretical interest appears limited;[32] yet the signs of his basic adherence to those principles are many. So, at *Ep.* 40.4, "speech which applies itself to the truth should be unaffected and plain," whereas "the popular style" that Seneca associates in this letter with the (otherwise unknown) philosopher Serapio "has nothing to do with the truth: its aim is to move the crowd and to captivate injudicious ears with its forcefulness; it doesn't submit to close scrutiny but is carried away [sc. by its own torrent]." Like Maecenas, Serapio apparently lacks the philosopher's "proper" compatibility of speech and character ("the philosopher's speech, just like his life, should be composed," 40.2). On reading Lucilius' new book, on the other hand, Seneca finds it full of wit (*ingenium*) and spirit (*animus*), with no "forced movement but an even flow, a style that was manly and chaste" while yet retaining the occasional mark of "that sweetness of yours, and, at the appropriate moment, that mildness" (46.2) – qualities signaling the "overall coherence" and "integrity of effect" of Lucilius' style,[33] but also, perhaps, the balance of the man himself. Just as the ideal Stoic stylist speaks the truth, so Lucilius will naturally hear the truth from Seneca (cf. *uerum audies*, 46.3) after, Seneca writes, he has given Lucilius' book a second perusal. In turn, Lucilius becomes the critic in *Ep.* 100: he has reportedly criticized the style of Papirius Fabianus (*c.* 35 BCE – *ante* 35 CE), Seneca's admired teacher, on the grounds that "his words are poured forth rather than driven home" (*effundi uerba, non figi*, 100.1). But any implication that Fabianus resembles the gushing Serapio in this way is dispelled by Seneca's defense of his teacher: he writes for the mind, not the

[30] Further, Smiley (1919, 50–1); Setaioli (1985, 789–90 = 2000, 126–7); Colish (1990, 58–9).
[31] So Diogenes of Babylon according to Diogenes Laertius in his life of Zeno, 7.26: Ἑλληνισμός, σαφήνεια, συντομία, πρέπον, κατασκευή. Further on these terms, Smiley (1919).
[32] Cf. Leeman (1963, 1.282): "At most, Seneca seems to have felt and stressed that he is not at variance with the Stoic principles."
[33] Graver (1998: 617–18).

ear (*animis .... non auribus*), shaping character, not mere words (*mores ....,
non uerba*, 100.2); avoiding timidity of expression ("An anxious manner of
speech does not befit the philosopher," 100.4), Fabianus was "not careless
in style, but assured" (*securus*, 100.5), avoiding "empty subtleties of argument" (*angustias inanis*, 100.5) and artificial contrivance ("his words are
well chosen and not strained for; they are not inserted unnaturally – *contra
naturam suam posita* – and inverted, according to current fashion"). Again,
the overall balance of Fabianus' style suggestively betokens the man: "But
look at the whole body of the work, how elegant it is: it is becoming (*honestum*)" (100.8).[34]

In *Ep.* 75, Lucilius has allegedly complained that Seneca's missives are
"rather carelessly written" (*minus .... accuratas a me epistulas*, 75.1) – a
charge that Seneca rebuts by asserting the naturalness of an epistolary mode
that is meant to be conversational in its ease, as if *sermo inlaboratus et faci-
lis* (cf. 75.1). Once more, natural sincerity is all ("Let us say what we feel,
feel what we say; let speech harmonize with life," 75.4); Seneca aims not to
please but to help (*non delectent uerba nostra sed prosint*, 75.5), and for his
eloquence to "display facts (*res*) rather than itself" (75.5). Certain incon-
sistencies have been alleged in Seneca's statements on style in and across
the *Epistles* (e.g., inconsistency between his disapproval of Serapio's rapid
delivery in *Ep.* 40 and his defense of the sweeping effectiveness of Fabianus'
style in *Ep.* 100), and also between Senecan theory and practice (e.g., inconsistency between his censure of excessive brevity and yet his own cultivation
of point and epigram). But such charges are not hard to parry;[35] and more
important in any case is the reflexive significance of Seneca's pronouncements on style as sampled (e.g.) in the infelicities that he imputes to Serapio
on the one hand, in the balanced composure of Lucilius and Fabianus on
the other. His emphasis on sincerity of expression, his prioritizing of *res*, not
uerba, Lucilius' alleged criticisms of his style, Seneca's balanced assessment
of the stylistic qualities of others: through these strategies, Seneca in effect
delivers a pledge of his *own* sincerity of voice and his *own* stylistic self-discipline in the *Epistles* (and beyond); since such *Epistles* as 40, 46, 75, 100, and
114 establish criteria by which we inevitably judge Seneca's *own* practice as
well, his reflections on style are ultimately inseparable from self-reflection
and self-policing. In this respect, stylistic (self-)commentary functions as yet
another aspect of the self-scrutiny that the *Epistles* promote above all else.

In contrast to "the vigor and sting necessary for oratory in public life,"
writes Cicero in the *Orator*, philosophy is an altogether more reserved affair,

---

34 Cf. of moral character *OLD honestus* 3a.
35 See already Merchant (1905, 57–9).

its style "gentle and contemplative.... There is no anger in it, no hatred, no ferocity, no appeal to compassion, no shrewdness .... And so it is called conversation (*sermo*) rather than oratory (*oratio*)" (62, 64). Seneca's lively shifts of pace, tenor, angle, and approach hardly characterize his philosophical style quite as the meek and restrained creature that Cicero describes. Already in *Ep.* 38, however, we have observed a form of *sermo* that at least approximates to the Ciceronian version: in contrast to the loud, jolting impact of lecture-hall *disputatio*, Senecan *sermo* is calmer and more private in its appeal and character, its subdued tones (*submissiora uerba*) better equipped to linger in the memory (38.1). This contrast between *disputatio* and *sermo* is further informed by the difference that Cicero draws between *contentio* and *sermo* in his *On duties*:

> Speech, too, has great power, and in two areas: one is in oratory (*contentionis*), the other in conversation (*sermonis*). Oratory (*contentio*) should be employed for speeches in legal proceedings, ... while conversation (*sermo*) should obtain in social groups, in philosophical discussions (*disputationibus*) and in gatherings of friends. (1.132)

Cicero's reliance in his *On duties* on the Middle Stoic Panaetius' celebrated *On duty* (Περὶ τοῦ καθήκοντος) has important implications for our discussion of Seneca. Even though *sermo* in Cicero is naturally more restrained than oratorical *contentio*, "it nevertheless sometimes happens that reprimands are necessary. In that case we perhaps need to use both a more rhetorical tone of voice (*uocis contentione maiore*) and sharper, more serious language ...." (1.136). Seneca, too, allows for a certain rhetorical/stylistic heightening according to circumstance: "Certainly, I don't want our conversation on matters of such importance to be barren and dry; for philosophy doesn't renounce all literary ability (*ingenio*). But not much attention is to be expended on mere words" (*Ep.* 75.3). For Aldo Setaioli, in his fundamental study of Senecan style, this double aspect of Senecan *sermo* – it is normally restrained and low key, but capable of rising when necessary to the more forceful capabilities of oratorical *contentio* – finds a suggestive precedent and putative model in Panaetius.[36] And beyond this flexible valence within Senecan *sermo* itself, the contrast between *disputatio* and *sermo* in *Ep.* 38.1 may offer its own telling differentiation of strains within Senecan discourse, the one impassioned, outward reaching and psychagogic in orientation, the other more measured, intimate and inward looking. This contrast of types is basic to the distinction that Alfonso Traina has so influentially drawn between what he presents as the two faces of Seneca's "stile drammatico,"

---

[36] Setaioli (1985, esp. 792–7, "Panezio e la teoria del *sermo*" = 2000, 130–6.

that of interiority on the one hand (cf. *sermo* in 38.1), of preaching on the other (cf. *disputatio* in 38.1).[37] Moreover, Setaioli connects the Senecan correlation between *oratio* and *uita* to Panaetius' practical emphasis on conformity to one's own nature (as opposed to traditional Stoic conformity to universal nature) and therefore on the key role of propriety (τὸ πρέπον, *decorum*) in the Senecan as well as the Panaetian aesthetic orders.[38] Other sources of Stoic influence are discernible, not least among them Posidonius, Panaetius' pupil;[39] but the cited factors indicate that Seneca's views on style were profoundly influenced by Panaetius in particular.

The Literary Context

Seneca's nurturing of a distinctive literary style is further conditioned by his role in the emergence of a Latin philosophical literature at Rome. Already in the first century BCE, Lucretius' *On the nature of things* and Cicero's prose treatises had popularized Greek philosophy before a Latin audience. Seneca furthers this popularization, but with a difference: he "stands out," asserts Brad Inwood, "for his striking choice to do what I would call primary philosophy (rather than exegetical or missionary work) in Latin."[40] Whereas Cicero renders Greek philosophical ideas in Latin, Inwood's Seneca "prefers to work his ideas out in Latin, in Latin terms, because that is the language he thinks in. Seneca, much more than Cicero, is thinking creatively and philosophically in Latin."[41] On this approach, Seneca's distinctive style expresses a pioneering habit of Latin thought, and he experiments widely in theme and genre by embarking (in his extant works alone) on the essay form of the *Dialogues*, on the extended treatise in his seven books *On benefits*, on a highly idiosyncratic blend of meteorological investigation and moralizing effusion in his eight-book *Natural Questions*, and on "a new branch of epistolography"[42] in the *Moral Epistles*. In the latter case Seneca responds partly to the Greek tradition of the philosophical letter but also to the weighty precedent of Cicero's letters. But, Seneca asserts in *Ep.* 118.1–2, in contrast to the news with which Cicero fills his correspondence, such as which candidate is in difficulties and who is contending on borrowed funds and who on his own resources, "it's better to deal with one's own troubles than with another's, to examine oneself, to see for how many things one is

---

[37] Traina (1987, esp. 9–41).
[38] Setaioli (1985, 798, 836–8 = 2000, 137; 187–91).
[39] Setaioli (1985, 800–1 = 2000, 139–41).
[40] Inwood (1995, 68 = 2005, 13).
[41] Inwood (1995, 74 = 2005, 20).
[42] Wilson (2001, 187); further, Inwood (2007a).

a candidate, and to vote for none of them." As Catharine Edwards nicely observes, "Roman public life, the primary concern of Cicero's letters, the context in which and from which the Ciceronian persona takes its meaning," is here "transcended, transformed into a vocabulary of image and metaphor through which the would-be philosopher's inner life can be articulated."[43]

This Senecan turning is symptomatic of the larger development of an introspective consciousness in the first century CE, and it is directly relatable to Greek elaboration of the same Stoic self-engagement in Epictetus' *Discourses* and Marcus Aurelius' *Meditations* in the first and second centuries.[44] Unprecedented in Latin literature, however, are the stylistic methodologies and program by which Seneca develops this introspective emphasis across his prose corpus. He creates a Latin style of the self, as it were; or, better, he forges what Traina terms "*il linguaggio latino dell' interiorità*," that introverted cousin of Seneca's extrovert "*linguaggio della predicazione*."[45]

Interiority and Senecan Style

Traina's "language of interiority" amounts to the realization in words of a particular style of thought. Fundamental to this system, he argues, are two recurrent metaphors, neither of them original to Seneca but both finessed by him in idiosyncratic fashion: interiority as possession and interiority as refuge.[46] The self-sufficient *sapiens* is free of all reliance on external goods, which too easily take possession of their possessor: *habere* [sc. *beneficia fortunae*] *nos putamus, haeremus* (*Ep.* 8.3: "We think we have fortune's favors in our grasp, but *we* cling to *them*").[47] For the *sapiens*, self-possession is all, and all is within him: "What can a man need from outside when he has gathered all that is his own in himself?" (*Dialogues* 7.16.3: *quid extrinsecus opus est ei qui omnia sua in se collegit?*). This rejection of externals is forcefully imprinted through Seneca's repeated use of the reflexive: our focus is turned to the self (*se*), which is objectified as if a textually real being in its own right – a self that is consciously owned (*se habere, On benefits* 5.7.5, *Ep.* 42.10), addressed (*se adloqui, Ep.* 26.4, 54.6), interrogated (*se interrogare, On benefits* 5.17.3, *Ep.* 13.6, 76.27), observed, and inspected (cf. *Ep.* 16.2: *excute te et uarie scrutare et obserua*).[48] As we loosen our grip

---

[43] Edwards (1997, 24 ± 2008, 86).
[44] Further, Edwards (1997, 24–6 = 2008, 86–8).
[45] Traina (1987, 11, 25).
[46] Traina (1987, 11). Further on this interiority Thévenaz (1944), Lotito (2001), Fasce (2002), and Traina (2006).
[47] Cf. for the thought *De vita beata* 22.5, 26.1, *Ep.* 98.2.
[48] Further, Traina (1987, 14–20, 54–60); Mazzoli (2006, esp. 457–9).

on externals, the reflexive adjective becomes identified not with "one's own (material) possessions" but with the *se* itself (cf. *nec quicquam suum nisi se putet*, *Dialogues* 2.6.3, of the sage who "regards nothing as his own except himself") – a conflation of identities completed in Seneca's favored formulation of *suus/meus/tuus esse* for "being one's own master."[49] His objectification of the self is made still more concrete by his appeal to everyday image, metaphor, and comparison,[50] such as when he casts "the reclaiming of the self" in the language of legal terminology (e.g., *non sumus sub rege: sibi quisque se uindicat*, *Ep.* 33.4, "We Stoics are subject to no despot: each of us lays claim to his own freedom");[51] when he likens philosophical therapy to medical intervention on the physical body;[52] or when he casts the truest liberation of the self in terms of emancipation from slavery: "He is free who has escaped slavery to himself (*seruitutem suam*) .... The most burdensome kind of slavery is to be a slave to the self (*sibi seruire*)" (*Natural Questions* 3 pref. 16–17).[53]

Paradox sharpens the verbal effect as the philosophical progressive grows away from externals and into himself.[54] In *On benefits* 7, *possessio* has two different applications:

> When, therefore, we look upon the mind of the *sapiens*, master as it is of all things and spread throughout the universe, we say that everything is his, although according to the common law it may happen that he'll be assessed as possessing no property at all. It makes a great difference whether we estimate his holdings (*possessio eius*) by the greatness of his mind or by the public register (7.8.1).

The lexical keys distinguished here – conventional *possessio* as opposed to the "higher" *possessio* of the *sapiens* – are juxtaposed much more concisely in (e.g.) *De providentia*, where, in god's imaginary words to privileged humankind, *non egere felicitate felicitas uestra est* (1.6.5: "Not to need happiness is your happiness"). Through epigrammatic formulations of this sort,[55] which well exemplify the brand of *sententia* that even Quintilian could admire in Seneca (*Inst.* 10.1.129), he amply indulges the wider Stoic taste for paradoxical point but with the added effect of contrasting very different conceptual orders, everyday and cosmically enlightened, in the two

---

[49] Traina (1987, 12); Lotito (2001, 155).
[50] See esp. Armisen-Marchetti (1989) with Steyns (1907) and (conveniently) Richardson-Hay (2006, 94–101).
[51] Cf. *Letters* 1.1 with Richardson-Hay (2006, 130–1); 33.4, 113.23, *De brev. Vit.* 2.4.
[52] So *Consolatio ad Helv.* 2.2; cf. 1.3.2 with Lanzarone (2008, 209).
[53] Cf. *Ep.* 8.7 with Richardson-Hay (2006, 286–7); 80.4–5, 85.28.
[54] Now Stewart (1997, esp. 12–15).
[55] Cf. *Ep.* 90.34, 98.1, 124.24 with Lanzarone (2008, 395) on *De prov.* 6.5.

parts of the verbal dyad. Beyond his cultivation of the paradoxical phrase, however, paradox is not so much a feature of Senecan style as a *precondition* of it, as if the style reflects a world outlook. After all, paradox underlies Traina's second key metaphor of interiority, that of refuge:

> In any case, the mind is to be recalled from all external objects into itself (*animus ab omnibus externis in se reuocandus est*). It must trust in itself, rejoice in itself, admire what is its own; it must withdraw as much as possible from the affairs of others and devote itself to itself (*recedat quantum potest ab alienis et se sibi adplicet, De tranq.* 9.14.2).

Here and elsewhere, withdrawal (*in se colligi, conuerti, reuerti, recondi, recurrere, secedere, recedere*)[56] is a forward step, a retreat by which we advance toward self-fulfillment and authenticity (cf. *Ep.* 124.24: "Only consider yourself happy when your every joy is born to you from yourself") – a paradoxical maneuver that complements the tendency already implicit in Traina's first possession metaphor: we think we possess externals, but they too easily possess us.

The Dramatic Style in Senecan Poetry and Prose

Seneca "took on almost every type of literature," writes Quintilian (*Inst.* 10.1.129); "for speeches of his, poems, letters and dialogues (*et orationes .... et poemata et epistulae et dialogi*) are all in circulation." This diversity of genres is accompanied by what James Ker well characterizes as "a continual embedding of one genre in another: a *consolatio* in book 6 of *Natural Questions*, a *fabula praetexta* hinted at in *De prouidentia*, a satirical mode employed in consolatory passages, a hymn uttered by Hippolytus at *Phaedra* 54–80."[57] Along with polygeneric change and admixture across his *oeuvre*, stylistic and tonal registers are themselves highly changeful from one work to another and often within the same work. In the *Natural Questions*, for example, outbursts of moral indignation (e.g., 3.17–18, 4b.13, 5.15, 18) disrupt the steady flow of his meteorological investigations, but there are other diversions: in Book 4a, for example, he embarks on a picturesque description, in some ways Herodotean in feel, of the Nile and its fauna, while at the end of Book 3, he unleashes the full dramatic force, in wave after narrative wave, of the vast cataclysm that ends one (Stoic) world-cycle before renewal begins afresh. Seneca may consistently apply favored stylistic features and turns (e.g., conciseness, epigram, *sermocinatio*, antithesis, etc.) across the

---

[56] See Traina (1987, 19–22, 63–4).
[57] Ker (2006, 31).

Natural Questions, but the work as a whole is engagingly *in*consistent in its stylistic modulations. Such internal shifts of modulation are hardly limited to the *Natural questions*; from an external standpoint, however, Seneca's shifts of modulation from one work to another arguably exploit generic and/or stylistic juxtaposition to highly provocative effect. The tragedies are an obvious case in point: in the violence of the passions they unleash and in the physical horrors they detail, they test the efficacy of Senecan (Stoic) reason and restraint as promulgated in the prose works; but the flamboyance of their often graphic, sensationalist style is also partly defined by contrast with the more measured stylistic demeanor that predominates in his prose. Then consider his *Apocolocyntosis*, on the "pumpkinification" of Claudius, in which Seneca's lampooning of the recently departed emperor fully bears the stylistic stamp of the Menippean tradition, including the use of colloquialism, vulgarism, dialogue format, and the insertion of verse-interludes (in a range of meters) within the prose format.[58] Beyond his scathing portrayal of Claudius, part of the humorous effect perhaps lies precisely in the shock of generic/stylistic adjustment to such a work after we have become acclimatized to the Seneca of the consolations to Marcia, to Helvia and to Polybius, for example, or the Seneca of *On anger*.

The verse interludes of the *Apocolocyntosis* constitute only one of several methods by which the poetic is incorporated in Senecan prose. Seneca frequently uses direct poetic quotation[59] to express or illustrate a given precept (e.g., *De prov.* 5.10–11, *De ira* 2.9.2, *De vita beata* 8.3, *Ep.* 12.9, 41.2, etc.); for "the same words are heard more carelessly and have less impact when they are delivered in prose; but when meter is added and when a noble idea is subjected to a fixed rhythm, that same thought is hurled forth with a more vigorous throw, as it were" (*Ep.* 108.10). He also deploys poetic diction, but here we tread carefully. The statistical and methodological challenges of deciding what precisely constitutes a true poeticism in the strong sense have only recently begun to be adequately addressed in modern scholarship;[60] in any case, it goes far beyond the scope of this chapter to address in detail the possible extent or nature of lexical and stylistic overlap between Senecan poetry and prose. But in one vital respect, the two forms are continuities of each other: whether through poetic coloration or any other of the stylistic strategies that we have surveyed in this chapter, Senecan prose amounts to an idiosyncratic *performance* of philosophy – one application of that "*stilo drammatico*" which goes

---

[58] Menippean features: Eden (1984, 13–14).
[59] See esp. Mazzoli (1970 with 1991).
[60] Now Hine (2005).

to different extremes in his tragedies, but there channels essentially the same powers of imagination and of verbal improvisation. Dramatization is all,[61] stylistic variation always at the service of that ordaining principle.

Further Reading

Continental scholarship has tended to make the most significant advances in the study of Senecan style. For the contrast between and the complementarity of Seneca's language of interiority on the one hand, the language of "preaching" on the other, Traina (1987) remains fundamental. The "everyday" dimension in Seneca's prose language is analyzed in detail by Setaioli (1980, 1981), but his more general account of "*Seneca e lo stile*" (Setaioli 1981) continues to be important; all three of these writings are now conveniently reassembled in Setaioli (2000). The importance of image and metaphor to Senecan discourse is minutely observed by Armisen-Marchetti (1989). Much of value is still to be gained from the detailed compilations of stylistic mannerism offered by Summers (1910) and Bourgery (1922). Hine (2005) provides many insights into poetic influence on Senecan prose diction, while Mazzoli (1970) remains fundamental on Seneca's frequent quotation of the poets in his prose. On the inseparability of literary form and meaning in Seneca's prose writings, Wilson (1987, 2001) is now usefully supplemented by Inwood (2007a).

---

[61] Cf. already Hijmans (1966).

II

MIREILLE ARMISEN-MARCHETTI

Seneca's Images and Metaphors

A quick glance at a single page of Seneca's writing already demonstrates the number of literary images it contains: metaphors, above all, but also similes, allegories, and even (more subtly) metonymies. The most remarkable among these images, the ones that produce the most vivid effect of distance from the literal, are definitely the metaphors and the similes.[1] In the limited space of this chapter, therefore, these figures in particular will occupy our attention, with the addition of a few words at the end about metonymy in the trage-dies. As a methodological guideline, we will use Seneca's own explicit princi-ples for the analysis of these figures; these are principles themselves derived from concepts in ancient rhetoric. This approach is designed to emphasize the intellectual environment of our writer and avoid anachronism.

Seneca's Theory of Metaphor and Simile

Seneca nowhere examines the working of metaphor or comparison in a sus-tained way, nor does he utter a single word about metonymy. Nonetheless, a few scattered remarks show that he adheres to the terminology and defini-tions of the rhetoricians. Thus metaphors are called *translationes verborum*, "transpositions of words" (*Ep.* 59.6). *Translatio* is the Latin rhetorical term for metaphor (*Rhet. Her.* 4.45; Cic. *De orat.* 3.155ff.; *Orat.* 134; Quint. *Inst.* 8.6.4). The term also shows that Seneca, in conformity with rhetor-ical classifications (e.g., Cicero, *Orat.* 134–6), includes metaphor (*transla-tiones*) among "ornaments of style" (*lumina verborum,* cf. *Orat.* 134) as opposed to "figures of thought" (*sententiarum ornamenta,* cf. *Orat. 136*). Elsewhere Seneca lists metaphors in a group of three terms, together with archaisms and neologisms, *verba prisca aut ficta* (*Ep.* 108.35; 114.10): this is a common grouping among the rhetoricians (Isoc. *Evag.* 190d; Cic. *De*

---

[1] Along with ancient theorists, we can here consider allegory to be a succession of metaphors.

orat. 3.152; 3.201; *Orat.* 80; Dion. Hal. *On the Arrangement of Words* 3.11; 25.8; Quint. *Inst.* 8.3.24).

When describing stylistic figures, the authors of the rhetorical treatises usually warn against the faults (*vitia*) into which these figures may fall. Seneca likewise evokes the perverse use of metaphor in bad contemporary writers: he complains that "audacious (*audax*) and frequent (*frequens*) metaphor is considered elegant (*pro cultu*)" (*Ep.* 114.10); elsewhere he speaks of "rash metaphors," *translationes temerarias* (*Ep.* 59.6). But what exactly is an "audacious" or "rash" metaphor? Thanks to Cicero, we know that it is one that relies on an insufficient likeness, a *dissimilitudo* (*De orat.* 3.162: this is an Aristotelian idea [*Rhet.* 3.2.1405a–b; 11.1412a11–12] repeated in all the writers of treatises); or one that employs an analogy "taken from far away," that is to say, one that is not clear enough (Cic. *De orat.* 3.163). Maecenas is the perfect model of the writer who uses metaphors badly: Seneca cites many of his abusive metaphors (*Ep.* 114.5), relating them to Maecenas's Asianist esthetic (and indirectly to his Epicureanism).[2] When we read these examples, we see that Maecenas' metaphors are too far-fetched even enigmatic; this is completely in line with Cicero's warning cited earlier. And if Maecenas strives for complicated metaphors, it is because of his general lassitude in the face of normative practices, a lassitude that affects not only his style but his entire existence. We can also point to his absurd striving for novelty (*Ep.* 114.10).

In contrast, Seneca's work contains no theories about simile. The terminology he uses to speak about comparison is in any case ambiguous. This is the case with *similitudo*, which is common in the rhetoricians. Sometimes Seneca uses this term to clearly designate a simile (*Ben.* 2.17.3, *Ep.* 13.3); at other times, by contrast, *similitudo* just means "resemblance," as in *Tranq.* 1.18 and *Ep.* 114.24, where the topic is the analogy on which a metaphor is based. Likewise, *imago* can refer explicitly to similes (*Ep.* 59.6–7, 72.8, 74.7, 92.21, 95.69), although this is not necessarily the case. Finally, we also find the term *parabole* (*Ep.* 59.6) without further specification but which, since Aristotle (*Rhet.* 2.1393a30ff.) designates a simile in the form of "in the same way as x, just so y" used for didactic purposes. But nowhere does Seneca analyze the way simile functions, or good or bad ways of using it. The only exception is at *Ep.* 59.6, where he praises Lucilius' style and congratulates him on using metaphors that are "not rash" in addition to similes (the latter are designated by the terms *imagines* and *parabolae*). Similes, he adds, were used by the "ancients," that is to say the ancient philosophers, *ut inbecillitatis nostrae adminicula sint*, "to serve as crutches for our weakness." We will

2 See Setaioli (2000, 225–74).

examine at a later point the meaning of this expression. But first, we must take a look at Seneca's practice and assess the metaphors and similes that figure in his writings.

The Choice of Images

There exist many general studies of Seneca's metaphors and similes: Steyns', which is worthy but incomplete,[3] Smith's, about the *Epistulae ad Lucilium*,[4] Canter's, which is limited to images from the stage,[5] and mine, which aims at an exhaustive treatment.[6] Nonetheless, caution is called for: while similes are easy to spot in the text, metaphors, in contrast, can be banal to the point of becoming difficult to detect. In the expression *amor sapientiae*, "love of wisdom," is *amor* a metaphor, or is it only a normal way of signifying a keen interest, without any reference to an erotic attachment? The answer depends on each individual's linguistic sensibility. But when, after a long allegorical description of the beauty of the wise soul, Seneca affirms that there is no one who "would not burn with love for it," *non amore eius arderet* (*Ep.* 115.6), the metaphorical sense of *amor* becomes indubitable. In short, there are many cases in which only the reader's linguistic intuition can decide whether a metaphor is present; doubt is only laid to rest when the metaphorical sense is revitalized by the context (here the description of the beauty of the soul) and/or by the presence of other metaphors that participate in the same semantic field (here the term *arderet*, "would burn," the image of the fire of love being one of the most common). The reader familiar with Seneca's texts should eventually develop a well-honed sensibility: after having encountered once or several usages of *amor* or *amare* where the metaphorical sense is marked by an explicit context, he will sense more easily the presence of the actual image in contexts that are not explicit or where the metaphor is reduced to an isolated term (*ama rationem*, *Ep.* 74.21; *virtutem adamare*, *Ep.* 71.5 and 94.8).

These precautions aside, this chapter can only sum up a few of the general conclusions drawn in the course of examining metaphors and similes in Seneca's work. Two observations should be made at the outset. The first is the contrast between the extreme abundance of images in the prose works and their relative rarity in the tragedies; we will return to this topic. The second is the very traditional character of these images. Only a few do not have

---

[3] Steyns (1907).
[4] Smith (1910).
[5] Canter (1925).
[6] Armisen-Marchetti (1989).

a previous history in Greco-Roman literary or philosophical texts. Seneca rarely unleashes his own imagination, even in the tragedies, and his metaphors rely on a limited creativity that refers back to a cultural heritage. This is not surprising if one recalls his warnings against metaphors that are too "audacious." Nonetheless, certain images appear more original. Among these are the ones borrowed from specifically Roman institutions – for example, gladiatorial games, with their methods of combat (*De ira* 1.11.1, 3.42.3; *De ben.* 5.3.3 and 4.1; *Ep.* 37.2, 117.25, etc.), the gladiators' condition (*De ira* 2.8.2), their courage (*De Const.* 16.2; *De tranq.* 11.4–5; *Ep.* 30.8), and so on. Still, one needs to exercise caution, since even the scenes which seem to rest on a particular sight, such as the defeated gladiator who offers himself up to the coup de grace (*De tranq.* 11.4–5; *Ep.* 30.8) can actually belong to an earlier tradition: the image of the dying gladiator can already be found in Cicero (*Tusc.* 2.41; *Phil.* 3.35; *Mil.* 92).

The selection of vehicles for imagery should not be confused with a personal interest in the realities that are being evoked: Seneca detested gladiatorial combat because of the sadistic passions it awoke in the public (*Ep.* 7.3–8). Another example is provided by the imagery borrowed from war and its techniques, which is very frequent and sometimes very detailed; and yet Seneca had never served in the army, and his convictions were pacifist.[7] The comparisons that feed the images are neither a direct transposition of experience nor of the values of the writer but were chosen for their expressivity and their efficacy in persuading.

When, then, Seneca draws from the stock of inherited images, his main concern is to be intelligible to the reader's intelligence and sensitivity. When he borrows metaphors from the Stoic tradition, then, he takes care to pair them, if they are clichés or too technical, with images taken from more meaningful and familiar circumstances. To express ethical value, Chrysippus used a commercial metaphor, *axia*, "price," "value." Cicero translated this by *aestimatio* (*aestimatio quae axia dicitur*, *Fin.* 3.34), which contains the same image. While using this translation himself (*De ira* 2.21.5, 3.12.3; *Ben.* 1.2.5, 4.10.5, 4.21.3; *Ep.* 76.32; etc.), Seneca more often has recourse to the everyday word *pretium*, "price" (*Ben.* 1.9.1; *Tranq.* 11.4; *Brev.* 8.1–2; *Ep.* 71.21 et 33; etc.). Most significantly, he introduces the word *census*, which, strictly speaking, refers to the censor's evaluation of a citizen's wealth, and the corresponding verb *censere*, terms which are here for the first time used metaphorically of moral values (*Ep.* 87.17, 95.58). In thus having recourse to a familiar and Roman reality, Seneca benefitted doubly: he gave life to images that had become trite, and he based them on his readers' environment.

---

[7] Armisen-Marchetti (2011).

Despite this, Seneca's creative personality shows up less in the introduction of new images than in the way he organizes the ones he has inherited into veritable symbolic networks. *Magnitudo animi*, "greatness of soul," is an image in use since Aristotle; in the Stoic system, *megalopsychia/ magnitudo animi* designates a subcategory of courage. At the same time, it is an archetypal image: in the human imagination, what is "great" or "high" has a positive connotation in comparison to that which is "small" or "low." Around this metaphor of the "greatness" of the soul, Seneca builds in his pages a complex system of imagery, reproducing in figural mode the logical relationships that tie together abstract philosophical concepts. The "greatness" of the soul of the wise man raises him to the height of the gods (*Ep* 41.4–5; see also *Helv.* 5.2; *Const.* 8.2; *Tranq.* 2.3; *Ep.* 31.9): a concrete transposition of the dogma that has gods and the sage sharing the same perfect rationality. This "greatness" allows him to "look down from above" or "despise" (*despicere*: the Latin verb superimposes both these meanings) the goods offered by Fortune (*Ep.* 9.13, 39.3, 74.6). In addition, because this greatness is too high to be affected by the evil-doing of the wicked, it assures the "constancy" of the soul (*Const.* 11.2). The connection between security and loftiness ("he who is placed in a safe spot sees everything underneath him," *Thy.* 365ff.) culminates in the image of the "fortress," *arx*, of the wise man's soul (*Ep.* 82.5, among others). There are other major symbolic frameworks: the sickness and the cure of the soul, the path and voyage of life, the loans of Fortune, the light of knowledge, and the like. But these frameworks are much less well represented in the tragedies, which leads us to suspect that the position and function of images are different in the philosophical texts and the tragic texts.

Functions of Imagery

To investigate these functions, we will once again take our start from what Seneca says of them himself, keeping in mind that he is generally speaking about metaphor and that he does so with reference to philosophical discourse, not tragic drama.

Terminology

Ameliorating the Poverty of Language: Catachresis
A properly Stoic discourse in conformity with the requirements of that doctrine should, in theory, be nothing but pure transparency, a direct expression of reality. Why introduce such improper material as metaphor? Seneca's first answer is: through necessity, because of the insufficiency of the Latin philosophical language. The problem of "the poverty of the language," *inopia*

sermonis, is an issue particularly in the *De beneficiis*, where the logic of "benefits" leads Seneca to reflect on lexical issues: "there is a considerable crowd of things that have no name, that we designate by non-specific terms that belong elsewhere and have been borrowed.... Because we have no means of assigning a name to each one, we borrow every time it is necessary" (*Ben.* 2.34.3). "Borrow," *abuti* (*Ben.* 5.11.2), corresponds to the noun *abusio*, which in the rhetoricians designates catachresis (Quint. *Inst.* 8.6.34). But the characteristic of a catachresis is to rapidly become normative language: this is the case for all the examples given by Seneca, the "foot" of the bed or the metrical "foot" (*Ben.* 2.34.2), expressions whose visual character is hardly felt or even not at all. However, this is not always the case. One very frequent example of catachresis in Seneca is the term *medicus* in the expression *medicus animi*, "doctor of the soul," to designate the teacher-philosopher who exerts himself to hold back his interlocutor from the passions. Neither in Greek nor in Latin is there a proper term for this spiritual activity, so that the metaphorical catachresis occurs as early as Democritus; it runs throughout the tradition of antiquity. But in spite of its age, this catachresis supplies a definite image in Seneca, for whom it constitutes the center of a very complex symbolic network that sets in detailed parallel the physical practices of medicine and those of the teacher of ethics.

Translation

In spite of the considerable work done by Cicero to translate Stoic terminology into Latin, Seneca still feels the need to return to the vocabulary at his disposal. This is because Cicero is interested in philosophical concepts and morals in a theoretical way, while Seneca is above all preoccupied by the transmission of morals and by practical applications. In contrast to abstract rendition, metaphor has the advantage of not only designating a concept but letting it have an intuitive grasp upon us, an intuition that is the more effective the more the comparand is familiar to the reader. For example, among the Greek Stoics, the *hegemonikon* (the term is derived from *hegemon*, leader) is the principal part of the soul. Seneca's translation, *principale* (*De ira* 1.3.7; *Ep.* 113.23; 121.10 and 13) maintains the Greek image, but in a particularly meaningful form for a contemporary reader, since this term, in the political lexicon of the Empire, designates what is related to *princeps*, "prince." Thus thanks to the metaphor, even a neophyte reader can form an approximate idea of the concept before started a real apprenticeship in doctrine.

"Rendering the Subject Matter Visible"

In *De beneficiis* 4.12.1, Seneca calls a benefit a "loan." His imaginary interlocutor leads him to remark that there is a large ethical difference between a benefit, which is a good in itself, and a loan, which is not a good in itself. As Seneca says, "When we say 'loan,' we are using an image and a metaphor.... We resort to these terms for the sake of 'rendering the subject matter visible'; when I say 'loan,' it is understood as '*like* a loan.'"

Seneca thus demonstrates that he is aware that a metaphor is inexact by nature and that this is in fact the very principle of the trope. In terms of modern linguistics, we would say that the speaker, when he creates a metaphor, selects a certain number of semes that are shared between the comparand and what is compared (in the case of the benefit and the loan, these are the semes connected to the idea of exchange) and neglects others (the ethical nature of each of these two notions). A metaphor is never entirely adequate to the concept it refers to and does not try to be; on the contrary, its very inexactness produces its expressive power. It is the same case when the analogy takes the form of a simile: the beneficiary of the benefit cannot be completely assimilated to a debtor, *debitoris exemplum dissimile est* (*Ben.* 7.14.5). This is the reason certain metaphors can clash with Stoic doctrine, for example, when Seneca says of the passions that they "enter" the soul, "occupy" it, or are "routed" (*De ira* 1.8.2, 2.13.3; *Const.* 5.3; *Ep.* 85.13, 94.68), or likewise that virtue "enters" the soul (*Ben.* 5.12.5), although in orthodox Stoicism, neither the passions nor virtue come from the exterior but are modifications of the rational part of the soul, the *hegemonikon*. But an inadequate image can also be rectified: by the correction of a seme (a benefit is a loan, but "I add that it cannot be paid back, although every loan can and should be paid back," *Ben.* 4.12.1); by recourse to complementary images (a game with a ball, to figure the exchange of benefits, *Ben.* 2.17.3–5, 2.32.1–4, etc.), to fill in the insufficiencies of the main image.

If Seneca has recourse to images despite their logical inexactness, it is *demonstrandae rei causa*, "to render the subject matter one is talking about visible." The same expression appears in *Ep.* 59.6 in regard to the *parabolae*, the explanatory similes used in philosophical discourse, Seneca says, *demonstrandae rei causa*, a formula he explains as follows: "to be crutches for our weakness, to put the speaker and the listener in the presence of the matter." It is, therefore, the limitation of the human spirit that makes necessary the recourse to images that allow one to imagine the concept via concrete analogies.

In fact, the image allows above all the visualization of what is invisible. This is particularly true for psychological realities.[8] When Serenus does not know how to express the psychological instability from which he suffers and for which he cannot find a name (*Tranq.* 1.4), he finally turns to a

[8] See Bartsch's chapter in this *Companion* on "metaphors of the self."

metaphor (*Tranq.* 1.18): "to exemplify it for you via a realistic analogy I complain of, I'm not troubled by the storm, but by sea-sickness." Just so in the tragedies, recurrent metaphors serve to describe the passions (the fire of love and of anger, the chill of fear, etc.), thus adding to the symbolic gestures of the Roman actor. But these images allow one also to reestablish psychological states too complex or too rare to be signified by the usual theatrical codes: the trouble that stays with Hercules once he emerges from his madness is compared by the choir to the sea, which continues to roar after the storm has abated (*HF* 1088–92).

The many similes of the *Natural Questions* represent a separate case. They depend on analogy, a procedure that is not unique to Seneca but goes back to Anaxagoras and thereafter runs through all of ancient science. Such analogies make it possible to represent and to study phenomena that escape human observation. Consider the treatment of wind in book five; it is defined as *fluens aer*, "air that flows" (*NQ* 5.1.1). Because it is impossible to see air, which is imperceptible to the gaze, an analogy is drawn with the movement of water, which is better known because it is observable; what is known about water is then transferred to the circulation of air by means of an explicit simile: "In rivers, it is the case that.... Similarly, the wind ..." (*NQ* 5.13.1–2). All of book 5 is fed by these comparisons between water and air, and the description and investigation of the causes (aetiology) of the phenomena of the winds are based on this. The *Natural Questions* abound with similes of this sort, through which they render visible what are no longer simple figures of style but a whole separate scientific method.

"Aiming at Happiness"

Seneca remarks that images allow us to be "in the presence of the thing itself" (the "signifying" thing, the "subject of discourse," *Ep.* 59.6, cited earlier). The formula clearly refers to the rhetorical notion of *evidential enargeia*, which designates language's ability to arouse vivid mental representations in our thought. This ability is particularly effective for persuasion ("enargeia ... seems to me not so much to tell as to show, and the emotions produced will be no different than if we were actually at the events themselves," Quint. *Inst.* 6.2.32). The image allows us to bestow clarity on the idea, but this clarity should still be subordinated to the moral: figures of style, including metaphors, are not to be sought for their own sake. One must write *ad propositum beatae vitae*, "aiming at happiness," that is, in the service of ethics (*Ep.* 108.35). Images participate in this project of moral persuasion, as much for the teacher who strives to persuade his student to adopt a good ethical attitude as for his student, who not only listens to his teacher but also persuades himself by reflecting on the dogma of the discipline and working on his own spiritual transformation. And here, the medium of the image is even more effective when it does not belong to the logical argument but, by its very nature, bypasses the resistance of the intellect. Thus, in the *De constantia*, the metaphor in which the passion of shame cannot "enter" a soul already occupied by virtue (*Const.* 5.3) transposes the Stoic logic of exclusion onto spatial terms. According to Stoic orthodoxy, the soul can only be in one of two states, perfect rationality or passion, each of the two excluding the other without any intermediary degree. But perhaps this idea seemed too rigid, and its result (that the sage cannot feel shame) is difficult to accept for the man not yet fully converted to Stoicism. As we've seen, the spatial metaphor, even if it is incorrect in doctrinal terms, allows one to picture to oneself the Stoic moral lesson, to feel it. It bestows on dogma a perceptible clarity that reiterates and reinforces its logical clarity.

It can also happen that reason surrenders completely to imagery. The thesis of the *De constantia* is that "the wise man is safe, he cannot be reached by any injury or insult" (*Const.* 2.4). It is a thesis that seems to contradict the obvious: many wise men have been insulted, so that Seneca's interlocutor Serenus three times withholds his agreement (3.1–2, 4.1, 4.2). The doctrinal response would be: the sage is safe from injuries not because he does not experience them but because they make no dent in his serenity. But instead of this, Seneca responds with metaphor: the wise man is inaccessible to injury because he is in an elevated place, out of everyone's reach (3.3–4, 4.1–2); because his soul is as hard as rock or iron (3.5); because he enjoys the security of a powerful general in enemy territory (4.3). The figural clarity of the image takes the place of logical argument.

Metaphor has one more function that we have not yet taken into account here. According to Cicero (*De orat.* 3.155–6), after metaphors began to be cultivated *inopiae causa* (because of the lack of literal expressions – that is to say, as catachresis), they became popular *delectationis causa*, to give pleasure, because "they bring vividness to speech." For his part, Seneca never mentions the pleasure of the image in his theoretical explanation. If nonetheless his writings contain images aimed above all at the pleasure of the reader or listener, that is to say, if his writings contain images that serve an aesthetic purpose more than any other function, it is in the tragedies that we have the greatest chance of finding them.

The Distinctive Feature of Tragic Images

As we have already mentioned, a catalogue of Seneca's images reveals an unexpected fact: the tragedies – where we might expect the writer to give freer rein to his imagination than in the philosophical works – in actuality contain many fewer metaphors and similes, and those that can be found are extremely conventional and almost always borrowed from the poetic and tragic literary tradition. The great metaphorical themes that tirelessly sustain the prose works, the sickness and remedies of the soul, the voyage of life, the battle against the passions, are much more rare in the dramas, even when the tragic framework could have made use of them. These metaphors serve above all to describe the psychological life of the characters, with this one detail, that they sometimes reflect the tragic plot: thus Medea's soul is ruled by the fire of her passions, the fire of hate (*Med.* 582), of rage (*Med.* 591), of grief (*Med.* 672); but at the same time, Medea herself physically handles the fire of revenge by means of which she will destroy her rival Creusa (*Med.* 817–39) and will finally bring about disaster for the palace and the city (885–890). The *evidentia* of the literary image becomes a striking part of tragic reality.

On the other hand, one finds here more than in the philosophical works the lengthy similes common in epic and tragedy since Homer, that take the form of "just as...., just so..." (*Ep.* 59.6). Most of the time the tragic images are borrowed from this tradition, and the comparands come from a limited number of domains: spectacles of nature, animals, religious cults, mythology. The role of these similes is essentially descriptive, whether they appear in narratives of offstage events (the ghosts of the dead rush up in numbers as great as the leaves in the springtime, as the waves of the sea, as birds in migration, *Oed.* 600–7) or whether they comment on events shown on stage, where they specify details and underline the importance of these events for the spectators. These latter images allow a focus on the facts that elude everyday experience: for example, a detail from a scene of divination compares the color of the sacrificial flame to the melting nuances of Isis's veil, *Oed.* 314–20; or the behavior driven by tragic *furor* (Medea is represented by wandering on the stage like a Maenad, *Med.* 382–6; or like a tigress, *Med.* 862–5).

However, the category of images that dominates the tragedies is metonymy (and its subclass synecdochy). The ancient rhetoricians failed to give us an individual description of this unobtrusive figure, and Seneca likewise does not analyze it. Metonymy consists in referring to one term by another through a relationship of proximity, whether in facts or in thought: Jakobson saw in it the mark of excellence of realism in literature. Here, the many metonymies allow the poet to focus attention on a significant detail of tragic *mimesis*. *Sceptro nostro famulus est potior tibi*, "a slave (i.e., Hercules) is worth more to you than my scepter," says Lycus to Megara (*HF* 430): the "scepter" (and indeed the actor is holding one in his hand; see verse 331) here stands for the status of king. In the same tragedy, the metonymy of the "hand," *manus* or *dextra*, figures royal power (*HF* 341, 740) or the bravery of Hercules (*HF* 528, 882, 1272, etc.). We also find many abstract synecdoches (the abstract in the place of the concrete) in the *sententiae*, where concision is key: *virtutis est domare quae cuncti pavent*, "a habit of bravery (that is, 'of the brave man') is to defeat what the whole world fears," *HF* 435).

The effect is such that the tragic poet seems to have been stingy with everything that could distract from the strict framework of theatrical *mimesis*: this is the case with metaphor and simile, which introduce vehicles that are potentially external to the components of the tragic myth. Seneca prefers to concentrate on the internal visual elements and to privilege metonymy and synecdoche, which focus the attention on a detail that is significant or even symbolic of the *muthos*. Clearly the metonymies of the tragedies would benefit from further study.

Further Reading

In the first part of the last century, Steyns (1907) and Smith (1910) attracted attention to the variety of images, both metaphors and similes, in Seneca's prose work, and Canter (1925) produced a partial list of their recurrence in the tragedies: all shared the view that these were no more than rhetorical elements, or indeed simple ornaments, of the author's style. Traina (1987), on the contrary, focuses on the essential role that certain metaphors and similes play in shaping Seneca's philosophical and pedagogical project, and Setaioli (1985), although not dealing specifically with images, has shown how style and philosophical project are intertwined. Armisen-Marchetti (1989) is specifically devoted to images in Seneca's poetry and prose (see also Armisen-Marchetti 2011 on the image of the *arx*). McCall (1969), Armisen-Marchetti (1991), Guidorizzi and Beta (2000), and Lau (2006) are useful on ancient rhetorical and philosophical views of metaphors and similes, providing a good picture of the cultural context and thus reducing the risk of anachronistic interpretations. A number of recent, innovative works highlight the philosophical and parenetic function of metaphors and similes, either in general (Lotito 2001, Inwood 2005) or focusing especially on the question of images (Bartsch 2009, Dressler 2012).

12

CEDRIC A. J. LITTLEWOOD

Theater and Theatricality in Seneca's World

"All the world is not of course a stage, but the crucial ways in which it isn't are not easy to specify."[1]

The theater has long offered a model for describing reality, from the roles that define us as persons to the dynamics of public performance and social spectacle. The erosion of the boundary between the real and the fictive or between more or less authentic constructions has long also been a source of moral and existential anxiety. Drama that exposes its own artifice – meta-drama – models both itself and, to the extent that the world outside the drama is conceived in theatrical terms, reality. This chapter offers three brief reflections on Senecan theatricality: "Roman Self-Fashioning" is concerned with Stoic persona theory and Seneca's philosophical use of dramatic personas in *Ad Marciam*; "Performing Power" discusses the theatricality of political power in Seneca's *Thyestes* and Julio-Claudian Rome; "The Grand Illusion" considers metadrama and the fictions of empire in *Troades*.

Roman Self-Fashioning

Stephen Greenblatt's influential reading of Thomas More as an actor improvising a life in the lethal pageantry of Tudor England is a compelling model for and from Seneca.[2] In a passage from *Utopia*, More prescribes for the statesman a civic-minded philosophy "which knows its own stage and, adapting itself, sustains its role harmoniously and appropriately (*cum decoro*) in the drama in hand ..." His interlocutor Hythloday argues that to be defined by the drama in hand is to become alienated from the values that should be most one's own.[3] More here revisits Cicero *De Officiis* 1.27–34 and the "four *personae*" theory

---

[1] Goffman (1969, 78) quoted by Easterling (1990), whose bibliography and discussion are invaluable.
[2] Greenblatt (1980, 11–73), Parrish (1997), and Edwards (1997, 35).
[3] Logan, Adams, and Miller (1995, 97–8) discussed by Greenblatt (1980, 35–6).

of the Stoic Panaetius, according to which the overall moral beauty or propriety (*decorum*) of our lives is determined by the success with which we perform and harmonize the various roles that nature and circumstance dictate.[4] Actors act appropriately when they perform well whatever roles their poet assigns, good or bad (1.38.98). Nature assigns to persons the role of constancy (*constantiae... partes*, 1.28.98) and a smaller range of legitimate performances.[5] It is then all the more striking to note that while More speaks of the statesman accommodating himself to the play in hand (*eique sese accommodans*, *Utopia* 96), Cicero speaks of actors choosing the plays that best accommodate them (*sibi accommodatissimas fabulas eligunt* 1.31.114).

The theatrical metaphor need not connote a life of insincerity[6] and hollowness, and clearly does not for Cicero. However, on a stage that offers only roles alien to our natural selves, life becomes inauthentic.[7] Shadi Bartsch has argued that although Seneca uses *persona* variously to connote both a legitimate role and a false mask, his frequent use of the term in the latter sense marks a subtle but significant shift from Cicero's practice.[8] This shift, running parallel with the political shift from Republic to Empire, may be associated with an inward turn from the external court of public opinion to an internal or internalized court of self-examination.[9] Alternatively, Nero's scripted and very public performance as *princeps* in *de Clementia* "combines political theater with courtroom drama" to present the imperial soul before the gaze and the judgment of his subjects.[10]

Seneca's ambivalence toward the stage has a distinguished heritage: the man who wrote the myth of the puppet-theater in the cave and coined the word "theatrocracy" (as a caricature of democracy) did so in dramatic dialogues.[11] *Ad Marciam*, which contains one of Seneca's more developed descriptions of life as a theatrical illusion (10.1–2), offers exemplary figures as roles to be imitated or avoided, quotes a line from the stage (9.5), and speaks in a succession of different voices.[12] Learning to construct *personae*,

---

[4] On the theory, see Gill (1988).

[5] See further Bartsch in this volume on Stoic consistency in life's performance.

[6] When Carlyle coined the word "theatricality" in 1837, he opposed it to "sincerity" (*French Revolution* II.i.ix.64).

[7] For examples from Seneca, see, e.g., *Thy.* 205–12, *Ep.* 76.31–2, 80.7–8, and Goldschmidt (1969, 180–6).

[8] Bartsch (2006, 216–29).

[9] On histrionic and juridic metaphor, see Fantham (2002) and Inwood (2005, 201–23). On interiority, see Traina (2006) and Williams in this volume.

[10] Star (2012, 118–20) and cf. Schofield in this volume

[11] Pl. *R.* 514a–517a (cave) and *Lg.* 701a3 (theatrocracy). See Weber (2004, 31–9) on theatrocracy and Rutherford (1995, 10–15) on the origins of the Platonic dialogue in mimetic art.

[12] On Seneca and the dialogue form, see Roller in this volume.

"a rhetorical fashioning of the self and others,"[13] played a central role in Roman education. Seneca's opinion that exemplary figures are rhetorically more effective than abstract precepts is characteristically Roman.[14]

At the beginning of *Ad Marciam*, Seneca offers contrasting sketches of Octavia's immoderate grief and Livia's restraint and challenges the bereaved Marcia to choose a model (3.3). To choose the right example is to be recalled to the model of ancient virtue that is her own character (*mores tuos velut aliquod antiquum exemplar*, 1.1). Seneca addresses Marcia in the persona of Areus, who (Seneca imagines) was Livia's interlocutor. The role playing is therapeutic: "exchange roles [with Livia] – he [Areus] was consoling you" (*muta personam – te consolatus est*, 6.1). A second persona, Nature, offers a broader perspective on mortality and the uncertainty of human affairs. A third, Marcia's father Cremutius Cordus, is now a spark in the divine fire that animates and shapes the cosmos. In the darkness of mortal life, Marcia cannot yet see as he does (26.3), but she must strive to act as if under his transfigured gaze (25.3). The sequence of personas does not correspond to the four *personae* of Panaetius and Cicero, but the fundamental principle, that Marcia must learn to play herself, conceived as an integrated plurality of roles, is the same.[15]

Fortune's goods are characterized in *Ad Marciam* as the glittering stage props of a rented world (10.1), but the contempt for display extends also to Seneca's use of personae. Seneca explains his decision to begin the dialogue with examples (*exempla*) and only later to offer precepts (*praecepta*) by saying that famous names have "an authority that does not leave the mind free, dazzled as people are by outward show" (*auctoritas quae liberum non relinquat animum ad speciosa stupentibus* 2.1). The philosopher employs the device of *prosopopoeia* and recalls Marcia to roles consistent with her true self, but not without acknowledging both the tyranny and the potential superficiality of images. It is an ambivalence that touches the philosopher-dramatist himself, whose suicide offered his friends both a derivative tableau after Socrates and Cato and "an image of his own life" (*imago vitae suae*, Tac. *Ann.* 15.62.1), at once a departure from the illusory stage and a showy performance upon it.[16]

Self-fashioning is to be found also within the tragedies, the most famous example being Medea's determination to become Medea (*Med.* 171, 910).

---

[13] Bloomer (1997, 59).
[14] Sen. *Ep.* 6.5 and Quint. *Inst.* 12.2.30 with Leigh (1997, 160–8) and Mowbray (2012, 396–9).
[15] Fournier (2009, 233).
[16] See Ker (2009a, 113–17), Edwards (2007, 155–9), and Braund in this volume.

Other characters, often also using their name as a standard, drive themselves to act and to be seen as acting in a worthy manner.[17] The self-fashioning of poetic constructs has a metaliterary aspect,[18] but one may also argue that the self-consciousness of dramatic characters is akin or even pointedly parallel to the Stoic role-playing of texts like *Ad Marciam*: the theatrical metaphor returns philosophized to the stage.[19]

Performing Power

populus ille, aliquando scaenici imperatoris spectator et plausor ... (Plin. *Pan.* 46.4)

(that people, once the applauding audience of an actor-emperor ...)

Julio-Claudian Rome and Neronian Rome in particular is commonly represented in ancient historiography through a theatrical paradigm by which the emperor and his subjects assume in alternation the roles of actors and audience in a series of false and degrading performances.[20] The actor-emperor and the actor-citizen confuse not just different but opposing roles in Roman culture.[21] Quintilian painstakingly distinguishes the speech and gestures appropriate to actors from those appropriate to public speakers (*Inst.* 11.3.14–185).[22] Tacitus refuses to shame the ancestors of the nobles whom Nero bribed onto the stage in the Juvenalia of CE 59 by giving their names (*Ann.* 14.14). Dio records that they performed under compulsion and envied the dead (61.19). But elsewhere Tacitus writes that Nero both coerced *and allowed* the appearance of leading Romans on the stage (*Ann.* 14.20). Clearly there is an important social distinction between the actor and the respectable citizen, but clearly also Nero the actor-emperor cannot be dismissed as a singular aberration.

A parallel site of confusion is the "noble gladiator." A performer of ill repute who exhibits his body might be an object of shameful desire,[23] but not, one would think, glorious. Yet Cicero and Seneca both describe gladiators as displaying a kind of martial virtue and steadfastness in the face of

---

[17] Fitch and McElduff (2002, 24–32) and Citti in this volume on Medea's self-affirmation in the modern theatrical tradition.

[18] Hinds (2011, 22–8).

[19] Bartsch (2006, 259–81), Star (2012, 62–83), and Trinacty in this volume.

[20] Bartsch (1994, 1–35).

[21] Edwards (1993, 123–36).

[22] Discussed by Fantham (2002, 370–3).

[23] E.g., Petr. 126.

death.[24] The "noble" gladiator often shames his social superior, but Seneca also uses the analogy to collapse the social distinction and represent everyone as performers in the games Fortune stages (*De brev.* 11.5).[25] Seneca's identification with the gladiator and the willingness of even elite citizens to appear in the arena uncoerced has been interpreted as an expression of aristocratic despair and humiliation under autocracy. In a world in which the martial display of a triumph was barred to all but the imperial family, the arena, real or virtual, could offer an alternative, abject glory.[26] How glorious, abject, or alternative the citizen-actor, senator, and future Stoic martyr Thrasea Paetus was considered to be when he sang in tragic costume in the games at Patavium (Tac. *Ann.* 16.21) is hard to say.[27] For Tacitus at least, that very ambiguity is the mark of a society morally and politically adrift.

Nero was represented as an emperor who preferred to be a performer. An alternative approach is to interpret him not as neglecting his position as *princeps* but as developing and performing it through public displays of monarchical, heroic, and divine power.[28] Nero noted that chariot racing was kingly and practiced by leaders of old and that Apollo was represented with a cithara not just in Greek cities but also in Roman temples (Tac. *Ann.* 14.14). He might have added that a triumphal *quadrigae* dedicated to Augustus stood in the Roman forum (*Res Gestae* 35), that Augustus had blended his own image with that of the solar charioteer and lyre player Apollo and had merged their dwellings on the Palatine hill.[29] Far from being a degenerate tyrant, Nero was a close student of the first *princeps* and his true heir.[30]

Cornelius Nepos comments with misleading clarity that to appear on stage and to display oneself to the people was a source of shame to the Romans but not to the Greeks.[31] Roman theater audiences accustomed to viewing

---

[24] Cic. *Tusc.* 2.17.41 and Sen. *Ep.* 70.27.

[25] On this passage, see Gunderson (1996, 138).

[26] Barton (1993, 25–31) and cf. Leigh (1997, 234–91) on "the disruption wrought by reference to the amphitheatrical" (243) in Lucan's inglorious wars. Gunderson (1996) and Edwards (2007, 46–77) question whether the noble gladiator is a particularly imperial phenomenon. See also Armisen-Marchetti in this volume.

[27] Discussed by Champlin (2003, 66). See Edwards (1993, 131–3) on legislation in the first century CE to prevent the elite performing as public entertainers.

[28] This is the revisionist thesis most fully articulated by Champlin (2003).

[29] Zanker (1988, 48–57). For Nero as "shining Apollo," see Champlin (2003, 112–44). See also Beacham (1999, 76) on the significance of Caesar's dedication of a chariot to Jupiter in 46 BCE.

[30] See further Feeney (2002, 183–4) on the "political theatre" of the Augustan principate and the literal theater as both substitute and template for public life.

[31] Nepos, *Vitae prf.* 5, discussed by Edwards (1993, 98–103) and Beacham (1999, 208–9).

(and booing and applauding) an elite seated just in front of a stage that lacked a proscenium arch might have found the boundary of the stage more elusive.[32] Nero watched plays from the top of the proscenium, halfway onto the stage (Suet. *Nero* 12). "Political theatre" in the loose sense, as manifested in such institutions as triumphs, weddings, and funerals, was long theatrical-ized in a stricter sense at Rome by its borrowing from the dramatic stage. Tragic quotation at Caesar's funeral and actors (*scaenici artifices*) rending garments from his triumphs were integrated parts of a complex performance over which the consul Antony presided.[33] Pompey's restaging in his own the-ater of his triple triumph through a performance of Agamemnon's triumph in the *Equos Troianus* in 55 BCE is a complementary example of the politi-cization of theater.[34] Some separation remains here between drama and real-ity as it does not in Nero's repetition in that same theater in CE 66 of king Tiridates' public act of submission performed moments earlier in the forum (Suet. *Nero* 13).[35] Nero allegedly drew inspiration for life from the theater, for example, by attempting to murder his mother in the kind of collapsible boat that he had seen on stage (Dio 61.12.2–3). After her death, masked as himself, he performed the dramatic role of the matricide Orestes (Suet. *Nero* 21.3). As the boundary between stage and reality dissolved, Nero became a creature of heroic myth.[36] Tacitus wrote his history as tragic through such theatrical cues as Nero "setting the stage" for a charge against his mother (*scaenam ... parat, Ann.* 14.7) and through allusion to Greek and Roman tragic texts.[37] There is particular irony in reading Seneca himself caught, in Tacitus and the ps-Senecan *Octavia*, in tragedies of his own making.[38]

Nero's public stage performances date from comparatively late in his reign (64 CE onward), and his long competitive tour of Greece in 66–67 CE suggests that the east provided him with an audience more accommodating of a performing *princeps*. But "the Macedonian drama" (τοῦ Μακεδονικοῦ δράματος, Plut. *Demetr.* 53.4) of the life of the Hellenistic king Demetrius is a reminder that power, theatrically costumed, could be represented as

---

[32] On seating arrangements, see Suet. *Aug.* 44. On the expression of public opinion at the theater, see Parker (1999, 171–6).
[33] Suet. *Iul.* 84 discussed by Dupont (1985, 167) and Boyle (2006, 97).
[34] Erasmo (2004, 86–91) and Boyle (2006, 156). See also Lucan's sympathetic but critical representation of Pompey lost in the dreams of his own theater (7.7–25). On resemblance between the theater complex itself and the old forum, see Purcell (1999, 187).
[35] Beacham (1999, 243–4) and Champlin (2003, 75).
[36] Dupont (1985, 432–7), Bartsch (1994, 38–50), and Champlin (2003, 84–111).
[37] On Tacitus' tragic history, see Woodman (1993) and Shumate (1997). On the *Oresteia* as a pattern for the dynasty, see Santoro l'Hoir (2006, 15–70).
[38] Ker (2009, 140–45).

imposture (41.3–4) by Greeks as well as Romans.[39] Demetrius' life is paired with that of the equally theatrical Antony, Plutarch's account of which ends with the observation that Nero was fifth in descent from Antony (*Ant.* 87.4).[40] The challenge of using the stage and theatrical effects to perform autocracy without appearing either an actor or an oriental tyrant is handed from one to the other and across the cultural divide supposedly separating Greece from Rome.

The performing tyrant is inscribed (if not also staged)[41] in Seneca's *Thyestes*, a play that probably dates from the second half of Nero's reign.[42] Art and spectacle are central to Atreus' revenge.[43] He wishes that he could make the gods observe the cannibal banquet from which they recoil (893–95) and pursues "something greater, larger than usual, beyond human limits" (*nescioquid animo maius et solito amplius / supraque fines moris humani*, 267–8). He achieves it in a grove at the heart of the royal palace where he "sings the lethal song/poem" (*letale carmen ... canit*, 692) and performs a Dionysiac sparagmos of Thyestes' children.[44] The Dionysiac grove is commonly characterized by a collision of cultures as the eastern god brings his ecstasy west, and this is significant for the characterization of Atreus' tyranny.[45] The palace surrounding the Tantalid grove recalls the palace of king Latinus (Verg. *Aen.* 7.170–91), and through it the palace of Augustus, but redrawn "in blatantly oriental colors."[46] In Alessandro Schiesaro's words, "Atreus shows the game [of the Roman god-emperor] for what it is."[47]

Insatiable appetite is the tragedy's dominant image for the pursuit of power, but another significant figure is that of the racetrack. Atreus breaks the cosmos by forcing the solar chariot off course (789–888) and celebrates his revenge in athletic metaphor: "now the true palm is won" (*nunc vera parta est palma*, 1097). Olympia, the site in the proem to *Georgics* 3 of

---

[39] von Hesberg (1999, 69–71).

[40] On Antony as actor, see Plut. *Ant.* 29.1–2, 54.3; as tragic figure, De Lacy (1952) and Leigh (1996).

[41] On stage performance, see Fitch (2000) on Seneca, and Beacham (1992, 117–98), Goldberg (1996), and Boyle (2006, 160–88, 221–38) on Roman theater.

[42] Nisbet (1990) with Fitch (1981, 303–5).

[43] Schiesaro (2003, 45–6) and Mowbray (2012, 399–403).

[44] Schiesaro (2003, 133–8) on Atreus as Dionysus, the god of this tragic stage.

[45] See Hunter (2006, 7–16) on "the cultural paradoxes of the *Bacchae*" (11).

[46] Tarrant (1985, 186, quote, and 183–86) on *Thy.* 641–664 and Pelops' Phrygian tiara. On Roman opposition to but also imitation of the Oriental in the imperial discourse of the *Aeneid*, see Reed (2007, 111–13 and 157–60). See also Kuttner (1999, 115) on Alexander, Antony, and "ethnically coded royal dress."

[47] Schiesaro (2003, 97, quote, and 70–138, esp. 130) on "the ethics and aesthetics of tyranny."

Vergil's assimilation of the triumphs of artist and emperor,[48] is in *Thyestes* the site of Pelops' victory and a foundation of the dynasty's power. The imagery of the chariot race and of appetite fuse in the description of the Argolid parched by Tantalid thirst (108–19). This passage draws on Ovid's description of the world burned by Phaethon's fatal chariot ride (*Met.* 2.214–64), and the discourse of Augustan power is implicated in Ovid's narrative of solar authority.[49] To read Seneca's intertextuality is to construct a relationship between Neronian and Augustan principates (see further Ker and Rimell in this volume).

The Grand Illusion

The dramatic illusion of Seneca's *Troades* breaks when the second chorus questions whether the soul survives the body:

> *Verum est an timidos fabula decipit*
> *umbras corporibus vivere conditis?* (*Tro.* 371–2)
>
> Is it true or a tale which deceives the fearful
> that shades live on when the bodies are buried?

Hell, it concludes, is "empty words and a tale like a bad dream" (*verbaque inania / et par sollicito fabula somnio*, 405–6). Such Epicurean disbelief is hard to reconcile with the Trojan women's celebration of Priam's escape from slavery into the sanctuary of Elysium (156–62) and harder still to reconcile with the apparition of Achilles' ghost (168–202). Commentators must resolve the awkwardness with a new chorus of Greek soldiers or embrace it.[50] To those who embrace it, the incoherence is symptomatic of the play's "disjunctive structure."[51] The word *fabula*, which appears pointedly at the beginning and the end of the ode, means "play" as well as "tale."[52] By breaking the illusion of the *fabula*, the chorus questions the fantasies that pass for reality on its stage.

Achilles' vengeful ghost personifies the influence of past events and past texts. Its apparition is immediately followed by an agon between Pyrrhus, Achilles' son, and Agamemnon and a "perverse repetition" of the famous

[48] Hardie (2002, 316–17) and Kuttner (1999, 117).
[49] Barchiesi (2005, 235–8). On Atreus and Nero as solar charioteer, see Volk (2006, 194–200).
[50] On the history of the problem, see Fantham (2000, 16–19).
[51] Boyle (1994, 172).
[52] *OLD* 665 and Feldherr (2010, 47–9) on *fabula* on the relationship between "real" power and the power of fiction, poetic and theatrical.

Homeric quarrel.[53] Agamemnon is forced to surrender Polyxena to the son as once he surrendered Briseis to the father and, in a different repetition, again to sacrifice a virgin princess in a pretended marriage to Achilles. Calchas rules that "the customary price" be paid: (*Dant fata Danais quo solent pretio viam* 360). What for the heroes is a memory of past events is for the reader a memory of past texts.[54] A very un-Homeric Agamemnon resists the patterns of fate and the tyrannical exercise of power:

> *ego esse quicquam sceptra nisi vano putem*
> *fulgore tectum nomen et falso comam*
> *vinclo decentem? (Tro.* 271–3)

> Could I consider sceptered power to be anything but a name overlaid with false glitter, a deceiving bond to adorn the hair?

This rhetoric of illusion anticipates the rejection of empty words in the following chorus, but Pyrrhus defeats the newly philosophical king. Achilles' ghost may be a mere fable and sceptered power a name overlaid with false glitter, but on the tragic stage, for those lost in a bad dream, their force is irresistible. Polyxena is surrendered like Briseis and dies like Iphigenia because these are the models, prescribed and prescribed, of mythic history.

Rome is implicated in these fictions. A Julio-Claudian audience was predisposed simultaneously to remember its illustrious Trojan past and to distance itself from the fallen city.[55] In Horace, *Odes* 3.3.57–60, Rome's success is contingent on Troy's extinction.[56] One may argue that in the *Aeneid*, it is through the sacrificial destruction of Troy that the city will later be reborn in Rome.[57] When Seneca's chorus wonders whether the soul survives death, it recalls a line of Horace:

> *an toti morimur nullaque pars manet*
> *nostri, cum profugo spiritus halitu*
> *immixtus nebulis cessit in aera*
> *et nudum tetigit subdita fax latus? (Sen. Tro.* 378–81)

> Or do we die utterly, so that no part of us remains, when the spirit with fugitive breath has mingled in the mists and passed away into air and the torch has been set to the naked flesh?)
> Cf.

---

[53] Wilson (1983, 34).

[54] See Boyle (1994, 27) on "the play's concept of "fate," *fatum* (lit. "what has been said")" and Cf. Trinacty in this volume on the *fata* of Oedipus and on Senecan intertextuality more generally.

[55] See Ker (2009a, 133–4) and his bibliography.

[56] See also Verg. *Georg.* 1.501–2 and Quint (1993, 50–80) on the dangers of repetition in the *Aeneid*.

[57] Bandera (1981, 236). Cf. Morgan (1999, 200–2) on the *Georgics*.

> *non omnis moriar multaque pars mei*
> *vitabit Libitinam; usque ego postera*
> *crescam laude recens, dum Capitolium*
> *scandet cum tacita virgine pontifex* (Hor. *Carm.* 3.30 6–9)

> I shall not entirely die and a great part of me shall escape
> Libitina; I shall grow ever renewed with praise, as long as
> the priest climbs the Capitol with the silent virgin[58]

The Horatian intertext is significant for its imperial and Roman concerns. The poet's immortality is tied to that of the priesthood of state religion, but the triumph of this self-styled *princeps* (3.30.13)[59] is undercut by the national anxieties of the preceding poem in which Maecenas is advised to stop worrying about the empire's frontiers because the gifts of Fortune do not last (25–52). *Odes* 3.29 contrasts honest poverty with the dangerous life of wealth and power and ends with the different fates of the overburdened ship and the little lifeboat in a storm. *Odes* 3.30 then begins with the eternal monument proof against the fury of wind and rain (1–4). The suggestion remains that the forces of change and decay do not end in Rome's eternal empire.[60]

As so often, Senecan tragedy amplifies the tensions of its Augustan predecessors.[61] Here Horace's guarantee of immortality, *dum Capitolium scandet cum tacita virgine pontifex*, finds its tragic echo as Polyxena, referred to by Calchas simply as a *virgo* (*Troades* 361) and a completely silent character,[62] climbs to her death on Achilles' tomb (1148–52). Of the singers echoing Horace, many will be lost in a storm at sea and all will be scattered like the pall of smoke that hangs, briefly, over the ruins of empire (1053–5). The chorus breaks the illusion of Fortune's drama to find security in extinction.[63]

At the tragedy's end, the messenger describes explicitly theatrical executions whose victims display a vital heroism that contrasts with the deathly existence of those doomed to survive.[64] The whole act is shot through with

---

[58] The silent virgin is the Vestal virgin, guardian of both the eternal flame and the Palladium brought from Troy.

[59] On "the displacement of motifs from poetry to politics" in this poem, see Lowrie (1997, 341).

[60] On the mutability of Rome, see Hardie (1992, 60–1) and Sen. *Ep.* 91.9–16.

[61] Putnam (1995) and cf. Hardie (1993, 75) on Vergil's epic successors.

[62] Polyxena speaks at her death in Seneca's models: see *Hec.* 546–52, 562–65 and Ovid *Met.* 13.457–73.

[63] *Spem ponant avidi, solliciti metum* (Let the greedy lay down their hopes, the anxious their fears, 399).

[64] Contrast the half-life of Andromache, *torpens malis, rigensque sine sensu* (without feeling, dazed and numbed by adversity, 417) or the impropriety of Hecuba surviving her people (1168–77) with the radiance of Polyxena (1137–46) or the heroism of Astyanax (1088–103).

theatrical language, none more direct than the description of the setting as "in the manner of a theatre" (*theatri more*, 1125).[65] The tragedy unites Greeks and Trojans: all weep for Astyanax (1098–100), all are moved by the spectacle of Polyxena meeting her death (1146).[66] For Florence Dupont, the uniformity of the audience makes a political point: Rome's imperial peace was preserved by the passivity of a people bound together in common subservience to the spectacle.[67] Astyanax and Polyxena walk clear eyed from the stage, but others remain its prisoner.

In this nexus of literary ghosts, bad dreams,[68] and moral falsehood, Seneca is preceded by Lucretius, the poet who so memorably described the hell humanity constructs for itself (3.978–1023) and who used the sacrifice of Iphigenia to call both religion and epic to account (1.80–135). After offering the sacrifice of Iphigenia as proof of religion's evil Lucretius warns:

> *Tutemet a nobis iam quovis tempore vatum*
> *terriloquis victus dictis desciscere quaeres.*
> *quippe etenim quam multa tibi iam fingere possunt*
> *somnia quae vitae rationes vertere possint* (1.102–5)

> You will yourself someday or other seek to fall away from me, overborne by the terrifying words of the priests. And indeed, how many dreams can they soon invent you, enough to upset the principles of your life.

Vatum ("priests/poets") looks back to Calchas, who demanded Iphigenia's death, and forward to Lucretius' next subject, Ennius, to whom Homer revealed the nature of reality in a dream. This revelation is a false *rerum natura*,[69] as deceitful and damaging as the visions that terrify the sick and the dreaming (1.132–5). From the physical error of Homeric epic, the belief that Acheron exists, comes fear, moral error, and the death of Iphigenia. The Trojan War is described in grand epic style as an example of something that did not exist in itself but was rather an accident of atoms (1.464–82). The "choice of the Trojan War ... seems to call into question the ethic of ambition and conquest embodied in the phrase *res gestae* (1.478).... The really important and lasting *res gestae* are those of the atoms and void."[70] The Trojan war is a great fiction – the greatest fiction – and a grand illusion.

---

[65] Boyle (1994, 224–32).
[66] On the embedded theater, see Mowbray (2012, 407–16).
[67] Dupont (1985, 419–20 and 456–62). The description of the inscribed audience as "plebeian" (*plebis* 1077) makes it anachronistically Roman.
[68] On dreams and literary fiction, see also Hor. *Ars* 6–9.
[69] On the "direct challenge" implicit in this phrase, see Gale (1994, 108).
[70] Gale (1994, 96).

Lucretius typically (though not invariably) influences tragic Seneca at one degree removed, via Vergil and lyric Horace.[71] If the *Aeneid* is a polemical reassertion of traditional epic (and Ennian) values, Lucretius is allusively present in it as an embedded and countervailing voice.[72] The memories of virginal slaughter that surround the sacrifice of Turnus at the problematic end of the *Aeneid* have their beginning in the tragic sacrifice of Iphigenia and the evils of false belief.[73] Lucretius made the killing of Iphigenia a paradigmatic case for Roman epic and empire to answer, and this Seneca inherits.[74]

The shedding of human blood is traumatic, but the sacrificial paradigm promises that it is not shed in vain, that there is renewal through the ritual act of violence. Renewal, however, is conspicuously denied in *Troades*, a play of inescapable repetition on Fortune's wheel. Andromache cannot see her son as anything but the image of Hector (461–8), encloses him in his father's tomb (508–12), and hears his body similarly ruined (1117). The *Aeneid* allowed its hero to leave Andromache and the shadows of Troy behind (*A.* 3.294–505). Hector's ghost promised a future beyond the fallen city (*A.* 2.268–97). *Troades* imitates the Vergilian dream of Hector's ghost (*Tro.* 438–60) only to deny its promise of renewal.[75] Like Lucretius, Seneca's Epicurean chorus invites the audience not to live with the dead and the dreaming. If the phantoms of Homer and Achilles show the power of insubstantial fables to shape reality, the disjointed structure of the tragedy, the fractures in the dramatic illusion, afford the audience/reader a means of resisting their influence.[76]

---

[71] See, e.g., Fitch (1987, 159–61) on *Her. F.* 125–204 and Tarrant (1985, 137–8) on *Thy.* 336–403.

[72] See, e.g., Hardie (1986, 213–29).

[73] Fowler (1987) and Hardie (1993, 27–8).

[74] See also Hardie (1995) and Segal (2001) on the redeployment of these same texts in Ovid, *Metamorphoses* 15.

[75] On the uncertain foundations of all proud empires, see the play's opening lines (1–6). On denial of closure in Senecan tragedy and its relationship with the *Aeneid*, see Putnam (1995, 277–8) and Schiesaro (2003, 65–9). For both critics, the boundlessness of tragic violence in Seneca unbalances the Vergilian tension between openness and closure.

[76] Marlowe's Faustus invokes the gods of Acheron, conjures Mephistophilis, and tells him, "I think hell's a fable" (*Doctor Faustus* II.i.130). The sentiment expressed and the damage done to the dramatic illusion are very similar to those of the second chorus of *Troades*. But for the other side of the coin – the will to play not to leave the stage – see Greenblatt (1980, 219), "Marlowe's heroes *must* live their lives as projects, but they do so in the midst of intimations that the projects are illusions."

Further Reading

For an introduction to the theories and history of theatricality see, for example, Davis and Postlewait (2003, especially 1–39 and 90–126). On metatheater, Abel (1963). On Senecan theatricality, Boyle (1997). On Nero, contrast Griffin's (1984) emperor, lost in fantasy by the end of his reign, with Champlin's (2003) more calculating performer of political theatre. On Nero's transformation into a tragic tyrant in the ps-Senecan *Octavia*, see Williams (1994) and Manuwald (2003). On the Romanness of Seneca's mythological worlds, see Tarrant (1995).

13

DAVID KONSTAN

Senecan Emotions

Seneca's writings constitute the fullest surviving evidence for the Stoic view of the emotions. Seneca was, however, a deep and original thinker, and it cannot be assumed that his accounts are always entirely in agreement with what the founders of the Stoic school, that is, Zeno and Chrysippus, or their later followers maintained; for this reason, I concentrate here on what we learn from Seneca himself, alluding to other Stoic writers only when they help to clarify Seneca's account. Writing under the early Roman Empire, where he held for a time positions of high importance, Seneca was naturally concerned with the passions of the powerful, above all the emperor (his treatise on clemency is addressed to Nero) but also members of the Roman nobility, who exercised enormous authority over their subordinates, not to mention their slaves, who were almost wholly at the mercy of their masters. Thus, unlike Aristotle, Cicero (in part), and Quintilian, for example, Seneca's concern with the emotions was not focused chiefly on oratory; he was interested in their effect on behavior and, more particularly, in the emotions appropriate to the sage. For, contrary to what is popularly supposed, the Stoic sage was not entirely emotionless but instead lacked certain kinds of passion (as we understand the term). An awareness of the distinction among types of feeling is crucial to understanding the views of Seneca and of the Stoics in general.

Though it may seem paradoxical, the best way to approach Seneca's conception of the emotions is by way of his discussion of sentiments that are not, strictly speaking, emotions at all. Near the beginning of the second book of his treatise *On Anger*, Seneca describes a set of responses that, he insists, are not emotions (*adfectus*) in the full sense of the term but rather "the initial preliminaries to emotions" (*principia proludentia adfectibus*, 2.2.6). These are defined as "motions that do not arise through our will" and are therefore irresistible and do not yield to reason (from Greek sources we learn that at least some Stoics applied the term *propatheia* to these movements). Seneca provides a lengthy and, at first blush, rather puzzling list of these proto-emotions, which include such responses as shivering or goose-pimples when one is sprinkled with cold water, aversion to certain kinds of touch (presumably slimy things and the like: the idea is that of disgust), the rising of one's hair at bad news, blushing at obscene language, vertigo produced by heights, responses to theatrical spectacles and narratives of historical events, songs and martial trumpeting, horrible paintings and the sight of punishments even when they are deserved, and contagious laughter and sadness – this last, he explains, is no more genuine grief that the frown evoked by seeing a shipwreck in a play, just as it is not real fear one feels when reading about the Roman disaster in the battle of Cannae.

Before we proceed to analyze this repertoire of reactions and attempt to see what they have in common, we may look at a passage in the first book of the same treatise, where Seneca distinguishes between human and animal responses in the following terms: "We must affirm that wild animals, and all creatures apart from human beings, are without anger; for since anger is contrary to reason, it does not arise except where reason has a place. Animals have violence, rabidity, ferocity, aggression, but do not have anger any more than they have licentiousness.... Dumb animals lack human emotions, but they do have certain impulses that are similar to emotions." Seneca goes on to observe that animals can utter sounds, but they do not have language; they perceive the outer shapes of things, by which they may be induced to attack, but these perceptions are muddy and confused: "thus, their onrushes and outbreaks are violent, but they do not have fears and worries, sadness and anger, but rather things that are similar to these" (*On Anger* 1.3.4–8; in the *Consolation to Marcia* 5.1, Seneca remarks that animals do not experience sadness and fear any more than stones do). In this passage, Seneca does not mention "preliminaries to emotions," presumably because in the case of animals, there is no further stage; but the connection between the two would seem to be clear. For example, immediately after he mentions the preliminaries to emotion, Seneca notes that "the ears of a soldier prick up at the sound of a trumpet, even when peace reigns and he is wearing the toga, and the noise of arms rouses army horses" (2.2.6). Animals, then, experience some proto-emotions, including no doubt such responses as shivering when doused with cold water, although other reactions that Seneca includes under this rubric cannot be attributed to them, for example, hair bristling upon hearing bad news or blushing at obscene language, since, as Seneca makes clear, animals lack language altogether. Because they do not have speech, which is equivalent, for the Stoics and ancient thinkers generally, to the absence of reason (recall that the Greek word *logos* means both "language" and "reason"), animals do not have true emotions; human beings, however, are susceptible to the kinds of affects that animals experience, such as instinctive aggression or other prerational impulses, but because they possess language, they are vulnerable even at this level to a wider range of responses, since even an account of war (which animals could not comprehend) can rouse a kind of proto-fear or martial spirit, and obscenity too can stimulate a type of proto-embarrassment to which animals are as immune as they are to the genuine and strictly human emotion of shame.[1] Darwin (1899, 354) wrote that "Blushing is the most peculiar and the most human of all expressions," and Mark Twain (1898, 159) quipped, "Man is the only animal that blushes. Or needs to."[2]

According to Seneca, then, if they are not to be mere impulses, emotions require reason and, correspondingly, a capacity for language, but a stimulus conveyed by means of language, as opposed to by direct perception, is not enough to qualify a response as emotional. An emotion is a voluntary reaction and differs from those that are not subject to our will (*voluntas*) and are, consequently, "invincible and inevitable" (*inuicti et ineuitabiles*, 2.2.1). An emotion requires willing assent. We can see how this works in connection with Seneca's treatment of anger, the emotion he analyzed at greatest length: "There is no doubt but that what arouses anger is the impression [*species*] that is presented of an injury [*iniuria*]" (2.1.3). This is in accord with Aristotle's view of anger as "a desire, accompanied by pain, for a perceived revenge, on account of a perceived slight [*oligôria*] on the part of people who are not fit to slight one or one's own" (*Rhetoric* 2.2, 1378a31–3), since the Latin word *iniuria* can mean an insult (cf. 1.3.3: "Aristotle's definition is not far from ours"); but it also conveys the sense of an unjust offense, and in this respect Seneca's definition conforms to Chrysippus' characterization of anger as "the desire to take vengeance against one who is believed to have committed a wrong contrary to one's deserts" (*SVF* 3.395 = Stobaeus 2.91.10; cf. Diogenes Laertius 7.113; also Posidonius fr. 155 Edelstein-Kidd = Lactantius *On the Anger of God* 17.13); indeed, Aristotle himself had already asserted that "anger resides in a perceived injustice [*adikia*]" (*Nicomachean Ethics* 5.8, 1135b25–9).

Now whether we speak of an insult or of a wrong "contrary to one's deserts," it is clear that anger, on both descriptions, requires a degree of judgment that already involves reason: animals are presumably not sensitive to slights, nor do they have beliefs about whether the ill treatment they may suffer is deserved or not. More generally, if animals attack furiously, it is not

[1] On shame and its problematic status as an emotion in Stoic thought, see Wray (this volume).

[2] In Mark Twain's book, *Following the Equator: A Journey around the World*, chapter headnotes are listed as taken from "Pudd'nhead Wilson's New Calendar" (of course, Twain made this up); the one on blushing is the headnote to part 3, chapter 27.

out of a desire for revenge but out of hunger or self-defense or some other instinctive motivation. For the Stoics, this factor of judgment takes the form not just of recognizing the nature of the wrong but of assenting to the proposition that it is a wrong. As Seneca states, "we are investigating whether anger follows immediately upon the impression itself and runs over without the mind agreeing, or is stimulated when the mind assents" (*De ira* 2.1.3).

Seneca immediately adds:

> We maintain that anger does not venture anything on its own but only when the mind approves; for to accept the impression of an injury that has been sustained and desire vengeance for it – and to unite the two judgments, that one ought not to have been harmed and that one ought to be avenged – this is not characteristic of an impulse [*impetus*] that is aroused without our will [*voluntas*]. For the latter kind is simple, but the former is composite and contains several elements: one has discerned something, grown indignant, condemned it, and takes revenge: these things cannot occur unless the mind consents to those things by which it was affected (2.1.4).

Seneca provides a more detailed summary of the three stages by which an emotion develops at 2.4.1–2, beginning with an involuntary motion that is like a "preparation for emotion" [*praeparatio adfectus*], then a willed but still not willful judgment, for instance that the person who harmed me should pay the penalty, and finally the moment when the passion vanquishes reason utterly.

We see, then, that an emotion for Seneca is a complex thing: one must be able to recognize the nature of the stimulus – an injury in the case of anger – and judge its merits, and both these processes involve voluntary mental acts, not merely instinctive reflexes, whether of the body or the mind. Now, we may wonder why Seneca and the Stoics go beyond Aristotle's recognition that the emotions involve judgments and hence are cognitive processes and insist on the voluntary nature of the mental act. Seneca himself poses the question – "Where, you say, is this question heading" – and he provides the answer: "that we may know what anger is; for if it arises in us without our willing it [*invitis*], it will never submit to reason" (*De ira* 2.2.1). Here is the crucial point: the passions must be amenable to reason, or else they are beyond our control. No one expects an animal to act contrary to its impulses, but in the case of emotions – not the initial preliminaries to emotions, but genuine human emotions – reason must be able to prevail. As Seneca says, "anger is put to flight by teachings [*praecepta*], for it is a voluntary vice [*vitium*] of the mind, and not among those things that are a consequence of some condition of our human lot, and which, for this reason, befall even the wisest; it is in this class that we must place that initial jolt to the mind that stirs us upon the mere opinion of an injury" (2.2.2).

The opinion alone is not enough: we must assent to it, for if this were not the case, we would not be in a position to withhold our assent and hence would be at the mercy of our passions.

One might have supposed that anger was an acceptable emotion, provided that it was controlled by or responsive to reason, but this is not in fact the Stoic view, nor is it Seneca's. Aristotle favored emotions in due measure, that is, proportional to the nature of the eliciting cause (an insult or unjust treatment in the case of anger, for example), and this doctrine was later referred to as *metropatheia*, from the Greek for measure (cf. English "meter") and *pathos*, the usual Greek term for emotion, though it also had the wider sense of anything suffered or experienced (for example, disease or misfortune; for Seneca's criticism of Aristotle on this score, cf. 1.17.1–2). The Stoics, however, sought to eliminate the *pathê* (plural of *pathos*) entirely, and hence they adopted the notion of *apatheia* or "lack of *pathos*" as their ideal. Thus, as we have seen, Seneca defines anger as "a voluntary vice of the mind," and the function of reason and instruction is to do away with the vice, not to moderate it. This view has given rise to the belief that the Stoics sought to eradicate all emotion, but, as we shall see, this is not the whole story. In any case, anger held a special place among the recognized emotions for its violence and intractability. Seneca affirms at the very beginning of his treatise that of all the passions, anger is the most vile and frenzied (*taetrum ac rabidum*, 1.1.1). Other emotions, he says, have some element of calmness in them – Seneca is doubtless thinking of sentiments such as pity, shame, and gratitude, though envy would rival anger for irrational ferocity – but anger, he says, is altogether impetuous, to the point that those who are angry will neglect their own interests provided that they can harm the other. This is why anger has been called a brief spell of madness (*breuem insaniam*, 3.1.2), for it is immune to reason and advice (*rationi consiliisque praeclusa*) and is provoked by groundless motives (*uanis agitata causis*, 3.1.2). It is the greatest plague, Seneca goes on to declare, and has caused the ruin of cities and whole peoples (Seneca gives some chilling examples of how anger inspires inhuman cruelty, for example, the story of Piso at 1.18.3–6). What is more, it is a useless passion, whether in war or to avenge even the worst kind of harm, such as the murder of one's own father. Of course, one will demand justice on behalf of dear ones and protect them (*uindicabit, tuebitur*, 1.12.2); but for this, reverence (*pietas*) is sufficient motive, Seneca avers, and does not require encouragement from anger (1.12.1).

Reason works to expel anger not merely by showing that it is unprofitable or tends to extremes but also by demonstrating that the ostensible motives for anger are baseless. For one thing, none of us is without blame (*neminem nostrum esse sine culpa*, 2.28.1), and we never fully know the motives of others; thus, we are in a poor position to judge what counts as an *iniuria*. This and other advice on how to avoid or assuage anger is addressed to people who aspire to be good but who are not Stoic sages (cf. *On tranquility of the soul* 11.1: "this speech of mine pertains to imperfect, middling, and unhealthy people, not to the sage"). For sages are unsusceptible to anger, since the only way to harm them is to deprive them of their virtue, which is, for Stoics, the only good; but the virtue of sages is unassailable (cf. *Epistle to Lucilius* 85; *On the constancy of the wise man* 5.5). Seneca invites all people to regard life this way when he observes that the cause of insane anger is that people take trivial matters to be of great importance (*exigua magno aestimatis*, 3.34.2).

When Seneca lists among the preliminaries to emotions not just dizziness caused by heights, contagious laughter, and the thrill a soldier experiences at the sound of military trumpets but also the response to seeing punishments "even when deserved," he is implicitly alluding to the common view, adopted by Aristotle as well as by the Stoics, that the pity is elicited by unmerited misfortune, not by suffering as such. The indiscriminate reaction to the sight of punishment is instinctive and hence a preliminary to emotion (this automatic response perhaps corresponds to what Aristotle, in the *Poetics*, labels "philanthropic"). As Aristotle and Cicero observe, we do not pity the convicted murderer who is being led out of the courtroom to suffer the penalty; pity is predicated on a moral judgment, and this is part of what constitutes it as an emotion proper. Although pity today is in bad odor, since it seems to imply condescension toward the wretched, it was universally listed among classical Greek and Roman inventories of the emotions. For a Stoic, however, this is just the problem: for however noble or justified pity may seem, certainly in comparison with anger, as an emotion, it too must be eliminated. But just as relinquishing anger and the desire for vengeance does not mean that one must tolerate offenses passively, for one will still defend oneself and exact punishment, albeit dispassionately and in the interest of justice, so too remaining unmoved by pity – in many respects, anger's opposite – does not mean that one must neglect the unfortunate or those who sue for mercy; for here too it is possible to respond out of a settled disposition of kindliness or benevolence, without the extra impulse of passion by which we are inevitably carried away (according to the Stoics) and so, despite Aristotle's confidence in an emotional golden mean, invariably exceed due measure. Seneca investigates the dispassionate disposition corresponding to pity in his treatise (partially preserved) *On Clemency*.

In the fragmentary second book of this essay (*De clem.* 2.3), Seneca offers several definitions of *clementia* in order to capture the sense of this complex idea. He begins by defining *clementia* as "mental self-control in one who has the power to exact revenge" (*temperantia animi in potestate ulciscendi*) and then adds the alternative description, "or mildness on the part of a superior toward an inferior in determining punishment" (*lenitas superioris adversus inferiorem in constituendis poenis*). Seneca then adds further qualifications, since a single formula may not fully capture the notion, and he states that *clementia* may also be described as "a tendency of the mind toward mildness in exacting punishment" (*inclinatio animi ad lenitatem in poena exigenda*). Seneca is at pains to show that clemency is an acceptable attitude for Stoics, whereas pity (*misericordia*) is, like anger, a vice, precisely insofar as it is an emotion. Thus, he writes: "it is relevant to investigate here what pity is, for many people praise it as a virtue and call a good person one who can feel pity [*misericors*]; and yet," Seneca hastens to add, "it is a vice of the mind" (2.4.4). He likens the difference between clemency or mildness and pity to that between religion and superstition and affirms that good men will avoid the latter as "the vice of a petty mind that collapses at the sight of the misfortunes of others," typical of old women who weep at the fate even of the most guilty. As he puts it, "pity looks to the condition, not the reason, whereas clemency assents to reason" (2.5.1). Seneca is aware that those with little knowledge of Stoicism see their posture as excessively harsh and unforgiving, making no allowance for human error (2.5.2). But this attitude rests on a misperception, and Stoicism is in fact the kindest of philosophies. For pity is a "disturbance of the mind [*aegritudo animi*]" resulting from the misery of others, whereas the mind of the sage is always serene and never subject to perturbation or grief, whether for the sufferings of others or his own (2.5.4–5). The sage never pities (*miseretur*) because pity is necessarily accompanied by misery (*miseria*) of the mind (2.6.1). It does not require pity to come to the aid of those in trouble: the sage performs all that is needed, but with a tranquil spirit: he does not pity, he helps (2.6.3). For the same reason, the sage does not pardon, which constitutes a remission of the just penalty, whereas clemency, though it may overlook offences, respects justice (2.7.3–4).

Scholars have brooded over the distinction that Seneca draws between pity and clemency, accusing him of attempting to wriggle out of the rigorous Stoic condemnation of pity (and all ordinary emotions) by substituting another term in its place. However, Seneca is right that clemency is not an emotion but a settled disposition: a good person acts out of kindness and not because she or he is struck by the impression of suffering in another. One judges calmly the misfortunes of others and comes to their aid because they deserve it; it is not necessary to be distraught in order to behave generously toward one who is worse off than oneself. The idea of clemency had, of course, a specific history in Rome, going back to Julius Caesar's calculated leniency toward his conquered enemies, and it came to be regarded as one of the primary virtues of emperors. We recall that Seneca addressed his essay on clemency precisely to Nero, to whom he had served as tutor. Clemency is thus especially associated with restraint on the part of the powerful in regard to punishment or revenge for offenses against oneself; as an antidote to acting out of anger (or some other base motive), it is better than pity, which, like all emotions, is whimsical and arbitrary.[3]

The concern to maintain a serene state of mind in all one's behavior also motivates Seneca's attitude toward fear. In his *Natural Questions* (*Quaestiones naturales*), Seneca pauses to consider fear in connection with the topic of earthquakes. He writes, "I had promised solace in respect to unusual dangers," and he proceeds to affirm that, since nothing that can perish is eternally at rest, "the fear of the foolish is without remedy, whereas reason expels terror from the wise" (*NQ* 6.2.1). "There is no greater consolation for death than mortality itself" (6.2.6): there is no sense in fearing thunder and lightning or the tremors of the earth when death is everywhere at hand. We must die somewhere, sometime (6.2.7). If death is met with equanimity, then fear is altogether banished (cf. *On tranquility of the soul* 11: "One who fears death will never do anything worthy of a living person"; also *Letter to Lucilius* 4.3–9).

One might have supposed that grief for dear ones we have lost would likewise be regarded as vice, like other emotions, but in fact this is not entirely the case. In the consolatory letter he wrote to his mother, Helvia, in order to assuage her sorrow over Seneca's exile, he explains that he hesitated to write sooner, since he knew that solace for pain that is still fresh may inflame the wound rather than alleviate it, and so he waited till it diminished in intensity and could bear the cure (*Cons. ad Helv.* 1.2). He is also worried about whether he is up to writing effectively and remarks that "every degree of anguish [*dolor*] that exceeds the mean [*modum*] necessarily undoes our choice of words" (1.3). There is the suggestion, then, that grief is not wholly to be repressed but must run its course, and that, like Aristotelian virtues but unlike Stoic emotions, it has a proper midpoint or norm. The fact that Helvia is a woman, Seneca avers, is no excuse for endless weeping; the ancestors stipulated a ten-month period of mourning for husbands, thus limiting rather than prohibiting grief (*luctus*): "for when you have lost one of your dearest, it is foolish indulgence to feel infinite pain [*dolor*], but to feel none is inhuman harshness. Best is a due proportion between regard

---

[3] Schofield (this volume) situates Seneca's essay on clemency in the tradition of treatises on kingship.

[*pietas*] and reason, both to feel the loss and to control it" (16.1). So too, in his *Consolation to Marcia* for the loss of her son, he complains that all the efforts of her friends have been in vain, and even time, which is nature's remedy for grief, has wasted its forces on her (1.6). For three years she has mourned without the least remission in intensity; like all vices that are not controlled, misery feeds on its own bitterness and the pain becomes a kind of perverse pleasure (*prava voluptas*, 1.7). The genre of the consolation is practical and is not given to precise philosophical analysis, and so one ought not to expect a strict Stoic definition of grief; in addition, the Latin word *dolor* is ambiguous between pain and sorrow or distress, and it is not always possible to catch the exact nuance of the term in a given passage. Pain surely is a sensation, not an emotion, whereas anguish at the loss of a dear one is more like a feeling. But does it require assent, or is it more like an initial preliminary to emotion, something that would affect even the sage, like the automatic response to witnessing the suffering of another? Seneca seems to regard grief as inevitable when the loss is recent, and only when it is prolonged and becomes a fixed state of melancholy does he regard it as excessive and even perverse. Perhaps it is only after a period of time has elapsed that one can speak of assenting to grief, and at this point it assumes the character of an emotion that ought to be eradicated (on grief, see also *Letter to Lucilius* 63).

As a Stoic, Seneca was committed to maintaining that the ordinary emotions were irrational and that the task of reason was not to moderate but to extirpate them; as he puts it, "That famous mean is false and useless, to be placed in the same class as someone saying that one should be moderately insane or moderately ill" (*Epistle to Lucilius* 85.9). It is clear too that he personally, and in his capacity as a political actor and thinker, harbored a deep suspicion of such passions as anger, pity, and fear, which took the form of powerful mental perturbations and rendered impossible the calm judgment that could only come from a mind that was serene and tranquil. Seneca illustrated the effects of inordinate passion in his tragedies, exhibiting in the *Thyestes* the extremes to which Atreus was driven by his lust for revenge against his brother (he kills his children and feeds their flesh to him) and the violence to which Medea was impelled out of anger at her husband Jason's betrayal. These concerns determined Seneca's choices and emphases in his treatment of the emotions. From other Stoic sources, we learn things about the emotions that Seneca fails to mention. For example, the Stoics classified or subsumed all emotions under four broad categories: pleasure, pain, desire, and fear; the first pair is present oriented (positively and negatively), whereas the second pair looks to the future. Every specific emotion was an inflection of one of these generic classes, involving assent to some particular judgment; thus anger was defined as a wish for revenge inspired by the impression of an injury (one must judge voluntarily that it is an injury) and so falls under the rubric of desire. What is more, the Stoics also described a set of good sentiments or *eupatheiai*, which were characteristic of the sage (the term seems to be a neologism of the same sort as *propatheiai* or proto-emotions). They argued that these came in only three kinds, corresponding to pleasure, desire, and fear (they labeled the positive counterparts to these, respectively, joy or good cheer, willing, and caution); there was no analogue, however, to pain, presumably because the sage was not distressed by anything in the present world, though he or she might take steps to avoid an unpleasant event in the future (on good sentiments and their relation to ordinary emotions, see Cicero *Tusculan Disputations* 4.11–14).

There has been considerable debate over whether these good sentiments are to be regarded as emotions at all: some maintain that they are wholly dispassionate states of mind, whereas others, looking among other things to the root *path-* in the coinage *eupatheia*, argue that they are indeed emotions but of the sort that are subject to reason, and in this respect they differ from ordinary *pathê*, which invariably are carried to excess, like headlong runners (according to the Stoic image) who overshoot the mark. Whichever view is correct (and since this chapter is on Seneca, it is not necessary to arrive at a final conclusion on the matter here), it appears that the popular image of the Stoic sage as cold and impassive is in need of modification. Seneca too gives evidence that the sage is in a state of good cheer with regard to the present, entertains wishes (as opposed to desires) – for example, for the well-being of others – and takes care with respect to things still to come. It is not clear, however, whether the reasonable wish that those who have committed an injustice be punished (though not in anger) or the application of clemency as opposed to the passion represented by pity are to be classified as suitable kinds of emotion (that is, equivalent to *eupatheiai*) or are simply forms of rational behavior. Seneca does allow, in connection with love, that one should indulge in the nobler emotions (*indulgendum est enim honestis adfectibus*, Ep. 104.3), and if he is not speaking loosely here, he may be thinking of the *eupatheiai*. But it would appear that Seneca was not concerned to insist on the emotional character of the sage's responses to external impressions, which would in any case have been invariably in accord with reason and never overstepping its dictates. The chief object of Seneca's teaching was to help people rid themselves of passions that were destructive of their own peace of mind and of social ties in general. To this end, he applied his brilliant skills at persuasion and showed by a wealth of examples and arguments that the emotions, once they took hold of one, were impossible to rein in and that the only remedy was to cut them off at the start by not assenting to the judgments that triggered them and recognizing their dreadful consequences.

Further Reading

The best book on the Stoic view of the emotions is Margaret Graver, *Stoicism and Emotion* (2007). There is a good discussion of Latin Stoic writers on the emotions in Gretchen Reydams-Schils, *The Roman Stoics: Self, Responsibility, and Affection* (2005). For Seneca's contributions to Stoic thought, see Brad Inwood, *Reading Seneca: Stoic Philosophy at Rome* (2005). Tad Brennan, *The Stoic Life: Emotions, Duties, and Fate* (2005) provides an excellent introduction to Stoic conceptions. Martha C. Nussbaum, *The Therapy of Desire: Theory and Practice in Hellenistic Ethics* (1994), offers an elegant and sympathetic treatment of Senecan Stoicism (see esp. chapters 10–12). Richard Sorabji, *Emotion and Peace of Mind: From Stoic Agitation to Christian Temptation* (2000), traces the development and influence of Stoic ideas on emotion and *apatheia*. Juha Sihvola and Troels Engberg-Pedersen's *The Emotions in Hellenistic Philosophy* (1998) collects some excellent essays with an emphasis on the Stoic tradition. Susanna Braund's commentary on Seneca's *De clementia* (2009), is indispensable for those who can read Latin. Simo Knuuttila, *Emotions in Ancient and Medieval Philosophy* (2004), gives an overview of thought about emotion over antiquity and the Middle Ages.

PART III
Senecan Tensions

14

SHADI BARTSCH

Senecan Selves*

Senecan Selves

What Seneca may have thought about the true nature of his self – the elements and agencies it controlled, the respective influences of family, lineage, and social forces, the shaping it owed to chance versus the extent it was up to him to control (*eph'hemin*) – this we will never be able to accurately reconstruct. However, there is no doubt that in the course of his lifetime he put on at least two contradictory performances to show who he was to two very different audiences. One Seneca was on display for the imperial court, in particular for his erstwhile student and eventual emperor, Nero, and also, in earlier days, for Caligula, Claudius, Agrippina, and others. The other Senecan "self" was for an audience of readers whom he cultivated throughout his writings, but especially with his works of the early 60s CE: that is, the readers of his *Epistles*, and their readers in posterity: us. Seneca's self-understanding in the *Epistles* (and, to a lesser degree, the other prose works) is there staged for us to see, preserved in his own words as he discusses the path of self-formation for the aspiring Stoic and offers up his own successes and failures in this regard. The probably fictitious correspondence with Lucilius[1] both articulates and represents its protagonist *carrying out* (much more so than the writings of his fellow Stoic Epictetus), an elaborate program for the sustained production of the ideal Stoic self as his life goal.[2] Unlike the dialogues, which are devoted to single topics, the letters cut across the entirety of a life, and the main actor in this program is Seneca himself, while his correspondent Lucilius and other addressees enter the picture to play their parts as students and interlocutors, to be exhorted and

---

* I thank Matthew Roller for his helpful comments on this essay.

[1] Cf. Griffin (1992, 416–19), Schafer (2011), Mazzoli (1989, 1846–55).
[2] See, for example, Edwards (1997); Foucault (1986, 37–68); Long (1991, 2009); Nussbaum (1994, 316–58).

encouraged in their progress toward this fully Stoic self or to hear Seneca's Stoic teachings on the nature of this self they are trying to reach.

In articulating "the fully Stoic self" as Seneca's self-professed endpoint in life, this corpus sets up a goal so sweeping and so exclusive of the normal business of Roman life and politics that it completely trumps other experiences once considered more traditionally constitutive of selfhood (e.g., at Cic. *De Off.* 1): *this* role was the one Seneca wanted to pass on to posterity more than any other, and he elides in these texts the life he lived at court, his life as a husband, and other roles he might have played. Seneca reminds us that any human can work toward the Stoic ideal and that that perfection, if ever attained, would not rest on a narrative of actions but on mental self-possession. But of course, a perfected Stoic Seneca is no more visible in these letters than is Seneca the scheming politician; this exists merely as a goal, a fantasy of self-sufficient and emotionally impervious perfection. When Seneca writes about it, he acknowledges that he has not reached this endpoint and that he is only a striver along that path (a *proficiens*), as are his fellow Stoics, those he knows and has heard tell of; the true Stoic sage is a rare man and may never have existed. It is the *pursuit* of the ideal that is portrayed in the *Epistles* as the full-time occupation of the actual Senecan self, so that Seneca's daily thoughts and actions in this direction, his rational deliberations, his awareness of error are what constitute his selfhood. We see an intellectual agent engaged in a constant struggle for self-amelioration; a self that practices a series of exercises, meditations, and second-order self-examinations in a constant and unabated effort toward a perfect serenity that we never see it gaining in any permanent way – even if Seneca speaks of individual wise decisions or knows theoretically what must be done. Not in a single letter does Seneca stand on the past heap of his personal history to announce, "Mission re self: accomplished."

The distinction between what we may call the proficient self and the ideal self[3] has been a major part of discourse on Stoic notions of selfhood since Michel Foucault reintroduced Seneca's philosophical struggles into the limelight in his work on the "care of the self." We owe it to Foucault's attention to practices of self-shaping and self-regulation in the ancient world (esp. Foucault 1986, 1988) that our once tarnished philosopher has emerged as

---

[3] The terminology of Stoic self-transformation has yet to be stabilized. Different writers have referred, for example, to the proficient self vs. the ideal self (as I have put it here), the occurrent self vs. the normative self (as Long, 2009, and Ker, 2009c, prefer), the actual self vs. the natural self (i.e., the rational self in accordance with nature, Gill, 2006) and the "mediated" self (Reydams-Schils, 2005), a different model in which this self "mediates" between the person's role in Roman society and the call of philosophical principles.

an object of serious study and not merely a flawed epigone. As Foucault's approach, along with the pioneering work of A.A. Long, Paul Veyne, and Pierre Hadot, has made abundantly clear, if for the Greeks "Know thyself" was an imperative that reminded us to know our limits and not to overreach (like, say, an Oedipus), for the Roman Stoics it was something significantly different, a project that addressed itself to the correct living of life as well as the articulation of theory and above all a project of coming to "know" the self that involved transformation as well as mere observation. As Foucault remarked, "What stands out in the texts of the first centuries ... is the insistence on the attention that should be brought to bear on oneself ... an intensification of the relation to oneself by which one constituted oneself as the object of one's acts," (1986, 41) the result of which would be self-correction and ever greater proximity to the rational life of the mind (cf. also Hadot 1995, 81–125).

This "intensification of the relationship to oneself" in Roman Stoicism, as subsequent scholars have elaborated, involved not so much practices of attention to the physical self and its care as a series of exercises, practices, and reflexive grammatical usages that focused upon the goal of aligning all one's judgments and choices with a purely rational perspective upon life. These complex acts of self-shaping that must go into the correction of the self are laid out (and described in practice) by Seneca himself: the *meditatio*,[4] the nocturnal self-review totting up the good and bad deeds of the day (cf. *De ira* 3.36; Ker 2009c), the repetitive anticipation of worst possible scenarios (*praemeditatio malorum*, cf. *Ep.* 30.18, 70.18, 114.27), the imaginary spectatorship of oneself by heroic figures, friends, or the divine principle itself ("God is near you, he is with you, he is within you," *Ep.* 41.2; cf. *Ep.* 92.30–1);[5] keeping notes and records of one's actions (*hypomnemata*, cf. Foucault 1997), internal dialogue and second-order queries about one's choices and desires (Inwood 2009b) – all marked by the unusual use of reflexive pronouns and quasi-paradoxical statements such as "*vindica te tibi,*" free yourself for yourself.[6] Poverty, humiliation, loss of life: as Seneca puts it in *De ira* 2.12.3, "There's nothing so difficult and demanding but that the human mind cannot overcome it and constant *meditatio* make it familiar." Diligent attention, he points out, can make even the curved beam straight again, and how much more pliable is the soul (*Ep.* 50.6)! All of this

---

[4] A reflection upon real and deceptive values in life, cf. Hadot (1969), Newman (1989), Armisen-Marchetti (2008).

[5] On self-spectatorship, Roller (2001, 82–8), Bartsch (2006, 183–215); on the divinity within, Russell (2004, 50ff).

[6] On reflexive forms, see esp. Traina (1987, 11–20, 52–66); on the slave metaphor, Edwards (2009).

was to lead to a state in which the ruling part of the soul (the *hegemonikon*) would consistently and naturally make the distinction between indifferents and what pertained to true wisdom; it was also to lead, as Seneca's writing makes so clear, to the cultivation of physical or emotional analgesia in the face of suffering. The goal was to privilege a philosophically informed perspective of the insignificance of societally driven values and mores in the face of more universal truths and in the path to wisdom and its correlative, happiness.[7]

Seneca uses the anecdotes and lessons of his prose writings to show us the proficient self (including his own) falling prey to bad judgments about the world around it. But he also shows us that because this self is open to and able to be influenced by self-command, *meditatio*, rational discourse, self-review, and other practices, it can eventually come to look more and more like the ideal self, the sage whose propositional judgments about the world are all consonant with the values of Stoic philosophy and are such as to never provoke passions or even internal conflict. Some features of this idealized sage emerge clearly from his writing: it would be a self in which the *hegemonikon* would rule over all the body's sensations, desires, appetites, and perceptions.[8] In as much as this rational principle shared the divine quality of the natural logos of the universe itself, it represented what was best about the human being and also his or her sole path to a happiness independent of the incidentals that come with life itself: health or sickness, wealth or poverty, good luck or bad, love or loneliness. In addition, Seneca suggests, attainment of the internal rule of rationality brought one close to god; sometimes he even offers the possibility of a rejoining with the divine.[9]

We must be clear that this mirroring attention to self is not in conflict with the orthodox Stoic notion of the unified self. Stoic theorizing on the unity of the self is in philosophical riposte to the Platonic view of the self as tripartite; it is also opposed to any form of psychological dualism positing that the rational mind and the emotions were two separate parts of the human soul. The Stoics held that the emotions were based on judgments – albeit bad ones – rather than constituting a physically different part of a multipartite self, and there is no reason to believe Seneca innovated in this regard.[10]

---

[7] The Pythagoreans and the Stoics likewise recommended that a few moments be set aside in the morning and evening for this self-examination, although we find Epictetus zealously recommending questioning one's judgment at all times of day (*Disc.* 3.10.1–5).

[8] For the *hegemonikon* as closest to our term "self," see Reydams-Schils (2005, 16–52); for a view of selfhood that privileges the irrational, see Schiesaro (2009).

[9] See for example *Ep.* 79.12; and cf. Russell (2004, 50ff).

[10] Supported by Inwood (2005); see also Gill (2009), with comments on *oikeiosis*, a process leading to interpersonal and internal order.

When we speak of the self-address of the self, then, we need not take these voices as representing psychological dualism of any form. As James Ker (2009c, 182) remarks, "the difference between the normative and occurrent selves is not an ontological division, but a discursive and practical division, one made for example along the axis of time of the pedagogical path toward perfection, or between the aspects of the self that are revealed through different methods of examination." However, it is true that if finally successful, these practices of self-review and self-rebuke would lead to the cessation of any need for inner dialogue; the sage would have complete control over his disposition toward the world around him and act in a naturally correct way. What is not so clear is the degree to which ideal Stoic sages would still retain recognizable and characteristic forms of individuality or "liberate oneself from one's individuality" (Hadot 1995, 210); whether Foucault's picture focuses too much on self-shaping as an artistic choice rather than a rule-bound product of clear rational imperatives (Nussbaum 1994; Harris 2001); whether the internalization of the idea of a judging viewer represents a continuation of or a break from features of the Roman culture of exemplarity and peer review (Roller 2001, 77–88; Bartsch 2006, 117–51). We can at least say that Foucault's emphasis on the institutional context of this activity, which constituted "a true social practice" (1986, 51), may be misplaced given the disregard for community evident in the letters (less so in the other prose works that preceded them).

What does the internal dialogue of the proficient Stoic look like? Seneca sometimes shows himself in imaginary conversation with an idealized interlocutor, for example a Cato, Laelius, Scipio, or a philosophical voice; at other times he takes on a voice consistent with that of the Stoic philosopher he is, rebuking others for their failings or uncertainties, reminding them that power and wealth are mistakenly valued by the contemporary Roman elite. And as the choice of interlocutors and "sides" within the self change, so too the context of this relationship is variously figured; Seneca now takes his metaphors from juridical procedures (*Ep.* 26.5, 28.10, etc.; now from accounting, now from other hierarchical interactions.[11] As Catharine Edwards (2009) points out, he will also use terminology taken from the institution of slavery in a reflexive way, so that the selves in discourse take on the roles of slave and master: the *Epistles* open with the startling phrase, "*vindica te tibi*," free yourself for yourself. And of course, as far as the *Epistles* are concerned, their genre ensures that there will always be an interlocutor for what Seneca has to say: Lucilius himself, more often than anyone else, is

---

[11] Foucault (1988;) Ker (2009c); Traina (1974).

the person whose questions and objections Seneca imagines as he urges his friend to virtue.

Metaphors of the Self

Seneca's writings offer a pedagogical route to the ideal self that not only shows us a proficient self engaging in exhortation but also uses metaphors to characterize both the shaping of the self and the ideal Stoic self (who has no need of further self-shaping or self-rebuke).[12] Seneca also turns to metaphor when he wishes to describe the relationship of the ruling rational principle to the physical body, and here he is not afraid to abuse in his figural language the orthodox Stoic claim that soul and body are in fact coextensive and that the divine *pneuma* that makes up the rational principle is in principle evenly spread out through the body.[13] Like his fellow Stoics Epictetus and Marcus Aurelius, Seneca turns to metaphors in which the secondary importance, even complete lack of importance and expendability, of the physical body is emphasized. Indeed, Seneca is consistently negative on the topic of human flesh. The body is at best the mere clothing of the soul, or an earthenware vessel (*vas*); worse, it is seen as decaying and decrepit dwelling (e.g., *Ep.* 65.17, 70.16–17, 58.35, etc.). It is a chain around our mental freedom (*Ep.* 65.21; *Ad Marc.* 24.5) and altogether unworthy of the mind (*Ep.* 120.14). In a philosophy that preaches that human pain and suffering are "indifferents" (even if nonpreferred indifferents), the body can have no other status, a fact that occasionally afforded mirth to other schools of thought when contemplating the Stoic philosopher being happy even on the rack.

Another common Senecan metaphor for the formation of the self is that of a potter or sculptor shaping clay or marble.[14] Shaping the self is a laborious process, he concedes, and yet we must begin to do so before its wickedness hardens it beyond molding (*Ep.* 50.5–6). Because Stoic orthodoxy held it that the soul was made up of a physical substance, *pneuma*, Senecan expressions such as *animos transfigurari* (*Ep.* 94.48), *se transfigurari* (*Ep.* 6.1), *se fingere* (*Ep.* 18.12), and *animum formare* (*Ep.* 50.5) can work simultaneously on the literal and metaphorical levels, on the one hand referring to the reshaping of the soul's *pneuma*, on the other pointing to the analogy between the man who works on perfecting himself and the sculptor who works on perfecting his statue. The outcome will be a soul that is

[12] Further on Seneca's use of metaphor, see Armisen-Marchetti in this volume.
[13] On such disjunctions, see Inwood (2005, 31–8).
[14] For example, *Ep.* 6.1; *Ep.* 25.5; *Ep.* 31.11; see Armisen-Marchetti (1989, s.vv); Bartsch (2009).

godlike – though not crafted in gold or silver, for the image of god cannot be expressed in this material (*Ep.* 31.11). In this use of artisanal metaphors, Seneca is innovating, even within the Stoic tradition. In Cicero, the sculptor Phidias is a metaphor for the orator-statesman who shapes the best *speech* (*Brutus* 228, *Orator* 8, *Or.* 235); in Seneca, we have the artisan of the soul instead, so that Cicero's analogy is transferred from the realm of civic activity to the self-shaping of the private philosopher. If the body is downplayed in Senecan Stoicism, so too (speaking again of the *Epistles* in particular) is the value of civil society and political participation.

A third metaphor for the struggle to become a good Stoic is particularly significant because it introduces us to a crucial issue in Roman Stoicism itself: the degree to which its philosophical stance may be accused of passivity and the ways in which the Stoics' own figural language strives to counteract this impression. As Seneca describes it, shaping the self involves a quasi-martial battle to resist the trials life brings and the weapons fortune showers on us. He thus often relies on military metaphors to characterize his "battle" against "fate," presenting the virtuous Roman as a fighter in a way that belies the Stoic emphasis on acceptance and presents him as facing overwhelming odds (nicely illustrated by Asmis 2009). We are to subdue our desires by storm, not circumvent them by logic (e.g., "*expugnare adfectus*," *Ep.* 87.41). Likewise, he will borrow language from the arena or athletic contests to characterize the Stoic's endurance or virtue. The philosopher is born "*sine missione*": his gladiatorial fight is lifelong. And while the gladiator can ask for pity, the philosopher must die on his feet and unconquered (*Ep.* 37.2). If the tamers of wild animals subdue beasts to the will of man, the philosopher tames exile, disgrace, and pain.[15] Here and beyond: as Matthew Roller (2001, 64–126) illustrates, other value-laden terms from the elite (bravery, honor, endurance) are overlaid onto the Stoic's battle with himself. Why the charge of passivity remained a problem for the Senecan self despite these efforts becomes clear as we turn to the tension between Stoic theater and the theater of fear.[16]

Actors and Acting

It has been noted often enough that Seneca's description of the path to wisdom also borrows from the language of the stage, an unintuitive choice of metaphorical vehicle to represent the Stoic sage in all his unshakeable

---

[15] *Ep.* 85 41; cf. *Ep.* 18.8, 28.7, 52.1, 66.1, 71.30, etc. For a full list, Armisen-Marchetti (1989) and Smith (1910 s.vv).

[16] For similar complexities with the notion of *patientia*, endurance, see Kaster (2002).

authenticity.[17] To be sure, the actor metaphor was (and continues to be) a popular one in common culture; all the world's a stage and always has been. In Seneca's treatment, however, the sage is the *best* of all actors – a quality Seneca bestows on him because his performance on the stage of life is marked by *consistency*. It is a great thing, he says, to play a single character and not to switch from one to another; all that matters is to stick to it, or, as Seneca puts it in another striking formation, to "be consistent with yourself" (*Ep.* 35.4).[18]

> It is a great achievement to play the part of just one man; no one can do it except the wise man; the rest of us take on too many different appearances. Now we seem worthy and serious, now wasteful and silly; we change our mask suddenly and put on a contradictory one. Demand from yourself therefore that you play that same role to the end in which you first presented yourself; and if you can't be praised, at least make sure you can be recognized.

In *Epistle* 77, the theatrical element reappears in terms of making a good ending: as in a play, so in life; it doesn't matter for how long but rather how well the role is performed. It's irrelevant at what point you stop; just have a good exit line.[19] Even the other actors are unnecessary in this drama of life: left alone on stage, the wise man can play to the end his own role (*Ep.* 109.6). In fact, Seneca's version of the good Stoic's consistency devolves upon the importance *of not changing your expression* no matter what happens. In his account, "Socrates himself, under the Thirty Tyrants, never changed his expression" (*Ep.* 104.28; cf. *Helv.* 13.4.4). Nor did Cato, even as the Republic fell around his ears (*Ep.* 104.30). In fact, no matter what happens to the Stoic wise man, the Stoic never lets himself visibly react: "Facing the torture machines of horrific men he holds his gaze steady; he changes nothing in his expression whether difficult or favorable outcomes are shown to him" (*De const.* 5.4). The wise man is not pushed around by the slings and arrows of Fortune nor the torture devices of tyrants but soldiers on without wavering, guided by rational principle alone and sporting a steady gaze.

There remains, however, another Senecan version of how one acts in the face of power, and it must be acknowledged that it has uncomfortable resonances with the wise man's unchanging mien. First, Seneca is willing to acknowledge that sometimes acting consistently is just – acting, for the

---

[17] On this topic, see the essay by Littlewood in this volume, which discusses theatricality in Stoic self-fashioning, imperial politics, and Senecan drama.

[18] The role of life is played before a general audience, and yet the most important thing is still "*ut constes tibi.*" Cf. *Ben.* 2.17.2 on the behavior of a Cynic philosopher: "*hanc personam induisti; agenda est.*"

[19] On the theater metaphor, see Smith (1910); Armisen-Marchetti (1989, s.vv with bibliography); Ker (2009a 113–46).

sake of ensuring one's safety, rather than playing out a wise and unchanging persona. In a passage from his essay *On tranquility of the soul* (dated to approximately 40 CE), Seneca observes that playing a consistent role is exhausting:

> Constant observation of oneself is torturous, and one fears to be caught out of one's usual role. Nor can we ever put down our cares, when we think we're being judged every time we're looked at. Many chance happenings can expose us against our will, and even granted that all this effort over oneself is successful, it's not a pleasant life, nor one free from anxiety, to live constantly wearing a mask. (*Tranq.* 17.1)

This is very different from the noble consistency of the stage as represented in the *Epistles*. The speaker is not the brave Stoic who barely flinches as the rack is winched tighter. It is instead the other self that Seneca staged: the one at court. It is in fact the Seneca whom Tacitus hints at in the *Annals*, who, when Britannicus was murdered, was "given no choice but to be *inter dissimulantes*" (Griffin 1992, 77), along with the rest of the audience at that dinner party, including even Agrippina and Octavia, who "had learned to hide her grief, her love, her every emotion" (*Ann.* 13.16). Adept at court life, Seneca likewise has to dissemble his true feelings with Nero upon the moment of his retirement instead expressing his gratitude. "Such is the end of all dialogues with an autocrat," Tacitus remarks wryly (14.56.1).

Given the ambivalence of the theater metaphor, it bears asking how the constancy of the sage's "self" manifests itself in difficult political times.[20] One might imagine that *deeds* rather than the exhibition of a poker face would here win the highest praise from Seneca, especially since there were Stoics who consistently opposed Nero, even unto death: for example, Thrasea Paetus, whose aspiring sagehood aimed at something more than the consistent performance of an essentially passive persona. Paetus walked out of the Senate in 59 CE while fulsome congratulations were being given to Nero for escaping his mother's "treachery;" and Paetus' public opposition to the Emperor continued until 62, when he left the Senate altogether. He thus provided (in Tacitus' words) an admirable example of *constantia* (*Ann.* 16.25) up to his suicide. Yet in his writings, Seneca steers clear of suggesting that *constantia* might look like ongoing defiance; for him, upon the failure of one's drama of life, it is death by suicide that is the ultimate political act,

---

[20] The ambivalence manifests itself even further when Seneca uses *negative* versions of the theater metaphor to show he is a good Stoic: e.g., *Ep.* 26.4–5, when he asks himself if his scornful words against Fortune were just a pretense, spoken as a mime-actor.

an "active" show of defiance that represents one's choice of *libertas* rather than fear.

The value of playing a part consistently seems, then, to map onto two Senecas, one at court and one retired. It was the former who first learned the value of never changing your expression: the grim stories of tyrants in Seneca's essay *De ira* remind us dramatically of what those years under Caligula were like and how much Seneca must have hoped, when he wrote *De clementia*, that Nero would not turn out the same way. This control over one's expressions and reactions was deemed invaluable by the professedly Stoic Seneca as well, even if figured completely differently now, as bravery before all forms of torture:

> If a man can look at flashing swords with unflinching eyes, if he knows that it makes no difference to him whether his soul leaves him through his mouth or through a wound in his throat, then call him happy [i.e., a sage]; call him happy too if, when bodily torture is in the cards (whether it comes about by accident or through harm inflicted by the more powerful) he can without concern hear about chains, exile, and all the empty fears of human minds. (*Ep.* 76.33)

It is at least suggestive of a fault line in Seneca's self-depiction that his brave man and his coward look alike from the outside: for both, the theater metaphor is brought into play; and on their stages, both play the same role with their carefully composed faces. The philosophical complexity of this partial overlap is far deeper than can be represented here. But it is interesting that the *political* theater of Seneca's earlier years ended up, in the *Epistles*, as a sort of *sage's* theater instead, marked by the same self-control called for when Britannicus fell poisoned from his couch – even if fear drove that response and bravery the Stoic sage's. Again in the *De ira*, we hear of a man whose son Caligula has recently murdered: invited to dinner by the emperor, he eats and drinks and sheds not a single tear (*De ira* 2.33.3–4). The political Seneca pipes in to praise his response: "Injuries from the more powerful must be borne with a cheerful face, not just with endurance; they will do it again if they believe they've done it once" (*De ira* 2.33.1).

Can we save Seneca by saying he at least *consistently* praises the wretched victims who manifest supreme self-control and *constantia* in the face of suffering, just as he commends the sages who do the same? We cannot, for the bivalence of this sort of acting does not escape Seneca himself; when in the same book of *De ira* Cambyses shoots an arrow through the heart of his friend Praexaspes' son, Praexaspes' calm praise of his unerring aim launches the philosopher into a frenzy of condemnation: "May the gods ruin such a man, more of a slave in soul than by rank! He praised an action that was already excessive to watch!" (*De ira* 3.14.2–3). For Seneca Pastor is a hero and Praexaspes a coward; but from both, the same reaction to abusive power. In one of the tragedies, on the other hand, we hear the much more commonsensical suggestion that the only person who is truly "happy" is the one who *can* change his expression as the circumstances demand – now that is freedom! (*Her. Oet.* 227–8, from the chorus).[21]

We may notice now how Seneca avoids commenting in the *Epistles* on his earlier, court self (whether to praise it or to denounce it)[22] in the way, for example, that Tacitus does in the *Agricola*, when he bitterly comments on his own cowardice in not speaking up against Domitian's murders of senators: "It was the worse part of our misery under Domitian to see and to be seen, when our sighs were recorded, when that savage and ruddy face was able to hold against them the pallor of so many men" (*Agr.* 45). The Senecan self that is elided in the *Epistles*, the one that lived during the years of subterfuge under the emperors Caligula, Claudius, and Nero (see Griffin, 1976, 68–172), must have labored under the constant awareness of an essential hypocrisy at the core of one's being, perhaps all the more so given the example of other imperial Stoics and the perks of being in the wealthy inner circle.[23] Indeed, of his fellow imperial Stoics, only Seneca had to endure this conjunction of politics and philosophy, hypocrisy and sincerity; Epictetus was never in a position of power, Marcus Aurelius, once emperor-Stoic, was never *not* in a position of power, and Thrasea Paetus, Helvidius Priscus, and others refused to be victims *or* to philosophize at length in writings but instead acted on their beliefs.[24]

What, finally, are we to make of the Senecan self depicted here and there in the dialogues but most richly so in the very long document that constitutes the *Epistles*? For this, we may hijack Tacitus' report of Seneca's final words at his forced suicide in 65 CE. As he cuts his veins, Seneca tells his followers that in his death he wishes to leave behind an *imago vitae suae* for them to inherit ("an image/model of his life," Tac. *Ann.* 15.62; this is also the title of Griffin's study of his character). This *imago*, untainted by the hypocrisy he had to live, is the Seneca that the philosopher emphasizes above all in the *Epistles*, where there is no Nero (unlike the *De clementia*),

---

[21] Further on the Stoic "actor" and the political one, Star (2012, 65–9).

[22] The closest he comes to this is the statement in *Ep.* 8.3, where he acknowledges that he has recognized the right path "too late, and tired out by error," but hopes to still show the path to others.

[23] For similar remarks on "self-disintegration," see Gill (2009).

[24] Is Stoic philosophy guilty of Zimmerman's charge (2000) that it teaches people to rationalize their suffering? Indeed, who can deny that Seneca may have turned to Stoicism because of his life situation?

little emphasis upon community (unlike the *De beneficiis*), not much by way of historical context (unlike the *Consolations*), but only the constant exercise of self upon self.[25] In the end, Seneca's most impressive act of self-shaping was not himself – though perhaps he got close between 62 and 65 CE – but his *portrayed* self in this work. For if Thrasea Paetus was brave in deed, Seneca, turning inward, chose a more passive form of Stoicism and left it for us to read and remember, articulated in words and on pages rather than in acts and at the imperial court.

Further Reading

Much interesting work has been done on the program of reflection and self-improvement that Seneca describes in his prose work. Important studies on the Senecan self in particular include Edwards (1997), Hadot (1969), Long (2009), and Reydams-Schils (2005); Bartsch and Wray (2009) contains essays that look at Senecan selfhood from literary and dramatic as well as philosophical angles. On the self in Hellenistic and Roman Stoicism, more generally, see Foucault (1986, 1988, 2005), Gill (2006), Newman (1989), and Nussbaum (1994). On the question of psychological dualism in Seneca's treatment of mind and other essays pertaining to the will, moral judgment, and self-assertion in his thought, see Inwood (2005).

On the philosopher's life and times, Griffin (1976, 2nd ed. 1992) is remarkably thorough; see also Veyne (2003) and Grimal (1978). Roller (2001) was one of the first studies to argue that Seneca deliberately uses traditional Roman values as a stepping stone for philosophical argument.

[25] See Ker (2009a) on the importance of Seneca's death to his identity.

15

DAVID WRAY

Seneca's Shame

The Latin word *pudor* captures a set of notions and experiences having at least as much to do with "honor" as with the set of destructive feelings based on self-condemnation that English speakers now usually designate by the word "shame" and often seek to minimize or eliminate therapeutically.[1] *Pudor*, like Greek *aidos*, was far more positive in connotation. Having it, in the right measure and the right way, counted as part of being equipped to live well. While ancient Greeks and Romans did find some negative things to say about shame, its absence was generally seen as license rather than liberation from unhelpful inhibition, a lack not only of every consideration of "honor" in the sense of propriety and respect (including self-respect) but also of all the kinds of restraint that allow human beings to live together in community.[2]

That Seneca has good things to say about shame is thus unsurprising, given his membership in what twentieth-century anthropology taught us to describe as a premodern "shame culture."[3] Ultimately, his take on shame, while uniquely Senecan in flavor and intensity, is also recognizably Stoic, albeit in some unexpected ways. But on a longstanding, widespread (and mistaken) view of their ethical system, shame can look like something a Stoic ought not to have regarded hospitably. Stoicism insisted that all items external to the soul's state of virtue or vice were neither good nor bad but indifferent. It posited *apatheia*, the absence of passionate emotion, as a necessary and essential characteristic of the happy life of the perfectly virtuous moral agent, the *sapiens* or "sage." It can thus easily be taken for a philosophy that disallows

---

[1] For examples of theoretical and therapeutic treatments of shame in the modern, broadly negative, sense, see Bradshaw (1988), Sedgwick and Frank (1995), and Nussbaum (2004).

[2] Having a muzzle that, like a dog's, never blushes is among the charges Achilles hurls at Agamemnon in their quarrel that opens the *Iliad* (1.149, 159).

[3] On "shame cultures" in anthropology and the study of classical antiquity, see Benedict (1946), Dodds (1951), Cairns (1993), and Williams (1993).

consideration of the kinds of things shame is most often about (externals) and pathologizes the kind of psychic event shame seems to be (an emotion). From this perspective, the fact that Greek Stoics classified *aidos* as a subcategory of *eulabeia* ("caution"), one of the *eupatheiai* ("commendable feelings") experienced by the sage, either will look like a fundamental self-contradiction in their doctrine or else will rouse the suspicion that Stoic "shame" must be a specialized philosophical term of art so far removed from the word's received meaning as to have no application in ordinary talk about lived experience.[4]

Whatever Seneca thought shame was, he obviously gave it an important place in ethical practice as well as in theory, as a survey of his prose writings suffices to confirm.[5] But if there is something special about Seneca's take on shame, we are not likely to find it through word study. The forms of *pudere* and its cognates circulating in his philosophical prose can hardly be taken as describing the eupathic inner life of an ideal agent. In fact, Seneca's philosophical use of shame terms sounds a lot like ordinary Roman *pudor*-talk. It fits comfortably into the taxonomy of "scripts" set up by Kaster in a study of *pudor* based on a review of all extant occurrences in classical Latin.[6]

Two examples from the *Epistles to Lucilius* are enough to show this. When Seneca asks his diatribe interlocutor "are you not ashamed of trying to heal your grief through pleasure?" (*non te pudet luctum uoluptate sanare? Ep.* 99.29), the shame he envisions corresponds to Kaster's script 6: "upon (or at the prospect of) seeing myself being seen in discreditable terms, I have an unpleasant psychophysical response, when the behavior or state of affairs that prompts the attention is 'up to me' and entails discreditable 'lowering' of the self."[7] What Seneca recommends to his interlocutor is clearly not to try and practice *apatheia* in the face of the imagined onslaught of a painful emotion but rather to feel its sting as an appropriate response to a blameworthy circumstance indicative of a blameworthy disposition and possibly as a means of exiting the circumstance and rehabilitating the disposition. Again, when Seneca professes to feel ashamed of humanity upon entering a school (*pudet autem me generis humani quotiens scholam intraui, Ep.* 76.4), the setting of his self-described response to the quality of education corresponds to Kaster's script 3, where the shame-inducing state of affairs is "not 'up to me' but is 'up to' another with whom I am somehow linked."[8]

4 Diogenes Laertius 7.116 is the source for the Stoic classification of shame as eupathic. See discussion at Graver (2007, 58–9).
5 A similar experiment practiced on the works of Epictetus and Marcus Aurelius, the other two extant major Stoic writers of the Roman period, produces a similar result.
6 Kaster (2005, 28–65).
7 Kaster (2005, 47–8).
8 Kaster (2005, 38–42).

Here once again Seneca might look to be straying from his Stoic line. The behavior of the entire human race, obviously, is not up to me. It lies outside the control of my faculty of choice (*prohairesis*). It has therefore no bearing on my state of virtue or vice, cannot therefore be a good or bad thing to me, and ought therefore, one might have thought, not to have given a Stoic cause for a second thought, let alone the "unpleasant psychophysical response" of shame.

In both those examples, the speaker of the epistle seems to be trying to shame his reader into a Stoic viewpoint, but the version of shame he enjoins sounds like a kind of experience Stoics are supposed to avoid. If we think we have caught Seneca in a contradiction, our first move will probably be to posit that Seneca's Stoicism was in tension with his culture as a whole and his social position as a member of it. This much seems not just correct but, given the fundamental anticonventionalism of what the Stoics taught, inevitable. Their ethical system was so "paradoxical," in the ancient sense of running counter to commonly held opinion, that explaining it to students or inserting its principles into public discourse necessarily entailed sometimes applying the most basic evaluative terms in ways that were, on the Stoic view, strictly false. Chrysippus had already acknowledged this expedient need for Stoics to talk sometimes in non-Stoic ways, and it is not hard to find Seneca doing just that.[9] As Roller has shown in an insightful study, not only does Seneca often assign evaluative terms according to the conventional Roman "regime of value" rather than the Stoic standard, he seldom seems at pains to distinguish clearly his references to these two competing standards of value, as we might have expected him to do if he thoroughly rejected the one and unambivalently embraced the other.[10] On the basis of this evidence, it would be easy to conclude that Seneca's philosophical commitments went only so deep and even easier to rush to the now familiar move, easily practiced on any canonical text, of unmasking Seneca's Stoic project as one of consolidating social privilege and political power by deploying prestigious cultural signifiers to disseminate ideology under cover of mystifying stealth.

The Roman and the Stoic in Seneca interact in ways more complex than a single model can exhaust. Without denying the possibility that new insights may yet come from hermeneutic modes that scrutinize his text for things like self-interest and self-deception, I am interested here in sketching an argument, if speculative and experimental, for a different kind of potential

[9] Plutarch, *De Stoicorum Repugnantiis* 1048A, 1034B = *SVF* 3.137, 3.698 = Long and Sedley (1987, 58H, 66B).
[10] Roller (2001, 64–126).

relation between Roman *pudor* and Stoic virtue, one that is visible only from a perspective willing to entertain provisional sympathy for precisely those radically intransigent aspects of the pair's two members that have most often baffled and repelled those evaluating them from outside. First, the intransigent moral perfectionism of Stoic ethics, by insisting that all virtuous states are equally virtuous and all nonvirtuous states equally vicious, seems at first blush to have consigned all ordinary human experience to utter degradation. Yet that same feature of the Stoic thought system opens up space for a developmental model of moral progress that turns out to look far less "perfectionist," in the ordinary understanding of the term, than the commonsense version of Greco-Roman ethics theorized by Aristotle. Second, the intransigent behavioral model of Roman honor and shame has often looked motivated by a vain grasping after aristocratic privilege, an aim that, once frustrated of attainment in the political and social fields of competition, quickly descends into the pathological realm of an obsessional fixation on suicide.[11] Yet that same model, throughout early modernity, also furnished a rich source of models of heroism and freedom that was productive in revolutionary politics as well as art.

Through a necessarily brief look at the splendors and miseries of shame as it circulates in his thought, with a closing look at how these play out in the life and death of his version of the tragic character of Phaedra, I want to suggest the location of a sublime potential within the thought and art of Seneca in which the grim grandeurs of both his philosophical and his dramatic writings participate in concert. Residing at the center of that potential, surprisingly, is what Seneca's culture called *pudor*. As Seneca had received the category, *pudor* was, both by its ambivalent valuation in philosophy and by its pervasive cultural presence in lived experience, more than just good to think with. It seems, for him, to have gone a long way toward making Stoicism feel like a habitable and hospitable container and a long way toward making a failed life like Phaedra's, and like that of every ordinary human agent when held up to the Stoic standard, look surprisingly worth celebrating in poetry.

Passionate Shame and Stoic Progress

Ambivalent valuation of shame was no Stoic invention. In Greco-Roman culture, we can trace it back to Homer, where the Iliadic Apollo qualifies shame as a thing "which is both greatly destructive and greatly helpful to men" (ἥ τ' ἄνδρας μέγα σίνεται ἠδ' ὀνίνησι, *Iliad* 24.45). But it is in the philosophy

---

[11] On Roman suicide and the socially constituted self, see Hill (2004).

of Aristotle that we find the readiest evidence of how subtly complex and potentially generative a valuation of shame Seneca had inherited. Aristotle's system had laid the framework broadly followed by the various Hellenistic philosophical schools, and his was an ethical discourse that proceeded by rooting itself in his culture's received ideas, theorizing and problematizing them but always referring back to them.

Aristotle's discussion of shame in the *Nicomachean Ethics* brings up the rear of a catalogue of ethical virtues, less as an afterthought than as an item on (and off) the list whose inclusion and exclusion both turn out to raise instructive problems (*EN* 1128b10–34). Shame, on Aristotle's productively fuzzy account of it, shares a number of functions with virtue and makes the judgments and decisions of the shame-based agent resemble those of the virtuous agent in some measure. Aristotle does cut a set of clear distinctions between shame and virtue, on the basis of category, structure, operation, and ethical status, but he also describes each distinction in a way that nuances and ultimately undermines each difference. Shame is "more like a feeling" than a disposition (ἕξις), but to put it that way is to imply that, for all the ways it differs from a disposition, it also in some way resembles one. Shame seems rooted in the body and its brute reflexes, but Aristotle's discussion brings out a sense in which it can be said to have propositionalizable cognitive content, as a consideration taken into account in rational deliberation about a contemplated action. Shame proceeds by painful constraint and regret, in contrast to the habituated optimal functioning of virtue, yet it can be, if only conditionally, called "appropriate" (ἐπιεικές), a way of naming human excellence whose roots go back to Homeric diction.

Shame, as Aristotle theorizes his culture's conception of it, straddles the definitional boundary between what does and does not count as an instance of virtue. It is for this reason that, as Burnyeat puts it in a crucial reading of this passage, shame can play the role of "the semivirtue of the learner."[12] It is not merely that shame is like virtue in some ways and unlike it in others. Rather, shame can serve as a provisional substitute for virtue in an individual development story, never neatly or without residue, but nonetheless as the nearest approximation to virtue of which a still maturing agent is capable. Its pervasive reach, from the lowest somatic reflexes all the way up to the highest cognitive functions, is what makes shame irreducible to a single precise definition. But this is also just what makes shame, as a complex set of events experienced differently at different psychic levels, uniquely fit for the role of a developmental ramp from a lower to a higher level of ethical functioning. Its potential for being experienced as thoroughgoing passion,

---

[12] Burnyeat (1981, 78).

an affective onslaught that grips and controls the agent subject to it, is what makes Aristotle exclude it from the optimal human functioning he defines as virtue. But this dangerous potential within shame is also just what makes it fully able to be integrated into the occurrent psychic lives of the creatures of passion that developing agents still are. In other words, ancient Mediterranean shame, as Aristotle theorizes it, turns out already to entail and contain within itself a potential for progress. If children whose psychic lives are properly shame based grow into virtuous adults in whose psychic lives shame properly plays no part, and if the attainment of virtue proceeds not through catastrophic transformation but by a developmental maturation, which is by nature gradual, then it follows that shame-based agents are able to make incremental progress toward virtue while still in their shame-based state and therefore still subject to passion.

Given the centrality of the notion of progress in Stoic ethics, it is not hard to see how this developmental model of shame, whether found in Aristotle's text or in vernacularized formulations circulating in Hellenistic schools, could have looked philosophically promising to Stoics. It is equally easy to see how Stoics might have modified the Aristotelian model to adapt it to the thoroughgoing moral perfectionism of their ethical system. What Aristotle claims about young people, that they live by passion and therefore fall short of the virtuous life, holds true on the Stoic view for nonsages, that is, all ordinary human agents. Aristotle's account offers reasons for thinking that some version of shame, for the mad slaves of passion that Aristotle thinks young people are and that Stoics think we nonsages are, is both occurrently appropriate and developmentally useful.

Having once gone deep enough into the Stoic position to see the potentially crucial role shame might be made to play in a Stoic story of progress toward virtue, we are also in a position to see that the two seemingly major impediments to incorporating shame into a Stoic developmental ethical model turn out to lack force. First, the objection that shame in a Stoic *progrediens* would entail caring too much about externals is one that might just as easily be raised against virtue in a Stoic *sapiens*. In both cases, the objection rests on an incomplete understanding of the underlying ethical teaching. Stoics think virtuous agents attach the utmost importance to decisions about things that are in themselves neither good nor bad. All decisions, in fact, are in this sense "about" preferred and dispreferred indifferent externals. But what the virtuous agent commits to in deciding is not the pursuit of a particular arrangement of affairs beyond the control of the agent but rather, simply, the pursuit of making a good decision. Seneca, in *Letter* 92 as elsewhere, works hard to make this point explicit, insisting that, for example, being an elegant dresser can count as an actualization of living in accord with nature, simply "because a human being is by nature an elegant and selective creature" (*natura enim homo mundum et elegans animal est, Ep. 92.12*), with the result that "elegant clothing is not something good in and of itself, but selecting it is, because the good of a selection resides not in its matter but its quality; it is our handling of things, not the things we handle, that can count as commendable" (*non est bonum per se munda uestis sed mundae uestis electio, quia non in re bonum est sed in electione quali; actiones nostrae honestae sunt, non ipsa quae aguntur, Ep. 92.12*).

To some, it may seem strangely decadent of Seneca to claim that "nonmoral" decisions about matters like clothing can count as opportunities for the exercise of optimal human functioning. But then, to many, it has seemed strangely intransigent of him to praise the Stoic who advised a man deliberating the highly "moral" question of whether to take his own life to stop tormenting himself as if he were deliberating about a matter of great importance (*de re magna, Ep. 77.6*). The two claims can look counterintuitive and mutually incompatible, but both depend on the same fundamental Stoic teaching. No decision is unimportant on the Stoic view, and the Kantian distinction between moral and nonmoral decisions is foreign to Stoic ethics, because every decision, whatever its matter, is either good – one that a virtuous agent would make – or not. But every decision involves a selection among items that, whether attractive or dreadful to the nonvirtuous, lie outside the soul's faculty of choosing and are therefore of themselves indifferent. It is only in the faculty of choice that Stoic virtue resides. Shame, then, can be said to approach virtue precisely to the degree that its constraints nudge the agent toward the choice a virtuous agent would have made in a given circumstance. In its ordinary and occurrent sense, shame might motivate a nonvirtuous agent to a decision that resembles a sage's closely enough to count as a *kathekon* or "appropriate action," but the ordinary fool's choice, however appropriate, never rises to the level of *katorthoma* or "right action."[13] The ideal shame imputed by Stoics to the sage presumably resembles what we ordinary fools mean by shame, in that it motivates and restrains but differs precisely in that it is a species of virtue, an instance of the *eupatheia* of caution rather than the *pathos* of fear.

The second objection to assigning shame a central role in Stoic progress toward virtue might seem to gather force just here. The fool's passionate shame, however cognitive its mode of operation and however impressively close to good choosing it may bring a progressing nonsage, still counts as passion. And the claim that passion has no place in the virtuous agent's life

---

[13] An especially clear explanation of this distinction is Brennan (2005, 169–80).

is so central to Stoicism that giving way on it can only amount to leaving off
being a Stoic. Stated in those terms, the objection can sound damning, but
some recent work has made it surprisingly easy to answer. The very notion
of progress toward virtue necessarily entails the possibility of comparing
different states of nonvirtue, different ways of being a passion-mad fool, and
ranking them as more or less advanced in progress and therefore more or
less preferable. One Greek source, Nemesius, defines *aidos* not as a species
of *eupatheia* but rather as the "finest" (*kalliston*) passion, and this surprising piece of evidence has led Kamtekar to speculate that at least some Stoics
may have explicitly formulated the kind of "double classification" of shame
sketched in the previous paragraph.[14] Graver, more recently, has offered a
simpler and stronger answer to the objection that the practice of encourag-
ing nonvirtuous moral progressors to feel shame (a pedagogical aspect of
their Socratic inheritance that all Stoic teachers, Seneca included, seem to
have perpetuated with gusto) clashes with the Stoic doctrine of *apatheia*.[15]
Sages do not get to passionlessness by shutting down their natural capac-
ities for passionate emotion. They get to it by attaining virtue, in which
state they never again lack or grasp after the good that produces happiness,
come what may, and never again experience or fear the evil that produces
misery. But the nonsage's life includes not just perceived evil but the actual
evil of lacking virtue. And in the face of present and future real evil, painful
responses like passionate shame and remorse, while absent from the sage's
life because their causes are absent, can count as both natural and appropriate for the rest of us.

The Sage's Vice and Phaedra's Virtue

This way of understanding Stoic moral psychology assigns shame a crucial
role in the life not just of practicing Stoics but of anyone trying to learn
how to live. It also suggests that, between the psychic functioning of sages
and nonsages, the continuities turn out to be at least as interesting as the
differences. Seneca seems to have had something like this thought in mind
when he describes a young man who, on first meeting, impressed him by
his clear signs of talent and character but even more by an excessive and
therefore suboptimal shamefacedness, as evidenced by an overwhelming
initial embarrassment followed by a persistent blush. From this vignette,
Seneca derives an altogether unexpected reflection about human flaws and
the attainment of sagehood:

[14] Kamtekar (1998) 140.
[15] Graver (2007, 191–211).

ubi se colligebat, uerecundiam, bonum in adulescente signum, uix potuit excutere: adeo illi ex alto suffusus est rubor. hic illum, quantum suspicor, etiam cum se confirmauerit et omnibus uitiis exuerit, sapientem quoque seque-tur. nulla enim sapientia naturalia corporis aut animi uitia ponuntur. quicquid infixum et ingenitum est, lenitur arte, non uincitur. (Ep. 11.1)

As he tried to collect himself, he could scarcely shake off his modest shame (a good sign in a young man): from so deep within came the blush that suffused him. My guess is that, even when he has gained strength, cast off all vices, become a sage, even then this trait will remain with him. For no natural vices of the body or the mind are set aside in sagehood. Whatever is fixed and inborn can be palliated through systematic work, but not overcome.

Seneca posits two related things about the young man's *uerecundia*, a word whose semantic range, as Kaster notes, broadly intersects that of *pudor*.[16] First, he speculates that it goes all the way down into his psychophysical organism, has resided there from birth, and is fixed. Second, he asserts that this shame reflex, like its supervening symptom, is outside the agent's power of choice, unlike most other visible emotions (skilled actors, he notes later in the letter, can weep, but not blush, at will). He further claims that if these two speculations are correct, a surprising but strictly logical conclusion follows. The defect (*uitium*) of body and mind that makes the young man redden and feel a kind of shame (*uerecundia*) in a situation where this response is suboptimal because misplaced counts as a "vice," but one whose possession would not bar him from attaining sagehood. In fact, it would remain with him even in that state of freedom from all "vice" in the ethical sense. The play on *uitium*, no equivocation, makes careful use of two philosophical senses of the word, general and ethical, both inherited from Platonic and Aristotelian use of the term *kakia*. Its point is to measure the wide range of psychophysical human imperfections Stoicism imputes to sages despite the perfection of their ethical virtue. These emphatically include cognitive and affective as well as physical defects.[17]

The continuities between a sage's ideal life and the occurrent life of us fools thus turn out to run in both directions, with negative as well as positive (not good and bad) traits present at both ends. Seneca's characterological imagination, as the eleventh letter portrays it, likes to think of ordinary occurrent human beings as sages *in potentia* (whether or not in the making),

---

[16] Kaster (2005, 61–5).

[17] This view of body–mind relations is entirely foreign to the high modern Cartesian model. No surprise that the eminent nineteenth-century philologist Nikolai Madvig emended the passage quoted previously by excising the words *aut animi*, on the tacit assumption that Seneca would not have located involuntary human defects elsewhere than in the body.

and this imaginative act entails pinpointing not just the seeds of virtue but also the indelible defects, the odd quirks, that a particular ethical subject would retain and carry across the threshold of wisdom's perfect attainment. This consideration, I suggest, points toward a more appealing and promising way of explaining Seneca's tragic characters and the prosopopoetic creative process of a dramatic poet who was also a Stoic philosopher, than more familiar attempts at cracking open this old chestnut.[18] Its explanatory value includes being able to account for what a critic like Marti was on to when she made Senecan tragic protagonists into proper Stoic *progredientes* (namely, that Seneca sees them as potential sages) as well as what more recent critics are on to when they make them into anti-Stoic perversions of sagehood (namely, that Seneca holds the Stoic belief that every approximation of virtue in a nonsage still counts, properly speaking, as thoroughgoing vice).[19] It allows us to say why both those critical models are somehow tempting and intriguing, because they are perspicacious in a way but also somehow unsatisfying, especially to readers who share Inwood's intuition that Seneca's plays, as serious dramatic poems, are inevitably informed by a Stoic sensibility without being mere protreptics disguised as theater, in something like the way that Graham Greene's novels are inevitably informed by a Catholic sensibility without being mere apologetics disguised as fiction.[20]

I close on the example of Phaedra, because the language of her Senecan drama seems to invite us to regard her as a kind of hero of *pudor*, a poetic representation of subjectivity that presses the potential as well as the limits of shame for advancing an ordinary wrecked human life toward the splendor of excellence. The ambivalence of her character, as reception history has evaluated it, takes on significance in this light precisely to the degree that we locate that ambivalence in the signifier *pudor* as it circulates in the text of the play itself. When her alarmed nurse reminds Phaedra that, while the best course is not to slip from the path, "shame – knowing a limit to straying – is a second best" (*pudor est secundus nosse peccandi modum*, 141), it is easy to take these words as the counsel of reason trying to talk madness off the ledge and easy to understand why some scholars have taken the nurse as a Stoic mouthpiece.[21] Yet this same utterance also reads as a counsel of hypocrisy, advising Phaedra to let shame teach her how to control and enjoy her vice by choosing outlets more readily concealed than the project of seducing

---

[18] Part of my claim here, that Seneca's depiction of his tragic characters "suggests the Stoic fortitude which they might display," is an observation already made by Littlewood (2004, 25).

[19] Marti (1945) and, e.g., Schiesaro (2003).

[20] Inwood (1991, 251).

[21] E.g., Lefèvre (1969) and Pratt (1983, 92).

a stepson. Both the Euripidean intertext and the subsequent actions of the Senecan nurse corroborate this construction powerfully, if inconclusively. When Phaedra, later in the same scene, answers the nurse's impassioned supplication with an assurance that "not all shame has departed from my freeborn spirit" (*non omnis animo cessit ingenuo pudor*, 250) followed by an announcement of her resolve to exit life, her moves are interpretable and have been taken by some scholars as manipulating a loving caregiver by a suicide threat sure to frighten the latter into willingness to do anything to save her mistress.[22] Indeed, even supposing that Phaedra's desire to be freed of her passion is sincere in the moment, none of the positive things Seneca says in his philosophy about the rational exit from life encourages us to suppose he disagreed with Aristotle's judgment that suicide to escape love is an instance of cowardice (*EN* 1116a13). And yet, however clearly her inner succumbing to erotic passion convicts her of a weakness that bars her from virtue, it is equally clear that his depiction of Phaedra's sudden impulse to die for the maintenance of her "freeborn spirit's" *pudor* bears a strong structural resemblance to suicides that Seneca admires as heroically intransigent acts done to preserve a noble freedom, like those of Cato and the captive Spartan boy who dashed out his brains rather than hold his new master's chamber pot.[23]

Phaedra is no sage, nor even a sage in the making (Seneca says this of himself).[24] But her tragedy, read in the light of what I have suggested here, invites us to imagine what she would be like as one by focusing on those aspects of her fierce, if disastrously fallible, commitment to *pudor* that might accompany her into the state where its object had become coterminous with virtue. If we think about moral progress as Seneca did, we will think that this commitment would still retain, in sagehood, some measure of that wild extravagance that renders her character recognizably Phaedra's. When she has confessed her love to Hippolytus and feels his sword drawn at her throat, her sudden outburst – that dying by his hand with her *pudor* intact (*salvo ... pudore*, 712) is a consummation beyond her devoutest wish – lies open to interpretation, certainly, as a pathological symptom of advanced sexual masochism or even, by a stretch, as a cunning stratagem based on cool certainty that Hippolytus was the kind of man who, on hearing such words, would throw down his sword and recoil in horror. But to the degree we are willing to take at face value her words spoken in the face of death, they enact an impulse, however disturbed in its manifestation, toward a hierarchy of

---

[22] Nisard (1834, 147) first among modern scholars.
[23] Cato: *De Providentia* 2 and elsewhere; Spartan boy: *Ep.* 77.14.
[24] *De Vita Beata* 17.3.

valuation organized by virtue. On this reading, it is as if Phaedra at sword's point suddenly learns a new thing about herself, namely that there is something in her love for Hippolytus that points, beyond the incestuous sexual hunger she feels and abhors, toward the actualization of an erotic friendship of the kind that the Stoics, as inheritors of the Socratic tradition, prized as one of the crowning excellences of the life of virtue.[25]

The closing scene of Phaedra's suicide over Hippolytus' shredded corpse corroborates this interpretation powerfully but again ambivalently, offering no positive resistance to the reader who prefers instead (like Theseus in the play) to take the action as merely grotesque and Phaedra as merely deluded.[26] Her earlier self-recognition as actually wanting to achieve, in a reality realer than her occurrent self, an intimate bond with Hippolytus in which shame is preserved intact, a bond like that of legitimate spouses, and her realization that death alone could bring her life's derangement to a near approximation of that aim, both come to fruition when she opens her guts over what remains of Hippolytus. Death, as she invokes it in a pair of lines in her dying speech that recall the Euripidean chorus's prescient narration of her suicide, is both her sick love's sole relief and the best restoration of dignity available for the self-inflicted injury to her shame.[27] Punishing herself for her hand in Hippolytus' destruction, she also commingles and joins herself with him in the deepest physical intimacy, where she will accompany him through the pyre and lie with him in the urn forever, like Achilles with Patroclus, in spite of Theseus' closing command to toss her abominable body in an unmarked ditch. The final scene's extravagant Senecan carnage, against which modern readers have tended to raise the defense of laughter, comes clad in a subtle dramatic poetry of conjugality. Phaedra dies on the word *uiro* (1198), referring to Hippolytus as a "man" or "hero," but also as a "husband," and her earlier use of that word in her speech (1184) had referred to Theseus under that description. More tellingly, her action of cutting a lock of her own hair in preparation for her self-immolation points toward the corresponding moment at the close of the Euripidean tragedy when Artemis, from the machine, reveals the aetiological significance of the play's mythic content: virgins of Attica on the eve of their wedding will sacrifice a lock of their hair to the hero Hippolytus, singing songs of mourning in which Phaedra too will have some share of commemoration.[28]

[25] Nussbaum (1995).
[26] E.g., Hill (2004, 174–5).
[27] Seneca *Phaedra* 1188–9; Euripides *Hippolytus* 771–5.
[28] Euripides *Hippolytus* 1423–30.

The Senecan Phaedra's death scene thus places her character, her desire, and her death in stark juxtaposition with the figure of a virgin bride, the flourishing of chaste conjugal love, and the heroic virtue of what Stoics called the rational exit from life. What kind of relation these juxtapositions signify is a question left open to interpretation. Readers who insist on finding only grisly parody and moral condemnation will not be explicitly gainsaid by the text. But even a provisional entertainment of the interpretation sketched here is enough to enable a reading of Seneca's tragedies as participating in his Stoic ethical project in an authentic and interesting way, by activating kinds of signifying power specific to dramatic poetry. In the ambivalent valuation of Phaedra's character and the potential for locating in that ambivalence a set of vectors passing, under the sign of *pudor*, through the degradation and madness of occurrent human life to the attainment of ideally optimal flourishing, Senecan tragedy offers a poetically fashioned life and world whose parallels to what Seneca and his philosophical tradition thought about shame shed light in both directions.

Further Reading

Kaster (2005) gives a rich account of shame and other constraining emotions in Roman culture. On shame in the specific context of Stoic philosophy, see Kamtekar (1998) and Graver (2007). Brennan (2005) offers a masterful sketch of the Stoic ethical system. Burnyeat (1981) is a classic interpretation of the role of shame in Aristotle's ethics. And Hill (2004) gives a stimulating (mostly hostile) discussion of *pudor* and suicide in regard to the character of Phaedra in Seneca's tragedy.

16

CAREY SEAL

Theory and Practice in Seneca's Writings

Seneca often writes that philosophy (*philosophia*) is the best or only way to attain virtue and thus happiness. In the first four books of the *Epistles* alone, he tells Lucilius that it is not possible to live well without philosophy (*Ep.* 16.3), that philosophy is to be preferred to all other arts (*Ep.* 29.12), and that philosophy offers the only way to be healthy, free of care, happy, and free (*Ep.* 37.3). What exactly would Lucilius, or anyone else who took Seneca's advice, spend his or her time doing? What are Seneca's reasons for thinking that the recommended activity, whatever it might be, is necessary and sufficient for happiness? This chapter aims first to sketch out an answer to these questions against the background of competing ancient conceptions of philosophy as a way of life. It then turns in sequence to three questions suggested by this sketch: How does Seneca understand the relationship between "theory" and "practice" in philosophy? How is this relationship registered in the form and texture of his writings? What effect does the Roman social and cultural environment have on Seneca's understanding and articulation of that relationship?

Seneca's Socratic Inheritance

In Plato's *Euthydemus*, Socrates secures the agreement of the young aristocrat Clinias to the proposition that knowledge is the only genuine good (282a). Everything else conventionally regarded as a good is only contingently valuable, since self-beneficial use of such goods depends on knowledge. For Plato's Socrates, the dependence of happiness on knowledge provides a warrant for claiming that the only life worth living would be spent in the pursuit of the sort of knowledge needed to live well (*Ap.* 38a). The picture of Socrates' activities that Plato presents in his so-called early dialogues offers a specimen of such a life, devoted to what Plato called philosophy.

Socrates' claim in the *Euthydemus* provides the germ of the Stoic doctrine that virtue, construed as a kind of knowledge, is the only good. But those who accept this Socratic proposition find themselves confronted with a number of questions: What kind of knowledge do we need to live a good life? How do we go about getting it? How do we know when we have attained it? What kind of balance should we aim to strike between learning how to live and actually living? Are learning and living well to any extent the same? That is, is there some value to certain kinds of intellectual activity, independent of their power to supply guidance in action?

Given the difficulty and complexity of these questions, it is no surprise that the answers they elicited from thinkers in the Socratic tradition were diverse. The Academic Skeptics, for example, translated Socrates' profession of ignorance into a habitual pessimism about the possibility of settled knowledge. The Cynics, meanwhile, held that the knowledge needed to live a good life was simply the understanding that ambient social values were pervasively corrupt and that happiness could be found by escaping the confines of convention into a genuinely natural existence. We can see these same aspects of the Socratic legacy in Stoic doctrine as well, though in a form compatible with the rest of the Stoic system. Socrates' emphasis on the difficulty of acquiring the knowledge we need to live well was answered by the Stoic doctrine that the individual who has fully acquired such knowledge – the sage – is vanishingly rare. On the question of what that knowledge is, the Stoic school was divided. The mainstream, represented by Chrysippus, affirmed the necessity of a three-part philosophical curriculum. Logic (including what we would now call epistemology), physics (the study of the natural world), and ethics all had their part to play in the philosopher's progress toward wisdom and thus happiness. The role of all three was instrumental to this progress toward happiness; unlike Aristotle, Chrysippus appears not to have believed that the pursuit of theoretical wisdom could be itself a constituent of the good life. Rather, a comprehensive understanding of the order of the universe, grounded in physical study and secured by the discipline of logic, aligns the agent with the world-mind that is identical with that order and thus makes possible, indeed certain, the rightness of the agent's actions. Not all Stoics agreed. Ariston of Chios reasserted, against Chrysippus, the Cynic elements that had been present in Stoicism from the beginning, arguing that only basic moral principles and not the disciplines of logic and physics were necessary for moral progress. In the late second and early first centuries BCE, Panaetius and Posidonius seem to have modified Chrysippan orthodoxy in the other direction, away from sweeping Cynicizing rejection of convention and toward an accommodation with convention, even to the extent of being prepared to accord external advantages the status of goods that Socrates had sought to deny them.

The Unity of Philosophy

In Seneca's prose works, we can see him grappling with this complex and contested Socratic inheritance and forging from it his own position on the vexed question of whether and how theoretical inquiry can and should be integrated with practice.[1] On the topic of logic, for example, Seneca walks a fine line: to give logical questions an independent importance, separate from the ability of logic to clarify for us the nature of the world order to which we must adapt ourselves, would be to retreat from the Socratic thesis that philosophy's urgent task is to guide action. On the other hand, to overemphasize this urgency is to risk collapsing into a Cynic-Aristonic repudiation of logic and thus of the equally Socratic idea that we need firm intellectual foundations for action. Seneca's tone when he explicitly mentions logic is often hostile (e.g., *Ep.* 45.13, 48.6–8, 49.5), but his objection is to indulgence in logical puzzles for their own sake, not to the use of logic in pursuing questions dictated by philosophy's practical agenda (*Ep.* 89.18).

Physics, too, is a focus of ancient debate about the connection between intellectual activity and practice. Socrates seems to have felt that our overriding need to put our own activity on a rational basis meant that there was no time for the natural inquiry that had been the dominant occupation of philosophers up to his own time (Pl. *Ap.* 19b–d, *Phd.* 96a–100a; Cic. *Tusc.* 5.10). The Stoics, by contrast, believed that a comprehensive understanding of the cosmos was itself an indispensable component of the knowledge Socrates believed we need (e.g., Cic. *Fin.* 3.73). Seneca advances this practical conception of physics as a necessary part of a well-reasoned life throughout his corpus. Sometimes, though, Seneca writes as if knowledge of how the universe works is an end in itself (e.g., *Ep.* 65.16–21; *NQ* 6.4.2, 1.praef.1–2), as it is for Plato (as distinguished from Socrates) and Aristotle. Brad Inwood has argued that these two understandings of the value of physics are subtly intertwined in Seneca's writing, as the theoretical drive for natural knowledge is repeatedly shown to serve a practical function by giving the agent the cosmic perspective he or she needs to live well.[2] Seneca's blurring of the lines between theory and practice can work both ways. In *On Leisure*, he argues that human beings are fitted by nature for study of the universe (*Ot.* 5); that is, theory is naturally and thus rightly part of our practice. Conversely, even in contemplative retirement, we still need, as human beings, to reflect on questions about the human good and human action (*Ot.* 4.2), so practice is rightly part of our theory as well.

---

[1] On Seneca's originality in the reception of doctrine, see Asmis' essay in this volume.
[2] Inwood (2009a).

Moral Theory and Philosophical Exercises

Seneca often mentions things that he does or that his addressee can and should do in the interests of moral progress. These include exercising the voice (*Ep.* 15.7), imagining one's own death (*Ep.* 26.8–10) or that one is observed in everything one does (*Ep.* 83.1), living on little to remove fear of poverty (*Ep.* 18.5–13), and conducting a daily review of one's actions (*Ira* 3.36). There has been much interest in the relationship of such "spiritual exercises" to the concept of self-fashioning that has underpinned a great deal of recent work in the humanities. Indeed, the work of Ilsetraut Hadot, Pierre Hadot, and Michel Foucault on the writings of Seneca, among other practical ethicists of the ancient world, played an indispensable part in articulating that concept. This work has raised important questions about the nature of philosophy in the ancient world and in particular about whether "philosophy" is to be thought of simply as rational inquiry or rather as a much broader range of activities aimed at securing wisdom and happiness by a variety of means including but not limited to rational inquiry.

A key question in this debate is to what extent Seneca's exercises form a body of practice separate from and independent of the theoretical reflection in which he also engages. Certainly, as recent work has shown, these exercises sometimes depend for their force on aspects of Roman social life that seem to have little to do with philosophical argument, for instance the authority wielded by the widely respected figures to whose imagined scrutiny one is supposed to submit one's actions (e.g., Cato and Laelius at *Ep.* 11.10). Also, Seneca's readiness to adapt such exercises from philosophical schools with theoretical commitments entirely opposed to his own, chiefly the Epicureans,[3] may suggest that they form a body of practice readily detachable from his doctrinal exposition. There is considerable evidence against this conclusion, though. Seneca explicitly affirms the value of higher-order moral principles and the need for practical advice to be referred to and constrained by them (*Ep.* 95). Indeed, Seneca's practice throughout his corpus gives an important place to moral theory, that is, for reflection on problems of choice abstracted from the particulars of practice. Theory in this sense, rather than in the Aristotelian sense of disinterested reflection, undergirds Seneca's efforts to modify his own practice and that of his readers, and in general he takes care to integrate his exercises into this larger argumentative structure.

Seneca's practice of philosophy in his writings unfolds in three steps, we might say: first a practical difficulty is introduced to motivate philosophical

---

[3] On this topic, see Schiesaro's essay in this volume.

inquiry, then points of theory are discussed and argued for in order to establish a framework for dealing with the problem, then on this basis exercises are recommended. Of course, this sequence of ideas does not always correspond to the order in which Seneca presents these operations in writing, but the three elements and their logical interrelationship can usually be discerned nonetheless. For instance, in *Epistle* 91, Seneca notes that a friend has been despondent over the destruction of his city by fire. He presents and argues for, in part through observations about the natural world, some points of Stoic moral theory that show such losses to be inevitable but not, in the end, relevant to genuine well-being. In the course of this exposition, he presents Lucilius with a way of warding off the grief that has overtaken their friend: he is to imagine such misfortunes and meditate on their inevitability. In this way, practice gives urgency and point to theory and is in turn guided by it.

We should think, then, not of a philosophy divided into rational and ascetic parts but rather of a practical philosophy in which the two parts of that phrase are mutually interdependent and interentailing, as they are for the Socrates of Plato's *Apology*. Seneca is always on guard against the danger that philosophy might come entirely unmoored from practical concerns, but he is equally insistent that those concerns can only be addressed through inquiry that seeks truth by argument (e.g., *Ep.* 82.6–7, 110.8); indeed, the quantity and quality of such inquiry throughout his corpus shows this principle to be the basic presupposition of his work. Scholars who claim priority and conceptual independence for the exercises are right to warn against simply assuming that Seneca or any other ancient writer meant by "philosophy" something close to the academic discipline we know today, the mainstream of which is defined by the argumentative pursuit of truth, But the differences are easily exaggerated, and in Seneca's case, at least, it is fair to say that they lie not so much in method as in avowed purpose: unlike most academic philosophers today, Seneca is explicit in his conviction that philosophy's rational search for truth conduces fairly directly to practical ends and can serve those ends uniquely well.

Writing Philosophy

When we enter into a discussion of how Seneca understood this connection between philosophical activity and the happy life, we are led very quickly from philosophical into literary questions. The orthodox Stoic doctrine, rooted in Socratic intellectualism, that both virtuous and vicious actions derived from beliefs, respectively true or false, leads to the supposition that changing belief by argument is sufficient to bring about moral change. One way to determine how completely Seneca subscribes to this doctrine, then, is to see how rigorously he confines himself to argument in his efforts to guide his readers toward virtue. We find a good deal of variety on this score. On the one hand, the letters and treatises contain long stretches of detailed, argumentative exposition, pursued for practical effect but with philosophical care and sophistication. On the other hand, there are many junctures at which Seneca seems to be aiming to induce moral progress through emotional rather than intellectual appeal. The very idea of doing this flies in the face of the Stoic doctrine that beliefs shape emotions, not the other way around. These passages, coupled with a broader suspicion of the putatively "rhetorical" character of post-Augustan writing at Rome, have often led critics to question not only Seneca's commitment to Stoic moral psychology but, more generally, his claim that philosophy, as represented and practiced in his writings, constitutes a method of moral instruction distinct from the processes of example and exhortation by which traditional, nonphilosophical moral teaching was transacted.[4]

Seneca himself confronts this question by drawing a distinction between on the one hand the actual work of moral guidance, which is accomplished by argument and patient discussion, and on the other the preliminary effort needed simply to capture the listener's attention, to jog him or her into giving attention to that discussion (*Ep.* 38.1). Indeed, Seneca's vivid rhetorical appeals generally operate in tandem with, not as a substitute for, much closer and more theoretically responsible argument. An example is the structure that we find in *On Mercy* and *On Anger*, both of which turn from strongly rhetorical treatments of their topics in their first books to more detailed and theoretical handling in the second books.[5] The intricate blending and overlay of these two modes in Seneca's work thus reflects not a lack of confidence in the ability of argument to push his readers along the path toward virtue but rather an awareness that philosophy has to vie for a hearing before its work can begin.

We might wonder how we are to fit Seneca's pervasive use of metaphor into this multimodal picture of moral guidance. The question of to what extent metaphor disrupts a text's aspirations to coherence is a complex one, and the potential contradictions involved are hardly confined to the Senecan corpus: witness the ongoing debate about whether Lucretius' manner of making the hidden workings of the natural world vivid and comprehensible imperils his poem's global agenda. It must suffice here to note that Seneca's metaphors, embedded in complex texts rich in detailed philosophical

---

[4] On this issue, see Wray's essay in this volume.
[5] This comparison is made in Kaster (2010, 134–5).

exposition, generally function not to close down or figure away a line of argument but rather to initiate one. That is, like Seneca's rhetorical stratagems more generally, they serve to direct attention to philosophical reasoning, not to displace it.

Each of Seneca's works exploits its generic background to encourage and demonstrate this approach to virtue through reason. The exceptions to this statement are the *Apocolocyntosis* and the tragedies. Certainly each of these has some philosophical *content* and deals with questions of central ethical importance. The tragedies in particular are the focus of ongoing controversy about their place in Seneca's philosophical project: Do they in some way enact the Stoic principles he expounds in his prose writings, or do they, instead, show the fundamental irrationality of the passions and the stark hopelessness of human life, demonstrating once again Seneca's supposed habit of self-contradiction? It is not taking part in this debate to observe that there is no place made for philosophical *method* in the dramas. Whatever the other ways in which the plays may spur moral progress, they do not do so by subjecting questions of action to rational scrutiny with the help of a developed apparatus of doctrine. It is precisely this operation, though, that is at the heart of the prose works.

In his letters to Lucilius, Seneca crosses the argumentative density of Epicurus' letters with the personal engagement of Cicero's. The result is a course of philosophical therapy that pays constant and nuanced attention to the relationship between theory and practice in moral guidance. Though the letters, unlike Cicero's, are clearly intended for readers other than just their addressee, Lucilius does not serve merely as peg on which to hang a series of philosophical harangues. Rather, discussions of Stoic doctrine are, in general, introduced by reference to some difficulty Lucilius has been having or to some objection he has raised to a previous point of Seneca's or simply by his unfolding intellectual engagement with philosophy. It would be an exaggeration to claim that we finish the preserved set of letters with a deep sense of Lucilius' character, but we see enough of his particular circumstances to establish Seneca's overarching point that philosophy takes its first impulses from the practical dilemmas of individual lives, however theoretically sophisticated it may need to become in its efforts to answer those dilemmas.

Seneca's letters, especially when considered as an ordered sequence, offer some of the advantages of the dialogue form:[6] they give a sense of what philosophical exchange is like, they show the uses of that exchange in making moral progress, and they encourage the reader to grapple with

[6] On Seneca's use of the dialogue form, see Roller in this volume.

the arguments made and to consider possible objections. Furthermore, by allowing the reader to see how philosophical guidance can be made therapeutically responsive to the needs of a particular individual, the letters give substance to the analogy Seneca repeatedly draws between medicine as an art of curing the body and philosophy as an art of curing the mind. This analogy has deep roots in both Greek and Roman attempts to describe the value and workings of philosophy (e.g., Cic. *Tusc* 3.1), but the broad canvas and protreptic specificity of the letters allow Seneca to show in detail how the medical model mediates between the singular and invariable truth that is the object of philosophy and the plural and varied human beings who are its subjects.

The so-called *Dialogues*, too, exhibit this therapeutic character, though despite their traditional title, the element of debate is muted in them by comparison with the dialogues of Plato or Cicero or even with the implied exchange of views in Seneca's letters. Seneca is able to give each of these works a definite practical orientation, though, that in each case ties the philosophical issue under discussion to the needs of the addressee and by extension his readership. He supplies this orientation most directly and naturally in the three consolations, each of which addresses itself to what would likely be acknowledged by the addressee as an obvious problem in need of remedy. In other cases, we are told that the addressee solicited help in dealing with a particular difficulty. *On Anger*, for instance, responds to Seneca's brother Novatus' request for a way of dealing with the passion of the title, while *On tranquility of the soul* presents us with a speech by the addressee, Serenus, in which he details his difficulties and requests a diagnosis and cure. The dialogue that makes the least effort to situate itself with respect to the needs of an addressee, *On leisure*, is also the one that addresses most directly questions of the interrelationship of theory and practice. Here Seneca deploys Stoic moral theory to mount a sophisticated rebuttal of the doctrine that philosophers must renounce wealth and of claims that philosophers fail to practice their own doctrines. It is a testament to Seneca's ingenuity that he is able to make this defense without retreating from the Socratic link between theory and practice.

A special case is the treatise *On Mercy*, addressed to Nero. Here Seneca must make the case for philosophy without the help of the medical model, since the suggestion that the emperor is in any way sick or deficient would be impolitic. Instead, Seneca suggests here another role for theory: it can confirm and make permanent good traits that proceed from instinct (*Clem.* 2.2.2). Seneca here relies on the Stoic doctrine, again one with Socratic roots, that each virtue must be grounded in a full understanding of the good. Nonsages do not possess this understanding, and so, however apparently virtuous their actions, they are merely accidently and contingently behaving in a virtuous way. The unstable epistemic foundations of their practice are always vulnerable to corruption and alteration, but theoretical reflection on ethical questions can bring those foundations closer to stability. Seneca does not make these premises explicit in *On Mercy*, for obvious reasons, but together with his claims about Nero's spontaneous clemency they generate a practical demand for his theoretical examination of that virtue. Of course, in light of what we know of Nero from other sources, it is tempting to suppose that Seneca intended a different kind of relationship between that examination and Nero's own behavior and that he hoped his discussion would prompt, rather than reinforce and consolidate, stirrings toward mildness on the emperor's part. In any event, it is clear that he regards detailed and argumentative examination of clemency as potentially having a morally ameliorative effect on Nero, from whatever starting point that amelioration proceeds.

The seven-book treatise *On Benefits*, too, deals with an ethical topic of far-reaching political significance, in this case the exchange of favors that structured Roman social and public life. Though the practical import of the subject as a whole is clear, Seneca's involved theoretical exploration of the moral questions surrounding reciprocity often bears little relation to any real dilemma of action, especially in the last three books, which, Seneca tells us, pursue for their intellectual interest strands of inquiry peripherally related to the central topic (*Ben.* 5.1.2). The treatise's connection to practice is perhaps best seen in light of the Stoic doctrine that the aspirant to wisdom should aim at a comprehensive grasp of the order that pervades the cosmos. Generally, as discussed previously and in what follows, this principle is understood as mandating attention to the standard topics of natural philosophy. Seneca, though, possibly following the example of Panaetius or Hecato or both, extends it to warrant a descriptive, not merely directly normative, *social* theory at the same level of sophistication that characterizes Stoic physics, and it is this that he provides in *On Benefits*.

The subject matter of the *Natural Questions* – physical and meteorological phenomena from rivers to lightning – might too seem to wander rather far from the tight link between theory and practice that we have been following through Seneca's corpus, especially in light of Socrates' aforementioned rejection of such study. The *Natural Questions* thus allow us to see in detail Seneca's understanding of the reasons for the Stoic grafting of natural study onto the Socratic model of philosophical practice. At the most basic level, Seneca makes the case that knowledge of the natural world gives us a sense of our place in the universe and thus of the responsibilities imposed on us by the cosmic order (e.g., *NQ* 6.32.1). Indeed, Seneca's argument throughout the *Natural Questions* for an ordered and providential universe, against the Epicurean picture of merely contingent order famously propounded by Lucretius, helps establish a warrant for his Stoic talk about such an order in the first place. But Seneca also lays recurring emphasis on the ethical function of the *activity* of studying or contemplating nature, as opposed to the knowledge gained by that study. That activity sharpens and trains our intellect for ethical reasoning (*NQ* 3.praef.18), and it offers us escape from morally corrosive environments (*NQ* 4a.praef.19–22). Aside from the independent value of natural knowledge, and even aside from their role in bringing us incrementally closer to the full understanding of the cosmos that we would need to be wise, physical study and the treatise itself are thus of immediate and direct moral benefit.

Seneca's prose writings are thus themselves philosophical exercises, in the sense that the reading of them is designed to stimulate and guide the rational inquiry that conduces to moral progress as well as to provide a model of that inquiry.

Rome and Philosophy

Seneca is committed to the ideal of the life guided by rational inquiry and in large part also to the traditional morality of the Roman elite. Often he seems to regard the two as compatible and, indeed, mutually reinforcing. Recent scholarship has profitably examined his use of exemplary figures and narratives from Roman history in arguing for Stoic claims, and, conversely, the ways in which those claims offer his aristocratic readers a means of reclaiming the dignity and autonomy they had lost under the principate. There is an obvious implicit tension between the two sources of moral norms, though, and that tension becomes especially evident when Seneca appeals to or offers praise for icons of Roman virtue who could not, as he and his readers know, possibly have been following the philosophical route to virtue that Seneca repeatedly endorses and that we have sketched out. Seneca's solution is to put forward an account of moral decline (see especially *Ep.* 95.14–39) that both accords with the deeply entrenched Roman view that things were, in general, better in the past and offers an explanation for why Seneca's contemporaries need philosophy when their ancestors, apparently, did not: philosophy is an art that develops to solve moral problems, which, Seneca maintains, grow more numerous and difficult as civilization develops.

The overt conflicts that appear in Seneca's writing between philosophically generated norms and those of the surrounding community are perhaps best viewed less as specific comments on contemporary Rome than as expressions of a more general opposition, visible in Plato and anticipated in the writings of the Presocratic thinkers Xenophanes, Heraclitus, and Parmenides, between the moral and epistemic claims of philosophy and those of the surrounding culture. It is this tension that Seneca has in mind when he wonders to what extent he and Lucilius ought to participate in the *Saturnalia* (*Ep.* 18) or worries that the unkempt appearance favored by some philosophers is gratuitously alienating to nonphilosophers (*Ep.* 5) or writes that he gave up his youthful vegetarianism, adopted under the influence of the quasi-Pythagorean Sextian school, because it diverged too conspicuously from general practice (*Ep.* 108.22). These concerns show a consciousness that the Socratic link between reflection and action necessarily generates substantial differences in mode of life between philosophers and others and at the same time a desire to contain the expression of those differences as much as possible. On a broader scale, his entire prose corpus can be seen as an effort on the one hand to assert the fundamental gulf between the way of life shaped by philosophical reflection and all other lives and on the other hand to take up the literary challenge of building a written bridge over that expanse.

Further Reading

There is detailed discussion of the Socratic principles adverted to in this essay, and of their implication that philosophy can and should be a way of life, in Cooper (2012, 24–69). Long (1988), Striker 1996a, and Long 1999 explore the import of Socratic ethics for Stoicism. On Seneca's attitude toward logic, see Barnes (1997, 12–23). On the relationship between physics and ethics in the Stoic system, see Inwood (2007b) and especially Inwood (2009a).

   One conception of ancient philosophy as a way of life, emphasizing philosophy's status as a practice and its mystical, communal, and somatic aspects can be traced through Rabbow (1954), I. Hadot (1969), and the essays collected in P. Hadot (1995), with a clear summation in P. Hadot (2002). This conception is adopted with significant modifications by Foucault (1986). The present chapter has stressed instead the centrality of argument and rational inquiry, and this alternative picture of philosophy as a way of life owes much to Nussbaum (1994) and Cooper (2012). Newman (1989) surveys Seneca's philosophical exercises. On self-scrutiny and self-examination in Seneca, see Bartsch (2006, 183–281) and Ker (2009c). The controversies surrounding the picture of the self presupposed by these exercises are best studied in Bartsch and Wray (2009), particularly in the introduction by Bartsch and Wray and in the essays by Long and Inwood.

For the ways in which genre inflects the relationship between theory and practice in Seneca's writing, see especially Williams (2012) on natural study as a philosophical exercise in the *Natural Questions* and Griffin (2013, 7–87) on the aims and context of *On Benefits*. Mayer (1991) examines Seneca's use of Roman exempla, while Roller (2001, 64–126) offers a nuanced political account of Stoicism's appeal to Seneca and his audience.

17

ELIZABETH ASMIS

Seneca's Originality

Seneca identified himself as a Stoic.[1] He also saw himself as making a philosophical contribution of his own. As is commonly agreed, this contribution lies in the field of practical ethics rather than theory. There is clearly something new in the way that Seneca puts theory to work. With the help of received ideas, Seneca stages a philosophical drama, which focuses on the individual trying to attain happiness. Taking on many guises (which stand, ultimately, for Seneca himself), this individual must fashion a journey of his own. He is aided by others; but he cannot progress unless he assumes responsibility for himself. Accordingly, Seneca sees himself not merely as a healer but as a healer whose job it is to motivate the patient to heal himself. It is here, I think, that we may find the root of Seneca's originality. Seeking to motivate, Seneca does not merely devise a new rhetoric; he takes a new look, above all, at the powers that an individual has within oneself to make a change.

In this chapter, I will first consider the originality of Seneca's philosophical writings as whole, then focus on what I consider the core of his originality. Dealing with the whole, the first two sections discuss, first, Seneca's own view of his philosophical independence, and, second, his actual independence in reconfiguring Stoic philosophy. The two final sections concern his aim as a philosophical healer: the first deals with two innovations in his moral psychology that have a bearing on practice; the second deals with the importance of wanting the right thing. Both of these sections concern an issue that continues to intrigue modern scholars: Seneca's emphasis on wanting (*velle*).

---

[1] He frequently refers to the Stoics as "us" or "our" (*nostri*), e.g., *De otio* 8.1, *De constantia* 2.1.

Seneca's Philosophical Independence

Seneca is profuse in acknowledging his debt to other thinkers. At the same time, he insists on his freedom to believe whatever he chooses. This freedom has two main aspects: he need not accept what previous Stoics proposed; and he can add whatever he chooses. On the first point, he proclaims: "We [Stoics] are not under a king; each person claims freedom for himself."[2] Thus he will not "bind" himself to any particular Stoic.[3] Although he "follows" earlier thinkers, he "follows a path of my own": "I am not a slave" to them, "but I give assent."[4] Consequently, he permits himself "to discover something, to change, and to leave aside." Elsewhere, he says that he will use the "old path" unless he "discovers one that is closer and more level."[5]

In his use of the term "assent," Seneca roots his independence in Stoic doctrine itself: having the power of assent, each person decides for himself what to believe. In addition, he views his independence as a right that he has as a Roman. Like any Roman citizen, Seneca will not be slave to a king. More specifically, he claims the prerogative of a Roman senator. As such, he holds the "right of opinion" (censendi ius): this is the right to approve or reject a motion, or divide it, or add to it.[6] However much the Greeks founded philosophical investigation, Seneca will continue this tradition as a Roman, making changes to it as he determines.

In Seneca's view, the Romans have already added much to the philosophical tradition. In one place, he lists (in order) the following "teachers of mankind": both Catos, Laelius the Wise, and Socrates together with Plato, Zeno, and Cleanthes.[7] Elsewhere, Seneca adds the Roman Stoic Tubero to the two Catos and Laelius.[8] Cato the younger, who committed suicide at Utica, is exalted by Seneca as possibly exceeding even the virtue of a Stoic wise man (Const. 7.1). What distinguishes the Romans in these lists is clearly their practice, not their theory. Seneca vehemently disclaims being a wise person or being anywhere near there. But his mention of Tubero and Laelius invites the reader to see Seneca, too, as qualified to join the list of those who show others how to move toward this goal.

Seneca aspired to make the philosophical tradition "greater" (ampliora, Ep. 64.7). Much, he says, remains to be done. There are two ways of making

---

[2] Ep. 33.4; cf. Ep. 45.4, 113.23, and 117.4–6.
[3] De vita beata 3.2–3 and De otio 3.1
[4] Ep. 80.1; cf. De otio 1.5.
[5] Ep. 33.11.
[6] De vita beata 3.2, cf. Ep. 21.9 and De otio 3.1.
[7] Ep. 64.10.
[8] Ep. 95.72 and 104.21; cf. 98.13.

a contribution: the addition of new discoveries or the use of past discoveries. The progression of discoveries is without end; there is always more to be added.[9] Suppose, however, that everything has already been discovered; still, the use of past discoveries is forever "new." Seneca calls this "the use, knowledge, and arrangement" of what has been discovered by others (*Ep.* 64.8). He goes on to explain that the "remedies of the mind" (*animi remedia*) have already been discovered; it is "our job" to determine how and when to apply them. Our predecessors "did (*egerunt*) much, but did not complete (*peregerunt*)" the job (*Ep.* 64.9).

By asserting that practice, too, is forever new, Seneca stakes out a claim for making a major contribution of his own. Seneca did not presume to equal his predecessors in the development of theory; but he did want to take his place among them as a moral guide, helping to complete what they began. In this endeavor, he developed a pedagogy that rivals the contributions of Plato, Aristotle, and others.

Reconfiguring Stoic Theory

How, then, did Seneca use the prerogative of cutting, augmenting, and changing the philosophical theories of the past? First of all, much of logic, one of the three parts of philosophy, falls by the wayside.[10] Further, Seneca eschews excessive learning of any kind.[11] The reason is that such studies have no practical value; they clutter the mind, which needs space to deal with important issues.[12] If his predecessors hadn't sought out what is superfluous, Seneca complains, perhaps they would have discovered what is necessary.[13]

As a topic of learning, morality, too, admits of being chopped up into ever-finer problems, leading to excess. Seneca, however, is much more tolerant of this kind of excess. In his largest moral treatise, *On Benefits*, Seneca admits that there is some superfluous analysis, lacking in practical value, in the last three of the seven books.[14] His excuse is that these intricacies offer relaxation and entertainment as well as sharpen the mind. One might add that to have a sharp mind on the topic of benefits was not without utility for the affluent Romans of Seneca's circle.

---

[9] In addition to *Ep.* 64.7, see *Ep.* 33.10–11, 45.4, 79.6, and n. 18.
[10] See *Ep.* 48.4–12; 49.6–12; 82.9 and 19; 83.9–17; 85.1–2, 24, 50; 106; 109.17–18; 111; and 113.
[11] See *Brev.* 13 and *Ep.* 88.36–45.
[12] *Ep.* 88.32–5.
[13] *Ep.* 45.4.
[14] *Ben.* 5.12.1–2 (together with 5.1–2) and 7.1; cf. *Ben.* 6.1 and *Ep.* 109.17.

Seneca not only leaves aside much of Stoic physics, but also reconfigures the whole into a much broader concern. His ambitious *Natural Questions* is an attempt to cover the whole of physics, from the pre-Socratics to recent thinkers. Taking the view that knowledge has grown and will continue to grow, Seneca makes a point of including theories that are outdated along with others that he considers wrong or even silly.[15] Toward the end of his work, he proposes to plunge into new, doubtful territory, without the help of teachers.[16] He disagrees with the Stoics a number of times, branding some of their theories "foolish."[17] In one place, he invokes the privilege of "adding an opinion" (*amplius censeo*); the addition consists of an analogy between the structure of the human body and the configuration of the earth.[18] This is not so very new; and, on the whole, Seneca seems to add few, if any, physical discoveries of his own.

This does not mean that Seneca's physics is derivative. The purpose that governs *Natural Questions* is Seneca's own: to raise the mind from the sordidness of human affairs to a union with god.[19] The message is influenced by Plato, but Seneca gives it a Stoic meaning. What is sordid is not our participation in the world but our repudiation of the divinity that permeates everything in the world. Throughout his work, physical investigation goes hand in hand with moral learning. To know the causes of lightning, for example, is not enough; one must strengthen one's mind not to fear it.[20] Likewise, Seneca keeps adding warnings against avarice, luxury, war,[21] sexual license, and the fear of death to physical explanations. In this interweaving of physical and moral themes, Seneca offers a deeply original counterpart to Lucretius' great Epicurean poem "On the Nature of Things."

Seneca is indebted to Plato in his ethical writings, especially in his recurrent depreciation of the body and inclination to view the mind as immortal.[22] He is also surprisingly hospitable to Epicureanism. Venturing "even into the camps of others" (*Ep.* 2.5) – though as a scout, he says, not a deserter – Seneca assimilates numerous sayings from Epicurus and his followers. Calling them "public" property,[23] he gives them a Stoic interpretation.

---

[15] On the growth of knowledge, see *NQ* 6.5.3, 7.25.3–5, 7.30–2; on including wrong views, see *NQ* 6.19.
[16] *NQ* 2.21.
[17] *NQ* 4B5–6; see also 1.8.4 and 7.22.1.
[18] *NQ* 3.15.1; cf. 2.57.1.
[19] *NQ* 1, Preface, and 3, Preface 18; cf. *Ad Helviam* 8.5–6 and 20.2. See further Williams 2012, esp. 2–10.
[20] *NQ* 2.59.1–2.
[21] *NQ* 5.18.
[22] See esp. *Ep.* 102.21–30.
[23] *Ep.* 8.8, 21.9, and 33.2.

Epicurus' maxim "a joyful poverty is a fine (*honesta*) thing" (*Ep.* 2.6), for example, becomes a description of the Stoic supreme good, called *honestum*; what is "fine," according to the Stoics, is moral goodness, and this is what gives "joy." Along with selected sayings, Seneca takes over Epicurean precepts and attitudes.[24] He appropriates the Epicurean doctrine that pleasure must be confined within natural bounds;[25] and he goes so far as to claim that Epicurus "teaches what is sacred and right" by reducing pleasure to something slight.[26] Seneca's withdrawal from public life, as set out in *On Leisure*, is another nod to Epicureanism. Friendship, too, looms large in his writings, as does the need for a mentor.

Last is a general reminder. It is one thing to identify what Seneca selects from previous philosophers. It is another to understand how he molds what he takes into something of his own. Seneca himself compares the work of learning from others to that of bees gathering materials for the production of honey; they must appropriate the materials they take by digesting them and making them their own.[27] In this process, the concepts and values that Seneca owes to his experience as a Roman have a transfiguring influence.

Two Issues of Moral Psychology

Two issues in Seneca's thought have provoked much interest recently. They also help to show what is original about his work. One concerns the structure of the mind, the other concerns the passions (Greek *pathê*).

The Structure of the Mind

Seneca offers a surprising division of the mind in one of his *Epistles* (92.1, 8). Here he divides the mind – called *principale*, the "directing" part of the soul (Greek *hegemonikon*) – into two parts: a "rational" and an "irrational part." The latter is in turn divided into (a) a part that is said to be "spirited, ambitious, uncontrolled" and to consist of the passions (*positam in adfectibus*) and (b) an indolent part, given to pleasure. This division occurs nowhere else in Seneca's writings. For the rest, he adheres to the early Stoic view of the mind as a unitary rational entity.[28] Traditionally, it was widely

---

[24] See Schottlaender (1955), Grimal (1970, 7–14) and Schiesaro's chapter in this volume.
[25] *De vita beata* 13.4 and 14.1; cf. *Ep.* 121.4.
[26] *De vita beata* 13.1
[27] *Ep.* 84; see further Castelnérac (2007).
[28] For example, Seneca states at *De ira* 1.8.3 that reason and passion (*affectus*) do not have separate locations but are a change of the mind for the better or worse.

held that Seneca owed the partition to Posidonius, who (it was believed, on the authority of Galen) followed Plato.[29] Recently, however, it has been argued that, instead of overturning the early Stoic view, Posidonius supplemented it by adding two irrational forces, spirit and desire, which serve as a source of energy for the passions. According to this interpretation, the passions remain acts of judgment (as posited by Chrysippus) but require, in addition, an irrational force to get started.[30]

Where does this leave Seneca? His division of the mind matches neither Plato's tripartition nor the new interpretation of Posidonius.[31] Seneca locates the Stoic passions (*adfectus*) in one irrational part of the mind, the spirit, while locating pleasure in the other irrational part; and he opposes these two parts to each other, the one as violent, the other as languid. Unlike Plato, he assigns these parts to the mind, not the soul; unlike Posidonius (on either the old or the new interpretation), he situates the passions (as violent kinds of feelings) within just one part, the spirit.

Seneca's partition, I suggest, looks very much like an attempt to adapt Stoic theory to a Platonic-Aristotelian framework. On behalf of such an adaptation, one might well argue that the early Stoics, too, recognized an irrational element within the mind: these are the passions, viewed as a perversion of reason. Seneca's third part of the mind is not the Stoic passion of desire (for, in his view, all passions belong to the spirit) but a nonrational attraction for pleasure, free from any act of judgment. It may reasonably be assigned to the mind as a feature that it shares with the whole living organism, which has a natural inclination toward pleasure. Seneca's partition, too, looks like a supplement to early Stoic theory, though different from the kind attributed to Posidonius: while retaining the claim that all passions are initiated by acts of judgment, it demarcates both a forceful antirational component, the spirit, and a feeble nonrational inclination for pleasure.[32] Among other questions, one may ask: does this supplement add a special motive force to the passions, or does it merely recognize the passions as a distinct

---

[29] See, for example, Voelke (1973), 165. Galen offers a lengthy polemic against Chrysippus and in support of Posidonius in book 4 of *On the doctrines of Plato and Hippocrates*; see Edelstein/Kidd fragments 34–5, 157–9, and 165.

[30] Fillion-Lahille (1984, 122–62) first proposed this view; she calls the irrational powers a "root" and "starting-point" (129–30, 135) and distinguishes them as an antecedent cause from the efficient cause, reason (154). Cooper (1998) subsequently analysed this position further (see p. 101, n. 8).

[31] Fillion-Lahille (1984, 161–2) attributes Seneca's partition to Posidonius.

[32] Even though Chrysippus denied that animals aim for pleasure, he admitted pleasure as a "by-product" (*epigennêma*), supervening on the attainment of natural goals (SVF 3.178). In agreement with Chrysippus, Seneca endorses pleasure as an attractive "addition" (*accessio*, Ep. 116.3).

type of mental activity, like the early Stoics? I shall return to this question in the last section of the chapter.

It is tempting to suppose that Seneca's supplement is, in fact, the one proposed by Posidonius. In that case, the current interpretation of Posidonius would need to be revised. The admission of a nonviolent desire for pleasure can readily be seen as an attempt to reconcile early Stoic views of pleasure with those of Plato and Aristotle. It also fits what Seneca says about pleasure elsewhere in his writings.[33] On a practical level, Seneca's analysis assigns two main tasks to reason: to defeat the passions on the one hand and to regulate pleasure on the other.

The Growth of a Passion

Seneca offers an especially fine-grained analysis of a passion in *On anger* 2.1–4. According to early Stoic theory, a passion (*pathos*) occurs when a person assents to a special type of "impulsive" presentation – one that involves a wrong evaluation of what one should do. In the case of anger, the presentation shows not only that an injury has occurred but also that one should take revenge. Seneca agrees. What is novel is that he now imputes a kind of willing, or wish, to the person who has the impulsive presentation. Preceding the act of assent, this kind of volition may be dispelled immediately by the intervention of reason (2.3.4):

> Anger must not only move, but run ahead; for it is an impulse, and impulse never occurs without assent of the mind, nor is it possible for revenge and punishment to occur without mental cognition. Someone has thought (*putavit*) himself injured and wanted (*voluit*) to take revenge, but when some cause dissuades him he has immediately settled down (*resedit*). I do not call this anger, but a motion of the mind that is obedient to reason; anger is that which has overleapt reason and snatches [a person] with itself.

As the perfect tenses of the verbs indicate, there is a succession of momentary responses: the thought of injury, the wish for revenge, the obedience to reason. There is a wish for revenge, but it passes immediately at the prompting of reason. Anger occurs only when the wish has been confirmed by assent; at that point, the wish has moved beyond the control of reason.

Seneca describes the same kind of situation a little later. He now offers a general analysis of the passions as a sequence of three kinds of motion, as exemplified by the passion of anger (2.4.1):

---

[33] See *De vita beata* 10.3, 12.2; and *Tranq.* 17.6. At *de vita beata* 12.2, Seneca distinguishes the mild, "languid" pleasures of the wise from the passion of pleasure.

Here is how you may know how the passions (*adfectus*) begin or grow or get carried away. The first motion is not voluntary, as though a preparation for the passion and a certain threat. The second is joined by a willing (*voluntas*) that is not stubborn (*contumax*), like: I should retaliate, since I have been hurt, or this person should be punished, since he has committed a crime. Third is a motion that is now out of control, which does not want to take revenge if it is right, but in any event, and which has overcome reason.

The three kinds of motion form a gradation: the first is involuntary; the second is joined by a volition that is still under the control of reason; and the third is no longer under the control of reason. As an example of the first motion, we might take the involuntary jolt triggered by the presentation of an injury; here, one has not yet formed a wish to take revenge. The second type comes with a conditional, "nonstubborn" kind of willing or wish (*voluntas*), for example, that I should take revenge. This, I take it, is the formation of an impulsive presentation; and it is not yet joined by assent. What makes the wish "nonstubborn" is that it can go either way: it may be either dispelled by reason or confirmed by assent. In the third type of motion, the wish has been transformed by an act of assent into an unconditional desire for revenge. This is the passion of anger; and it is no longer subject to the control of reason.[34]

As Seneca now shows, the distinction between two kinds of willing applies to all the passions: there is a preliminary, conditional willing that occurs at the stage of the presentation; and it is succeeded by a fixed willing that is due to an act of assent and constitutes the passion. Although some passions, such as anger, fall technically under the category of one of the main Stoic passions, "desire" (*epithymia*), all passions are marked by desire in a loose sense. Take another main passion, fear: there is, first, a conditional wish to run, let us say, from the enemy, which is not yet a passion; it is succeeded by a fixed determination to run, which is a passion. There is no technical Stoic vocabulary that marks the distinction between the two kinds of willing. Yet the distinction is of enormous practical significance: for it pries open a critical space for intervention. The wise person is immune to even the first kind of willing; though susceptible to physical jolts, he won't even momentarily entertain the thought of taking revenge. But all nonwise people are besieged by inappropriate wishes at the stage at which they are still considering a course of action, before they have given assent; and their well-being depends

---

[34] My interpretation agrees with that of Sorabji (2000, 61–3). Following Fillion-Lahille (1984, 181), Graver (2007, 125–32) takes the second stage to correspond to anger and the third to an especially vicious condition, "brutishness"; this seems to me in conflict with Seneca's view of anger as something that is out of control.

on being able to resist these inchoate wishes. It is too late when they have given assent; the damage is done. At that stage, one can only review the past in order to learn to intervene at the right point the next time.

From the beginning, the Stoics warned against giving assent rashly. Seneca agrees, but with new specificity. What he adds is the recognition that temptation is fine – it is not just inevitable but useful; for the mere thought of doing something inappropriate is another signal (in addition to purely physical reactions) for the need of intervention.[35] Seneca makes a virtue (loosely speaking) out of a vice (loosely speaking): by watching our desires before they erupt into full-fledged passions, we can put a stop to them.

Pedagogy and Moral Willing

It is time now to close in on the individual whom Seneca proposes to train. How can he turn from wrong desires to desiring what is right?

First, Seneca insists repeatedly on the need for a moral guide.[36] "Virtue is difficult to find," he says, "it needs a director (*rector*) and leader (*dux*)."[37] Theoretically, it is possible to find virtue by oneself; but Seneca has no faith in this possibility.[38] He distinguishes two kinds of guides: previous thinkers, who have left behind books, together with their example; and contemporaries, who may address a general audience or take a particular person under their guidance. Seneca calls for the student to "live" with both types of guides – both dead and living – as intimate friends.[39] This is not a hierarchical relationship but a community of equals, whereby each inspires and learns from the other.

Why is it so important to have a guide? As Seneca points out, every person who wants to become virtuous starts out not from a position of neutrality but from a position of evil. Although we are born without any moral flaw,[40] we are necessarily imbued with evil before we ever start attempting to become good: "A good mind comes to no one before a bad mind; we have all been occupied beforehand."[41] Following Chrysippus,[42] Seneca recognizes two external sources of corruption: persuasive images and indoctrination (*katêchêsis*, something like "ear bashing"). As he keeps emphasizing,

---

[35] See *De ira* 2.22.2–4 and 3.29–30.3 for examples of how to preempt anger by making appropriate judgments.

[36] *De vita beata* 1.2; *Ep.* 52.2; *Ep.* 94.50–6; and *Ben.* 5.25.5–6.

[37] *NQ* 3.30.8.

[38] See *Ben.* 5.25.5 and *Ep.* 52.3.

[39] *Ep.* 52.7–8, *Brev.* 14, *Constantia* 13, and *Ep.* 104.21–2. On Seneca's relations with Lucilius, see *Ep.* 35.2, 40.1, and 55.11.

[40] *Ep.* 22.15 and 94.55–6.

[41] *Ep.* 50.7; cf. 97.10.

[42] SVF 3.228–9a.

presentations have the power to deceive us;[43] and the "crowd" has the power to infect us with its opinions.[44] By "crowd," he is careful to note, he does not mean a certain social level; he means the overwhelming number of humans, regardless of social station, who have become sunk in a moral morass.[45]

These external influences go along with inner vulnerability. The reason that they can corrupt at all is that our rational faculty is necessarily weak through the entire process of development by which it moves, first, to the acquisition of full rationality (at age 14, according to some Stoics) and, second, to the attainment of perfect rationality. Although the rational faculty keeps growing, it is liable to lapse until the very moment at which it attains perfect rationality.[46] Further, the more we are infected by evil, the more difficult it is to expel it.[47] Yet, as Seneca also keeps insisting, we are ourselves to blame for not getting rid of it. We do not try hard enough, and we do not listen to wise counsel. The main reason is that we are too self-satisfied.[48] We are ignorant of the evil within us (*Ep.* 50.3–4); indeed, we are enamored of our faults (*Ep.* 116.8). We make the excuse that we can't do it, not recognizing that the real reason is that we are unwilling (*nolle*), not that we lack the ability (*posse*).[49] We delight, too, in the wrong that we do, even though an innate sense of the good disturbs even the most vicious among us.[50]

A mentor, therefore, needs to counteract both the external sources of corruption and our inner sloth. Seneca innovates on both fronts. Against deceptive presentations and brainwashing, he summons all the techniques of ordinary rhetoric. It is often said that what Seneca adds to Stoic doctrine is rhetorical elaboration; and this tends to have a negative ring.[51] Seneca's rhetoric, however, serves his personal philosophical purpose as a moral healer; and even if it gets in the way of argument, it need not take anything away from the philosophical endeavor to establish a firm foundation of truths by which to guide one's life.

I will cite just two examples of Seneca's use of rhetoric, one dealing with Seneca's choice of subject matter, the other with expression. The Stoic sage had long before become an object of ridicule; or if not that, he had been dismissed as an unrealizable ideal. Seneca resuscitates him, depicting him in

---

[43] See *Ep.* 87.33, 94.13, and 118.8; *Helvia* 6.1; *Ben.* 4.34.1; *De ira* 2.22.2; *Tranq.* 12.5.

[44] *Ep.* 123.6–9, with warnings against the crowd at *Ep.* 5.2–3; 25.7, etc.

[45] *De vita beata* 2.2.

[46] *Ep.* 94.13 and 97.10.

[47] *Ep.* 50.4–7 and 59.9.

[48] *Ep.* 59.9–11; cf. *Tranq.* 1.16.

[49] *Ep.* 116.8

[50] *Ep.* 97.10–12.

[51] Opinions range from the very negative (Cooper 2004) to a positive evaluation of Seneca's purpose (Hadot 1969).

new glory as one who combines the attributes of a warrior with those of a god. The sage is not a mirage: he is there in real life, as exemplified – even to excess – by Cato.[52] Firm, unshaken, generous, and kind, Seneca's sage is serenely happy. What we see is not intellectual fixity but indomitable contentment and joy.[53] Drawing on traditional Roman notions of *virtus* and influenced, too, by an Epicurean ideal of happiness, Seneca transforms the Stoic sage into an object of emulation, inspiring the beholder with a yearning to become just like him.

Seneca also sought to pack as much persuasive power as possible into verbal expression. A basic concern is to put together individual letter sounds into a well-sounding whole, or what we might call the art of "sound bites." Poetry provides a starting point. Following Cleanthes, Seneca held that metrical rhythms impress a moral message especially forcefully on the mind. As evidence, he points to what happens in the theater: even the worst scoundrels applaud moral pronouncements. That is why philosophers should intersperse poetry in their discourse.[54] Seneca seeks to achieve the same effect by his use of prose sayings, *sententiae*.[55] They punctuate his prose persistently as a means of making an immediate impact. The problem is that the effect of such sound bites is short lived: it needs to be reinforced by philosophical instruction.[56]

In general, the force of rhetoric or any other external stimulus is not enough: the student must be prompted to engage in an effort of his own. It is the basic job of a guide to rouse the student's own capacity for moral action. In this endeavor, he has a crucial ally: the moral sensibility that is inborn in every human being. Seneca calls it a "sense of the good" (*boni sensus, Ep.* 97.12); and it consists of both a natural "desire" (*cupiditas*) for the good[57] and a natural "aversion" (*aversatio*) from evil (*Ep.* 97.16.). No one becomes good without it, and it inheres even in the worst of us.[58] Despite the difficulty of eradicating moral evil, "it is easy to stir the listener to a desire for what is right (*cupidinem recti*); for nature has given to all the foundations and seed (*semen*) of the virtues" (*Ep.* 108.8). When these "seeds" are stirred by admonitions, for example, virtue is aroused within us just as a spark is fanned into a flame by a light breath; in short, "virtue is aroused when touched and impelled."[59]

---

[52] *Constantia* 7.1.
[53] See, for example, *Ep.* 41.5, 45.9, 59.14, 115.3–6; and *Clementia* 2.5.2–5.
[54] *Ep.* 108.8–12; on Cleanthes, see Philodemus *On Music* 4 col. 142.5–22 (Delattre).
[55] *Ep.* 94.27 and 43; cf. *Ep.* 108.6–7.
[56] *Ep.* 108.7 and 12.
[57] *Ep.* 108.8; *De vita beata* 1.1.
[58] *Ep.* 97.12; cf. *Ben.* 3.1.4.
[59] *Ep.* 94.29, cf. *Ben.* 6.16.5–7.

This moral sense belongs to our nature as rational animals. As the term "seeds" implies, our inborn power of reason is not something inert; it is a force that grows by its own nature. Derived from god and striving toward god, it is inherently something divine. Calling it a "god," or "sacred spirit" (*sacer spiritus*), Seneca personifies it as an "observer and watchman (*observator et custos*) of our evils and goods," who "treats us as it is treated by us."[60]

Although it is inevitable, therefore, for the mind to be corrupted by external influences, it has both an awareness of its own moral condition and the power to improve it. Seneca, I suggest, provides us with the evidence to distinguish three levels of moral awareness. Although he does not distinguish them explicitly or shape them into a theory, they offer a new perspective on how to heal oneself or others.

In the first place, every living creature has an inner cognition (*conscientia, suneidêsis*) of its constitution, together with an affinity (*oikeiosis, conciliatio*) toward itself and an alienation (*allotriôsis, aversatio*) from its destruction.[61] In the case of humans, this is an awareness of our condition as rational beings, resulting in an affinity ("desire," as Seneca puts it) for the good and alienation from evil. In common with our other powers, we have an awareness of our power of reason before we ever use it. This is the most basic level of self-awareness, underlying the rest.

Second, we have an awareness of our moral development, consisting of a gradation of discomfort about our inner evil and (when we finally become good) unshakeable tranquility.[62] Our moral sense is now in use, and we are aware of how it is functioning. Our discomfort ranges from acute torment to insecure reprieves. As we make moral progress, our torment is increasingly alleviated; but we continue to fluctuate from one condition to the other until we reach the perfect haven of our final goal.[63] Seneca labels the awareness we have when we act badly "bad conscience" (*mala conscientia*) and the awareness we have when we act virtuously "good conscience" (*bona conscientia*).[64] Only the wise person has "good conscience" in a strict sense. These two concepts are of central importance in Seneca's pedagogy. They constitute a rudimentary form of "conscience" as we might call it: we feel anxiety when we act badly, and we feel tranquility when we act well.

Third, we come to know our moral condition by making it an object of attention. This is the stage of self-examination, leading (in the case of the

---

[60] *Ep.* 41.2; cf. 83.1.
[61] SVF 3.178–186; and *Ep.* 121.5–24.
[62] Some examples of Seneca's emphasis on inner torment are at *Ep.* 48.7, 81.23, 97.15; *Tranq.* 17.1, and *Brev.* 10.2.
[63] See esp. *Tranq.* 2.6–15, 12.1–7; *Ep.* 56.9–10.
[64] See *Ep.* 12.9 and 43.5; *De vita beata* 19.1 and 20.4; *Ben.* 4.12.4; *Clem.* 1.15.5.

nonwise) to a recognition of the need for self-improvement.[65] This kind of awareness is no longer passive (as the first two stages); nor is our moral sense merely in use (as in the second stage); we now use our moral sense to assess and improve our condition. This is "conscience" of a higher sort: we do not merely feel good or bad; we judge ourselves to be good or bad and, if we are bad, in need of becoming good. Seneca describes both the second and third levels when personifying our inner spirit as an "observer and watchman." At the second level, our spirit merely registers the good and evil within us; at the third, it tells us what is to be done. It "treats us as it is treated by us" by either making us feel how we act (at the second level) or taking charge of our feelings (at the third).

At all three levels, there is a desire for the good; but it is only at the third stage that we try to influence our desires. This is the stage of doing moral work.[66] As Seneca sees it, there is need of an enormous effort. The reason is that we must reorient our desires, or wanting, from mistakenly pursuing advantages (such as life, health, wealth) as goods to pursuing the real good. Our mind must become "intent (*intenta*) on the desire (*cupiditas*) for the good alone."[67] This requires not just a subordination of advantages to the good, but, wrenchingly, a change toward fully wanting disadvantages when they are necessary.[68] We must embrace fate by wanting what we naturally shun. This is basic Stoic theory; but Seneca gives new emphasis to the clash of desires. He depicts a moral upheaval. From "voluntary slavery,"[69] we must fight for the freedom of wanting what we have desired, unwittingly, all along.

Scholars have drawn attention to Seneca's focus on wanting (*voluntas, velle*).[70] "What is wisdom?" he asks. The answer is: "always to want (*velle*) the same thing and not want (*nolle*) the same thing" (*Ep.* 20.5). What one needs to be good, he says, is to "want" (*velle*) it;[71] and there are many other striking locutions of this kind. Seneca imputes "good will" (*bona voluntas*) not only to persons whose wanting has become fully good but to all who

---

[65] See esp. *De ira* 3.36; *Ep.* 13.6–13, 16.2, and 28.9–10.

[66] See *Ep.* 50.5.

[67] *De ira* 3.41.1. *Intenta* corresponds to the Epicurean notion of *epibolê*.

[68] *Ep.* 61.2–4, cf. 54, 82.15–16; *Prov.* 5.

[69] *Ep.* 47.17 and 22.10–11.

[70] See esp. Pohlenz (1941, 111–17; 1948, 319–20); Voelke (1973, 161–90 and 198–9); and Donini (1982, 181–210, esp. 202–3). I agree with Voelke (p. 198) that Seneca "*tend à faire de la volonté l'élément déterminant de la moralité*" without offering "*une doctrine systématiquement élaborée.*" Inwood (2005) opposes the notion of "summary will," which he assigns to Seneca, to that of "traditional will," which he takes some scholars to attribute to Seneca.

[71] *Ep.* 80.4; cf. 71.36.

merely want to be good. Comparing it to the dormant power of sight that lies within eyes that are closed (*Ben.* 5.25.6), he demands that it be transformed into a "good mind" (*bona mens*).[72] It becomes in this way what the early Stoics termed "will" (*boulêsis*), a condition that applies only to the wise.[73] Seneca extends an appropriate kind of wanting to all three levels, using ordinary language to do so. The result is a new view of our moral path as a continuum of wanting: we must turn our inborn wanting into a deliberate wanting by overcoming the wrong kind of wanting. By emphasizing the power of wanting (right or wrong), Seneca emphasizes the struggle that is needed to make moral progress. Reason doesn't just deviate or get back on track: it is expelled from its path and must force its way back.

How much of a change, then, did Seneca make to Stoic moral theory? His emphasis on wanting offers an answer to an earlier question. Did Seneca assign a separate force to the passionate part of the mind, the spirit, analogously to what has been proposed for Posidonius? I suggest not. The power of willing that goes along with our nature as rational animals is sufficient. It is in our nature to have both a desire for advantages (to preserve us) and a desire for the good. Desire of the first kind, when it exceeds the bounds of reason, accounts for the passions; no other force is needed. In the same way, our inborn desire for the good requires no other internal power to move us toward the good.

Seneca's emphasis on wanting may be viewed merely as an elaboration of early Stoic theory; but we can also, I think, see a new theory in the making. Seneca does not himself offer a new theory, complete with new terminology. What he does is to prepare the ground for a new theory. Michael Frede has suggested that Epictetus' notion of *prohairesis* is the first notion of a "will" in antiquity.[74] In my view, Seneca contributed at least as much to the notion of a "will." Epictetus retooled an Aristotelian term, *prohairesis* ("choice"), to designate the power of decision making that exists at the third level that I distinguished. What Epictetus emphasizes is our intellectual freedom. Seneca gives much more emphasis to the power of willing, which he chose to call by the ordinary Latin term *voluntas*.

Further Reading

Hadot (1969) is a pioneering work in the study of Seneca's originality as a teacher of philosophy. Subsequently, Inwood (2005) focused on the

[72] *Ep.* 16.1.
[73] SVF 3.431–2, 438.
[74] Frede (2011, 46).

originality of Seneca's treatment of various themes in Stoic philosophy. Inwood (2007a) also contributes many insights to Seneca's pedagogical procedure in his *Epistles*, as does Schafer (2009). Graver (2007) is indispensable toward an understanding of Seneca's moral psychology.

18

ALESSANDRO SCHIESARO

Seneca and Epicurus: The Allure of the Other

A complex relationship with Epicurus and his philosophy spans much of Seneca's *oeuvre*, with admiration, critique, imitation, and competition vying for primacy in different works and at different times. These approaches are based on direct knowledge of the complete or partial text of some Epicurean letters (at least five) and of a collection of maxims probably arranged by topic (*gnomologium*).[1] Direct knowledge of other Epicurean texts cannot be ruled out. References to Epicurean doctrines and citations of Epicurus' works can be found throughout Seneca's philosophical corpus from the *Dialogi* to the *Epistles*, where they become particularly frequent, but Epicurean concepts are voiced in the tragedies as well.[2] Lucretius, both as the foremost Roman interpreter of the Greek philosopher and as a master of Latin poetry, plays a distinctive role in Seneca's negotiations of Epicureanism and Stoicism, his influence being particularly strong in the *Epistles to Lucilius* and *Natural Questions*.

The Boundaries of Eclecticism

Seneca's reference to and quotation of Epicurean concepts invites a certain amount of special pleading, given Epicurus' distance from core Stoic doctrine. Our author justifies his flexible approach to such a counterintuitive model in both specific and general terms. Specifically, Seneca points out that Epicurus has attracted a worse reputation than his doctrine deserves, once his teaching is properly analyzed. In general, he theorizes that the philosopher's attitude to past "discoveries and discoverers of wisdom" should resemble the way a good *paterfamilias* manages inherited properties: they should be not only preserved but expanded with a view to the future (*Ep.*

---

[1] Scholarly opinion on direct knowledge has varied widely: see Setaioli (1988: 171–82) for a thorough discussion. He is right to argue that Seneca had access to an anthology containing some full *Letters* as well as a collection of *sententiae*, albeit not to the whole corpus.

[2] 2 See, e.g., Pierini (1996) and Marino (1996), with further bibliography.

64.7). Those who have preceded us in the search for the truth should therefore not be regarded as masters but as guides (*Ep.* 33.11).[3] So, when Seneca offers Lucilius an Epicurean maxim early on in the *Epistles*, he points out that he has come across it more as an explorer (2.5 *explorator*) than as a traitor (*transfuga*); Epicurus' exhortations to virtue are, after all, "public property" (21.9 *publicae sunt*), or even, at a later stage, not just "public" but effectively "Stoic" as well (33.2 *publicae sunt et maxime nostrae*).

This display of open-mindedness and goodwill[4] belies a shrewd approach to a largely incompatible doctrine. Reliance on *sententiae* disconnected from a larger argumentative framework limits from the outset the scope for doctrinal contamination, although authoritative scholars have argued in the past that Seneca "crosses over" to Epicureanism in important respects.[5] In privileging Epicurus' teachings on ethics while silencing or criticizing his physics, Seneca tames the disruptive potential of his doctrine and aligns himself with the prevailing *Zeitgeist*. The stark anti-Epicurean worldview articulated in Cicero's philosophical corpus has made way for a more widespread acceptance of some Epicurean precepts on the part of, at least, the Roman upper classes,[6] a success due both to the different attitudes towards public life evolving in the early Principate and to a diminished emphasis on Epicurus' and Lucretius' problematic views on physics.[7] Rather than looking at it in terms of orthodoxy or lack of it,[8] Seneca's attitude towards Epicureanism, which is more nuanced than it might at first appear, provides an interesting test case for assessing central aspects of his work and his *persona*: issues relating, for example, to Seneca's "eclecticism"[9] in the process of reshaping Stoic philosophy for a Roman imperial audience, to the strong dialogic tendency of much of his work,[10] and to the tensions, in both thought and style, between self-restraint and inspired excitement.

Epicurus' presence in the *Epistles* is especially prominent, with Posidonius, Zeno, and other Stoic masters well behind him, and all but six of the first twenty-nine *Epistles* contain direct quotations of Epicurean maxims.[11] Much

---

[3] On Seneca's reception of prior philosophers, see Asmis in this volume.
[4] Freise (1989, 533–6).
[5] Marchesi (1944, 301–10).
[6] Innocenti (1972, 134–7).
[7] On the cultural milieu and potential audience of Seneca's philosophical work, see Inwood (1995).
[8] A comprehensive treatment of the issue appears in Rist (1989).
[9] See Castelnérac (2007), and Asmis' chapter in this *Companion*, with further bibliography.
[10] See Roller's chapter in this *Companion*.
[11] Motto-Clark (1968, 39). Some items, evidently anonymous in the author's source, are not attributed to the Greek philosopher.

as he criticizes the role Epicureans assign to *voluptas*,[12] Seneca insists on a positive appreciation of the founder's temperate lifestyle (*Ep.* 18.9–10) and near-heroic death (*Ep.* 66.47),[13] which guarantees his enduring fame (*Ep.* 79.15) even if his school attracts followers beholden to pleasure rather than to virtue. Such positive evaluation makes it possible for Seneca to endorse several aspects of Epicurean teachings about ethics, with a preference for topics such as the limitation of desire, the importance of friendship,[14] and the rewards of a life based on the search for wisdom.[15] A partial convergence with Epicurean theories of *otium* can also be observed, which is perhaps less surprising in light of the fact that the *Epistles* mark Seneca's final disengagement from active politics.[16]

Quotations and references of Epicurean maxims especially in the early part of the collection alert readers to the importance of Epicurus' own letters as a literary and didactic model for Seneca's collection.[17] Their distribution across the work also plays a significant structural role. While almost all of the twenty-nine letters in Books I to III quote Epicurus regularly, in *Ep.* 30 to 97 he is mentioned much less frequently (eleven times in total), while neither quotations nor even his name appear from *Letter* 98 to the end. This distribution is in itself significant, since it puts on display the notion that even other sects can provide germs of truth useful to the spiritual growth of the *proficiens* especially at the early stages of his training, while Stoic doctrine represents the true goal of Seneca's teachings. As instruction acquires a more organic and theoretical form, the space for heterogeneous authorities correspondingly declines, up to the point when the mature *vir*, secure in his new knowledge, will no longer need to rely on memorable, if unconnected, *praecepta* (33.6–7).[18] In this progression from maxims (*sententiae*) to increasingly broader and more theoretical discussions, Seneca follows the teaching methods advocated by the Epicurean school, which used the master's *Capital Sentences* as the first installment in a process of education leading to his *Epitome* and, eventually, to the massive *Peri physeos*.[19] Moreover, if Lucilius had indeed displayed Epicurean leanings,[20] the frequent

---

[12] On this particular strain of anti-Epicurean polemics, see also *Ben.* 4.2.1–4, with Griffin (2013, 233).

[13] Further references to Epicurus' death at 92.25 and possibly 87.2, cf. Ker (2009a, 148).

[14] Schottlaender (1954–5).

[15] A detailed analysis of all the quotations in Setaioli (1988, 171–248).

[16] Mutschmann (1915, 321). The Epicureans' position on political engagement, at any rate, was less one sided than anti-Epicurean polemics liked to maintain: see Roskam (2007, 45–56).

[17] Rosati (1981, 5–7); Inwood (2007a, esp. 142–8); Wildberger (2014).

[18] Mazzoli (1989, 1862–3).

[19] Hadot (1968).

[20] Griffin (1976, 315); Setaioli (1988, 201).

acknowledgment of the Greek philosopher's importance in the early part of the *Epistles* can be seen as a form of *captatio benevolentiae* in some way parallel to Lucretius' careful induction of Memmius into distant and potentially unwelcome truths in the *DRN* (a work that also displays a progression from compact, memorable tenets in the first books to a more open, abstract approach in its later parts). The Stoic master Chrysippus had indeed recommended that the teacher adapt his mission to the specific needs and beliefs of the pupil, without excessive recourse to dogmatism at an early stage.[21]

Agreement with some aspects of Epicurean ethics coexists with scathing criticism, a strategy exemplified in *Ep.* 90.35, where Epicurus is not named but accused of having "placed citizens outside their homeland, gods outside the world and given over virtue to pleasure." Seneca summarizes here the vast doctrinal distance that keeps Epicureans and Stoics apart on key matters. The Stoics believe in a cosmos ruled by divine agency, which the Epicureans roundly deny; they encourage participation in public unless impossible, as opposed to a life of serene seclusion interrupted by political commitment only under extreme circumstances. The last item reflects a wide-spread criticism of Epicureanism, since the Stoics identify *virtus*, not *voluptas*, as the highest good.[22] Yet even on this topic, Seneca develops elsewhere a more nuanced evaluation as he (correctly) points out that this "teacher of pleasure" (18.9 *magister voluptatis*) promotes a notion of *voluptas* as the absence of pain that is far removed from the pursuit of pleasure *per se*; he eats sparingly to test "whether he thereby falls short of full and complete happiness" and whether any effort to get closer to the goal would actually be worth its while (18.9). Moreover, in his exhaustive discussion of the nature of virtue in *Ep.* 66, Seneca implicitly rebukes his own accusations that Epicureans are beholden to pleasure. While their *virtus* lacks the theological foundations of the Stoics' (a point over which, however, he does not linger), its behavioral implications are comparable: both Stoic *virtus* and Epicurean *voluptas* are predicated on "following nature," a recipe for restraint rather than excess.

Seneca had elaborated this point at greater length in an earlier work, *De vita beata*, which contains his most explicit judgment on Epicurus' philosophy and its reception. Here, taking pains to distance himself from the majority view held by his fellow Stoics (13.1), Seneca judges Epicurean teachings "venerable" and "upright," and, upon closer inspection, even "austere" (13.4 *sancta, recta, tristia*), since the pursuit of pleasure is subjected to the limits of nature and would thus be insufficient to satisfy vice (13.4). Serious damage

[21] *SVF* 3.474.
[22] Freise (1989, 544–5).

to Epicurus' reputation has been inflicted by followers who bring along their own immoderate and un-Epicurean notion of pleasure as "slothful idleness" (13.3) and who join the school only because it appears to support their inclinations. Thus, Seneca concludes, Epicurus' sect is not a "teacher of vice" (13.2), but he has undeservedly acquired a bad name, since a true understanding of Epicurean *voluptas* is limited to the cognoscenti. The simile with which Seneca structures his reasoning is revealing. Epicurus, he claims, is like a man who dresses up as a woman: his honor and virility are intact, but he carries a tambourine in his hands just like a priest of Cybele and thus invites negative, if unfounded, opinions about his morality. This unexpected reference to the quasi-Bacchic *furor* of a frenzied Oriental cult that blurs the boundaries between genders paves the way, in the *Epistles*, for a more elaborate set of associations between Epicurean theories of pleasures and sexual mores and also establishes a link with the problematic nature of inspiration and the stylistic aspect in which philosophical teaching is couched.

In *Ep.* 108.8–9, Seneca focuses on the peculiar emotive impact of *sententiae*, which strike hearers and spectators with great force and spur them into action in the same way poetry does. Epicurus' apparent effeminacy had been signaled metaphorically by his holding a tambourine; now the excitement of listeners who "are stirred by high-sounding phrases" (*magnificas voces*) just like "the emasculated Phrygian priests who are roused by the sound of the flute and go mad to order" (108.7) is proposed as a positive response to important philosophical teachings, in contrast to a form of superficial listening that has no effect on the soul and therefore entails no learning and no ethical progress. The emotional impact of resounding (indeed sublime)[23] precepts is a precondition for spurring listeners to self-improvement and is described in terms that recall the traditional lexicon of Bacchic ecstasy, such as *furor*, *rapio*, and *instigo*. *Sententiae*, even if couched in prose, are a form of poetic expression, with which they share the ability to "strike" the mind of hearers, that is, of providing the emotional *ictus* that is then subjected to rational assent.[24] In his *On the Tranquillity of Mind*, Seneca had developed a similar line of thought with specific reference to Plato's theory that "the sane mind knocks in vain at the door of poetry." Since "no great genius has ever existed without some touch of madness," as Aristotle puts it,[25] only "an excited mind" (17.10 *mota mens*) can "soar aloft fired by divine inspi-

---

[23] On *magnificus* in connection with the *megalopsuchia* of the sublime, see Mazzoli (1990, 92).
[24] On *sententiae* in Seneca's prose, see Traina (1987, 26–7), and Asmis's chapter in this volume.
[25] Further discussion in Schiesaro (2003, 23–4).

ration" and attain a "sublime and difficult height" (*sublime quicquam et in arduo positum*).

At an earlier stage in the didactic journey charted in the *Letters*, Seneca had cautioned against the limitations and potential dangers of *sententiae*, with a discussion that also mobilizes sexual analogies. *Letter* 33 marks a watershed after the extensive use of Epicurean maxims in the first group of the letters and the transition to longer and more complex texts. Here, in the framework of a discussion about philosophical modes of expression, Seneca points out to Lucilius that the Stoic masters have never bothered with *flosculi* – memorable maxims[26] – but the whole texture of their writings is manly (*virilis*), and "such thoughts as one may extract here and there in the work of other philosophers run through the whole body of our writings" (33.3). Epicurus' strong utterances are more noticeable because they stand out in an uneven context, an ungenerous if typical criticism of his doctrine's supposed lack of systematicity. This "flaw" may at least in part be the reflection of sources available to Seneca but also offers a very convenient foil at a stage in his career where not just the *Epistles* and *Natural Questions* but also the contemporaneous (and now lost) *Books on Moral Philosophy* (*Moralis philosophiae libri*) attest to a concerted effort to attain a coherent and systematic whole. What is most relevant, however, is the implicit parallelism posited between manliness and systematicity on the one hand and a "womanly" interest in resounding maxims that capture the attention of the reader on the other. This parallel becomes clearer once we notice that Epicurus' *praecepta* are compared to poetic utterances: both are memorably compact.[27] As Seneca points out at *Ep.* 94.25, "advice (*admonitio*) is not teaching," but it does "engage the attention and rouses us (*excitat*)" in the same manner in which poetry and theater can stir audiences into action. Thus an approach to ethical teaching that, like Epicurus', is heavily reliant on maxims and can be approved of only if the stimuli it affords are later reined in by thoughtful, systematic reasoning. Otherwise they would constitute an incitement to passions ultimately devoid of true philosophical worth.

A more extensive critique of Epicurus' style is to be found in *Letter* 114.[28] Seneca discusses why at certain times a "degenerate style of speech" (*corrupti*

---

[26] Before its occurrence in Seneca (twice in *Ep.* 33 and nowhere else), *flosculus* in a rhetorical sense is first found at Cic. *Sest.* 119, already with a somewhat negative connotation (it is considered incompatible with *gravitas*). Quintilian follows up on Seneca's connection between *flosculi* and depravity; see 2.5.22 (*ne* [sc. *pueri*] *capti voluptate prava deleniantur*) and esp. 12.10.73.

[27] *Ep.* 33.6: "for single maxims sink in more easily when they are marked off and bounded line a line of verse (*carminis modo inclusa*)," cf. Traina (1987, 40).

[28] On which see esp. Graver (1998), an excellent paper.

generis oratio) becomes popular, for instance, one that appears "mincing and modulated like the music of a concert piece" (*infracta et in morem cantici ducta*) and favors "disconnected phrases" (*abruptae sententiae*). The answer is that "man's speech is just like his life," and "wholesome, well-ordered, serious and restrained" souls produce a "sound and sober" style (114.1–3), an argument that is buttressed by an extensive criticism of the life and style of Maecenas, an Epicurean follower who is here attacked with arguments that had likely been used against Epicurus himself.[29] Maecenas (literally) embodies a corrupted form of eloquence, which reflects unacceptable personal mores: his "looseness of speech" (114.4 *oratio soluta*) is the consequence and the equivalent of his own "ungirt attire" (*discinctus*); his words are as *recherché* as, among other things, his clothes or his house. Seneca's strictures focus on Maecenas' excessive recourse to contorted sentences and to unusual metaphors, all indications of the fact that an excess of prosperity had "turned his head" – *motum ... caput* (114.8) also recalls the "Bacchic" *mota mens* of *Tranq.* 17.11.

The barrage of criticism directed against Maecenas – seen as a representative of the "vulgar" aspects of Epicureanism the founder had been able to keep at bay – is as intriguing as the double-edged attitude displayed in the other passages quoted earlier in connection with Epicurus' use of *sententiae*. Seneca reiterates that his style aspires to simplicity and directness (75.1–2), yet his epigrammatic sententiousness is one of the most noticeable aspects of his writing, both in prose and in poetry, and – a neat *contrappasso* given his criticism of Epicurus – one of the chief reasons for the memorability of his precepts and their lasting success.[30] Indeed, although he approves of his "excellent *sententiae*" on moral grounds (10.1.129), Quintilian's criticism of Seneca's style[31] insists precisely on these shortcomings in terms that mirror the philosopher's strictures against the Epicureans and especially Maecenas: "his style is for the most part decadent (*corrupta*), and particularly dangerous because of the seductiveness of the vices with which it abounds"; he displays a "longing for the perverse (*prava*)"[32] and "breaks up his weighty ideas in his tiny little epigrams (10.1.130, *minutissimis sententiis*)."[33] Quintilian's assessment highlights the contradictory nature of Seneca's expostulations

[29] See Setaioli (2000, 255–74).
[30] See, e.g., Fitch (1987, 59–60) on the popularity of *florilegia* of *sententiae* culled from the tragedies.
[31] About which see Williams' chapter in this volume.
[32] *Prava* is Sarpe's conjecture for the mss. *parum*.
[33] As he points out in general terms elsewhere, an excessive recourse to *sententiae* yields "a fragmented effect" (8.5.27 *concisam ... orationem*) and leads to a "broken style" (*soluta ... oratio*), cf. 12.10.48.

against the self-indulgent and uncontrolled style of Maecenas and calls into question the solidity of the argument, developed in *Letter* 33, that the Stoics' superiority over the Epicureans consists in the ("manly") premium they put on a systematic exposition as opposed to an excessive pursuit of attractive *sententiae*. Seneca may indeed be protesting too much, or, as elsewhere, he may be displaying his ambivalence between the allure of "ecstatic" inspiration and the demands for rational self-restraint.

Sublimity and the Will to Knowledge

The scope and structure of Seneca's *Natural Questions* have much in common with Lucretius' didactic poem.[34] Both authors promote the investigation of natural phenomena as a means to ethical improvement,[35] and in both works, the proems, which to a certain extent are autonomous from the rest of each book, focus on comparable themes. Lucretius devotes most of his proems to a praise of Epicurus, Seneca to the importance of studying nature. The proem to *DRN* 2, an exaltation of philosophy, finds a parallel in *NQ praef.* 1, while some of the self-reflexive themes of the programmatic proem to *DRN* 4 are echoed at the outset of *NQ* 3.[36]

These broad structural and thematic affinities highlight the crucial theoretical differences underlying the two works, whose ultimate goals remain irreconcilable, since the understanding of nature's workings is, for Lucretius, a means to "exclude the gods from earth" (*Ep.* 90.35), while, in Seneca's eyes, the wonders of nature are a powerful reminder of divine providence (indeed, "theology is the culmination of physics").[37] These differences permeate important aspects of the narrative, and I will focus here on two key issues, causation and the sublime, where overlap between the different approaches of the two authors is marked and instructive.

Seneca's explicit intention is etiological: he aims to "embrace the whole universe" and to bring out its "secret causes" (3 *praef.* 1), and his investigation into natural phenomena strives for a degree of exactitude in many respects higher than that required in the Epicurean system when it deals not with the basic laws of nature but with specific phenomena, such as those discussed in Book 6 of *DRN*. Since these phenomena do not allow for a univocal explanation, Lucretius offers a variety of alternative theories, all of which are consistent with observable facts and all of which rule out

---

[34] Lana (1955, 12–19), in an opening chapter titled "On Lucretius' footprints."
[35] See esp. Berno (2003) and Williams (2012).
[36] Significant points of contact link the concluding sections of the two works: Lana (1955, 13).
[37] Inwood (1999) 23.

divine agency, a method called *pleonachos tropos*. Even if we cannot ascertain, in the absence of tangible evidence, which one of these explanations is the operative one, we can rest assured that one of them is certainly valid, and there is no need to "refer events to the dominion of the gods, and to yield them the place of kings" (6.54–5). Seneca, too, aims to eradicate the fear caused by phenomena such as lightning and earthquakes,[38] and since "heaven and earth are not shaken by divine anger: these phenomena have their own causes" (6.3.1), assigning to Jupiter the power to cause lightning is no more than a "poetic excess" (2.44.1). Although Seneca does believe in natural laws[39] and not in the arbitrary power of irritable gods, he nonetheless parts company with Lucretius once the search for causes reaches its final stages. He, too, lists a number of alternative explanations, generally in the form of a doxography, but rather than leaving all plausible options open, he identifies the one explanatory model he considers correct. The contrast with the Epicurean-Lucretian method is clear, for instance, at *NQ* 6.20.5–7,[40] where Seneca quotes Epicurus' five possible theories about earthquakes, since it is "difficult to promise certainty when dealing with issues which can only be attained by conjecture," and concludes by approving Epicurus' preference for air as the most likely explanation (6.21.1). However, rather than comparing the relative merits of the alternatives available, he harks back to the assumption that "in nature there is nothing more powerful, nothing more vigorous than air," the *spiritus* or *pneuma*. Seneca's preference for the pneumatic theory is based on the general notion that *spiritus* enables other natural elements such as fire and water to preserve their strength (6.21.1) and innately contains (*inesse*) a "natural power of movement" (*naturalem vim movendi*). Since causes are "portions of breath"[41] that act on inert matter and shape it at will (*Ep.* 65.2), an ultimately theological explanation resurfaces in Seneca's reasoning in spite of the initial disclaimer.

This different methodological approach is consistent with the underlying foundations of Seneca's system, where causes are linked to each other in a *longus ordo rerum* (*Prov.* 5.7). There is no room for the random results of colliding atoms that dominate the Epicurean universe: here "cause is linked with cause" (*Prov.* 5.7 *causa pendet ex causa*), with God and Fate being the final resting point in the search for causes. When Lucretius (2.1153–6) disparages the notion that mortal creatures may have descended from

---

[38] Cf. 1 *praef.* 12: once the mind has risen to contemplate the universe, it can watch natural phenomena "without fear" (*secure*).

[39] Citti (2012).

[40] On Seneca's treatment of earthquakes, see esp. De Vivo (1992, 83–9), and specifically on this section Williams (2012, 246–7).

[41] Aetius 1.11.5 (*SVF* 2.340; Long and Sedley [1987, 2.336]).

the sky by sliding along the golden rope, he probably has in mind a more comprehensive critique of the Stoic allegorical interpretation of the rope linking heaven and earth at *Iliad* 8.19, which in the Homeric image represented "destiny" *(heimarmene)*.[42] For the Epicureans, the space between first principles and fundamental *foedera* on the one hand and myriad individual events on the other can only be filled by plausible speculation based on the observation of natural laws. For a Stoic, at least in theory, it should be possible to reconstruct a unique and indisputable chain of causal connections leading back to the ultimate cause, since "at the beginning of each world cycle a causal nexus is providentially planned and initiated, by virtue of which *every* detail of the subsequent world process is predetermined."[43] The *NQ* display a strong tendency toward a "totalizing worldview"[44] that in its import and outlook is directly comparable to the Epicurean unification of all natural phenomena under a very limited number of general laws, but, unlike Epicurus' and Lucretius' *ratio,* these are ultimately guaranteed by divine authority.

In this respect, Seneca can be seen to follow a distinguished line of authors who displayed the same ambivalent reaction to Lucretius' poem, combining respect for his poetic achievements with skepticism about the foundations of his system and the consequences it entails for the relationship between human beings and the gods. Like Vergil and Ovid, Seneca marks his distance from the model by using a Lucretian passage in a more circumscribed, literal fashion, thus altering its original import and meaning.[45] *NQ* 4b.3.4 quotes Lucr. 1.313 *stilicidi casus lapidem cavat* ("dripping water falling on stone hollows it out"), a quasi- proverbial expression that, in the context of Lucretius' argument, is meant to prove the key point that visibility is not a necessary property of atoms. Seneca, incongruously, puts the line to work in an attempt to demonstrate that individual kernels of hail are round in shape,[46] although nothing in the original text allows for such an inference. The same approach is found in the *Epistles.*[47] At 106.8 he quotes another verse drawn from Lucretius' lengthy attempt to prove the existence of invisible atoms. Seneca agrees that "nothing can touch or be touched, except body" (Lucr. 1.304), but in a wholly different context, dealing not with atoms and their nature but with the attempt to show that both virtues and vices are "bodies" in so far as they can act on bodies. Even when agreement

[42] Furley (1966).
[43] Long and Sedley (1987, 2.343).
[44] Williams (2012, 3–4) and *passim.*
[45] A list of parallel passages in Mazzoli (1970, 206–7).
[46] Althoff (2005, 17).
[47] See Althoff (2005), who highlights the points of agreement between the two authors.

would be possible, Seneca distances himself from the model he quotes. For instance, he refutes outright Lucretius' seemingly innocuous assertion that the light of *ratio* can dispel the vain terrors of the mind, which make us tremble in broad daylight like children scared of the dark (110.6 *sed falsum est, Lucreti, non timemus in luce*), insisting that only a proper understanding of human and divine matters, including the role of providence, can rescue us from moral darkness (110.7).

The important role played by the sublime in both Lucretius and Seneca[48] makes a comparison between their different approaches particularly fascinating. Both authors identify sublimity as an essential cognitive tool that has to be mastered if the philosopher-poet hopes to incite his audience to a heightened understanding of truth and to moral self-improvement. Yet they hold different views on the relationship between sublimity and the gods on the one hand and the interplay of excitement and rational understanding on the other. Lucretius' sublime is first and foremost an etiological strategy, a cognitive tool for apprehending natural causes that has a liberating and exhilarating effect. The emotional consequences attending sublimity, *divina... voluptas atque horror* (3.28–9 "divine delight and shuddering"), are subordinated to this cognitive process. Contemplation of nature as such holds no comparable aesthetic or emotional gain. Indeed, a dispassionate consideration of the basic features of the natural world leads to the conclusion that the world was not created for our benefit and is singularly packed with obstacles and dangers, as Lucretius expands at 5.200–34 in order to show that *natura rerum* is laden with faults (5.199). At the zenith of Epicurus' voyage across the universe, we find not the contemplation of our world's smallness and irrelevance but an insight that revolutionizes traditional views on religion. Since Epicurus is now able to understand and convey to us the basic laws of nature that govern all phenomena (*nihil ex nihilo*, "nothing comes from nothing" and *nihil in nihilum*, "nothing dissolves into nothing"), he can overcome the power of religion and grant us a definitive victory over superstition and fear (1.78–9). Seneca, on the contrary, argues that intellectual prowess, the ability to penetrate the innermost secrets of nature (1 *praef.* 3 *secretiora*) and to derive pleasurable contemplation from this activity (1 *praef.* 12 *delectant*) is "proof of the divine nature" of the soul. Indeed, the *sapiens'* investigations into truth and nature lead him, unlike animals who see but do not understand, to perceive the presence of divinity. The "law of life" (*vitae lex*) consists not merely in knowing the gods but in following them (90.34 *nec nosse tantum sed sequi deos*).

[48] See Mazzoli (1990). On sublime in the tragedies: Schiesaro (2003, 127–32); in *NQ*: 222–30, 255–6.

In the Epicurean system, laws of nature are the ultimate causes of the phenomena that surround us. What is at stake is not the validity of these laws but how they apply to specific events. The pleasure of contemplation will derive, therefore, from the explanatory power that follows this groundbreaking acquisition. Seneca's Stoic sublime is different. The search for causes is proleptically voided of any true epistemic value, because all causes, in their apparent variety, depend on and resolve into one, the decrees of Fate. A more detailed understanding can therefore acquire a moral dimension, in so far as it confirms human beings' belief in the ultimate agency of Fate, or an aesthetic dimension, because contemplating the order of the universe is in itself a source of intellectual and aesthetic pleasure, but it can never alter the relationship between God and mortals. The search for causes is thus more a form of intellectual *otium* and pride than a journey into the unknown that can stimulate a radical change of perspective on the structure and workings of the cosmos.

Seneca shows an awareness of this basic feature of his intellectual investigation at *De otio* 5.6, where he engages an important Lucretian intertext. "Our thought bursts through the ramparts of the sky" (*cogitatio nostra caeli munimenta perrumpit*) because it is in our (better) nature not to be satisfied with the understanding of "what is visible." We are drawn to investigate "what lies beyond the world," a set of fundamental cosmic issues, such as the boundaries of space or the existence of atoms, comparable to the totalizing ambition of Lucretian physics.[49] Seneca appears to allude here to Lucr. 1.70–1, where Epicurus' "lively power of mind" manages to "shatter (*effringere*) the confining bars of nature's gates" so that he is able to "march far beyond the flaming walls of the world (*moenia mundi*)." From this extensive scientific program, however, Seneca draws a conclusion that is far removed from Lucretius': the limitations of human time make such an ambitious endeavor impossible, and "man is too mortal to comprehend things immortal" (5.7). Living according to Nature implies "surrendering to her" and becoming its "admirer and worshipper" (*admirator cultorque*), living a life of "unbroken contemplation" (5.8) with no practical consequences, which can be pleasant and charming.

Seneca's emphasis on admiration and contemplation attempts to deprive the etiological and rationalistic aspirations – and methods – of *NQ* of their potential disruptiveness. Nature, however sharply investigated, should prove to be a coherent whole pervaded by an overarching *ratio* that is not threatened by the relentless search for explanations. Yet Seneca's sublime retains a provocative edginess. Excitement, philosophical or otherwise, always

[49] Indeed, some are couched in Epicurean terms: see Williams' commentary *ad loc.*

involves some loss of control, a danger to which the Epicureans, in spite of their founder's best efforts, are especially prone, both in their life and in their writings. This is what makes them the ideal other onto which desire and repulsion can be inscribed. If the ultimate goal of philosophy, as of life, is wisdom based on reason, the ultimate risk must be that of falling into "that famous chaos of the Epicureans," the "void without end" of a doctrine that assigns far too much importance to chance (*Ep.* 72.9). Then both the philosopher and his disciple would face the fate Seneca's tragic characters repeatedly voice as a fear or a curse: that of bringing *chaos* onto earth.[50]

Further Reading

A detailed analysis of Epicurus' presence in Seneca is offered by Mutschmann (1915), Schottlander (1954–5), André (1968) and Setaioli (1988a: 171–248), who also parses Seneca's quotes of Epicurus and highlights significant aspects of style and interpretation. On *de beneficiis*, see Lo Moro (1976), and now Griffin's (2013) excellent treatment; on *Naturales quaestiones* the important contributions by Berno (2003) and Williams (2012). A general study of the Epicurean elements in the tragedies is missing. Innocenti (1972) and Inwood (1995) place the debate between Stoics and Epicureans in a larger historical and cultural context. On causation: Inwood (1995) and Althoff (2005).

[50] See, e.g., *Th.* 1009 *ad chaos inane*, with Tarrant *ad loc.*

PART IV

The Senecan Tradition

19

ALDO SETAIOLI

Seneca and the Ancient World

Seneca as a Public Figure

Seneca was not merely a writer but also a statesman who served for several years as Nero's advisor and, for a time – with the support of the prefect of the *praetorium* Afranius Burrus – as the real power behind the throne. So we shall start with the way he was seen and judged as a public figure. From this point of view, the first document is possibly the only *praetexta* that has come down to us in its entirety, the *Octavia*, in which Seneca appears as a character. This play was probably composed at a time and in a milieu close to Seneca. Although Seneca appears here in his capacity as Nero's advisor, the *Octavia* clearly idealizes him and avoids presenting him as the statesman who so often had to come to terms with the demands of power. The Seneca portrayed here is not the historical one but rather an uncompromising philosopher, though the author does not lend him the attitudes and ideas consistent with the Stoic positions familiar from his own writings.

We sporadically find other judgments of this kind: according to Lucan's *Vita* attributed to Vacca Seneca was endowed with all the virtues, and Juvenal has no doubt that people would prefer Seneca to Nero if they could have their say (8.211–12). Seneca's contemporary and countryman Columella calls him a man of excellent nature and great learning (3.3.3) but also mentions a vineyard he owned that, according to Pliny the Elder (*NH* 14.51–2), he had purchased at a great price just for the sake of owning it – a veiled hint at the contradiction between Seneca's life and his philosophical principles. Pliny does recognize, however, that Seneca was the most learned man of his time.

The most interesting testimonies are to be found in the works of the historians who covered the time of Seneca's activity: Tacitus, two generations later, and Cassius Dio, in the third century CE. Tacitus' sources were Pliny the Elder, Cluvius Rufus, and Fabius Rusticus: the latter, as Tacitus realized, was a friend of Seneca's and tended to be favorable to him. Tacitus' attitude to the philosopher is on the whole fair and well balanced. He does not fail to stress that Seneca's literary vanity (*Ann.* 13.11.2) – a detail we also find in Quintilian (10.1.126) and Suetonius (*Nero* 52) – played into the hands of his enemies, such as Suillius (Tac. *Ann.* 13.42.3) and of those who slandered him at Nero's court (Tac. *Ann.* 14.52.3). Although Tacitus does report the many charges leveled at Seneca during his collaboration with Nero, he never openly endorses them and often takes pains to mention a favorable or justificatory version as well. In the rhetorically elaborate dialogue in which Seneca asks for Nero's permission to retire from public life, the historian is clearly on Seneca's side, with Nero portrayed as a hypocritical villain (*Ann.* 14.53–6).

Tacitus' climactic description of Seneca's death (*Ann.* 15.60 ff.) puts the final seal on the historian's assessment of this "distinguished man" (*egregius vir*: *Ann.* 15.23.4). True, the scene is not devoid of melodrama, but this is meant to enhance the rhetorical effect, not to detract from it. Those who regard this description (as well as Tacitus' overall attitude to Seneca) as negatively ironic[1] disregard the fact that Tacitus puts into the mouth of the dying Seneca words that express an idea very close to one the historian himself formulates while addressing his father-in-law in the spirited allocution at the end of the *Agricola*. Tacitus' Seneca says to his friends: "I bequeath you the image of my life", while Tacitus says to the dead Agricola: "Call us to the contemplation of your virtues" (*Agr.* 46.1).

In Cassius Dio, we find a quite different and markedly negative attitude. His picture of Seneca, however, is not completely consistent. He calls him the most learned and the wisest of the Romans (59.17.7; cp. 61.3.3; 61.4.1); but later on we witness a drastic change: Suillius' charges are presented as well founded (61.10.1–6); Dio even adds further accusations of his own and, in particular, endorses the reproach that Seneca lived in a way that was inconsistent with his philosophical doctrines – a widespread criticism which Seneca himself had tried to counter in his *De vita beata*. Elsewhere he presents Seneca as an accomplice to, or even as the mastermind behind Nero's crimes (e.g., 61.12.1). Possibly Dio followed two different sources, which he appears not to have reconciled with each other, although it should not be forgotten that from book 61 on, his work is only known through excerpts. As a consequence, his portrait of Seneca hardly appears credible or reliable.

---

[1] Such as, most recently Schmal (2008).

Seneca as a Writer

The diffusion of Seneca's writings is documented in antiquity not just in literary texts, but also in a few direct testimonies. Seneca's name (*Lucius Annaeus Senecas* [sic], with *Annaeus* corrected from *Annus*: CIL IV, Suppl. 4418) was graffitoed on the walls of Pompeii, where we also find a line from one of his tragedies, the *Agamemnon*: *Idai cernu nemura* (CIL IV, Suppl. 6698: cp. Sen. *Agam.* 730 *Idaea cerno nemora*). The change from *Idaea* to the archaic genitive *Idai*, which transforms Seneca's trimeter into a senarius, suggests that the author of the graffito failed to recognize the poet's metrical innovations. Quite possibly, another line from the same play might be recognized in a second graffito immediately above, if we are to read in *set cur sacratas*, the beginning of Sen. *Agam.* 693 *sed cur sacratas deripis capiti infulas?*[2]

Some scholars believe that these graffiti prove that Seneca's tragedies were actually staged and performed in Pompeii, but the level of knowledge they suggest may also be explained by public recitations. Some Pompeian wall paintings and even reliefs on sarcophagi have also been thought to represent scenes from Seneca's tragedies, but again such interpretations are based more on wishful thinking than on convincing evidence. A fragmentary sheet of parchment containing lines 663 through 704 of Seneca's *Medea* was recently discovered in Egypt (P. Mich. inv. no. 4969, fr. 36). It was part of a codex and should probably be dated in the fourth century CE.[3] There are corrections by a second hand and marginal notes in Greek; colometry is respected and the lyric lines of the chorus (vv. 663–9) are indented. This fragment is also important for establishing the text, as it provides by far the earliest testimony of the play. We can gather from all this that Senecan drama may have been more widely known and influential than his philosophical prose works were.

The Influence of Seneca's Philosophical Thought

It may come as a surprise that Seneca's philosophical thinking has left hardly any trace in later philosophical texts, even in authors like Epictetus and Marcus Aurelius, who belonged to the same philosophical school as Seneca. There are, to be sure, several conceptual similarities, but they are more naturally accounted for through their common philosophical mold

---

[2] Lebek (1985).
[3] Editio princeps: Markus and Schwendner (1997).

ALDO SETAIOLI

than by assuming the influence of Seneca's writings. Such influence only becomes apparent in Christian authors writing in Latin.

Several different explanations are possible. First of all, Seneca's purpose was not to provide a complete and consistent system of philosophy. This may be the meaning of Quintilian's charge, when he states that " [Seneca] was not a good enough scholar in philosophy, but he was nonetheless an outstanding castigator of vice"[4] (10.1.129). His main purpose was to promote his own and his readers' moral progress rather than to advance philosophical theory *per se*. Another reason is that he wrote in Latin, whereas the usual language of philosophy was Greek. In the imperial period, we do occasionally hear of Roman philosophers who wrote in Latin, such as Sergius Plautus and Seneca's own teacher Papirius Fabianus, but most wrote in Greek regardless of their nationality. Not just the Greek Epictetus, but also the Roman Sextius (the founder of the so-called "school of the Sextii"), as we learn from Seneca himself, as well as Musonius Rufus and even the Roman emperor Marcus Aurelius. In Seneca's own circle, the bilingual Annaeus Cornutus commented on Vergil and wrote about grammar in Latin but wrote his philosophical works in Greek.

Finally, Stoicism had been all but completely superseded by Platonism by the third century CE. It is interesting to see how the Roman Neoplatonist Macrobius, in his commentary on Cicero's *Dream of Scipio* (1.21.34), uses imagery and terminology taken from Seneca (*Ep.* 41.5) but transforms their basically Stoic and materialistic meaning to express the Neoplatonic conception of the soul that Porphyry had formulated with an image akin to Seneca's: sunbeams reach the earth despite the fact that the sun stays in the sky (Porph. F 261F, p. 288–9 Smith).

Seneca's thinking, however, did leave recognizable traces in subsequent texts seriously engaged in tackling problems to do with different levels of human experience. In the *Octavia*, Nero's arguments in support of tyrannical whim in his dialogue with Seneca are precisely those the philosopher had refuted in his *De clementia*, whereas in other authors, both Latin and Greek, *clementia* loses the central importance it had in Seneca's political theory. This happens, for instance, in Pliny the Younger's *Panegyricus*, in Dio Chrysostom's orations *De regno*, and also in Musonius Rufus, Epictetus, and Marcus Aurelius, while *clementia* retains its central position in the poet Statius (especially in *Thebaid* 12) and in the later *Panegyrici Latini*.

The most interesting philosophical confrontation, however, takes place between Seneca and his nephew Lucan, the pagan writer most deeply engaged with Seneca's legacy of thought. Lucan, no doubt, had been brought

[4] Griffin (2000, 535).

258

up in Seneca's milieu, and his poem suggests an author much influenced by Stoicism, even though he has come to call into question even its basic tenets – to lose his Stoic faith, so to speak.[5] Whereas Seneca preached the acceptance of all that fate, identified with the Stoic god, has in store for us, Lucan reacts against the higher will that seems to guide the world to catastrophe through a path of evil. His hero, the younger Cato, whom Seneca had elevated to a symbol of the ideal Stoic sage, is very much unlike Lucan's *sapiens*, in that he opposes his own will to that of the gods. Perhaps Lucan merely develops the embryonic elements of contradiction that may already be detected in Seneca's thought, such as the contrast between the wise man's struggle with fortune and his abiding by the Stoic god's will, which human beings can perceive only in its manifestation as fortune; even more probably, he was influenced by Seneca's tragedies, which depict a world utterly devoid of a *logos* capable of guiding nature and man toward a rational goal (though it may be disputed that this bleak picture unreservedly corresponds to Seneca's own view).

Other writers appear to have benefited from Seneca's teaching but, on closer inspection, are found to have done so only in a superficial way. So, for example, Martial often appears to versify Senecan ideas, but in reality he turns them into a very down-to-earth ideal of worldly enjoyment. While in Seneca the loaded meaning given to words like *vivere* and *vita* defines life fully in tune with one's devotion to philosophy and to self-improvement, in Martial the same vocabulary depicts a life dedicated to material gains and pleasures, not unlike Trimalchio's goal in Petronius' *Satyrica*. And Pliny the Younger often expresses ideas akin to those found in Seneca's *De beneficiis* and even appears to echo him when he calls the house a miniature state in which slaves should enjoy right of citizenship (Plin. *Ep.* 8.16.2; cf. Sen. *Ep.* 47.14). In all these authors, however, there is no trace of the theoretical underpinnings of the behavior Seneca advocates.

Literary Relationships

Reference to Seneca, although almost invariably unacknowledged, is near-obligatory for the writers of his time and can sometimes be gleaned in later authors, too. The bucolic poet Calpurnius Siculus clearly reworks in his *Eclogues* (4.138–41) some lines of the *Apocolocyntosis* in which Seneca describes the three Fates spinning the golden thread of Nero's life (*Apoc.* 4.3–9, 19–21). More contacts with the same work and also with the *De clementia* may be detected elsewhere, and this ensures the poet's link with Seneca,

[5] Due (1970, 214).

even if we are not prepared to recognize the latter in the bucolic character of Meliboeus. The author of the *Laus Pisonis* is also familiar with Seneca.

We have already spoken about the *Octavia* and Lucan. Here we shall only add that although the parallels between the *Octavia* and Seneca's genuine tragedies (and even his prose works) are innumerable, the author varies the usual pattern of Senecan plays: unlike most Senecan victims, Octavia reacts and inveighs against Nero, who, on his part, is not driven by incontrollable fury, like most Senecan tyrants, but only by self-interest, and reasons coolly with Seneca. Lucan, although on the whole he questions his uncle's philosophical stand, does use Seneca's prose work as a source of information (e.g., the *Naturales quaestiones* about the Etruscan methods of divination and the sources of the Nile – at the beginning and the end of the *Pharsalia*, respectively), and also the tragedies, especially when a gloomy atmosphere is evoked. As we shall see, he thus paved the way for Seneca's use by the poets of the following generation.

The satirical poet Persius, as we know from his *Vita* (ch. 5), got to know Seneca (or, more likely, his works) late in his short life and was not much impressed by his *ingenium* – a term that covers all aspects of Seneca's writing and in particular his distinctive style. Persius, who makes it very clear that he does not appreciate the bombast of epic and tragedy, may have Seneca's *Thyestes* in mind in his fifth satire, when he parodically demotes the cauldron used by Atreus to prepare Thyestes' cannibalistic meal to a homely kitchen pot (*olla*). Seneca had called it *aenum*, a term appropriate to high-style poetry.

The pseudo-Vergilian *Aetna* is an interesting case in point. The majority of Senecan parallels can be found in the *Naturales quaestiones*, but some concern other Senecan works both in verse and prose. Several verbal correspondences (e.g., *Aetna* 270 and Sen. *Ep.* 92.31; *Aetna* 233 and Sen. *Phaedr.* 333) and the final tale of the brothers from Catania (cp. Sen. *ben.* 3.37.2 and 6.36.1) point to direct contact, and the fact that they draw on several Senecan texts suggests that the poet of *Aetna* is alluding to Seneca rather than vice-versa. The poem, if not by Lucilius, must have been written by someone who was close to Seneca and familiar with his writings.

Were we to single out the most fascinating literary relationship in Seneca's own time and environment, it would surely be Petronius' *Satyrica*. To begin with, Seneca's own *Apocolocyntosis* may have influenced Petronius' mixture of prose and verse – a legacy of the Menippean satire which had been introduced to Latin literature by Varro – even though a papyrus scrap containing a lewd narrative that includes a speech in verse (the so-called *Iolaus*, POxy 3010) may suggest that this form was not unknown to what we conventionally call "Greek novels." There are indeed several parallels between Petronius and the *Apocolocyntosis*, but those between the *Satyrica* and Seneca's serious writings, in verse as well as in prose, are even more numerous. Although Seneca is never named, the reader often suspects comic parodying of either Seneca's moral teaching or of his most pathetic tragic scenes. When Trimalchio says, "Slaves too are men" (Petr. 71.1), for example, it is impossible to miss the connection with Seneca's "They are slaves; rather, they are men" (*Ep.* 47.1).[6]

We have touched upon one of the most blatant Senecan parodies in Petronius, when the rich freedman Trimalchio utters humanitarian ideas concerning the treatment of slaves, echoing Seneca in intentionally atrocious Latin. But the allusions to Seneca are innumerable, so much so that some passages, such as Encolpius' speech on the corpse of Lichas (115.9–10, 12–19), may be regarded as veritable pastiches of Senecan ideas. Almost invariably, Senecan materials appear in Petronius in ridiculous or unseemly situations – a clear mark of parodic intention. The parody extends to Seneca's tragedies, too. There are many such instances, and one of the two extended poems in the *Satyrica*, the so-called *Troiae halosis* ("Capture of Troy"), recited by Eumolpus at chapter 89, apes Seneca's plays in both meter and expressive mannerisms such as the frequent repetition of words – not to mention the numerous verbal parallels – even though Petronius does not grasp all the metrical subtleties of Seneca's tragic trimeter.[7]

This literary interaction was probably not one sided. There are passages in Seneca that may be construed as anti-Petronian lampoons, and they are late enough to allow for Seneca's knowledge of the *Satyrica*. The attack on those who exchange the roles of day and night (*Ep.* 122.2) may also be directed at Petronius, who, according to Tacitus (*Ann.* 16.18.1), lived at night and slept by day. An even clearer anti-Petronian skit may be seen in a Senecan passage (*Ep.* 123.10–11) in which the philosopher places in the mouths of disreputable bons vivants who hate philosophy words that seem to echo the materialistic life idealized by Trimalchio (e.g., Petr. 34.10), who – it should not be forgotten – boastfully declares that he has never listened to a philosopher (Petr. 71.12). While it is probably overdoing it to glimpse a caricature of Petronius in Seneca's unfriendly portrait of Maecenas, Augustus' minister,[8] this portrait, as well as some other Senecan figures, may have suggested certain details for Trimalchio's portrayal in the *Satyrica* (Sen. *Ep.* 114.6; cp. Petr. 27.3; 32.2).

---

[6] The parallel, suggested by Smith (1975), with Herod. 5.15, where a mistress tells her slave: "I was the one who made you a man among men") hardly fits Petronius' context, though it is akin to a different passage in the Cena (74.13).

[7] Cervellera (1975).

[8] Byrne (2006).

The pseudo-Ovidian *Consolatio ad Liviam* shows clear influences of Seneca's *Consolations* but also of the *De clementia,* the *De vita beata,* and the *Epistulae* (*Ep.* 85.29), and is clearly dependent on him. Statius admired Lucan (*Silv.* 2.7.30–2) and, like him, transplanted the bleak atmosphere of Senecan tragedy into his epic, where many of his characters are governed by a *furor* that leads to a *nefas* reminiscent of Seneca's plays. There are many close parallels between the *Thebaid* and Senecan tragedy, such as the scene of necromancy at 4.406–645 (cf., e.g., Sen. *Oed.* 530–658). The Theban subject links the poem with Seneca's *Oedipus* and *Phoenissae,* but there are also close parallels with his *Thyestes,* a play that portrays the unrelenting enmity between two brothers. Even Statius' other, less bleak epic, the *Achilleid,* is influenced by Seneca's tragedy, especially the *Troades.*

In Valerius Flaccus' *Argonautica,* themes from Senecan tragedy (the hero's conflict with tyrannical figures, the lust for power driven by *furor,* Medea's love as a tragic fault – *nefas* – etc.) are grafted onto the old myth. Valerius' Medea is not the young and still innocent woman of Apollonius of Rhodes but the powerful, frightening figure of the tragic tradition, which focuses on a later phase of her story. There are several verbal parallels with Seneca's *Medea* (7.461 and Sen. *Med.* 280; 7.461–2 and Sen. *Med.* 900; and several others), and whole scenes are modeled on this tragedy, such as Medea's last speech (8.414–6), which is reminiscent of the words uttered by Seneca's Medea at *Med.* 204–51 and 447–89.

Silius Italicus uses Senecan tragedy, along with Vergil and Ovid, primarily in his description of the underworld, in *Punica* 13 (especially *Herc. f.* 658–829, but also other parts of that tragedy and *Oed.* 171–3). In Juvenal, there are several parallels with Seneca's tragedies and prose works, and one literal repetition (9.96 *ardet et odit* = Sen. *Med.* 582). Even Hosidius Geta's *Medea,* despite being a Vergilian *cento,* is influenced by its Senecan namesake in its structure and in the choice of Vergilian expressions, which are as close as possible to Seneca's, especially at the beginning and the end of the scenes. The last pagan poet in which Senecan influence may be recognized is Rutilius Namatianus, who shows traces of his acquaintance Seneca's tragedies and may have derived his views on the Jews (*de red.* 1.397 f.) from Seneca's *De superstitione.*

We would probably recognize a strong Senecan influence on the prose writers if more of the prose works of his time had been preserved. As it is, Seneca's traces are less clearly visible in imperial prose than they are in poetry. In Pliny the Younger, although the avowed model of his letter collection is Cicero, each letter tends to turn into a self-contained essay, as in Seneca, who, however is mentioned only once (5.3.5.), as the author of light verse. Tacitus may have been influenced by Senecan tragedy in the highly theatrical staging of some episodes, such as the murder of Agrippina, and the *De ira* may have suggested some traits of the *Germania*.

One of the last pagan writers, Macrobius, never mentions Seneca by name but was certainly familiar with his work. His commentary on the *Dream of Scipio* has a Senecan flavor, and a more extensive engagement is to be found in his *Saturnalia*. Aside from some minor reminiscences (e.g., *Sat.* 1.7.6 and Sen. *Ep.* 10.5), Macrobius uses extended parts of Seneca's *Ep.* 84 in the introduction and of *Ep.* 47 (on the slaves) at *Sat.* 1.11.7–16. Alhough Macrobius obviously adapts Seneca's words to his own purposes, his importance for establishing Seneca's original text deserves more attention than it usually receives. If his adaptation of *Ep.* 84 misunderstands Seneca's promotion of an organic assimilation of knowledge, he at least engages Seneca at the level of cultural content rather than of rhetorical form, and is more in keeping with Seneca's meaning than his rhetorical opponents.

Ancient Judgments on Seneca's Style

As we have seen, Persius was not impressed by Seneca's *ingenium*. The satirist must have been an exception, if we can trust Quintilian's testimony, according to which Seneca was all the rage in his own time, whereas he tried to stem this fashion by preaching a return to Ciceronian patterns. Even Tacitus, writing a generation later, remarks that Seneca's *ingenium* was pleasing and suited to his own times (*Ann.* 13.3.1). Seneca was already in vogue by the reign of Caligula, as Suetonius testifies (*Calig.* 53). The same author, however, attests the first of a long series of severe criticisms of Seneca's style. According to Caligula, Seneca composed "mere display pieces" (*commissiones meras*) and his prose was "sand without lime" (*harena sine calce*). This latter statement undoubtedly refers to Seneca's broken composition, made of short, pithy sentences, a poor mortar to keep the whole together; the mishmash of chopped-up phrases – *minutissimae sententiae* – was later criticized by Quintilian (10.1.130). The term *commissio* meant "spectacle" in Seneca's time (it is also found at *Ep.* 84.10), but Caligula's judgment would be more effective if the first metaphor, like the second, also referred to the architectural realm. In this case, *commissiones meras* could mean "mere juxtapositions" – a meaning taken up and explained by the following *harena sine calce* and highlighted by the repetition of the prefix (*com-missiones ... com-ponere*).[9]

---

[9] Alhough the verb *committere* has this meaning in classical Latin, *commissio* in this sense does not appear till very late (TLL III 1900, 40–9), but it is used in connection

Quintilian does recognize "fullness" (*copia*) in Seneca's style (10.1.128; 12.10.11) and quotes his *Medea* (9.2.9). In his most detailed assessment (10.1.125–31), he strives to be fair to him, recognizing his talent and appreciating him as a moralist but criticizing his "vices" (*vitia*) that appealed so much to the younger generation. Quintilian tries to redress what he believes to be a corrupt taste. He does so on the basis of a predefined rhetorical pattern, without understanding Seneca's originality in granting a central role to the personality of the individual writer ("if you correct what the rhetoricians call vices, you destroy the work of great writers," says Seneca: *Ep.* 114.12). Actually, Quintilian's criticism of Seneca is close to the Elder Seneca's strictures against Ovid – another literary innovator (Sen. rhet. *contr.* 2.10.2: "Ovid was not unaware of his vices; rather he loved them"; cf. Quint. 10.1.130: "if Seneca had not loved everything he wrote …").

It is hardly surprising that the archaizing writers of the second century CE should attack a "modernist" like Seneca, taking Quintilian's judgment to an extreme in the process. Whereas Quintilian had conceded that there was something good in Seneca, for Fronto, whose criticism is closer to insult than to rational argument, Seneca's talent is very occasional, so much so that it can be compared to the silver coins sometimes found in sewers (*de orationibus* 3). He does point out one evident characteristic of Seneca's writing: the frequent repetition of the same idea in different forms, yet he completely misses the didactic motivation behind this device, i.e. the need to drive home his moral teaching: "What is never learned well enough is never repeated too often" (*numquam nimis dicitur quod numquam satis discitur*: *Ep.* 27.9).

In the preface to his *Noctes Atticae* (*praef.* 9), among many miscellaneous works like his own, Gellius mentions *Epistulae morales*, undoubtedly those of Seneca. When he does refer specifically to Seneca, however, Gellius finds virtually nothing worth saving (12.2). Like Fronto, he disregards the pedagogical purpose of Seneca's style, and resorts to insult even more freely (*insulsissime, nugator, ineptus, insubidus*). He is especially offended by the negative judgment Seneca (in a letter lost to us) directs against the classics, Cicero and – to a lesser extent – Vergil, and against Ennius, the poet revered by the champions of the archaizing tendency.

The virulence of these attacks suggests that Seneca probably still had admirers at this time. Much as his stylistic manner was later to experience a

with architecture (Cassiod. *hist.* 9.34 *lapidum iuncturas et commissiones*). If we could take Caligula's utterance as the first example of this meaning, there would be no need to correct *commissiones* into *commissuras*.

revival, too, beginning with the Christian writers, it was primarily Seneca's thinking that enjoyed a renewed influence.

Further Reading

The fundamental work on Seneca's reception in antiquity is Trillitzsch (1971), which, however, ignores on the whole his impact at the literary level. A good discussion of the figure of Seneca at the court of Nero as depicted in the *Octavia* may be found in Armisen-Marchetti (1998). An in-depth investigation of Lucan's relation to Seneca is offered by Narducci (2002); on *aemulatio*, see Castagna (2003). On Senecan echoes in the *Aetna*, see De Vivo (1989).

The many points of contact between Seneca and his contemporary Petronius are discussed by Sullivan (1968), Rose (1971), Smith (1975), and, more recently, in Schmeling (2011), Setaioli (2011) and Star (2012).

Statius' borrowings from Senecan tragedy are treated by Frings (1992). Quintilian's judgment of Seneca as a writer is well analyzed by Calboli (1999). Fleury (2000) offers a study of Fronto's criticism of Seneca's style.

20

CHIARA TORRE

Seneca and the Christian Tradition

Seneca's journey toward becoming one of the most significant writers and thinkers in the European tradition begins with the reception of his works by Christian writers, from the Apologists to the sixth-century Martin of Braga. In the wake of Trillitzsch's masterly essay,[1] a great deal has been published over the last forty years by scholars keen to survey Seneca's presence in the ancient Christian tradition and to detail numerous possible correspondences between Seneca's works and the writings of the Fathers. Existing bibliography is brimming with data and unverifiable hypotheses, but the overall picture remains vague, with many questions left unanswered.[2] We urgently need a more thorough and precise assessment of Christian authors' familiarity with and use of Seneca.

Dynamics of Reception

Perhaps the best evidence for the reception of Seneca in Late Antiquity can be found in the pseudo-correspondence of St. Paul and Seneca. This text will be my starting point, but I sidestep problems to do with authorship, dating, the identity of the addressee, structure, and genre and will focus instead on the larger problem that grew out of the first Humanists' interpretation of the letters and that went on to shape the entire history of Seneca's Christian reception. As Momigliano argues,[3] the Humanists' approach to Seneca developed in direct relation to their reading of the pseudo-correspondence with St. Paul. The first Humanists failed to reject the testimony of Augustine (*Letter to Macedonius* 153.14) and Jerome (*On Illustrious Men* 12) and thus attempted to account for the Apostle's familiarity with Seneca by creating a crypto-Christian philosopher. This strategy sets the tone for future studies,

---

[1] Trillitzsch (1971).
[2] Traina (1987, 188).
[3] Momigliano (1955, 13–32).

to the extent that most scholars – both those who argued for the letters' authenticity and the more numerous ones who denied it – were inclined to claim a Christian Seneca, or at least to affirm that he was spiritually in tune with Christian doctrine. This critical status quo proved stubbornly self-perpetuating: wherever critics identified a strong overlap with Christian themes in passages of Senecan prose, these instances were immediately collated as evidence both of the notion that the Fathers made extensive use of Seneca's works and of the view that they recognized him as a fellow Christian.

Yet Seneca's reception among Christians was not necessarily tied up with ideological involvement. Of greater relevance is the crucial historical and geographical overlap among three key figures at the height of their careers, all of whom became martyrs under Nero: Seneca (Nero's counselor), Peter (Christ's heir), and Paul (the Pagans' Apostle). This synchronicity was a hugely significant factor in making Seneca an icon in the Christian tradition, and it had little to do with a straightforward ideological investment in or agreement with Senecan thought, as Augustine's mistrust of Seneca makes clear. Christian writers did not necessarily engage in depth with the content of Seneca's work, especially when we compare the reception of Seneca to that of other classical authors in the same period. The pseudo-correspondence with St. Paul as well as other texts (see, for example, Lactantius, *Divine Institutes* 6.24.13–14; Jerome, *On Illustrious Men* 12) rather suggests that Seneca is regarded more as a historical and political figure than as a philosopher and thinker.[4] In the absence of clear evidence to this effect, we should be careful to assume that the Fathers were inclined to draw substantially from Seneca's works and thought.

It may be significant that the Fathers appear to have echoed Quintilian's famous evaluation of Seneca, which was well known in schools.[5] Here Seneca is placed at the end of a list of philosophers but not *among* them, for he lacks sufficient "accuracy" (*diligentia*) and is thereby not considered an intermediary figure in the assimilation and cultural transmission of Stoic thought in Rome. However, this perception doesn't seem to have been carried over to any great extent into Late Antiquity. Jerome gives biographical

---

[4] A large part of Seneca's reception in the Ancient World as a whole (not only in the Christian Tradition) pertained to his role as a public figure and outstanding witness of his own times rather than as a writer or thinker: see Setaioli's chapter in this volume, especially 317–9.

[5] Quintilian, *Institutes of Oratory* 10.1.125–131, also discussed in this *Companion* by Braund (29), Williams (168–70), and Setaioli's chapter in this volume (320, 328–9). Lactantius, *Divine Institutes* 5.9.18, hints at this passage. Quintilian's canon of authors as a whole is frequently echoed: for instance, the list of philosophers Jerome holds up as examples of the disputation style in the epistle to Pammachius (*Letters* 49.13.3–4) follows Quintilian's list of *Socratici*.

details of Seneca's career, yet only Lactantius explicitly defines him as a Roman Stoic (and a shrewd one: Seneca is "most penetrating," *acerrimus*, and "acutest," *acutissimus*), and we should note that the Stoic label serves a specific purpose in the context – the section of *Divine Institutes* in which Lactantius analyzes ancient philosophers' false opinions on the nature of God. More generally, however, Seneca is considered a Pagan thinker and is not referred to specifically as a Stoic. Yet many scholars have taken for granted the notion that the reception of Seneca in Late Antiquity was guided by the strong presence of Stoicism in Christian thought – another misconception for which evidence is missing. Quintilian described Seneca as a superb critic of vice (*egregius insectator vitiorum*), and indeed the reception of Seneca in Late Antiquity was focused not on Stoicism as such but around moral topics such as anger, superstition, and continence, with special attention devoted to individual works dealing with specific ethical issues (for instance *On Anger*, *On Superstition*, *On Marriage*).

Quintilian also portrays Seneca as an unrivalled stylist known for his captivating and aphoristic prose and poetry, and Christian writers seem to have understood and packaged Seneca in similar terms. Hence the reception of his works seems to have been filtered by means of gnomologies, starting at least from the sixth century, when the *Liber de moribus* (an anonymous compilation of Senecan *sententiae*) and the *Formula for an Honest Life* of Martin of Braga were composed. Seneca's idiosyncratic style was not exactly revived in Christian texts, at least up to the fourth century or even later (perhaps in part because of Quintilian's negative judgment), but some of its features are recognizable – in the innovative style of Ambrosius' homilies, for example, as well in Augustine's energetic, post-Platonic writings on introspection. Much research remains to be done in this area. Some aphoristic snippets of Senecan tragedy can also be detected in the Christian authors, although they are rarely attributed to him. We might glimpse a more nuanced reception of the tragedies in Prudentius: the staging of Hippolytus' death in the *Phaedra*, for instance, seems to have inspired the narrative pattern of St. Hippolytus' martyrdom (*Peristephanon* 11), and critics have noted the influence of Seneca's dramatic techniques in the hymn for St. Romanus (*Peristephanon* 10).

The distinction between Seneca the philosopher and Seneca the dramatist was increasingly emphasized in Late Antiquity, resulting in two distinct branches in the Christian reception of his corpus. Other Senecan texts known and studied by the Fathers were probably selected for their cultural significance (the *Exhortations*, for example, as a paradigm of protreptic writing) or for their exemplification of systematic structure (the *Libri moralis philosophiae*, "Books of Ethics," possibly designed as a list of questions and answers, may in turn have been used as a resource for scholastic maxims or *placita*). Perhaps the Fathers also had access to other Senecan works lost to us, for instance the "commentaries" (*commentarii*) to Lucilius mentioned in *Letter* 39.1, which were already arranged systematically.

Rather than offering a broad survey of possible traces of Seneca's works in the Fathers' texts, I will focus in what follows on a selected group of authors and themes, with a view to developing a sharper methodology for interpreting the mass of information at our disposal. I will therefore discuss some Christian authors whose engagement with Seneca is not limited to the appropriation of a few aphorisms but reflects a deeper understanding of his works.

When Tertullian writes that Seneca "is often one of ours" (*Seneca saepe noster*) in a passage that also cites Seneca's *On Benefits*, he signals this kind of engagement.[6] While as a rule the Fathers use *noster* in connection with a classical author in order to set up an opposition between Latin and Greek writers, this may well be the one instance in which the adjective marks a distinction between Christian and Pagan authors. Moreover, Tertullian is arguably deploying a full-fledged strategy of appropriation of Pagan philosophy. The relevant passage from *On Benefits* discusses the theory of the "seeds" (*semina*) of all notions that are inborn in the mind as well as the role of God as the teacher who cultivates them. Tertullian explicitly appropriates this theory in order to argue that all natural properties of the soul are inherent in it as parts of its divine substance and therefore grow and develop accordingly.

Theological and Moral Issues

I will begin with theology, and specifically Seneca's critique of what he sees as false and superstitious Pagan practices and his argument for the creation of a true, spiritual cult, in fragments of the *On Superstition* (Fragm. 65–74 Vottero) transmitted by Augustine (*City of God* 6.10–11). Other traces of Seneca's text can be found in Tertullian (*Apology* 12.6, 16.11, 46.4), Minucius (*Octavius* 25.8, 28.7), and Lactantius (*Divine Institutes* 1.20). According to Augustine, whereas Varro distinguished between the false "mythical" aspect (*theologia fabulosa*) of Pagan religion and its more reliable "civil" or "political" aspect (*theologia civilis*), Seneca aims to convince his readers that Pagan civil theology is just as fake and theatrical as mythical theology. The heart of Senecan polemics might lie in the use of theatrical imagery. On the one hand, he could have argued, theatre is the place where

[6] Tertullian, *A Treatise on the Soul* 20.1, quoting Seneca, *On Benefits* 4.6.7.

false, mythological, and poetic representations of gods are popularized; on the other, it also represents the fictional realm in which civil cults are celebrated during periodic *ludi*, so that the theatre may come to symbolize the gap between superstition – which relies on appearance – and authentic religious experience.

Augustine, in turn, denounces Seneca's stance against *superstitio*, drawing attention to his own hypocritical emphasis on the theatricality of public life, in which the wise man is an actor who must portray superstitious beliefs even though he does not accept them in his heart: "Seneca preferred, as the best role to be followed by a wise man [*has partes ... elegit Seneca sapienti*], to feign respect for them in act, but to have no real regard for them at heart."[7]

The Fathers may have incorporated and critiqued other Senecan passages in their collection of arguments against Pagan religion. Some passages from Seneca's extant writings[8] are echoed in Arnobius;[9] Lactantius may have used three lost Senecan writings (*Exhortations*, *Books of Ethics*, and *On untimely Death*) as theological doxographies pertaining to the opinions of various Pagan authors on God and his true cult. Indeed, five out of fourteen quotes from the *Exhortations*,[10] two out of three from the *On untimely Death*,[11] and two out of four from the *Books of Ethics*[12] are concerned with the topic of divinity.

Of all the moral issues analyzed by Seneca in his prose works, the Fathers seem to have been particularly intrigued by debates on anger and chastity. In his *On the Anger of God*, Lactantius employs several (unattributed) Senecan allusions and quotations, particularly from the *On Anger*, which he reads selectively according to his own theological agenda. The text defends the biblical concept of God's anger against the concept of divine impassivity (*apatheia*), which had been established by the theology and ethics of the Pagan philosophers and had also gained some currency in Christian thought. Instead of focusing on biblical exegesis, Lactantius chooses to discuss ancient philosophical positions, especially those of the Epicureans and Stoics, and attempts to distinguish between good anger (a product of reason, proper to God as well as to the *pater familias*) and bad anger (born of instinct, proper to men and beasts), which must be removed. Lactantius apparently selected certain items from his source and organized them by topic: all the

---

[7] Fr. 71 Vottero.
[8] See, e.g., *Letters* 95.47–50, 123.16; *On Benefits* 4.19.1, 4.25.1–3.
[9] *Against the Pagans* 4.30–2, 6.2–3, 6.24.
[10] Fragm. 84, 86–9 Vottero, quoted in Lactantius, *Divine Institutes* 1.5, 1.7, 2.8, 6.24–5.
[11] Fragm. 61–2 Vottero, in *Divine Institutes* 1.5, 3.12.
[12] Fragm. 93–4 Vottero, in *Divine Institutes* 1.16, 2.2.

passages have been rewritten and recontextualized, their meaning and function transformed. Interestingly, allusions to Seneca's *On Clemency* are interwoven with quotes from the *On Anger*, suggesting that Lactantius – like many modern critics – read the two texts as connected and complementary. Seneca himself had excluded anger as a tyrannical passion from the realm of good government based on the principle of clemency, whereas according to Lactantius, anger, such as the "just anger" (*iusta ira*) that fills a man with healthy fear, is essential for effective government of the *domus*, the State and the world.

Seneca on anger may have underpinned the debate between Lactantius and two other Christian authors: Arnobius, who according to Jerome was one of Lactantius' teachers, and Martin of Braga, who composed a refined epitome of Seneca's *On Anger*. In several passages of the *Against the Pagans*,[13] Arnobius asserts that God is immune to anger, being immune both to its causes (God's nature cannot be touched by the pain of insult or by the desire for revenge) and to its effects (anger is always blind fury, far removed from God's perfect embodiment of the good). For Arnobius, the theme of God's *apatheia* is at the center of a tapestry whose threads all lead to Seneca and specifically to his thoughts on the *apatheia* of the wise man, on the monstrosity of anger,[14] and on divine nature.[15] Arnobius' views on anger are almost directly opposed to Lactantius', which can partly be explained by the different historical contexts in which the two authors were writing: Arnobius wrote just before Diocletian's persecution, while Lactantius composed his treatise after Constantine's edict, as he anticipated God's revenge on the persecutors of the past.

Martin's epitome of the *On Anger* follows Seneca closely in discussing the effects of anger and how it should be avoided or cured. The epitomist is engaged not only in trimming his model by making dozens of small morphological, syntactical, lexical, and stylistic changes but also in rebuilding it according to a new, structural framework that intertwines ancient philosophical thought with notions about deadly sins derived from the monastic tradition. Martin's decision to use only this Senecan dialogue to condemn anger as a deadly sin may betray the intention to mount a counterattack against Lactantius' thesis as well as to attract a broader, lay audience for his epitome. The text was probably conceived as a draft of homilies for laymen and dedicated to his friend, the bishop Vittimer.

---

[13] See 1.17, 1.23, 7.5–7, 7.23.
[14] *On Anger* 1.1–2, 1.1.4–6, 1.5.3, 3.3.2; *On the Firmness of the wise man* 3.3, 9.3, 13.3–5.
[15] See especially *Letters* 95.47–50; *On Benefits* 4.7.2, 4.9.1, 4.25.1–3.

In contrast to Martin, when Jerome weaves fragments of Seneca's *On Marriage* into chapters 41 to 49 of book one of *Against Jovinianus* (the number of passages cited ranges from thirty-two to forty-four depending on the edition), his own imposing presence prevails over a fading Seneca. After examining the Old and New Testaments, Jerome summons Pagan history, philosophy, and religion to argue that Christian ascetic doctrines had not introduced anything new. Among Pagan witnesses in favor of virginity and chastity, according to Jerome, Seneca also wrote about marriage. Although only three of these passages are explicitly labeled by Jerome as Senecan, several scholars have been spurred on to seek out further Senecan allusions or citations in the *Against Jovinianus*, and various reconstructions of Seneca's work have been proposed.

The complex web of sources in *Against Jovinianus* as a whole allows us to verify whether Seneca acted as an intermediary between Pagan authors and the Fathers. For Jerome, both the Bible and Pagan texts constitute a vast repository of anecdotes, *exempla*, and memorable phrases. This is also true of properly philosophical sources quoted in his work: not only Seneca but also Plutarch, Aristotle, Plato, Theophrastus, Chrysippus, and Epicurus are important not so much for their doctrines as for their roles as paradigmatic wise men.

We might detect a certain uniformity, then, in Jerome's use of *testimonia* or *exempla*. We could even argue that Jerome manipulated Pagan sources for his own polemic purposes, just as he was shown to have done with the Holy Scriptures (evidence of this can be found in his distortion of several passages taken from Plutarch's *Advice to the Bride and Groom*). Seneca too may have been subjected to a similar kind of corruption.

Indeed, the rhetoricity of many of Jerome's *testimonia* in the *Against Jovinianus* might suggest that some of these could come from the gnomologies; some others might precisely issue from Seneca's *On Marriage* as the only intermediate source. This might also apply to the so-called *Eclogue* of Theophrastus (*ecloga Theophrasti*),[16] which according to Jerome is a substantial extract from a lost "Golden Book of Marriage" (*aureolus liber de nuptiis*) by the Greek philosopher Theophrastus. However, some scholars have proposed that Jerome translated directly from Theophrastus or read the fragment in a (lost) work of Porphyrius (as he certainly did in the second book of *Against Jovinianus*, plagiarizing Porphyrius' *On Abstinence*).

The *Eclogue* reads as a collage or pastiche: philosophical elements are blended with and perhaps counterbalanced by nonphilosophical ones, possibly deriving from comic or satirical texts, and Seneca's lost *On Marriage*

---

[16] *Against Jovinianus* 47 (Seneca, *On Marriage* Fragm. 54 Vottero).

might also play a role. The philosophical topic of marriage is introduced at the beginning of the work via a question – To what extent is marriage reconcilable with philosophical life? – and the text ends by reasserting the wise man's calling to a contemplative life devoted to the divine.

The first part appears to be far more Theophrastean. A set of circumstances is laid out, which, if they were all to occur simultaneously, might still allow the wise man to marry but which, given their rarity, represent obstacles. We are not therefore dealing with Stoic debate on the criteria for choosing a wife, for the emphasis is rather on circumstances determined by Fortune. All this leads up to Theophrastus' reservations on the political engagement of the wise man, to which he had set strict limits, depending on circumstances, if Cicero's testimony is to be trusted.[17] The *Eclogue*'s conclusion, therefore, which promotes the ideal of the wise man's spiritual solitude, perfectly matches Seneca's thought and style (see Fragm. 54 Vottero, 57–62).

The middle part of the work has an aphoristic flavor: it includes a long list of *sententiae* about how to choose a wife, as well as about the many difficulties marriage entails. Echoes of Seneca are also scattered here and there.

Overall, it is possible that in his original dialogue, Seneca debated Theophrastus' theory that the wise man could marry in exceptional circumstances. He may also have contested the resulting constraints on the wise man's autarky, as he does elsewhere, by attacking Theophrastus and the Peripatetics. It looks likely that Seneca's strenuous defense of self-sufficiency did not entail a complete ban on marriage for the wise man. Jerome failed to detect the direction Seneca's criticism of Theophrastus was going, or perhaps he did not want to: as a result, he flattens out Seneca's multifaceted polemic, reducing it to a straightforward and philosophically superficial attack on marriage.

Another major influence on the Christian literary tradition was exercised by Seneca's protreptics, and in Lactantius as well as in Martin's *Formula for an Honest Life*, we find traces of his lost *Exhortations*, a text mentioned by Seneca in a passage (*Letters* 16.1–6) that also gives us some idea of the structure of the work. Cicero's lost protreptic dialogue *Hortensius*, of which we have some fragments, many from Lactantius himself, offers clues as to the contents of the *Exhortations*, and the fragments quoted by Lactantius[18] add to the picture. By quoting Seneca, Lactantius takes pains to explain the extent to which Seneca can help us progress on the path of truth and firmly

---

[17] Cicero, *Ends of Goods and Evils* 5.11. See also Diogenes Laertius, *Lives of Eminent Philosophers* 5.45.

[18] Fragm. 76–89 Vottero, coming from books I, II, III, V, VI of *Divine Institutes*.

establishes the boundaries beyond which Seneca cannot lead us. He echoes Seneca in pouring ridicule on arrogant, so-called philosophers (Fragm. 76 Vottero), in denouncing the contradiction between their words and actions, and more generally in condemning the immortality of all those unworthy people who claim to be able to do philosophy (Fragm. 77 Vottero, a text that Minucius, *Octavius* 38.5 also hinted at). He is also in full agreement with Seneca on the key role of the conscience as a guide to individual morality (Fragm. 81 Vottero, imitated also by Minucius, *Octavius* 35.6) and on the presence of the divine in the soul (Fragm. 89 Vottero); and, like Seneca, he extols the wise man's magnanimity.[19] Lactantius, however, refutes Seneca's definition of philosophy as a rule, theory, method, or knowledge (*regula, ars, ratio, scientia*) of living ethically (Fragm. 82 Vottero) and suggests that in the face of the true wisdom given to humans by God, Seneca's *Exhortations* cannot be considered a rulebook for leading a fully moral life (*regula bene honesteque vivendi*).

The *Formula for an Honest Life* of Martin of Braga, a synopsis on ethics that may have been derived from a lost Senecan work, appears, whether this was its aim or not, as a belated answer to Lactantius on this point. The *Formula*, a guide to the good use of power composed to educate King Miro and his courtiers, marks the final stages of Late Antiquity's reception of Seneca, and also represents the first piece in the puzzle of his Medieval reception, especially in pseudoepigraphic writings. Indeed, during the Middle Ages, a shortened version of the *Formula* came be known as Seneca's *On the four cardinal virtues* (*De quattuor virtutibus cardinalibus*),[20] while yet another version, supplemented by a collection of Seneca's *sententiae* and also attributed to Seneca, was given the title *De copia verborum* ("On Abundant Style"). Correspondences between the *Formula* and Seneca's writings were detected early on, although no specific model was identified. Today, scholars are inclined to believe that the text relies heavily on and possibly represents a reshaping of a lost work, perhaps, as a passage at the beginning of the *Formula* about the relationship among the four virtues and moral duties would suggest, Seneca's *On Duties* (*De officiis*).[21]

While we cannot establish with any degree of certainty the relationship between the *Formula* and Seneca's *On Duties*, we may get further if we investigate the influence of the *Exhortations* on the *Formula*. The notion

---

[19] Fragm. 78 Vottero, doubtfully assigned to the *Exhortations*; it matches Fragm. 96 well, which in turn comes from the *On Untimely Death*.

[20] See Stacey's chapter in this volume.

[21] To be sure, Cicero and Ambrosius in their respective *On Duties* as well as Seneca himself in *Letters* 94–5 debated this topic. However, too little of Seneca's *De officiis* survives to substantiate this claim.

that the *Formula* is dependent on or influenced by Seneca's *Exhortations* is suggested by a number of points: both texts define philosophy as "a set of rules for living a good, honest life" (*regula bene honesteque vivendi*, Fragm. 82), and the same idea is reflected in the title of Martin's treatise (*formula vitae honestae*); discussion of the four virtues, as a fragment of *Hortensius* confirms,[22] was a popular topic in protreptic writings; finally, the topic of moral duties in itself, connected to the discussion of how many circumstances and elements of judgment should be taken into consideration in distinguishing between false and true virtues, is found in both the *Formula* and the *Exhortations* (Fragm. 79–80 Vottero).

In general, however, Martin of Braga seems to draw on Senecan texts as tools and models for a secularizing moral pedagogy. This use of Seneca may also be relevant for the so-called trilogy *Driving away Vanity, On Pride* and *Exhortation to Humility* (*Pro repellenda iactantia, Item de superbia, Exhortatio humilitatis*), which is usually regarded as the grouping together of monastic collations. These writings contain several echoes of Seneca, all related to the theme of adulation. The secular *Exhortation to Humility* separates the trilogy from the monastic tradition, which nonetheless stands in the background; at the same time, it bridges the gap to the *Formula for an Honest Life*, in which the theme of adulation is also present. Like the *Formula*, then, the trilogy might also be interpreted as a Christian *speculum principis* for King Miro, and it may even have constituted the next stage of the king's *institutio* after the teaching of the *Formula*.

Two key points emerge from our analysis. First, the Fathers were not just interested in Seneca as an aphoristic writer, despite the fact that his texts mostly circulated in the Christian tradition in the form of extracted gnomes; Senecan texts were also an important part of the vast pool of doxographical writing from which the Fathers regularly drew. Secondly, it is important to assert that the reception of Senecan texts in the Fathers is part of a wider picture in which a small number of Christian authors interacted with a trio of Pagans –Seneca, Cicero and Varro– who were of particular interest because they had dealt with moral and ethical debates in their philosophical works. Seneca is explicitly associated with Varro and Cicero on at least two occasions, by Augustine and Lactantius, and both authors[23] draw on this relationship as a basis for the structure of their own books. In the sixth book of the *City of God*, Varro's fragments frame chapters 2 through 9, whereas those of Seneca's *On Superstition* structure chapters 10 and 11; in the third

---

[22] Fragm. 110 Grilli, transmitted by Augustine, *On the Trinity* 14.9.12.
[23] Seneca's *On Superstition* in Augustine's *City of God* 6.10; and Seneca's *Exhortations* in Lactantius' *Divine Institutes* 3.15–6.

book of *Divine Institutes*, fragments of Seneca's *Exhortations* are found in those chapters in which there are also references to Cicero's *Hortensius*. What we glimpse from these observations is a cultural genealogy in which Seneca occupies a crucial position, linking the Latin *auctoritas* of Cicero and Varro with Christian doctrine.

Further Reading

The major general surveys of Seneca's influence in Christian late antiquity are Martina (2001), Moreschini (2013), and the magisterial study of Trillitzsch (1971). In English, see also Ross (1974). On the pseudo-correspondance of Seneca and St. Paul, see Bocciolini Palagi (1985), Mara (2001), Fürst, Fuhrer, Siegert, and Walter (2006), and Mazzoli (2008); in English, Panizza (1976) and Abbott (1978). On the reception of specific tragedies, see Gasti (1993, 215–29), Henke (1985), Mazzoli (2010), Trillitzsch (1981). Under "personaggi citati" the database www.Senecana.it offers a list (with further bibliography) of possible traces of *lectura Senecae* in Latin Christian authors.

21

ROLAND MAYER

Seneca *Redivivus*: Seneca in the Medieval and Renaissance World

Transmission through the centuries of Seneca's writings produced paradoxically opposite results: a good deal that was genuine was lost, whilst the corpus ballooned into a "super-Seneca,"[1] with the accretion of misattributions and falsifications, along with epitomes of or extracts from the genuine works in new formats and under new titles. The Middle Ages inherited this bulging Seneca, who would in due course be reduced in scale by the more scholarly High Renaissance. Removal of the surplus did the emerging genuine Seneca no harm. His now-recovered Stoic thought, his engaging prose style, and his flexible literary formats ensured his popularity both with readers and with writers in the increasingly prominent vernaculars of Europe. The discovery of historical information also helped to put biographical flesh on the literary bones, so that by the end of the period discussed here, Seneca had been transformed from a bloodless *auctor* into a living presence who had a profound influence on life.

The Middle Ages

A brief survey of the availability and diffusion of Seneca's writings in the late Middle Ages will set the scene.[2] Most of the genuine texts that survived antiquity had very restricted diffusion until the late eleventh century; from then on, works are gradually rediscovered and copied for wider distribution. First come the *Epistulae*. *Epistles* 1 through 88 had been fairly widely available from the Carolingian period, but a combined tradition of them plus *Ep.* 89 through 124 took off in the early twelfth century, and there were once more than 500 manuscripts of the *Epistles* (in varied groupings) down to the invention of print.[3] Then, in the last decade of the eleventh

---

[1] The phrase is owed to Hinds (2004, 162).
[2] Reynolds (1965, 112–24) and (1983, 358–9), De Robertis and Resta (2004).
[3] Fohlen (2000).

century, *De beneficiis* and *De clementia* emerge and detonate an "explosion of interest" in the twelfth.[4] In the early twelfth century, the *Naturales quaestiones* become available, and in the second half of the thirteenth century, the *Dialogi* (excerpts had been known earlier), of which there are now around 100 manuscripts.[5] The *De ira* does not seem to have attracted much interest,[6] and the consolations presumably offered the Christian reader very little. The *Apocolocyntosis* likewise deserves no more than a word, since its influence was minimal.[7] The very lateness of its first printing (1513) shows what little notice it attracted compared to the other works. Still, the existence of about forty manuscripts suggests a degree of diffusion,[8] and it figured in some early biographies of Seneca.

The tragedies become known in the second half of the twelfth century and spread rapidly only from the beginning of the fourteenth.[9] Finally, the rhetorical works titled *Controversiae*, really the work of Seneca the Elder, continued to circulate under the son's name; the excerpted tradition is larger than that of the authentic text. Some of the imaginary "cases" set for debate were a source for tales in the *Gesta Romanorum*.[10]

During this period of rediscovery, Seneca's works enjoyed polar forms of presentation. On the one hand, *florilegia* of extracts were compiled, one of the most influential, especially in Spain, being Luca Mannelli's *Tabulatio et expositio Senecae*, commissioned by Pope Clement VI (mid-fourteenth century).[11] On the other, *corpora* of a variety of texts were constructed. Epitomes were not always identified as such, thus betraying readers into the belief that they had a complete text.[12] The largely ethical *florilegia*, which drew chiefly on *De beneficiis*, *De clementia*, and the *Epistles*, served varied purposes. Some seem designed for personal meditation or for education.[13] The *florilegium Gallicum* is apparently a source book of philosophical material, whereas the *florilegium Angelicum* supplied preachers with snappy aphorisms.[14] This filleting of Seneca's moral works removed their particular

[4] Reynolds (1983, 364), Brugnoli (2000, 240); for *De clementia*, Braund (2009, 77).
[5] Reynolds (1983, 366–8).
[6] Brugnoli (2000, 230–1).
[7] But see Colish (1976).
[8] Reynolds (1983, 361–2).
[9] Tarrant (1983, 378–81).
[10] Müller (1887, VII, n. 1), Friedländer (1921–3, II: 205 = Eng. trans., London 1913, III: 16 with examples in the appendix in IV: 297–8).
[11] Blüher (1969, 98–102).
[12] Munk Olsen (2000,164–5).
[13] Meditation: Delhaye (1964), Munk Olsen (2000, 163, and cf. Sen. *Ep.* 84); education: Ross (1974, 137).
[14] Nothdurft (1963, 156–60), Lapidge (1988, 94–5).

philosophical color. Even the newly recovered works were epitomized, thus further diluting the Stoic message. The assembly of his works into *corpora*, on the other hand, did serve to focus attention more on Seneca as an individual and as something of a systematic thinker, with a definite doctrine to impart.

We need also to reckon with what are called paratexts. Mediaeval readers were not content with a bare text. Manuscripts did not remain plain for long but tended to be equipped with comments, either for private study or with a view to wider dissemination, perhaps as aids to the university *lectura* on Seneca. In the tradition of the *accessus*, the writer's life preceded his text,[15] and for Seneca this was provided by the exiguous reference in Jerome's *De viris illustribus* 12 to his correspondence with the apostle Paul and to his death, ordered by Nero.[16] Walter of Burley (1274/4 – ca. 1344), if he is the author of the encyclopaedic *De vita et moribus philosophorum*, was the first to exploit Suetonius' biographies of the emperors and he drew up a list of Seneca's works (ch. 117).[17]

For the mediaeval reader, Seneca was essentially a moral authority,[18] his role validated by Jerome, among others. Whilst many of his maxims could have been ascribed to anyone, Seneca's name guaranteed their probity. An attractive feature of his moralizing was his engagement with particular situations, as described above all in the *Epistles*. What mattered at this time was the message, less the messenger: the historical Seneca had largely "disappeared behind his morality."[19] Some scholars, however, argue for rather more in the way of an interest in ancient Stoicism,[20] but the available Senecan texts will not have been as useful as Cicero's philosophical treatises, in which interlocutors were charged with comprehensive expositions of the tenets of the different schools. To some extent, this deficiency is the fault of transmission, since the works of Seneca's that reached the Middle Ages were never designed to provide a thorough account of Stoic doctrine on any particular topic. The *Epistles* and *Dialogues* offered instead "Stoicism lite" and so provided rather less to those, if any,[21] who sought an understanding of Stoic ethics. During this period, Aristotle reigned supreme, and the philosopher Seneca had little to contribute to scholasticism; it would be some time before his Stoicism would become fashionable.[22]

[15] Fohlen (2002), Albanese (2004).
[16] Ker (2009a, 187–97).
[17] Fohlen (2002, 3).
[18] Spanneut (1990, 587–91).
[19] So Reynolds (1965, 115). On this topic, see also Torre in this volume.
[20] Verbeke (1983), Smiraglia (2000).
[21] Ross (1984).
[22] Ross (1974, 139–40).

The morally acceptable doctrines of Stoicism had anyway long before been appropriated by the early Fathers of the Church, so that by the Middle Ages, it was hard to disentangle them from Christian orthodoxy.[23] What chiefly attracted in Senecan morality was his emphasis on *virtus* and a simple life lived in accordance with nature. What exactly a Stoic meant by *virtus* and *natura* will not have been known to most of Seneca's mediaeval readers. No matter; the *Epistles* offered William of Saint-Thierry a platform for an ascetical exhortation to the monks of Citeaux, and the encouragement of simplicity appealed strongly to Cistercians.[24] In the secular world, the developing genre of the "mirror of princes" owed a good deal to Seneca, especially William of Conches' *Moralium dogma philosophorum*, dedicated to Henry II of England.[25] Some aspects of Stoic teaching, however, were anathema, for instance, the justification of suicide, and Seneca's own suicide raised some hackles.[26] The *Natural Questions* offered a new facet of his learning with its information on cosmology and the physical environment. This work fed a growing appetite for scientific research and speculation in the twelfth century.[27] But in this department of knowledge, too, Aristotle was the ancient authority whose work was sought out, translated, and interpreted.[28]

Pre-Humanism and Renaissance

One sphere of Seneca's literary activity has so far not been brought into the reckoning: the dramas. His plays had become available during the late Middle Ages, but their diffusion and use were pretty restricted.[29] In turning to them, we effectively move into the age of the so-called pre-humanists, which glides into the Renaissance of letters.[30] The textual tradition of the tragedies long produced confusion thanks to misattribution: the manuscripts provided up to three first names (Marcus, Lucius, and even Publius), and so occasionally in the early Renaissance the corpus was dismembered like Hippolytus and parcelled out among them. An additional difficulty was the inclusion in the genuine corpus of two plays, *Octavia* and *Hercules Oetaeus*, the first of which cannot be Senecan, whereas the second may be, at least in part. The genuine corpus was only identified in 1592 by the Jesuit editor

[23] Nothdurft (1963), Lapidge (1988, 84 and 89), Smiraglia (2000) and Berno's chapter in this volume.
[24] Lapidge (1988, 96–7).
[25] Lapidge (1988, 95–6).
[26] Lapidge (1988, 95), Ross (1974, 138–9).
[27] Lapidge (1988, 102–3).
[28] Stok (2000, 363).
[29] Trillitzsch (1978).
[30] Spanneut (1990, 591–4), Monti (2008, 113–32).

Martin Delrius (1561–1608).[31] The influence of the tragedies did not, however, depend upon their attribution. Their enduring service was in providing a model of the formal tragic drama of antiquity for imitation, and this marks a change of direction in the use to which Seneca was now being put.

It was in the late thirteenth century with the discovery of the Codex Etruscus by Lovato dei Lovati (1241–1309) that the text of the tragedies began to be copied in real earnest; some 400 manuscripts were produced through to the end of the fifteenth century.[32] The plays presented their first modern readers with hurdles to be surmounted, and so to facilitate comprehension, the English Dominican monk Nicholas Trevet (1258–1328) was commissioned at Avignon to compose commentaries on them, a work completed around 1315.[33] The fourteenth century saw a marked development of interest in the plays in Padua and Avignon. The Paduan Albertino Mussato (1261–1329) equipped the plays with a biography of the writer (about which more will be said in what follows), arguments, and a sketchy commentary.[34] Further inspired by their recovery, Mussato speculated on the nature of tragedy.[35] But his chief claim to fame was the composition of the first modern tragedy in Latin along Senecan lines, the *Ecerinis*, in 1314–15. *Ecerinis*, a historical drama based on *Thyestes* and *Octavia*, relates the expulsion of a Paduan tyrant. Recited (not performed) annually at Christmas, it secured its author considerable renown[36] and set something of a fashion in Italy for Latin tragedies on historical themes. The tragedies provided a model not only for new works in Latin, especially plays performed in colleges and universities,[37] but they were also influential in shaping drama in the emerging vernaculars of Europe.[38]

Imitation, however, was not the sole fruit of the enthusiasm for Senecan drama; it also generated a desire to perform the plays on a stage. Seneca's *Phaedra* was the first ancient tragedy to be performed in modern times in about 1486;[39] its success in Rome inspired other performances across Europe. Since music was composed for the choral passages, this revival must be seen as paving the way to opera. The performance of an ancient tragedy in a palace courtyard seemed inadequate, and so construction of a

---

[31] Mayer (1994), Caviglia (2001), Machielsen (2014).
[32] Grund (2011, xiv–xx).
[33] Caviglia (2001), Clark (2004), Grund (2011, xv–xviii).
[34] Megas (1969).
[35] Grund (2011, xxiii).
[36] Grund (2011, xx–xxiv).
[37] Binns (1974), Questa (1999).
[38] For Spain, see Blüher (1969, 244–52); for Shakespeare, Braden (1985), Paratore (2011), and Citti's chapter in this volume.
[39] Mayer (2002, 99–101).

dedicated theatre building on Roman lines was at least considered. It was only to be realized a century later by Andrea Palladio's Teatro Olimpico in Vicenza.

Engagement with the tragedies sparked a wider interest in Seneca as a man of flesh and blood. The old-fashioned *accessus* was undernourished, and anyway, by now ever more ancient evidence about Seneca and his times was becoming available. Mussato composed a fuller life as preface to his own text of the tragedies.[40] The discovery of Tacitus' *Annales* in 1374 and the wider circulation in Italy of Suetonius' *Lives* added fresh details about Seneca's life and brought it into sharper focus. But that sharper focus also raised issues about the probity of Seneca's character and behavior, issues his apologists would have to face. The burgeoning biographical tradition also perpetrated an unfortunate (but not universally held) belief among the pre-humanists that at the end of his life, Seneca was a crypto-Christian. Why had Jerome included Seneca "in the catalogue of the saints"? It was not because he regarded Seneca as a Christian (he is silent on that point) but because he recognized the widespread popularity of the (bogus) correspondence between Seneca and Paul. Jerome was apparently never misunderstood in the Middle Ages, but wishful thinking by some later biographers ranked Seneca among the redeemed.[41] This blunder caused an unexpected difficulty for some readers of the *Epistles*, as we will see. Another, but amusing, error was generated by the long-standing amalgamation of the elder and the younger Seneca: the combined product must have lived about one hundred and fifteen years! Many biographies accepted this marvelous longevity as fact.

We may now return to the engagement with Seneca's prose writing and the pivotal figure of Petrarch (1304–74).[42] Petrarch was as devoted to Seneca as he was to Cicero. He seems to have been the first to bother to sift the genuine out of the baggy inheritance of "Senecan" texts, and so he repudiated *De quattuor virtutibus* and *De moribus* whilst accepting the correspondence with Paul. He still ascribed to him his father's rhetorical works, and more tellingly, he used the spurious *De remediis* as a springboard for his own *De remediis utriusque fortunae*. This points to a still weak appreciation of Seneca's urbane rhetoric and literary prose style. Petrarch shared the contemporary biographical interest in Seneca, which took the (for him) characteristic form of a personal letter to the ancient Roman. For Petrarch, Seneca is a living figure who in his time as a courtier did not always set an

[40] Panizza (1984), Fohlen (2002, 4).
[41] Panizza (1987, 323), Fohlen (2002, 5–6).
[42] De Nolhac (1907/1965, II 115–26), Bobbio (1941), Billanovich (1947/1995, 109–16).

impeccable moral example; in particular, his huge wealth was something of a stumbling block.[43]

At this point the diffusion of Seneca's works should again be noted.[44] Manuscripts continue to be written, and from about 1474, printed editions appear.[45] Translations into the vernaculars become commoner, especially and not unexpectedly into Hispanic languages.[46] Lectures or professorships in Seneca continue in the universities. To assist professors and students, commentaries are composed,[47] most notably by the Dominican friar Domenico da Peccioli (1320–1408), who wrote the first complete commentary on the *Epistles* as well as a new biography of Seneca.[48]

Since considerable attention has recently been paid to these works, a particular word may be said about the widely circulated commentary of Gasparino Barzizza (ca. 1360–1431). Barzizza was at heart a "Ciceronian," but like many Ciceronians, he was rather dazzled by Seneca's panache. He composed commentaries on his works to serve as the basis for a series of university lectures in Milan in the early fifteenth century.[49] Barzizza is seen to be often at sea when explaining Seneca's philosophical "doctrine." One source of difficulty has been mentioned already, the belief that he was a Christian. This prompted an entirely futile search in his *Epistles* for hints of his conversion and its effect upon his thought. But there were other hazards. The urbane, informal epistolary mode was not what readers brought up on scholastic philosophy expected. Seneca was not systematic but discursive, hortatory, persuasive. It was hard to extract a coherent doctrine from what remained of his writings, so some pretty un-Senecan constructs were produced on the basis of the *Epistles*. Finally, and somewhat surprisingly, many had trouble with Seneca's Latinity; for instance, some commentators could not really understand the idiomatic expression *aliud agere* in the first letter.[50] Their misunderstanding produced some far-fetched efforts at interpretation, later ridiculed by Erasmus, who of course knew that the expression meant "to be careless/heedless."[51]

The early Renaissance registered something of a decline in Seneca's popularity, chiefly because the star of Cicero was in the ascendant as a prose

---

[43] De Nolhac (1907/1965, II 122–4).

[44] De Robertis and Resta (2004) remains an indispensable guide.

[45] Reynolds (1983, 360, n.14).

[46] Bolgar (1954, 534–7), Blüher (1969, 94–117), Fothergill-Payne (1988, 7–13).

[47] Fohlen (2002, 22–4).

[48] Marcucci in De Robertis and Resta (2004, 227–9).

[49] Panizza (1977), Fohlen (2002, 46–50), Albanese (2004) in De Robertis and Resta (2004, 239–41 and 242–3), and Stacey's chapter in this volume.

[50] Panizza (1983, 54–9).

[51] Panizza (1987, 326–7).

model. Seneca's style was known to have been severely criticized in antiquity, and so it was generally felt that however valuable his moral doctrine, his style could not serve as a model. That the dip in popularity was only slight, however, is shown by the number of incunable (i.e., pre-1500) editions issuing from the busy presses of Europe and especially of Spain.[52] A good deal of effort during this period was expended on sorting out what was genuine and what not and which ancient works belonged to which Seneca. Seneca's role as moral guide remained as unchallenged as before, and even his style was beginning to attract attention and apology, most significantly from Desiderius Erasmus (1466/9–1536).[53]

The Seneca of Erasmus is decidedly not the Seneca of the Middle Ages, thanks to the marginalization in his editions of the spurious works (though the rhetorical works were still ascribed to him) and to greater focus on his prose style.[54] In the preface to his second edition of Seneca's prose works in 1529, Erasmus was not uncritical of Seneca's Latinity, which, in designating it "silver," he felt inferior to Cicero's "gold," perhaps chiefly because its brevity was too often enigmatic.[55] But it was style that now clinched Erasmus' conviction that the correspondence with Saint Paul could not be genuine, since the Senecan letters were so clumsily written; he had printed the correspondence in his edition of 1515, allowing that Jerome knew it to be spurious, but he now repudiated it with reasons given.[56] The capital factor in the difference between the Seneca of the Middle Ages and of Erasmus was the new medium of diffusion, print. Print created the need for critical editions of texts, providing as authentic a version as possible. This Erasmus tried to do on three occasions, in 1515, 1529, and posthumously in 1537. In the preface to his first edition of 1515, he claimed to have removed, sometimes by conjecture, no fewer than four thousand errors.[57] By way of popularization, in 1528, Erasmus produced a *florilegium* of Senecan passages, of course only from the genuine works; a preliminary index handily listed the topics to be found in the selection. Erasmus had no interest in Stoicism, and for him Seneca was still simply a moral guide.[58]

---

[52] Periti in De Robertis and Resta (2004, 166–7, 224–5, and 281–2), Fothergill-Payne (1988, 16–25).
[53] Phillips (1970, 15–17).
[54] Trillitzsch (1965), Carabin (2006, 42–55, esp. 46–52).
[55] Allen (1934, 31–7, no. 2091, 128–33, 259–74).
[56] Allen (1934, 40–1, no. 2092).
[57] Allen (1910, 52, no. 325).
[58] Carabin (2006, 55).

High Renaissance and Baroque

The High Renaissance and Baroque periods (late sixteenth and seventeenth centuries) see the tide turning at last in favor of Seneca's prose style. The forerunner was Marc-Antoine Muret (Muretus, 1526–85), professor of moral philosophy at the University of Rome, La Sapienza, whose partial edition of Seneca was published there in 1585, the year of his death. In 1575, Muretus lectured on the *De providentia* and defended Senecan prose style, especially for its density and brevity.[59] Another paladin was Henri Estienne (Stephanus, 1528/31–98),[60] who in his *Ad Senecae lectionem proodopoeia* (Geneva, 1586) defended Seneca's style from the cavils of antiquity and previous editors. He listed the technical terminology of Stoicism to be found in Seneca's works and went on to analyze the characteristics of his style, such as sentence structure (described as *membratim* and *incisim*), antithesis, parenthesis, imperatives directed to the reader, asyndeton, short, sharp sentences, and the use of imaginary thoughts and objections. He considered too the organization of the thought and argument, noting that printed editions often obscured the correct structure by making faulty divisions. His point was that Seneca constructed a fluid argument, often dispensing with the logical signposts that might otherwise guide a reader along the path. In further sections, he discussed Seneca's vocabulary and use of metaphor. All is designed to illustrate the high merit of Seneca as a writer. Unfortunately this work seems to have been little noticed by contemporaries,[61] but it nonetheless demonstrates both the growing interest in Senecan Stoicism and a more favorable assessment of his prose style.

Seneca's outstanding champion was Justus Lipsius (1547–1606). Two features of his enthusiasm for Seneca need separate discussion, Stoic philosophy on the one hand and Seneca's idiosyncratic style, imitated in Lipsius' own Latin, on the other. Stoicism was difficult to revive in or revise for a Christian society.[62] Nonetheless, Lipsius resorted to Senecan Stoicism as an antidote to the religious strife of the period. His international bestseller *De constantia*,[63] *On steadfastness* (first edition, 1584) was not designed to expound or revive the Stoicism of antiquity but to provide an alternative to contemporary sectarian discord. The work struck a chord and generated a neostoic movement that spread rapidly through Europe,[64] enlisting

[59] Carabin (2006, 70–7), Kraye (2007, 834).
[60] Carabin (2006) and (2007).
[61] Carabin (2007, 7–8).
[62] Ross (1974), Kraye (1988) 361–74, Long (2003), Carabin (2006, 83–96).
[63] Young (2011).
[64] Morford (1991), Moreau (1999), and Citti's chapter in this volume.

even such figures as Peter Paul Rubens, who not only depicted the death of Seneca[65] but a group portrait of Lipsius and his dog with his closest students, including the artist.[66]

As a philologist, Lipsius had edited two of Latin literature's prose masters, Tacitus and Seneca. Both he and his readers knew that in antiquity, Seneca's style had been criticized, so part of his agenda was to rehabilitate it in a brief prefatory essay to his 1605 edition. He there offered a point-by-point refutation of the chief indictments of Seneca's manner. For Lipsius, this was more than an academic exercise, since he had himself abandoned Cicero as a model for Latin prose composition and adopted what came to be known as a "hopping" style, much indebted to the authors he edited.[67] The choice of this style was not fundamentally aesthetic, as if it were no more than a matter of personal taste how one wrote, so long as the Latinity was correct. The Senecan style was chosen for psychological reasons. In the dreadful times of religious strife through which he was living, Lipsius felt that serious writers needed a less balanced manner of writing Latin, a less public voice than Cicero's. He sought an alternative in a new emotional language that would reflect the spontaneity and authenticity of thought as it arises in the individual mind.[68] Seneca's style proved ideal for this impressionistic mode of writing, especially in the epistolary genre, which should not be carefully combed. As Ciceronian style was appropriate to the public oration, Senecan style came to be seen as appropriate to the letter or meditative essay, like Seneca's twelve so-called *Dialogi*. Lipsius' advocacy of this "unbuttoned" prose induced Michel de Montaigne (1533–92) to attempt something similar in vernacular prose.[69]

Montaigne was drawn less to Seneca's Stoicism than to his psychological insight, as a student of the self and how to master and guide it.[70] As a writer, Montaigne owed to Seneca both the essay as the medium of ethical discourse and an informal prose style, developed now for the first time in a modern vernacular. Montaigne compared Seneca and Plutarch, whom he regarded as the more substantial, in Essay II 10 (and cf. III 12), and he defended Seneca the man and the thinker against the charge of hypocrisy in Essay II 32.[71] In Essay II 17, he admits his inclination towards "le parler de Sénèque," which

[65] Ker (2009a, 212–15), and Citti's chapter in this volume.
[66] Papy (1999), Ker (2009a, 301–4).
[67] Williamson (1951), Mouchel (1990, 179–211), Kraye (2007, 834–5).
[68] Mouchel (1990, 181).
[69] Hay (1938), Simone (1968, 246–8).
[70] So Friedrich (1991, 60–6) against the classic work of Villey (1933).
[71] Tarrête (2004, 905–6).

means something like "the spoken style," because Cicero's was too public a voice for moral reflection and analysis.[72] Montaigne was recognized by his contemporaries as a French Seneca, whose expressive spontaneity reproduced something of the Roman's easygoing style. Of course he was capable of seeing the merit of the Senecan manner for himself, but as a correspondent of Lipsius', he was also influenced by the great scholar's rehabilitation of the personal style.[73]

This was the third and last high point of Seneca's reputation and influence as a prose writer. Thanks to Montaigne, the essay as a literary form was taken over by other writers in the European vernaculars, and his novel style, informal and exploratory, offered an appealing alternative to the more heavily rhetoricized models then in fashion.[74]

Conclusion

During the period described in this chapter, Seneca's trajectory from moral *auctor* to champion of Stoicism has been charted. It may be suggested that no classical author underwent as thorough a transformation as Seneca did thanks to the removal of spurious texts and the increased availability of genuine ones. In the Middle Ages, "super-Seneca" provided little more than generalized moral guidance through both authentic works and the penumbra of texts more or less indebted to his genuine writings. The number of authentic works increased in the Middle Ages, and Seneca was even found to provide information on the physical world as well as ethical guidance. *Florilegia* further spread his reputation, and university lecturers expounded his doctrine. Biography was initially hampered by lack of hard evidence. Finally, on the threshold of the Renaissance, the tragedies were added to the corpus of his writings and demonstrated the impressive range of his literary achievement.

Pre-humanist and Renaissance scholars pruned away the pseudepigrapha and tidied up the genuine texts for the age of print. Important for biography was the disentanglement of the two Senecas, father and son, thus assigning the "rhetorical" works and even in due course the tragedies to their true authors. The dramas now fired enthusiasm for imitation and performance. Fuller biographies were being written thanks to the increased range of early

---

[72] Friedrich (1991, 375–6), Tarrête (2004, 906–7), Carabin (2006, 99–101), Kraye (2007, 836).
[73] Magnien (2004). I wish particularly to thank my colleague Emily Butterworth for assistance in dealing with Montaigne.
[74] Summers (1910), Williamson (1951), Carabin (2006, 102).

source material, but the notion that Seneca was a Christian stymied interpretation (as it had not done in the case of the poet Statius). Elaborate
commentaries come to replace the earlier indices of contents and notable
topics.[75] So by the end of our period, we have a rounded human being with
a reliable biography and a corpus of genuine texts.

Thanks to this recovery of the individual Seneca, he became "good to
think with," not just a storehouse of moral wisdom. His role as moral guide
remained firm, but now too his style – a matter of fundamental importance
during the period of the "revival of letters," which had long proved something of a stumbling block – was gradually perceived to offer advantages
the more elaborate prose of a Cicero lacked: flexibility, spontaneity, and
informality. That style used in a compatible format of letter or essay generated what gave an impression of being unfiltered products of the mind. In
the High Renaissance, a concentration on Senecan ethics foregrounded the
Stoic element, and with Lipsius' espousal of Senecan Stoicism, a movement
of considerable importance, neostoicism, was generated and spread across
Europe.

Further Reading

Continental European scholars have engaged much more extensively with
the reception of Senecan writing than their Anglophone colleagues have (and
the library of the Warburg Institute in London is an invaluable storehouse
of that scholarship). The superbly illustrated catalogue of De Robertis and
Resta (2004) is just one example of this. Nonetheless, Ker (2009), by focusing on the theme of death, offers an ambitious and successful account of
the reception of Seneca more generally than his title might suggest. Braden
(1985) and Paratore (2011, a collection of essays mainly from the 1950s
and 1960s) provide useful starting points for the appropriation of Senecan
drama in the early modern period. Morford (1991) charts the genesis of the
neostoic movement. Williamson (1951) remains a fine survey of the influence
of Senecan prose on High Renaissance Latin and the emerging vernaculars.

In the recently published Brill *Companion to Seneca*, M. Laarmann (2014)
surveys the reception of his philosophical writings in the period covered in
this chapter on pp. 55–66, and on pp. 75–82 W. Schubert (2014) tackles
reception of the dramatic works.

---

[75] Fohlen (2002, 30).

22

PETER STACEY

Senecan Political Thought from the Middle Ages to Early Modernity

One reason for the increasing interest among intellectual historians in the part played by Seneca's work in shaping various political ideologies and theories of the postclassical period has been a concern to impart a greater degree of complexity to our understanding of the character and the content of the pervasive debt European political thought owed to distinctively Roman philosophical sources and, in so doing, to reverse some of the effects of its gradual occlusion from the historiography of European political thought since the Enlightenment. Diderot was perhaps the last European thinker to take Seneca seriously as a political philosopher of public importance – and even he seems to have been out on a limb among his contemporaries.[1] With the increasing preeminence enjoyed by Greek philosophy in nineteenth-century political thought and the corresponding denigration of Roman intellectual culture, only Cicero retained his stature as a Roman political theorist of consequence – and the amalgam of beliefs that underpinned this altered perspective has quietly informed the reconstruction of the Greco-Roman sources of later political theory with remarkably unhelpful resilience until recently.

The tendency to skate over Seneca's contribution to political theory as slight and second-rate may be well founded, but it is nevertheless relatively modern. Seneca was a revered political authority from the medieval to the early modern era, particularly – though certainly not exclusively – among theorists of monarchy. Some indication of his standing is glimpsed in accounts of Machiavelli's famous deathbed dream – assuredly apocryphal but no less revealing for that – which began to circulate after his death. Horrified by his glimpse of a band of appallingly dressed Christians enjoying the spiritual rewards of heaven, Machiavelli is said to have promptly plumped for the company of the solemn and majestic group of ancients he saw damned to hell – "Plato, Seneca, Plutarch, Tacitus and others" – all discussing "matters

---

[1] For recent discussions, see Andrew (2004); Russo (2009).

of state."[2] Once we recover the basis of this considerably loftier vision of Seneca's place in the political firmament, we can also begin to identify some of the ideological and intellectual elements of the explanation for the historical slippage in his status within the canon.

Although only a partial picture of the pattern of Senecan debts in later political thought has so far emerged, several of its features are worth underlining because they illustrate some of the complexities in determining which parts of the corpus – and which combinations of texts – to track. Every work was scoured by his readers for authoritative classical opinions with which to construct or sustain their politics. Humanist writers educated in the *ars rhetorica* were especially adept at excerpting Senecan material and transplanting it to amplify their political discussions. That practice extended to numerous pseudo-Senecan texts; of this body of *spuria*, the most consequential for the history of political thought were *De quattuor virtutibus cardinalibus* (also called the *Formula vitae honestae*) and *De remediis fortuitorum*. The former – a sixth-century tract shot through with Senecan content – became popular in the literature on city government and the duties of magistrates in the Italian communes.[3] Giovanni da Viterbo's *Liber de regimine civitatum* (1250s) and the *Li Livres dou trésor* (1266) of Dante's mentor, Brunetto Latini, cite its analysis of the virtues verbatim.[4] *De remediis fortuitorum*, a dialogue in which Reason personified responds to a series of impassioned laments about the effects of chance occurrences, was valued by Dante himself.[5] Its structure was adopted and refined by Petrarch in his *De remediis utriusque fortunae* (1366), an immensely influential guide to the psychotherapeutic benefits of self-mastery in the face of fluctuating luck.[6]

But extensive political arguments about the character of good government – and the importance of good self-government in its provision – were derived from two Senecan texts especially: *De clementia* and, to a lesser extent, *De ira*. Since they left the deepest mark upon concerted thinking about the conduct of public affairs, I shall concentrate on an exploration of that fact here. The following discussion is broadly organized into medieval, Renaissance, and early modern sections. The last is briefer, partly because the Senecan commitments of the early modern period are well observed already, but also because my underlying aim is to provide some material with which to construct a deeper historical explanation of those commitments than is currently available.

---

[2] Villari (1895–97) 3.370, n.1.
[3] See Berno's chapter in this volume.
[4] For detailed discussions, see Skinner (2002, 17–30, 41–92); Stacey (2007, 95–110).
[5] Mezzadroli (1990, 79–82).
[6] See Panizza (1991).

It is certainly true that the political dimensions of Seneca's social philosophy in *De beneficiis* also attracted considerable attention among political thinkers with differing theoretical interests in this period. In the thirteenth century, the jurist Albertano da Brescia begins to cite it regularly in his work.[7] Latini's reliance upon its authority is especially evident in Book 2 of *Li Livres dou trésor*. It looms large in Italian Renaissance discussions of the need for liberality in civic life, particularly in princely regimes, a point helpfully underlined by Benedetto Varchi for his patron Eleonora of Toledo, the wife of Duke Cosimo I de' Medici, in the dedication of his 1546 translation of the work into the Tuscan *volgare*.[8] And its contentions were also expounded elsewhere – by Christine de Pizan, for instance, in her description of princely virtue in *Le Livre du Corps de Policie* (1406).[9]

De beneficiis was well known in the scholastic tradition, too. In his discussion of the limits of political obligation in the *Secunda Secundae* of his *Summa*,[10] Aquinas singled out a passage, destined to become heavily annotated, in which Seneca had claimed that "it is a mistake to think that slavery penetrates the entire man" since "the better part of him is exempt ... bodies can be assigned to masters ... but the mind ... is its own master (*sui iuris*) ... that inner part can never come into anyone's possession."[11] Seneca's account of human liberty is inflected by its local context. It is framed in terms of the Roman civil definition of a free person as *sui iuris* rather than *in aliena potestate*, subject to the jurisdictional power of another. But Seneca substitutes a civil conception of *ius* for a metaphysical one, thereby conveying the Stoic view that freedom consists in adherence to reason and therefore natural rather than positive law. His Stoic ontology notwithstanding, Seneca's formulation appears markedly dualist, a tendency that surfaces elsewhere in his work, making it more easily assimilated to Christian and Platonic positions.

The subsequent use to which this doctrine was put in different discursive domains illustrates an important aspect of the history of Seneca's philosophy. On the one hand, his descriptions of *homo liber* facilitated the "remarkable intrusion of the language of Roman law into the domain of moral psychology" recently observed in the work of Justus Lipsius, for whom freedom is similarly defined as "the mind being *sui iuris*."[12] But on

---

[7] For Seneca in Albertano, see Stacey (2007, 100–4).

[8] Seneca (1554: A ii).

[9] Pizan (1994, 27, 1.14).

[10] Aquinas (2002, 69, ST IIaIIae 104, art.5).

[11] Sen., *Ben.* 3.20.1–2.

[12] For this point and the relevant passages (in Lipsius' *Physiologia Stoicorum*), see Sierhuis (2013, 53).

the other hand, the implications of Seneca's treatment of reason as *lex natu-ralis* were pursued by Hugo Grotius in a fully juridical idiom, using elements of Seneca's "wise philosophy" in the construction of a theory of natural right around his own vision of man as "free and *sui iuris*."[13] This approach grounds Grotius' endorsement of Seneca's penology in *De clementia* and *De ira* in his *Commentary on the Law of Prize and Booty* (1603) and allows him to use *De beneficiis* as an important point of departure for his account of human sociability in the "Preliminary Discourse" of *De iure belli ac pacis* (1625).[14] The *fortuna* of *De beneficiis* remains little understood, but the fact that Seneca's thinking hinged upon a conception of reason as a form of natural law enabled it to be pressed into legal as well as moral arguments; and that bifurcation is part of a wider story about the reception of Seneca's philosophy.

The Middle Ages

De clementia reappeared in Europe, together with *De beneficiis*, in the early 800s. It was the only surviving attempt to theorize the Roman monarchy to any significant degree, and the earliest extant classical text to refer to itself as a *speculum principis*, or mirror for the prince. This latter characteristic secured it a seminal role in galvanizing the rhetorical structure of an entire genre of political literature whose origins are still regularly misdescribed as medieval. But it is the former fact about the text that ensured its ideological utility to European monarchical governments. Its imperious opening state-ment of princely power was accompanied by a robustly absolutist theory of monarchy designed to legitimate the new sovereign order under the Roman Principate.

During the surge in Seneca's popularity in the twelfth century, *De cle-mentia* was read as a document about royal power. In *The Topography of Ireland* (1188), Gerald of Wales praised the English king Henry II for arm-ing himself with Senecan remedies in his handling of the recent rebellion against him: "you had also frequently in your hands the book which Seneca addressed to Nero 'On Mercy', nor were you mindless of the counsel he so worthily gave to the emperor. 'Follow,' he said, 'the practice of physi-cians.'"[15] Gerald's association of royal behavior with a Senecan ideology of clemency was traceable to the terms of the text itself. Seneca repeatedly

---

[13] Grotius (2006, 24, 28).
[14] E.g., Grotius (2006, 25, 28, 46, 1.2, 1.3); Grotius (2005, 145 n.2, "Preliminary Discourse," 8), citing Sen., *Ben*. 4.18.1–4.
[15] Gerald of Wales (2000, 87).

equates *princeps* with *rex* (and *civitas* with *regnum*), on the grounds that constitutional definitions and nomenclature are irrelevant in the assessment of good and bad government. For "what distinguishes a tyrant from a king are his actions, not the name"; and "no one could conceive of anything more becoming to a ruler than mercy, whatever the manner of his accession to power and whatever its legal basis."[16] The regal terminology used throughout *De clementia* guaranteed its utility to royal regimes for centuries to come.

Seneca's medieval readers correctly identified these assertions as the core of his theory, in which the permanent attribution of *imperium* to a ruler is held to be a good and just organization of political power only if that individual embodies a specific moral *persona*. Conscientiously committed to the cultivation of reason, the Senecan prince was equipped with a specific set of virtues. Clemency is the preeminent characteristic of a monarch, a supralegal and divine quality exercised in accordance with the one law that matters in the Stoic moral universe: the *lex naturalis*, as Seneca calls it.[17] But magnanimity, moderation, and humaneness are also said to be particularly fitting in view of the monarch's providentially determined role as the sole bearer of *imperium*.

Seneca's theory had already been introduced into the political thought of the English realm by John of Salisbury, another student of Seneca, in his *Policraticus* (1159). John's debts to *De clementia* have barely been acknowledged, but they are profound. The most obvious of these lies in his use of the metaphor of the body politic. Since John cites a fictitious work of Plutarch, the *Institutio Traiani*, as his principal classical source for the idea in Book VI, it is often supposed that John himself created the imagery of his monarchical theory.[18] But his description of the polity, from its head to its feet, is clearly parasitic upon *De clementia*, in which Seneca elaborately reconfigures the picture of the *corpus reipublicae* inherited from Cicero and Livy, telling his prince that "your *res publica* is your body and you are its mind" and informing him that "the gentleness of your mind will be transmitted to others ... diffused over the whole body ... All will be formed in your likeness. Health springs from the head."[19] Seneca further explains that, just as "the body is entirely at the service of the mind ... hands, feet and eyes do its business, the skin that we see protects it," so "in the same way this vast multitude of men surrounds one man as though he were its mind, ruled by his spirit, guided by his reason; it would crush and shatter itself by its own strength without the

[16] Sen., *Clem.* 1.12.1; 1.19.1.
[17] Sen., *Clem.*1.19.1.
[18] John of Salisbury (1990, 103, 6. *Prologue*).
[19] Sen., *Clem.* 1.5.1; 2.2.1.

support of his discernment."[20] The relationship of dependency is emphatically underlined: the prince is the "bond which holds the *res publica* together, the breath of life ... the mind of the empire."[21] This part of Seneca's theory runs like a rich seam through centuries of European monarchical thought. John's distinction lies in being one of the first thinkers to rework it.

The metaphor reemerges in Gerald's endorsement of the medical analogy in Seneca's argument. For Seneca, clemency is a "gentle medicine," applied to the body politic by a princely doctor who "reveals his reluctance to apply harsh remedies" by hesitating to apply the knife and resorting to punishment only when "he has run out of remedies."[22] This is the "practice of physicians" to which Gerald is referring. In so behaving, Seneca had added, the prince acts like any good father, who "would be slow to sever one of his limbs ... while doing so, he would groan and hesitate long and often."[23] But again, John's *Policraticus* had led the way in rearticulating these thoughts. In Book IV, John agrees that the prince must correct his subjects' errors "in medical fashion." No monarch should be so "strong as to amputate a part of his body without pain ... he grieves, therefore, when he is asked for the required punishment of the guilty, yet he executes it with a reluctant right hand ... in tormenting parts of the body of which he is the head, he serves the law mournfully and with groans."[24]

A spectacularly public use of Seneca's *De clementia* is visible in the *Constitutions of Melfi*, three books of legal codes issued for the Sicilian kingdom by Frederick II in 1231, which remained in force until the Napoleonic era. The prologue of the *Constitutions* places the words of Seneca's prince in the mouth of his medieval descendant:

> Princes of nations were created ... as arbiters of life and death for mankind to decide, as executors in some way of Divine Providence, how each man should have fortune, estate and status. The king of kings and prince of princes demands above all from their hands that they have the strength to render account perfectly of the stewardship committed to them ...[25]

As its earliest commentator, Marino da Caramanico, declared in his gloss, "these are the words of Seneca in the first book of *De clementia* to Nero, where he says: 'Have I, of all mortals found favour and been chosen to act on earth in place of the gods? I am the arbiter of life and death over

---

[20] Sen., *Clem.* 1.3.5.
[21] Sen., *Clem.* 2.4.1.
[22] Sen., *Clem.* 1.17.1; 1.13.4; 1.14.1.
[23] Sen., *Clem.* 1.14.3.
[24] John of Salisbury (1990, 50, 4.8).
[25] *Constitutionum Regni Siciliarum* (1999, 4). For discussion of the document in context, see Stacey (2007, 75–81, 90–5).

peoples ...'"[26] The Sicilian king's incorporation of the Senecan *persona* was a response to the recent invasion of his realm by papal forces under the banner of a crusade aiming at Frederick's removal. Seneca's account of the unmediated character of secular authority allowed the Sicilian monarch to claim that, as vicegerent of God, he held the kingdom in the form of a trust and that he owed an account of its administration to God alone as his representative.

This particular passage in the prologue of Seneca's theory that relayed the idea of the *res publica* as a divine trust also had an illustrious future in absolutist thought. Bodin would cite it in Book 2 of *Six Livres de la République* (1576), observing that its account of "soveraigne authoritie" is articulated by "Seneca speaking in the person of Nero his scholler."[27] Seneca's *princeps* bore the crucial "marks" of sovereignty, and Bodin draws upon *De clementia* throughout his text.[28] From the thirteenth century onwards, *De clementia* was a rich source of doctrine for civilian lawyers. Since Seneca's sovereign *persona* was the embodiment of Stoic *ratio*, *De clementia* could contribute to discussions of the princely powers conducted in terms of his adherence to the *lex naturalis*. For "Seneca," explained Andrea da Isernia, a fourteenth-century Neapolitan lawyer, "was the finest jurist, as is patently clear to anyone who reads him."[29]

The Renaissance

Humanists from Petrarch onwards developed Seneca's arguments in a moral language. Seneca offered them a theory and a genre with which to instruct princes on their duties. But he was also thought to possess an unrivalled capacity to stimulate change in moral behavior. Seneca's reflections on the role of rhetoric in moral exhortation were duly noted; and his style of preceptive reasoning – characteristically reliant upon exemplification and figurative language – praised and emulated. The leading Senecan scholar of the early Italian Renaissance, Gasparino Barzizza (ca. 1360–1431), regarded Seneca as an unparalleled source of wisdom – "the *princeps* of all the Greeks and Latins" – because his writings about the welfare of the soul demonstrated a commitment to rendering philosophy practical.[30] Seneca

---

[26] *Constitutionum Regni Siciliarum* (1999) 4, n.(h).

[27] Bodin (1962, 221, 2.5).

[28] Bodin (1962, 20, 1.4), (Sen., *Clem.* 1.16.2); 22 (1.4) (*Clem.* 1.14.3); 24 (1.4) (*Clem.* 1.23.1 and 1.15.2–7; 32 (1.V) (*Clem.* 1.14.2); 36 (1.5) (*Ira* 3.40.2, but c.f. *Clem.* 1.18.2); 221 (2.5) (*Clem* 1.1.2); 426 (4.1) (*Clem.* 1.24.1); 512 (4.6) (*Clem.* 1.19.2–3).

[29] Cited from Kantorowicz (1957, 473 n.56).

[30] Barzizza (1977a, 349). On Barzizza, see Mayer's chapter in this volume.

was a Latin Socrates, an identification subsequently strengthened by the Plutarchan pairing of their lives in Giannozzo Manetti's *Vitae Socratis et Senecae* (c.1456). In Barzizza's view, Seneca "is quite rightly called the greatest teacher of life by everyone in our time."[31] That judgement was held to be particularly applicable to political life. Having insisted upon the primacy of Scripture in the syllabus outlined in his *Education of the Christian Prince* (1516), Erasmus declared that Plutarch should top the list of the classical authorities his prince (the future Charles V) should read; but he "easily assigns the next place to Seneca," whose "writings admirably excite and inspire the study of what is honourable, and carry the soul of the reader away from sordid cares to a sublime height, especially in their repeated denunciation of tyranny."[32]

The humanists also explored the conceptual connections between *De ira* and *De clementia. De ira* had returned into circulation in the eleventh century. In its new Christian context, Seneca's lessons about self-rule became a guide to self-subjection, applied to a soul now partitioned and vitiated, and with no hope of eradicating the emotions but nevertheless intent upon restraining them. Seneca's account of anger's lethal effects upon political society thrived. Pre-humanist writers cite it at length, cross-fertilizing its precepts with those of *De clementia* in their advice to their elected magistrates.[33] They are exercised by the level of civic discord in their communes, exacerbated by a form of social violence to which the theory of *De ira* was well attuned: the vendetta. This practice embodied the disposition – the desire for revenge – that Seneca's text aimed to expunge, and the political literature accordingly rehearses its argument attentively. Although many communes collapsed amid spiraling disorder and submitted to monarchical rule, *De ira* remained crucial to the emerging princely ideology, which revived Seneca's narrative of the restoration of the *res publica* and its *libertas* under the Principate. *De clementia* had envisioned a *res publica* formerly torn apart by civil war but now unified and restored to "supreme liberty" under the government of a perfectly rational princely *mens*. The rearticulation of that ideological assertion went hand in hand with *De ira*'s argument.

From Petrarch onwards, both texts were mined to produce an increasingly introspective monarch. *De clementia*'s opening depiction of the prince examining his conscience demonstrated the political importance of internalising the lessons of *De ira*, which described the practice as a matter of

---

[31] Barzizza (1977b, 352).

[32] Erasmus (1997, 62, 2.15).

[33] For further discussion of *De ira* in this literature and its context, see Stacey (2007, 100–10).

"daily pleading my case at my own court" by placing oneself before the "judge" of "reason."[34] The formation of a Christian conscience from Origen onwards was indebted to this imaginative conceptualisation, which now emerged among humanists.[35] Petrarch read Seneca on a daily basis, and although he wrote to him to criticize his association with Nero, he reiterated Senecan political doctrine in a succession of texts.[36] His letter of 1373 to Francesco da Carrara, the ruler of Padua, offered "to show what the ruler of a country should be, so that, by looking at this as though looking at yourself in the mirror ... you may experience joy."[37] The Senecan conceit gives Petrarch room to construct the *persona* of the prince while simultaneously praising his audience for already embodying it. Francesco is naturally prone to clemency and utterly averse to cruelty; in the case of the latter, Petrarch observes that "for no one is it harder to struggle against his nature than it is for you to think, let alone do, anything cruel ... a vice alien to the nature of man and especially of a prince."[38] He exercises the power of life and death over his subjects, as Seneca counsels, in benevolent fashion, as a Roman father and true *Pater Patriae*.[39] The Senecan image of the body politic is then invoked: "you must love your citizens as though they were limbs of your body, or parts of your soul: for the republic is one body and you are its head."[40] Given that the *res publica* has been "committed" to the prince as its administrator and not its owner, Petrarch stresses that Francesco "will be giving an account" of his conduct "to God, if not to men," and concludes his strikingly absolutist picture on a Senecan point: "what does it matter that someone is not held accountable to another person? For the soul is beholden to itself and its conscience."[41]

Petrarch's *De remediis utriusque fortunae* offered an equally Senecan account of the wise man's war with *Fortuna*. Dedicating his work to Azzo da Correggio, the *signore* of Parma, Petrarch recurs to the familiar conceit, inviting the ruler to "behold the profile of your mind as in a looking-glass."[42] His text aims to arm Azzo with "short and precise statements, as if with a handy coat of mail ... protecting you against all assaults and sudden attacks ... for we fight a twofold duel with *Fortuna*."[43] Petrarch agrees with

---

[34] Sen., *Ira* 3.36.1–38.2; 128–9; *Clem.* 1.1.1–4.
[35] For further discussion, see Stacey (2011a, 23–6).
[36] Petrarca, *Fam.* 24.5.
[37] Petrarca (1978, 770).
[38] Petrarca (1978, 802).
[39] Petrarca (1978, 776, cf. Sen., *Clem.* 1.14.1–3).
[40] Petrarca (1978, 778).
[41] Petrarca (1978, 794–6).
[42] Petrarca (1975, 68).
[43] Petrarca (1975, 56).

Seneca's providentialist point that "death, imprisonment, burning, and all the other missiles of *Fortuna* ... are not evils, but only seem to be."[44] But he warns that Fortune's smile is equally treacherous. All the Senecan resources at his disposal are mobilised to depict the battle for a rational perspective in a world whose moral contours become blurred by passional responses.

The imagery of *Fortuna* in Seneca had been political as well as martial. His *Fortuna* governs slaves in the cruellest of kingdoms, whose jurisdiction the wise man despises.[45] She is "a mistress that is changeable and passionate and neglectful ... capricious in both her rewards and her punishments."[46] The Florentine chancellor, Poggio Bracciolini, adopts this perspective in his *De miseria humanae conditionis*, dedicated to Sigismondo Malatesta, the ruler of Rimini (1455). Another assiduous reader of Seneca, Poggio denounces "that truly vain passion for *Fortuna*'s gifts, which are so injurious to mankind."[47] Even "the highest positions – principalities, kingdoms and empires – are nothing more than the blandishments of *Fortuna*."[48] Her capricious command can make "a king of a slave and a slave of a king."[49]

In his correspondence of 1506, Machiavelli similarly recalls the fickleness of Fortune's rule over men.[50] In his poetry, the Florentine develops the conventional imagery to "sing of the kingdom of *Fortuna* and of her chances favourable and adverse."[51] We enter a realm ruled by a "shifting creature" and "a cruel goddess" who "sits on high above all," enthroned in a palace from which she commands.[52] But in *Il Principe* (1513), Machiavelli's assault on the metaphysics underpinning the traditional account of princely government consists in radically reworking this imagery. For Machiavelli, the idea that *Fortuna* can be overcome by mental exertion is dangerously delusional. The conventional lessons about self-conquest only make sense in a providentialist world emptied of the contingencies that, as Machiavelli sees it, must be countered by a truly *virtuoso* prince. In chapter XXV, Machiavelli rejects the Stoic and Christian belief that God and *Fortuna* can somehow be aligned. Evacuating God from the picture, he ventures that "*Fortuna* is the arbiter of half our actions, but that even she leaves the government of half of

[44] Sen. *Ep.* 85.26.
[45] For the *regnum* of Fortuna in Seneca, see *Brev. Vit.* 10.4; *Vit. Beat.* 25.5. For *Fortuna*'s jurisdiction, see *Brev. Vit.* 10.2; *Ep.* 36.6.
[46] Sen., *Cons. Marc.* 10.6.
[47] Bracciolini (1997, 18
[48] Bracciolini (1997, 19).
[49] Bracciolini (1997, 21).
[50] Machiavelli (1971, 1083).
[51] Machiavelli (1971, 976).
[52] Machiavelli (1971, 976–9).

them – or thereabouts – to us."[53] Only upon grasping this fact and grappling with the very real forces *Fortuna* represents will we recuperate our ability to govern states successfully.

Getting to grips with *Fortuna* meant dramatically reconceptualizing *virtù*. Since "Fortuna is a woman," if "you want to control her it is necessary to treat her roughly ... she is more inclined to men who are impetuous ... she is always well disposed towards young men ... they are less cautious and more aggressive, and treat her more boldly."[54] For Machiavelli, dispassionate Stoic constancy is a desperately imprudent form of rigidity, rendering a prince impotent when confronted with sudden changes in *variazioni* of time and circumstance. The moral absolutism that had grounded the unswerving commitment to clemency and humaneness vanishes. Scandalous considerations of the virtues of cruelty emerge in a systematic reversal of Senecan doctrine.[55] The benefits of "gentle medicine" are substituted for calculations about the viability of "strong medicine."[56] The princely medic's reluctance to draw blood is now condemned as frequently fatal for the body politic: "if the first signs of trouble are perceived, it is easy to find a solution; but if one lets troubles develop, the medicine will be too late, because the malady will have become incurable."[57] Seneca's recommendation that a captured ruler survives "to the glory of his saviour" had been embraced by Renaissance moralists, who agreed with Seneca that "to owe one's life is to have lost it" already. Given their indebtedness, such captives should be spared rather than "snatched from sight."[58] But as Machiavelli observes, the problem with placing princes in your debt is that they may well have some credit left with their former subjects. So one must learn how to "extinguish the family of the ruler" who had previously governed in states you conquer.[59] With them "extinguished, no one else remains to be feared, since the others do not have any credit with the people."[60] Machiavelli's talk of extinguishing enemies replaces the metaphor of enlightened monarchy in *De clementia*. But it is also the language of debt cancellation.

---

[53] Machiavelli (1988, 85 [amended], Ch. 25).
[54] Machiavelli (1988, 87, Ch. 25).
[55] For a detailed treatment, see Stacey (2007, 267–93).
[56] Machiavelli (1988, 7, Ch. 3).
[57] Machiavelli (1988, 11, Ch. 3).
[58] See Sen., *Clem.* I.21.2.
[59] Machiavelli (1971, 259, Ch. 3). "*E chi le acquista, volendole tenere, debbe avere dua respetti: l'uno, che il sangue del loro principe antiquo si spenga....*"
[60] Machiavelli (1971, 263, Ch. 4): "*il quale spento, non resta alcuno di chi si abbia a temere, non avendo li altri credito con li populi...*"

The Early Modern Period

Almost no subsequent monarchical theorist could contemplate embracing this moral vision, not least because it had eliminated any trace of a princely conscience. In some quarters, it made no obvious impact. A year after publishing his first edition of Seneca's works (1515), Erasmus relayed the duties of a Christian prince as a matter of constant conscientiousness:

> When you visit your cities, do not think to yourself like this: "I am the master of these; they are at my disposal; I can do what I like with them." But if you want to think about it as a good prince should, do so along these lines: "Everything here has been put in my trust, and I must therefore keep a good watch over it so that I may hand it back in better condition than I received it."[61]

The articulation of Senecan precepts had become highly imitative. Seneca's image of the princes as a merciful father figure divinely authorized to rule over errant subjects had migrated easily into Christian political culture; it remained lodged there, attracting the young Calvin, who probably commenced his extensive commentary on *De clementia* during his final year of law at Bourges in 1529.[62] The greatest Senecan scholar of the period, Lipsius, certainly saw the force of Machiavelli's prudential thinking. But he nevertheless remained wedded to Seneca's monarchical theory, describing clemency in the *Politica* (1589) as the Moon of Government, while insisting in the *Monita et exempla politica* (1605) that the "two golden books" of *De clementia* were required princely reading.[63]

Perhaps the most unsettling feature of Machiavelli's work was its demolition of the contention that a prince ruled over a *res publica*. There was no trace of liberty in any of Machiavelli's principalities. They were revealed to be structures of domination governed by princes as their possessions and occupied by quite categorically unfree subjects. That was an abhorrent picture for monarchists. They continued to rely on the Senecan architecture of absolutism to prop up their vision of "free monarchies," as King James I of England called them, presided over by "a loving Father and careful watchman ... countable to that great God, who placed him as his lieutenant over ... them that are committed to his charge."[64] And, as Judith Shklar underlined, Seneca's *De clementia* played a principal role in sustaining "the Augustan charade" of the *ancien regime*, in which Augustus' seventeenth-

[61] Erasmus (1997, 38, 1.79)
[62] For the intellectual background, see the *Introduction* to Calvin (1969, 3–140).
[63] For these points, see Soen (2011, 208).
[64] King James VI and I (1994, 65).

century successors "posed as the saviours of the republic," asserting that the prince "is the republic now."[65]

But with the gradual recession of a humanist culture in which Seneca's reputation had been secured, reservations about Seneca's intellectual rigor and his style were expressed with increasing frequency, chipping away at centuries of accumulated authority. Nevertheless, any explanation of the twists and tergiversations in taste that culminated in Macauley's disdainful aside that reading Seneca's prose was "like dining on nothing but anchovy sauce" must consider the growing ideological aversion to his work. Not only were his writings implicated in royal absolutism; elements of his moral philosophy that advocated the benefits of a philosophically tactical retreat from the turbulence of public life had also been assembled to construct a markedly quietist political subjectivity by early modern neo-Stoic writers from Lipsius onwards. Neither development helped endear Seneca to revolutionaries or reformers.

Besides, the terrifying dependency of subjects in Senecan monarchies was amply evident in early modern theatre. The European political imagination came to be haunted by the depiction of tyranny in Seneca's tragedies. Notwithstanding the fissuring in the Renaissance *fortuna* of Seneca's works caused by the belief that Seneca *moralis* and Seneca *tragicus* were different authors, his portrayal of the carnage wrought by rulers and their relations when gripped by passional states – vengeful rage, especially – captivated generations of admirers and imitators. The Senecan themes of Kyd, Marlowe, Jonson, Webster, Corneille, and numerous other playwrights have been identified; so, too, has the presence of Senecan political ideas in Shakespeare.[66] Richard II, for one, well knew that kings sought the true image of royalty in the mirror, not in the trappings of office. But Senecan monarchs were only guaranteed a glorious reflection if they genuinely embodied the quality of mercy. And if the benefits of a clear conscience were said in *De ira* to guaranteed a restful night's repose, then in the case of kings, as *De clementia* emphasized that meant "never having shed a citizen's blood – it means spotlessness."[67] As Lady Macbeth came to see – over the course of perhaps the most Senecan work in Shakespeare's oeuvre – killing your rivals would make your sleep fitful to the point of somnambulism. Testing the truth of Seneca's warning that "no one can wear a *persona* for long – pretences fall back into their true nature" made for riveting drama. Only Machiavelli

---

[65] Shklar (1990, 265–6).
[66] For an excellent new discussion, see Burrow (2013, 162–201).
[67] Sen., *Clem.* I.11.2.

seems to have been prepared to ridicule the thought – and even he ended up cast as a villain on the stage.[68]

Further Reading

An increasingly detailed account of the fertile relationship between Senecan philosophy and postclassical political thought is now emerging. Essential items in the medieval transmission of *De clementia* and *De beneficiis* are Mazzoli (1978) and Mazzoli (1982). For Seneca's letters, see Reynolds (1965) and Panizza (1977). For the tragedies, see Villa (2000). For Seneca's identity and the *spuria* attributed to him in this period, see Martellotti (1972) and Meerseman (1973). De Robertis and Resta (2004) is an exhibition catalogue that provides extraordinarily rich information on the textual histories of the Senecan and pseudo-Senecan corpus from manuscript to printed page; it is usefully read in conjunction with Niutta and Santucci (1999), which contains excellent material on the iconography of Seneca.

The essays in Dionigi (1999) investigate a wide range of Senecan themes from the Middle Ages to the modern period. The importance of *De clementia* and *De beneficiis* to Renaissance humanist political theory has long been asserted by Quentin Skinner (see, e.g., Skinner (1981) 29, 36, 45–6); the role of *De clementia* is the focus of Stacey (2007) and (2011b) (which also underlines the centrality of *De ira*). Some brief but important new points about the afterlife of *De beneficiis* are in Chapter 9 of Griffin (2013). The scholarship of Jill Kraye (esp. Kraye 2005, 2001/2) is crucial to understanding early modern neo-Senecan philosophy; for recent groundbreaking work on Seneca in Lipsius, see Papy (2002) and the contributions in de Bom *et al.* (2011), especially that of Soen. Seminal studies of neo-Senecan tragedy from Mussato to Shakespeare and beyond are Braden (1985), Miola (1992), and Mayer (1994). For Seneca at court in Jacobean England, see Salmon (1991). A brilliant new analysis of Shakespeare's debts to Seneca is in chapter 5 of Burrow (2013); while Tilmouth (2009) examines the visibility of Seneca's conscientious self in Shakespeare's portrayal of Lucrece and Macbeth in particular. Blüher (1969), meanwhile, remains a fascinating history of Seneca's reception in Spain.

---

[68] Sen., *Clem.* 1.1.6.

23

FRANCESCO CITTI

Seneca and the Moderns

The seventeenth and eighteenth centuries – with the annotated editions by Lipsius, Gronovius, Scriverius, and Farnabius, the multiple Elzevier impressions, and vernacular translations – established the definitive consecration of Seneca and his influence. Since then, three main lines of Senecan reception are evident. First, there is the work of Seneca the philosopher and naturalist, which is reread primarily for its rationalistic moralism, sometimes contaminated with Christian ethics (and more recently with existentialism) or watered down as some sort of cure for the soul. His *Epistles* and *Dialogues* are a stylistic model for the modern philosophical essay, while the epigrams in which Seneca highlights his key concepts (withdrawal, brevity of life, *meditatio mortis*) have become part of a traditional repertoire. Secondly, Senecan tragic theatre, with its dark setting and explicit violence, is widely imitated, except for a brief period between the nineteenth and early-twentieth centuries. And thirdly, there is Seneca himself, a troubled and contradictory man, who by his suicide becomes the subject of a variety of iconographic, literary, and even film adaptations, sometimes dramatic, sometimes parodic. Seneca's influence is so broad and pervasive that "we have all become Senecans without knowing it":[1] that is to say, not infrequently the reception of Seneca is an imitation in the second degree: the philosophical works and his prose style are mediated through Augustine, Petrarch, Montaigne, and Diderot, while his drama comes down to us through Corneille, Racine, and Shakespeare.

Seneca the Philosopher

The seventeenth century is definitely the acme of the diffusion of Seneca's works and more generally of Stoic thought throughout Europe. Central to this phenomenon was the figure of Lipsius, editor of Seneca and a student of

[1] Quinn (1979, 218).

FRANCESCO CITTI

Stoicism, a doctrine of which his dialogue *De Constantia* (1583) offers a new version largely relying on Seneca. His Neostoicism[2] is based on a new idea of Christian providence, which reconciles the determinism of the divine plan and the rationality of the individual: man is naturally oriented to seek tranquility and peace and to escape the passions, just as the false good and evil. This view is shared by the German Caspar Schoppe (*Elementa philosophiae stoicae moralis*, 1606) and Joseph Hall, who emphasizes from a Christian perspective the need to moderate the passions and to obey Providence (*Characters of Vertues and Vices*, 1608; *Heaven upon Earth*, 1606). Similar approaches were adopted by the Spanish Francisco de Quevedo (1580–1645) – author of *Moral Doctrin* (1612) and also of four fictional Letters to Lucilius – and by the Jesuit Baltasar Gracián (1601–58).[3] The latter not only affirms that "The sage should be self-sufficient" and "virtue is the link of all perfections, the center of all the felicities" (*The Art of Worldly Wisdom* 137, 300) but also imitates Seneca's style, which he regards as perfectly suited to the philosophical issue at hand and aligned with the Baroque predilection for sententiousness.

During this period, Seneca prevails over Cicero as a stylistic model; his epistolary form also appears appropriate for modern philosophical reflection. According to Francis Bacon, "Seneca's epistles to Lucilius, if you mark them well, are but essays, that is, dispersed meditations." Special attention was then given to consolatory themes associated with the control of the passions and the exercise of virtue. We might mention in particular the *Treaty on the constancy and consolation for the public calamities* by Guillaume du Vair (1589), Pierre Charron's *On wisdom* (1601), and François de Malherbe's lyric *Consolation to Mr. du Périer on the Death of his Daughter* (1598). In the *Consolation* Malherbe, who translated the *Epistles*, *De beneficiis*, and *Naturales Quaestiones*, displays his excellent knowledge of Seneca. Martin Opitz also followed in Seneca's footsteps; he not only translated *Troades* (1625) and echoed various passages from *Naturales Quaestiones* (including the famous vision of the earth from heaven, 1 *Praef.* 8–11) in his poem *Vesuvius* (1631) but also made use of Senecan themes and expressions in *Poems of Consolation in Adversities of War*. Here the wise man "binds his ship to the anchor of virtue," is indifferent to earthly glory, constant and unchanging; his *Zlatna, or Tranquility of the soul* takes after Seneca's *De tranquillitate*. The Elizabethan poet Ben Jonson (1572–637) saw in Seneca not only a literary model for his theater but also a teacher of ethics and even of political practices;[4] it is no coincidence that echoes of *De beneficiis*

[2] Spanneut (1980, 388–99); Lagrée (1994).
[3] Blüher (1969, 326–443); Crosby (2005, 58f).
[4] Evans (1995, 57–88), for the copy of Seneca owned by Jonson.

resound in his *Underwoods* and particularly in the *Epistle to Sir Edward Sacvile* – but also in *Poetaster*, *Sejanus*, and in the prose *Discoveries*, where the poet expresses his appreciation for the *brevitas* of Seneca's epistolary style. Jonson appropriates some Senecan epigrams, too: from *Naturales Quaestiones*, for instance, (1 *Praef.* 5: *O quam contempta res est homo nisi supra humana surrexerit!*) he picks up "O how despised and base a thing is a man, / If he not strive t'erect his groveling thoughts / Above the straine of flesh!" (*Cynthia's Revels* 1.5.33–5).[5] The reading of *Naturales* is also recommended by John Milton (*Of Education*, 1644), who in his political works is inspired by *De clementia* and in *Paradise Lost* and *Paradise Regained* repeatedly alludes to Seneca.[6] *Naturales Quaestiones* is appreciated for the ethical reflections mainly contained in the prefaces rather than for its scientific content: the physicist and chemist Robert Boyle (1627–91) had an isolated interest, extracting quotes and insights on scientific methods. The appearance of comets in 1577 and 1604 awakens the consideration of many scientists, including Kepler and Galileo, for the *Naturales Queastiones*, whose Book VII is devoted to comets (quoting, inter alia, the discussion on geocentrism and heliocentrism of 7.2.3).[7]

Even the protagonists of modern philosophy, such as Descartes, Spinoza, and Leibnitz[8] – while not interested in the genealogy of their theories – are nevertheless influenced by Stoic thought: there are numerous Senecan quotations in *Studium bonae mentis* and *Cogitationes privatae* by Descartes, who addressed a letter on morality to Princess Elizabeth Charlotte (1645), commenting on large passages from *De vita beata*. Criticism of Seneca is frequent in Pascal (1623–62), La Bruyère (1645–96), and Boussuet (1627–704), who in the *Sermon on providence* (1656) rejects Seneca's pomposity. Attacks multiply with Malebranche (1638–718) and the *Maxims* of La Rochefoucauld, where Senequism is indicated as a "contagion which has infected an infinity of shallow-minded free-thinkers."

Seneca's influence shrinks in the eighteenth century,[9] although the philosopher David Hume (1711–76) was an avid reader of his philosophical works, of which d'Holbach promoted a translation into French: started by La Grange and finished by Naigeon (1795), the work was preceded by the large treatise by Diderot (*Essay on the Life and Works of the Philosopher Seneca, and on the Reigns of Claudius and Neron*, 1778). Especially in the

[5] Nanni and Pellacani (2012) 197, 200.
[6] See e.g. 3.61–3 "when God / Looking on the earth, with approbation marks / The just man," possibly an allusion to *prov.* 2.9.
[7] Nanni and Pellacani (2012, 203, 216); Gauly (2012, 143–59) on Kepler.
[8] Long (2003), Rutherford (2004).
[9] Spanneut (1980, 400–3); André (1999).

first part of the *Essay*, Diderot – who understood the difficulty of political commitment in the troubled experience of enlightened despotism –
defends the philosopher who "even before the spectacle of depravity and
crimes" offered by the tyrant does not escape his ethical and civic duty.[10]
Rousseau also considered Seneca among his favorite authors: he translated
the *Apocolocyntosis* and echoes in *Emile* and his *Discourses* Senecan themes
such as Cato's Socratic suicide, the praise of primitive man, the attack on
corruption and luxury, as well as reflections on the use of time. By contrast,
La Mettrie's *Anti-Seneca or the Sovereign Good* (1748), originally conceived
as an introduction to *De vita beata*, is a rejection of Seneca's philosophy and
identifies the aim of life not as virtue but as Epicurean delight.

Both because his rationalism was far from romantic sensibility and
because the professional philosophers regarded his work as moralistic and
poorly systematic, the nineteenth century and the beginning of the twentieth marked a crisis in the fortune of Seneca the philosopher, followed by a
rediscovery between the two world wars. Goethe's case is peculiar: in the
Theory of Colours (1810) and in *Paralipomena* (1851), he appreciates the
Naturales Quaestiones as a scientific treatise, while echoes of other works
are scattered in *Maxims and Reflections*.

Individual quotations of incisive formulations can then be detected in
Schopenhauer (1788) and Kierkegaard (1813–55), who, however, purchased
a copy of the philosophical works in translation only as late as 1850, thus
relying up to that point on second-hand quotations only.[11] The judgment of
Hegel (1770–831) is critical and sarcastic at times, as is that of Nietzsche,
who defines Seneca as a "toreador of virtue" and in an epigram (34) included
in the *Prelude* to *The Joyful Wisdom* dismisses his work as chatter: "They
write and write (quite maddening me) / Their 'sapient' twaddle airy, / As if
'twere *primum scribere*, / *Deinde philosophari*."

Even in the twentieth century, the survival of Seneca's philosophy is dis-
continuous: dubious affinities were indicated between Heidegger's ideas of
care and being-toward-death and Seneca's conceptualization of *cura* and
meditatio mortis;[12] also uncertain is Seneca's influence on the concept of
time developed by Emmanuel Mounier and the existentialists. The Spanish
Senecanism of Maria Zambrano (*Seneca's living thought*, 1944), during the
civil wars, expressly refers to Seneca as a model of intellectual dissenting
power, and identifies notions of meditation and resignation as the basis of his

---

[10] On Diderot, see Stacey's chapter in this volume.
[11] Bruun (2009); von Albrecht (1999).
[12] Seneca is explicitly mentioned in *Being and Time*, 42; see Perelli (1994). In general on
Seneca the philosopher in the twentieth century, Citti and Neri (2001, 15–79).

bitter philosophy, almost a real *ars moriendi*. After the war, a Christian interpretation of Seneca is proposed again by Gustav Thybon, who considered him a privileged witness of human nature and a doctor of the soul. A more general revitalization of Stoicism is enacted by theological thinkers such as Dietrich Bonhoeffer, Paul Tillich, and Jacques Maritain who in his *Moral Philosophy* (1960) recognizes in Seneca "a kind of kinship with Christian themes." Special attention to the thought and style of Seneca is also given by Foucault's fundamental studies on Stoicism and the *Care of the Self*.[13]

Seneca's sententious style was bound to provide a repertoire of maxims, anthologized or quoted by essayists and novelists. Among countless examples, we can recall collections of aphorisms such as the *Breviary* of Giovanni Reale (1994), Georg Schoeck's *Seneca for Managers* (1970), a manual of practical philosophy, and *The Consolations of Philosophy* by Alain de Botton (2000), who attributes the cure for frustration to an actualization of Seneca's thought, as well as the numerous quotations by the Spanish novelist Camilo José Cela (1916–2002). A striking case is represented by Günter Grass' *Local anesthetic* (1969), a sort of novel-confession, in which the protagonist, Professor Starusch, while talking to his dentist, uses numerous quotations from Seneca, presented as a kind of painkiller for spiritual anxieties and as a guide to address problems such as political commitment, compromise with power, and the difficulties of working as an educator.

Seneca the Dramatist

After the 1484 *editio princeps* Seneca's tragedies were frequently reprinted, commented upon, translated into different languages and staged as well. In Italy, the tragedians Giambattista Giraldi Cinzio and Sperone Speroni were inspired by him; in France, the playwrights of the siècle d'or, in particular Routrou (*Dying Hercules*, 1634), Corneille (*Medea*, 1635), and Racine (*Fedra*, 1677).[14] No less important is Seneca's more or less direct influence on English tragedy from Kyd, Chapman, Marlowe, and Marston, up to Shakespeare, centering on themes such as revenge, blood, wrath, and tyranny. Shakespeare drew from Seneca stories focused on violent revenges of Thyestean proportions (*Hamlet, Titus Andronicus*), scenes of witchcraft (*Macbeth*) and madness (*Othello, King Lear*), and more generally the macabre taste and the theme of the contrast between inner freedom and tyrannical power (*Richard III*).[15] Later on, in the atmosphere of pre-Romanticism,

[13] Foucault (1986); see also Bartsch's chapter in this volume.
[14] Braden (1985, 115–52); De Caigny (2011); Paratore (2011, 181–209).
[15] Lucas (1922, 110–33; Braden (1985, 153–223).

the same ideal was to inspire Vittorio Alfieri's political tragedies. Even the declamatory style of Seneca is imitated, with his soul-searching monologues, the verse broken by stichomythia, wordplays, and epigrams. The famous line of the murderous Lady Macbeth – "All the perfumes of Arabia will not sweeten this little hand" (5.1.50–1) – echoes Hercules' words: *Quis Tanais aut quis Nilus aut quis Persica / violentus unda Tigris … / abluere dextram poterit?* (*H.F.* 1323–6).

After this great flowering of translations and operistic rewritings (including Cherubini's *Medea*, 1797) a period of decline follows in the Romantic period. A. W. Schlegel's judgment is harsh. The tragedies, he claims, "are beyond description bombastic and frigid, unnatural both in character and action, revolting from their violation of propriety, and so destitute of theatrical effect, that I believe they were never meant to leave the rhetorical schools for the stage."[16] However, there are exceptions, such as Swinburne's *Phaedra* (in *Poems and Ballads*, 1866), in which Phaedra confesses her love to Hippolytus (as in Seneca but not in Euripides).

In the twentieth century,[17] the tragedy of Seneca is appreciated by Eliot, poet and literary critic, to whom we owe the influential dictum that "In the plays of Seneca, the drama is all in the word", and is therefore rediscovered, studied, translated and performed once again. Ted Hughes' *Oedipus* (1968), a powerful rewriting which emphasizes the wordplay and repetitions of his model, is particularly influential. Seneca's reinterpretations range from the "theatre of cruelty" by Artaud (*Tantalus Torture*, from *Thyestes*) and the postwar Anouilh (*Medea*, 1946) to the postmodern Hugo Claus (*Thyestes*, 1966, *Oedipus*, 1971, *Phaedra*, 1980). Spanish writers reinterpret the tragedies in a Christian or Francoist light (Unamuno, Pemán) or choose to see in Medea's drama a foreshadowing of the golden, and finally catastrophic, age of the conquistadors (Bergamín, *Poetry's Infernal Frontiers*, 1959; Carpentier, *The Harp and the Shadow*, 1979).

Seneca's influence on the theatre is too extensive to analyze in detail: here we will examine just a few examples of the reception of *Oedipus*, *Phaedra*, and *Medea*. In the Oedipus tradition, Seneca's version is notable for the original treatment of some aspects of the mythical plot,[18] a greater emphasis being reserved for the episodes of the plague and the Sphinx, the presence of prodigious scenes of sacrifice and of evocation, and finally the reversal of the finale, with Jocasta's heroic suicide (with a sword) following the blinding of Oedipus. The shift of scenic focus from the action to the words and

---

[16] Schlegel (1846, 11).
[17] Citti and Neri (2001, 81–148).
[18] Paduano (2008, 79–192); Citti and Iannucci (2012, xxi–li).

the psychological interiority is also distinctive in Seneca. Consequently, the truth is not discovered, as in Sophocles, through a progressive examination of the evidence, but it is sensed by the protagonist, shrouded from the outset in doubt, fear, and the sense of guilt. These elements are also found in Corneille (*Oedipus*, 1659), who however reduces violent incidents and the macabre (eliminating sacrifice and extispicy) and, in accordance with the taste of his time, inserts the love story of Theseus and Dirce, daughter of Laius, the legitimate heir to the throne. The romantic subplot thus turns into a tale of dynastic conspiracy, and the contemporary theme of the king's legitimacy prevails over that of patricide and incest. The end is a combination of Sophocles and Seneca: Jocasta stabs herself with a dagger before Oedipus blinds himself. The baroque author Emanuele Tesauro (1661) follows Seneca's text more closely, retaining, for instance, much of the sacrifice scene, but reinterprets it from a Christian point of view. In his play Tiresias, as an inspired priest (unlike his hesitant Senecan model) approaches the discovery of the guilty party through the interpretation of sacrifice. Once again the priest is tasked with banishing Oedipus, who is accused of not having been able to avoid his fate. The *Oedipus* of Dryden and Lee (1678) is an elaborate fusion of Sophoclean, Senecan, and Jacobean elements, while the subplot, whose protagonists are Adrastus and Eurydice, is derived from Corneille. Their love story is complicated by the incestuous rivalry of Creon (uncle of Eurydice), a typical Shakespearean villain, who plots against the king. Oedipus' public character as a just and God-like (1.1.341) heroic ruler who comes back in triumph from war harks back to Sophocles. Seneca inspire various miraculous events and the evocation of Laius' ghost, as well as the insistence on the details of the plague and self-blinding. The scene in which Jocasta kills the children, followed by the double suicide of the protagonists, is modelled on the *Medea*. Seneca is behind Oedipus' private character, that of man tormented by doubts, the victim of a storm that torments him at both a physical and psychological level. These features, which dominate in *Medea* and *Agamemnon*, deeply affected the psychology and atmosphere of *King Lear*. In the post-Freudian age, Senecan elements are to be found in Gide's *Oedipus* (1936), with his maniacal concern for the subversion of parental roles, and in Cocteau's *Infernal Machine* (1932), which, by the appearance of the ghost of Laius on the walls of Thebes, also alludes to *Hamlet*.

Racine claims that his *Phaedra* is modelled on Euripides, but dramatic plot derives from Seneca, as had already been the case in the previous *Hippolytuses* by Garnier (1573) and La Pinelière (1635). Racine derives from Seneca, among other elements, the face-to-face scene where Phaedra confesses her love for Hippolytus; the use of Hippolytus' sword as evidence of his guilt; Hippolytus' bloody death before Phaedra's admission of guilt and her suicide by poison, however, and not by sword (as in Seneca) in order to reduce the violence. The story, complicated by a romantic-political subplot (the love of Hippolytus for Aricie), was affected by the Jansenistic concept of predestination, which easily fits in with the Stoic notion of fate: Phaedra's destiny is hereditary, going back to the union of Pasiphae and the bull, and the heroine is therefore destined to struggle in vain against her fate. D'Annunzio will emphasize this titanic aspect of Phaedra in his own tragedy by the same title (1909).[19]

The *Medea* by Pierre Corneille (1635), Franz Grillparzer (in the trilogy *The Golden Fleece*), and Jean Anouilh (1946)[20] take after Seneca's plot with some variations: Corneille reintroduces the Aegeus scene (which featured in Euripides, but not in Seneca), with tragicomic overtones; the scenes dominated by Jason and Medea are reduced (but will be expanded again by Anhouil, where they occupy fully a third of the play); and Medea's characterization as a foreign and barbaric sorceress bent on achieving revenge is intensified (Anhouil will turn her into a gipsy).

A recurrent motif in Seneca's tragedy is the interplay between key words such as *Medea, malum, mater, monstrum*. At the beginning, when the nurse asserts that "there is no loyalty in your husband, and nothing remains of your great wealth," Medea responds without hesitation: *Medea superest,* "Medea remains" (166). A loaded exchange follows: Nurse: *Medea* – Medea: *Fiam* N. *Mater es.* – M. *Cui sim vides.* ("Medea – :: I shall become her :: You are mother :: You see by whom," v. 171). In the final monologue, after she has already decided to kill her children, Medea can finally claim that she has become 'herself': *Medea nunc sum; crevit ingenium malis* ("Now I am Medea: my genius has grown through evil," 910). This stylistic and psychological trait, perhaps the most characteristic of Seneca's *Medea*, appears at the beginning of Corneille's tragedy, in the dialogue between Medea and Nerina (1.5.320f.) "*Dans si grand revers que vous reste-t-il ? :: Moi: / Moi, dis-je, et c'est assez*"; and then in the dialogue with Aegeus, when Medea is finally ready for revenge: "*C'est demain que mon art fait triompher ma haine ; / Demain je suis Médée*" (4.5.1250f.). But Medea's egotism is even more pronounced in Grillparzer, where the protagonist, who in the opening scene has buried a chest containing all the instruments of her magic, feels lost and alien even to herself, and therefore asks Jason, "But who shall give Medea back to me?" (2.1055). Only after digging up the chest and

[19] Wanke (1978, 211–20); De Caigny (2011, 907–18); Paratore (2011, 253–72), on D'Annunzio.
[20] Wanke (1978, 196–207; 221–6); Friedrich (1967, 46–54).

310

recovering her magical powers does she regain her full identity ("Medea, I am once more," 4.1953). Even in Anouilh, who writes his tragedy after the war, Medea is in search of her identity, torn between oppression and freedom. Medea's self-affirmation is thus repeated obsessively a dozen times throughout the tragedy,[21] which ends with the death of the heroine in the flames of her caravan.

Seneca as a Character

Tacitus' historical account, as well as the more critical one by Dio Cassius, but also the *Octavia*, together with the numerous autobiographical references in Seneca's works, are the basis of the rich literary tradition that portrays his contradictions: the austere Stoic philosopher, who proclaims detachment from riches whilst being greedy and unscrupulous, who recommends withdrawal and *meditatio mortis* but is engaged in politics as Nero's tutor, and finally through his Socratic suicide manages to make peace between his words and his works.[22] His death is widely immortalized by the figurative tradition, according to two iconographic schemes already codified by Rubens:[23] the first is that of *Seneca dying* (1612–5: Figure 1), where the suicide appears accompanied by the soldiers who had informed him of Nero's order to kill himself, the opener of his veins, and a scribe who takes note of his last words. Seneca's figure, standing in a small basin, with cruciform arms and eyes serenely facing the sky, seems to recall a type of *Christus patiens* and therefore suggests the idea of a Christian Seneca, as outlined not only by the patristic tradition but also by Lipsius, a close friend of Rubens. This scheme is adopted, among others, by Gerrit van Hothorst (1622–7) and Luca Giordano (1699 ca.: Figure 2), who depicts Seneca partly recumbent, in a pose reminiscent of Christ's washing of feet. An alternative iconographic scheme focuses on the isolated figure of Seneca: divulged by the engraving made by Cornelis Galle from a drawing by Rubens and reproduced in the 1615 Lipsius edition (Figure 3), this pattern is repeated several times by Luca Giordano, who depicts an emaciated and seated Seneca, with the same face as the engraving by Theodor Galle for the 1605 Lipius edition; the eighteenth-century Seneca by Francesco Pittoni (1714) is more muscular and meditative, like that of Guercino, submerged to mid-torso in the bath (1640).

---

[21] Citti and Neri (2001, 103–7, 140).

[22] For a fuller account of the sources on Seneca's biography and death, see Braund's chapter in this volume.

[23] On Seneca's death in literature and art, Hess (2009); Ker (2009a, 179–244).

Figure 1. Rubens, Peter Paul (1577–1640). The dying Seneca. Oil on wood, 185 × 154.7 cm. Inv. 305. bpk, Berlin / Alte Pinakothek, Bayerische Staatsgemaeldesammlungen, München, Germany / Art Resource, NY.

Justus Lipsius is the dedicatee of the neo-Latin tragedy *Nero* by Matthew Gwinne (1603), who depicts the falls of Claudius, Britannicus, Agrippina, Octavia (after her death she appears as a ghost), and finally of Nero; Seneca is represented in his role as a counselor who is ultimately driven to suicide by his Prince: reminiscences of Tacitus are clear, but there are also allusions to Seneca's own works. *The coronation of Poppea* by Claudio Monteverdi, based on a libretto by Francesco Busenello (1643), echoes the *Octavia*,

Figure 2. Giordano, Luca (1634–1705). The death of Seneca. Lucius Aennaeus Seneca, Stoic philosopher (4 BCE-65 CE) forced by Emperor Nero to commit suicide. Canvas, 155 × 188 cm. M.I. 871. Musée du Louvre, Paris, France. Erich Lessing / Art Resource, NY.

albeit not explicitly.[24] The *Coronation*, like the Octavia, stages the contrast between Fortune and Love, but in the opera the character of Seneca is more developed. He embodies virtue and tries to oppose Nero's plans, who, because of his love for Poppea, divorces Octavia, dismisses his tutor and sentences him to death. Seneca's suicide is only announced to his friends and servants, who prepare the bath, while there is no mention of Paulina's. The words of friends urging Seneca not to commit suicide (*"Non morir, non morir, Seneca,"* "Do not die, do not die, Seneca": 2.3) probably reflect the Christian condemnation of suicide and the Counter-Reformation harsh judgment of a philosopher full of contradictions. Tristan l'Hermite's *Seneca's death* (1643), which is intended rather as a continuation of *Octavia*, stages Seneca's withdrawal from politics without Nero's consent and his suicide, now reinterpreted in a Christian light: the dying Seneca commits his hopes

[24] Rosand (1985).

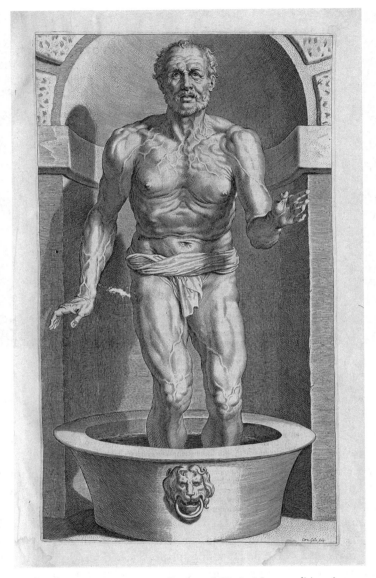

Figure 3. T. Galle, Dying Seneca, engraving from J. Lipsius' Seneca edition, Antwerp 1615 (Bayerische Staatsbibliothek München Res/2 A.lat.b. 648).

to the same God Liberator of Paul of Tarsus, thus crediting the tradition of their epistolary.

Eighteenth-century German drama appropriates the theme, with Friedrich von Creutz' *Seneca* (1754) and the homonymous play by Christian von

Figure 4. David, Jacques Louis (1748–1825). The Death of Seneca. Oil on canvas, 122.5 × 155 cm. Dutuit 1154.Photo: Bulloz. Musée du Petit Palais, Paris, France. © RMN-Grand Palais / Art Resource, NY.

Kleist (1758): in both, his wife Paulina regains her role, committing suicide like Seneca, who in turn is presented as a hero of great stature. In Kleist, Seneca's death, like that of Christ, is accompanied by cosmic disturbance and is presented as a necessary fulfilment of the philosopher's destiny: hence he refuses the help of Polybius, who would like to die in his place. Even in France, in the wake of Diderot's *Essay*, Paulina plays a lead role in the crowded paintings by Pierre Peyron and Jacques-Louis David (1773; Figure 4).

With few exceptions, such as the lyrical drama *Three dead* by Apollon Majkov (1856) – a dialogue among Seneca, the Epicurean Lucius, and Lucianus – the nineteenth century witnesses a fading of Seneca's figure, obscured by that of Petronius, as showed among others in Henry Sienkiewicz' *Quo vadis* (1896) and its film version by Mervin Le Roy (1951), set against the backdrop of a grand battle between Christianity and decadent paganism.[25] The duplicity of Seneca, in his private life and political decisions, is

[25] Citti and Neri (2001, 149–93), also about Seneca in the novel.

underlined by Riccardo Bacchelli's *Dialogue of Seneca and Burrus* (1920) and also in Giovanni Papini's *Universal Judgment* (1944). Seneca then takes on almost caricatured features in the historical novel set in the age of Nero: in Hubert Monteilhet's *Neropolis* (1984) and in Robert Graves' *I, Claudius* and *Claudius the God* (1934), Seneca is presented as a contradictory multimillionaire, willing to resort to every form of flattery in order to be able to return to Rome from Corsica. In Mika Waltari's *The Roman* (1964), Paulina is saved from suicide, just because Seneca is distracted as he makes final corrections to his works. He is then consigned to a secondary role in the novels about Pisonian conspiracy by American authors during the Cold War, such as Vincent Sheean (*Beware of Caesar*, 1965) and John Hersey (*The Conspiracy*: 1972). Seneca's suicide is then the basis for numerous theatrical rewritings in postwar Germany.[26] In Hermann Gressieker's *Seneca and the golden Age* (1951), Seneca discovers the closeness of his own thought with that of Christ, and his suicide is likened to the persecutions of Christians. Similarly, Stephan Hiebel's *Seneca* opens with the day of Christ's crucifixion and closes in 68 CE, with a group of women at the tomb of Nero, which seems to recall the scene of the resurrection. A Seneca intent on claiming freedom and dignity under tyranny is the protagonist of the tragic farce of Peter Hacks' *Seneca's Death* (1978) and of the homonymous play by Heiner Müller (1992). The farcical tone is also adopted by the Hungarian playwright Miklós Hubay for his "variations on the theme of the tyrant comedian": *The youngest son* (1970) refers to the matricide of Agrippina approved by a cynical and unscrupulous Seneca. In the *Transformation of a god into a pumpkin, transformation of a pumpkin into a God*, Nero – while trying to learn the eulogy for Claudius – recites passages from the *Apocolocyntosis*, playing with marionettes of Claudius, Hercules, and Hermes.

Further Reading

Due to the magnitude of Seneca's reception an overall review is still missing. In the vast bibliography available, the philosophical and dramatic spheres are usually considered separately; there are also numerous essays on individual episodes of imitation (especially theatrical).

The seventeenth- and eighteenth-century editions are carefully analyzed, from a bibliographic and iconographic point of view, in the exhibition catalogues edited by Niutta and Santucci (1999) and De Robertis and Resta (2004). Brief general introductions to the influence of Seneca the philosopher

[26] von Albrecht (1999, 289–95); Ziolkowski (2004); Ker (2009a, 238–40).

in the modern age are provided by Gummere (1922, 114–38) and Ross (1974, 147–52); more details in Spanneut (1973, 255–389, in general on Stoicism, and 1980, 389–407, in particular on Seneca); see also Laarmann (2014, 65–71), mainly on the German area. Von Albrecht (1999) and Ziolkowski (2004; the latter limited to the twentieth century) are also devoted to Seneca the philosopher and literary character in Germany, while Blüher (1969) focuses on Spain until the seventeenth century. Extensive surveys by Hine (2010a) and Nanni and Pellacani (2012) are devoted to Seneca the scientist; Gauly (2012) focuses on the sixteenth and seventeenth centuries (on Galilei, Tycho Brahe, and Kepler), as does Hirai (2012, especially on Lipsius).

The *Nachleben* of Seneca's tragedies from Antiquity to the present is briefly outlined by Schubert (2014); Lefèvre (1978) contains more extensive profiles divided by area; a new assessment of the fortune of Senecan drama in "Scholarship, Literature, and Performance" will be offered by Dodson-Robinson (forthcoming). On English classical theatre, see Lucas (1922) and Braden (1985); on the French, de Caigny (2011) and Paratore (2011). A detailed analysis of the fortune of *Medea* and *Oedipus* in the subsequent dramatic tradition is provided by Boyle in his commentaries (2011, lxxxviii–cxvi and 2014, cxix–cxli); on *Oedipus*, see also Paduano (2008). The representations of Seneca's death, in theatre and art, are examined in detail by Ker (2009a) and Hess (2009, for the seventeenth and eighteenth centuries); on Seneca's character (but also on *Octavia*) in opera, see Schubert (2003) and Manuwald (2005 and 2013). Citti and Neri (2001) deal with many aspects of Seneca's reception as a philosopher, playwright, and character in the twentieth century.

GENERAL BIBLIOGRAPHY

Aalders, G. J. D. 1975. *Political Thought in Hellenistic Times.* Amsterdam.

Abbott, K. M. 1978. "Seneca and St. Paul," in D. C. Riechel, ed., *Wege der Worte: Festschrift für Wolfgang Fleischauer,* 119–31. Cologne.

Abel, K. 1967. *Bauformen in Senecas Dialogen.* Heidelberg.

——— 1991. "Die 'beweisende' Struktur des senecanischen Dialogs," in P. Grimal, ed., *Sénèque et la prose latine* (Entretiens Hardt 36), 49–97. Vandœuvres and Geneva.

Abel, L. 1963. *Metatheater: A New View of Dramatic Form.* New York.

Ahl, F. 2000. "Seneca and Chaucer: Translating both Poetry and Sense," in S. Harrison, ed., *Seneca in Performance,* 151–72. London.

——— 2008. *Two Faces of Oedipus: Sophocles' Oedipus Tyrannus and Seneca's Oedipus.* Ithaca, N.Y.

Albanese, G. 2004. "La *Vita Senecae,*" in T. De Robertis and G. Resta, eds. 2004, Seneca: una vicenda testuale, Florence, 47–54.

Alexander, W. H. 1935. "The Professor's Deadly Vengeance," *The University of Toronto Quarterly* 4: 239–58.

Allen, P. S. et al., eds. 1910. *Opus epistolarum Des. Erasmi Roterodami,* vol. II. Oxford.

Allen, P. S. et al., eds. 1934. *Opus epistolarum Des. Erasmi Roterodami,* vol. VIII. Oxford.

Althoff, J. 2005. "Senecas Naturales questiones, Buch 2, und Lukrez," in Th. Baier, G. Manuwald, and B. Zimmermann, eds., *Seneca: philosophus et magister. Festschrift für Eckard Lefèvre zum 70. Geburtstag,* 9–34. Freiburg im B.

Altman, J. G. 1982. *Epistolarity: Approaches to a Form.* Columbus.

André, J. M. 1968. "Sénèque et l'Épicurisme: ultime position," in *Actes du VIII Congrès de l'Association G. Budé,* 469–80. Paris.

——— 1999. "Arti liberali e pedagogia: l'eredità di Seneca in Francia," in I. Dionigi, ed., *Seneca nella coscienza dell'Europa,* 198–214. Milan.

Andrew, E. 2004. "The Senecan Moment: Patronage and Philosophy in the Eighteenth Century," *Journal of the History of Ideas* 65: 277–99.

Annas, J. 1992. *Hellenistic Philosophy of Mind.* Berkeley.

Aquinas, T. 2002. *Political Writings,* ed. R. W. Dyson. Cambridge.

Arce, J. 2010. "Roman Imperial Funerals *in effigie,*" in B. C. Ewald and C. Noreña, eds., *The Emperor and Rome: Space, Representation, and Ritual* (Yale Classical Studies 35), 309–23. Cambridge.

Armisen-Marchetti, M. 1989. Sapientiae facies: *étude sur les images de Sénèque.* Paris.

1991. "La métaphore et l'abstraction dans la prose de Sénèque," in P. Grimal, ed., *Sénèque et la prose Latine* (Entretiens Hardt 36), 99–139. Vandoeuvres and Geneva.

1995. "Sénèque et l'appropriation du temps," *Latomus* 54: 545–67.

1998. "Le Sénèque de l'*Octavie*," in M. H. Garelli-François, ed., *Rome et le Tragique. Colloque international 26, 27, 28 mars 1998*, 197–209 (*Pallas* 49). Toulouse.

2006. "*Speculum Neronis*: un mode spécifique de direction de conscience dans le *De Clementia* de Sénèque," *Revue des études latines* 84: 185–201.

2008. "Imagination and Meditation in Seneca: The Example of *Praemeditatio*," in J. G. Fitch, ed., *Seneca (Oxford Readings in Classical Studies)*, 102–13. Oxford. (Originally published as "Imagination et méditation chez Sénèque: l'exemple de la *praemeditatio*," *Revue des Études Latines* 64, 1986: 185–95.)

2011. "Murailles, citadelles et sièges chez Sénèque le philosophe," *Technai* 2: 53–66.

Armstrong, D. 2011. "Epicurean Virtues, Epicurean Friendship," in J. Fish and K. R. Sanders, eds., *Epicurus and the Epicurean Tradition*, 105–28. Cambridge.

Asmis, E. 2009. "Seneca on Fortune and the Kingdom of God," in S. Bartsch and D. Wray, eds., *Seneca and the Self*, 115–38. Cambridge.

Austin, R. G. 1948. *Quintiliani Institutionis oratoriae liber XII*. Oxford.

Bakhtin, M. M. 1986. *Speech Genres and Other Late Essays*, tr. V. W. McGee. Austin.

Bandera, C. 1981. "Sacrificial Levels in Virgil's *Aeneid*," *Arethusa* 14: 217–39.

Barchiesi, A., ed. 2005. *Ovidio, Metamorfosi*, Volume I (Libri I–II). Rome.

Barnes, J. 1997. *Logic and the Imperial Stoa*. Leiden.

Barthes, R. 1972. "Tacitus and the Funerary Baroque," in *Critical Essays*, tr. R. Howard, 162–6. Evanston, Ill.

Barton, C. A. 1993. *The Sorrows of the Ancient Romans. The Gladiator and the Monster*. Princeton.

Bartsch, S. 1994. *Actors in the Audience: Theatricality and Doublespeak from Nero to Hadrian*. Cambridge, Mass., and London.

2006. *The Mirror of the Self: Sexuality, Self-Knowledge, and the Gaze in the Early Empire*. Chicago.

2009. "Senecan Metaphor and Stoic Self-Instruction," in S. Bartsch and D. Wray, eds., *Seneca and the Self*, 188–217. Cambridge.

Bartsch, S. and D. Wray, eds. 2009. *Seneca and the Self*. Cambridge.

Barzizza, G. 1977a. *Vita Senecae*, ed. L. A. Panizza, in "Gasparino Barzizza's Commentaries on Seneca's Letters," *Traditio* 33: 342–50 (Appendix II).

1977b. *Prohemium, Comentarii in Epistolas Senece*, ed. L. A. Panizza, in "Gasparino Barzizza's Commentaries on Seneca's Letters," *Traditio* 33: 350–7 (Appendix III).

Bauman, R. 1983. *Lawyers in Roman Republican Politics: A Study of the Roman Jurists in Their Political Setting, 316–82 B.C.* Munich.

Beacham, R. C. 1992. *The Roman Theater and Its Audience*. Cambridge, Mass.

1999. *Spectacle Entertainments of Early Imperial Rome*. New Haven.

Benedict, R. 1946. *The Chrysanthemum and the Sword: Patterns of Japanese Culture*. Boston.

Benferhat, Y. 2005. *Ciues epicurei: les épicuriens et l'idée de monarchie à Rome et en Italie de Sylla à Octave*. Brussels.

Béranger, J. 1952. *Recherches sur l'aspect idéologique du principat*. Basel.

Beretta, M., F. Citti, and L. Pasetti, eds. 2012. *Seneca e le scienze naturali*. Florence.

Bergmann, B., and C. Kondoleon, eds. 1999. *The Art of Ancient Spectacle*. New Haven.

Berno, F. R. 2003. *Lo specchio, il vizio e la virtù. Studio sulle Naturales Quaestiones di Seneca*. Bologna.

ed. 2006. *L. Anneo Seneca, Lettere a Lucilio LibroVI: Le lettere 53–7*. Bologna.

2010. "Seneca, *Naturales Quaestiones*," in C. Walde, ed., *Die Rezeption der antiken Literatur. Kulturhistorisches Werklexicon*, 875–89. Der Neue Pauly. Supplemente Band 7. Stuttgart and Weimar.

2012. "Non solo acqua: elementi per un diluvio universale nel terzo libro delle *Naturales Quaestiones*," in M. Beretta, F. Citti, and L. Pasetti, eds., *Seneca e le scienze naturali*, 57–68. Florence.

Berthet, J.-F. 1979. "Sénèque lecteur d'Horace d'après les *Lettres à Lucilius*," *Latomus* 38: 940–54.

Bickel, E. 1905. "Die Schrift des Martinus von Bracara *Formula vitae honestae*," *Rheinisches Museum* 60: 505–51.

1915. *Diatribe in Senecae philosophi fragmenta I. Fragmenta de matrimonio*. Leipzig.

Billanovich, G. 1947/1995. *Petrarca letterato* I. Rome.

Billerbeck, M., and E. A. Schmidt, eds. 2004. *Sénèque le tragique*. Entrétiens Hardt 50. Vandoeuvres-Geneva.

Binns, J. W. 1974. "Seneca and Neo-Latin Tragedy in England," in C. D. N. Costa, ed. *Seneca*, 215–24. London.

Blänsdorf, J. 1986. "Senecas *Apocolocyntosis* und die Intertextualitätstheorie," *Poetica* 18: 1–26.

Bloom, H 1997. *The Anxiety of Influence: A Theory of Poetry*. 2nd ed. Oxford.

Bloomer, W. M. 1997. "Schooling in Persona: Imagination and Subordination in Roman Education," *CA* 16.1: 57–78.

Blüher, K. A. 1969. *Seneca in Spanien. Untersuchungen zur Geschichte der Seneca-Rezeption in Spanien vom 13. bis 17. Jahrhundert*. Berne and Munich (= 1983. *Séneca en España*, Madrid).

Bobbio, A. 1941. "Seneca e la formazione spirituale e culturale del Petrarca," *Bibliofilia* 43: 223–91.

Bocciolini Palagi, L. 1978. *Il carteggio apocrifo di Seneca e san Paolo*, ed. Leo S. Olschki. Florence. (New expanded edition in Palagi L. Bocciolini, ed., *Epistolario apocrifo di Seneca e San Paolo*. Florence 1985.)

Bodin, Jean. 1962. *The Six Bookes of a Commonweale*, ed. K. McRae, tr. R. Knolles [1606]. Cambridge, Mass.

Bolgar, R. R. 1954. *The Classical Heritage and Its Beneficiaries*. Cambridge.

Bonner, S. F. 1949. *Roman Declamation in the Late Republic and Early Empire*. Liverpool.

Bourgery, A. 1922. *Sénèque prosateur. Études littéraires et grammaticales sur la prose de Sénèque le philosophe*. Paris.

Boyle, A. J., ed. 1994. *Seneca's* Troades, with tr. and comm. Leeds.

1997. *Tragic Seneca: An Essay in the Theatrical Tradition*. London and New York.

2006. *Roman Tragedy*. London.

ed. 2011. *Seneca: Oedipus*. Oxford.

ed. 2014. *Seneca: Medea*. Oxford.

Bracciolini, P. 1997. "On the Misery of the Human Condition," in J. Kraye, ed., *Cambridge Translations of Renaissance Philosophical Texts*, vol. I, 18–28. Cambridge.

Braden, G. 1985. *Renaissance Tragedy and the Senecan Tradition. Anger's Privilege*. New Haven.

Bradshaw, J. 1988. *Healing the Shame That Binds You*. Deerfield Beach, Fl.

Braund, D. C. 1980. "The Aedui, Troy and the *Apocolocyntosis*," *Classical Quarterly* 30: 420–5.

Braund, S. M., and P. James 1998. "*Quasi homo*: distortion and contortion in Seneca's *Apocolocyntosis*," *Arethusa* 31: 285–311.

Braund, S. M., ed. 2009. *Seneca, De Clementia*. Oxford.

Braund, S. M. 2013. "Haunted by Horror: The Ghost of Seneca in Renaissance Drama," in E. Buckley and M. Dinter, eds., *A Blackwell Companion to Neronian Literature and Culture*, 425–43. Malden, Mass.

Bravo Díaz, J. R. 1991. "*Spiritus*: estudio de un término científico (*Naturales Quaestiones* de Séneca)," in A. Ramos Guerreira, ed., *Mnemosyne C. Codoñer a discipulis oblatum*, 15–28. Salamanca.

1995. "*Aer, aether, caelum, sublimis*: estudio del vocabolario técnico utilizado para designar el cielo en las *Naturales Quaestiones* de Séneca y otros escritores científicos," *Voces* 6: 9–39.

ed. 2013. *Séneca, Cuestiones Naturales*. Madrid.

Brennan, T. 2005. *The Stoic Life: Emotions, Duties, and Fate*. Oxford and New York.

Brink, C. O. 1971. *Horace on Poetry: The "Ars Poetica."* Cambridge.

1989. "Quintilian's *De causis corruptae eloquentiae* and Tacitus' *Dialogus de oratoribus*," *CQ* 39: 472–503.

Brock, R. W. 2013. *Greek Political Imagery from Homer to Aristotle*. London.

Brugnoli, G. 2000. "La 'Lectura Senecae' dal tardo-antico al XIII secolo," *Giornale Italiano di Filologia* 52: 225–47.

Brunt, P. A. 1965. "Amicitia in the Late Roman Republic," *Proceedings of the Cambridge Philological Society* 11: 1–20. Reprinted in *The Fall of the Roman Republic and Other Essays*, 351–81. Oxford.

1975. "Stoicism and the Principate," *Papers of the British School at Rome* 43: 7–35. Reprinted in *Studies in Stoicism*, 275–309. Oxford, 2013.

Bruun, N. 1990. "Neue Bemerkungen zur Apocolocyntosis des Seneca," *Analecta Romana Instituti Danici* 19: 69–78.

2009. "Seneca: *Disjecta Membra* in Kierkegaard's Writings," in J. Stewart, ed., *Kierkegaard and the Roman World*, 111–24. Farnham and Burlington.

Burnyeat, M. 1981. "Aristotle on Learning to Be Good," in A. O. Rorty, ed., *Essays on Aristotle's Ethics*, 69–92. Berkeley and Los Angeles.

Burrow, C. 2013. *Shakespeare and Classical Antiquity*. Oxford.

Busch, A. 2009. "Dissolution of the Self in the Senecan Corpus," in S. Bartsch and D. Wray, eds., *Seneca and the Self*, 255–82. Cambridge.

Buzzi, F. 2001. "La filosofia di Seneca nel pensiero cristiano di Giusto Lipsio," in A. P. Martina, ed., *Seneca e i Cristiani. Atti del Convegno Internazionale*, 365–91. Milan.

Byrne, S. N. 1999. "Maecenas in Seneca and Other Post-Augustan Authors," in S. N. Byrne and E. P. Cueva, eds., *Veritatis Amicitiaeque Causa: Essays in Honor of Anna Lydia Motto and John R. Clark*, 21–40. Wauconda, Ill.

2006. "Petronius and Maecenas: Seneca's Calculated Criticism," in S. N. Byrne, E. P. Cueva, and J. Alvares, eds., *Authors, Authority, and Interpreters in the Ancient Novel. Essays in Honor of G. L. Schmeling*, 83–111. Groningen.

Cairns, D. 1993. *Aidōs: The Psychology and Ethics of Honour and Shame in Ancient Greek Literature*. Oxford and New York.

Calboli, G. 1999. "Il giudizio di Quintiliano su Seneca," in I. Dionigi, ed., *Seneca nella coscienza dell'Europa*, 19–57. Milan.

Calvin, John. 1969. *Commentary on Seneca's De Clementia*, ed. and trans. F. L. Battles and André Malan Hugo. Leiden.

1999. *Constitutionum Regni Siciliarum libri III*, vol. I., ed. Andrea Romano. Catanzaro.

Cancik, Hildegard. 1967. *Untersuchungen zu Senecas Epistulae morales*. Hildesheim.

Cannadine, D., and S. Price, eds. 1987. *Rituals of Royalty: Power and Ceremonial in Traditional Societies*. Cambridge.

Canter, Howard V. 1925. "Rhetorical Elements in the Tragedies of Seneca," *University of Illinois Studies in Language and Literature* 10: 1–185.

Carabin, D. 2004. *Les idées stoïciennes dans la littérature morale des XVIe et XVIIe siècles 1575–1642*. Paris.

2006. *Henri Estienne, érudit, novateur, polémiste. Étude sur Ad Senecae lectionem Proodopoeiae*. Paris.

2007., ed. *H. Estienne, Introduction à la lecture de Sénèque 1586*. Paris.

Castagna, L., ed. 1996. *Nove studi sui cori tragici di Seneca*. Milan.

2003. "Lucano e Seneca: limiti di una *aemulatio*," in I. Gualandri and G. Mazzoli. *Gli Annei. Una famiglia nella storia e nella cultura di Roma imperiale*. Como. 2003, 277–90.

Castelnérac, B. 2007. "'Eclecticism' in Plutarch and Seneca," *Hermathena* 182: 135–63.

Castiglioni, L. 1924. "Studi intorno a Seneca prosatore e filosofo," *Rivista di Filologia e di Istruzione Classica* 52: 350–82. Reprinted in A. Traina, ed., *Seneca: letture critiche*, 97–126. Milan, 1976.

Caviglia, F. 2001. "Commenti di ecclesiastici a Seneca tragico: Trevet e Delrio," in A. P. Martina, ed. *Seneca e i Cristiani. Atti del Convegno Internazionale.*, 351–63. Milan.

Cervellera, M. A. 1975. "Petronio e Seneca tragico," *Rivista di Cultura Classica e Medievale* 17: 107–19.

Champlin, E. 2003. *Nero*. Cambridge, Mass.

Chevallier, R., and R. Poignault, eds. 1991. *Présence de Sénèque*. Paris.

Citti, F., and C. Neri. 2001. *Seneca nel Novecento*, Roma.

2012. *Cura sui. Studi sul lessico filosofico di Seneca*. Amsterdam.

Citti, F., and A. Iannucci. 2012. "Edipo classico e contemporaneo: la Sfinge, i piedi, il dubbio," in *Edipo classico e contemporaneo*, xxi–li. Hildesheim, Zürich, and New York.

Clark, J. G. 2004. "Trevet, Nicholas (*b.* 1257x65, *d.* in or after 1334)," in *Oxford Dictionary of National Biography*. Oxford.

Codoñer, C., ed. 1979. *L. Annaei Senecae Naturales Quaestiones*, Consejo superior de investigaciones científicas. Madrid.

Codoñer Merino, C. 1983. "El adversario ficticio en Séneca," *Helmantica* 34: 131–48.

Coffey, M. 1976. *Roman Satire*. Methuen, London, and New York.

Coleman, K. M. 1990. "Fatal Charades: Roman Executions Staged as Mythological Enactments," *Journal of Roman Studies* 80: 44–73.

Coleman, R. 1974. "The Artful Moralist: A Study of Seneca's Epistolary Style," *Classical Quarterly* 68: 276–89.

Colish, M. L. 1976. "Seneca's *Apocolocyntosis* as a Possible Source for Erasmus' *Julius Exclusus*," *Renaissance Quarterly* 29: 361–8.

   1990. *The Stoic Tradition from Antiquity to the Early Middle Ages*. 2 vols. Leiden.

Connors, C. 2005. "Epic allusion in Roman satire," in K. Freudenburg, ed., *The Cambridge Companion to Roman Satire*, 123–45. Cambridge.

Conte, G. B. 1994. *Latin Literature: A History*, revised D. Fowler and G. W. Most, tr. J. Solodow. Baltimore.

   1996. *The Hidden Author: An Interpretation of Petronius's Satyricon*. Berkeley.

Cooper, J. M. 1998. "Posidonios on Emotions," in J. Shivola and T. Engberg-Pedersen, eds., *The Emotions in Hellenistic Philosophy*, 71–111. Dordrecht, Boston, and London.

   2004. "Moral Theory and Moral Improvement: Seneca," in *Knowledge, Nature, and the Good*, 309–34. Princeton.

   2012. *Pursuits of Wisdom: Six Ways of Life in Ancient Philosophy from Socrates to Plotinus*. Princeton.

Cooper, J. M., and Procopé, J. F. 1995. *Seneca. Moral and Political Essays*. Cambridge.

Costa, C. D. N., ed. 1974. *Seneca*. London.

Crook, J. 1955. *Consilium Principis*. Cambridge.

Crosby, J. O. 2005. *Nuevas cartas de la última prisión de Quevedo*. Woodbridge.

Cugusi, P. 1983. *Evoluzione e forme dell'epistolografia Latina nella tarda repubblica e nei due primi secoli dell'impero*. Rome.

Cupaiuolo, G 1975. *Introduzione al De Ira di Seneca*. Naples.

Currie, H. M. 1966. "The Younger Seneca's Style: Some Observations," *Bulletin of the Institute of Classical Studies* 13: 76–87.

Damschen, G. and A. Heil, eds. 2014. *Brill's Companion to Seneca*. Leiden.

Darwin, C. 1899. *The Expression of the Emotions in Man and Animals*. New York.

Davis, T. C., and T. Postlewait, eds. 2003. *Theatricality*. Cambridge.

de Bom, E. et al., eds. 2011. *(Un)Masking the Realities of Power. Justus Lipsius and the Dynamics of Political Writing in Early Modern Europe*, Leiden.

de Caigny, F. 2011. *Seneque le Tragique en France (XVIe–XVIIe siècles). Imitation, traduction, adaptation*. Paris.

De Lacy, Ph. 1952. "Biography and Tragedy in Plutarch," *American Journal of Philology* 73: 159–71.

de Nolhac, P. 1907. *Pétrarque e l'humanisme*. Reprinted in 1965. Paris.

De Robertis, T., and G. Resta, eds. 2004. *Seneca: una vicenda testuale*. Florence.

De Vivo, A. 1989. "Considerazioni sull'*Aetna*: rapporti con Seneca, epoca di composizione, *Vichiana* 18: 63–85.

   1992. *Le parole della scienza. Sul trattato De terrae motu di Seneca*. Salerno.

   2012. "Seneca e i terremoti (*Questioni naturali*, libro VI)," in M. Beretta, F. Citti, and L. Pasetti, eds., *Seneca e le scienze naturali*, 93–106. Florence.

Degl'Innocenti Pierini, R. 1981. "Motivi consolatorii e ideologia imperiale nella *Consolatio ad Polybium* di Seneca," *Quaderni di Filologia Latina* 1: 115–47. Reprinted in *Tra Ovidio e Seneca*, 213–48. Bologna, 1990.

1990. "Seneca, Ovidio e il diluvio," in *Tra Ovidio e Seneca*, 177–210, Bologna.

1996. "Venit ad pigros cana senectus (Sen. *Herc. F.* 198). Un motivo dei cori senecani tra filosofia ed attualità," in L. Castagna, ed., *Nove studi sui cori tragici di Seneca*, 37–55. Milan. Reprinted in *Tra filosofia e poesia. Studi su Seneca e dintorni*, 59–77. Bologna.

Delhaye, P. 1964. "Florilèges médiévaux d'éthique," in *Dictionnaire de spiritualité* 5: 465–72. Paris.

Desan, P., ed. 2004. *Dictionnaire de Michel de Montaigne.* Paris.

Dionigi, I., ed. 1999. *Seneca nella coscienza dell'Europa.* Milan.

Dodds, E. R. 1951. *The Greeks and the Irrational.* Berkeley.

Dodson-Robinson E., ed. forthcoming. *A Brill Companion.* Leiden and Boston.

Dolganov, A. forthcoming. "The Epicurean Republic of Letters," in I. Gildenhard and P. Ceccarelli, eds., *Configuring Communities: The Socio-Political Dimension of Ancient Epistolography.* Oxford.

Dominik, W. J. 1997. "The Style Is the Man: Seneca, Tacitus and Quintilian's Canon," In W. J. Dominik, ed., *Roman Eloquence: Rhetoric in Society and Literature*, 50–68. London and New York.

Donini, P. 1982. *Le scuole, l'anima, l'impero: La filosofia antica da Antioco a Plotino.* Turin.

Dressler A. 2012. "'You Must Change Your Life'; Theory and Practice, Metaphor and *Exemplum*, in Seneca's Prose," *Helios* 39: 45–92.

Due, O. S. 1970. "Lucain et la philosophie," in M. Durry, ed., *Lucain. Sept exposés* (Entretiens Hardt 15), 203–32. Vandœuvres-Geneva.

Dupont, F. 1985. *L'Acteur-roi, ou Le théâtre dans la Rome antique.* Paris.

Dyson, S. L. 1970. "The Portrait of Seneca in Tacitus," *Arethusa* 3: 71–84.

Easterling, P. 1990. "Constructing Character in Greek Tragedy," in C. Pelling, ed., *Characterization and Individuality in Greek Tragedy*, 83–99. Oxford.

Eden, P. T., ed. 1984. *Seneca: Apocolocyntosis.* Cambridge Greek and Latin Classics. Cambridge.

Edwards, C. 1993. *The Politics of Immorality in Ancient Rome.* Cambridge.

1997. "Self-Scrutiny and Self-Transformation in Seneca's *Letters*," *Greece and Rome* 44: 23–38. Reprinted in J. G. Fitch, ed., *Seneca* (Oxford Readings in Classical Studies), 84–101. Oxford, 2008.

1999. "The Suffering Body: Philosophy and Pain in Seneca's Letters," in J. Porter, ed., *Constructions of the Classical Body*, 252–68. Ann Arbor.

2005. "Archetypally Roman? Representing Seneca's Ageing Body," in M. Wyke and A. Hopkins, eds., *Roman Bodies: Antiquity to the Eighteenth Century*, 13–22. London.

2007. *Death in Ancient Rome.* New Haven.

2009. "Free Yourself! Slavery, Freedom and the Self in Seneca's *Letters*," in S. Bartsch and D. Wray, eds. *Seneca and the Self*, 139–59. Cambriedge.

Eliot, T. S. 1950. "Seneca in Elizabethan translation" (originally 1927), in *Selected Essays*, 51–88. New York.

Elsner, J., and J. Masters, eds. 1994. *Reflections of Nero.* London.

Erasmo, M. 2004. *Roman Tragedy: Theater to Theatricality.* Austin.

Erasmus. 1997. *The Education of a Christian Prince*, ed. and tr. L. Jardine. Cambridge.

Evans, R. C. 1995. *Habits of Mind. Evidence and Effects of Ben Jonson's Reading*. Lewisburg, London, and Cranbury.

Fairweather, J. 1981. *Seneca the Elder*. Cambridge.

Fantham, E. 1975. "Virgil's Dido and Seneca's Tragic Heroines," *Greece and Rome* 22: 1–10. Reprinted in J. G. Fitch, ed., *Seneca* (Oxford Readings in Classical Studies), 272–85. Oxford, 2008.

1982. *Seneca's* Troades: *A Literary Introduction with Text, Translation and Commentary*. Princeton.

1996. *Roman Literary Culture*. Baltimore.

2000. "Production of Seneca's *Trojan Women*, Ancient? And Modern," in G. W. M. Harrison, ed., *Seneca in performance*, 13–26. London.

2002. "Orator and/et Actor," in P. Easterling and E. Hall, eds., *Greek and Roman Actors: Aspects of an Ancient Profession*, 362–76. Cambridge.

Fasce, S. 2002. *Letteratura e psicologia. L'espressione del linguaggio interiore*. Genoa.

Feeney, D. C. 2002. "*Una cum scriptore meo.* Poetry, Principate and the Traditions of Literary History in the Epistle to Augustus," in A. J. Woodman and D. C. Feeney, eds., *Traditions and Contexts in the Poetry of Horace*, 172–87. Cambridge.

2007. *Caesar's Calendar. Ancient Time and the Beginnings of History*. Berkeley, Los Angeles, and London.

Feldherr, A. 2010. *Playing Gods: Ovid's* Metamorphoses *and the Politics of Fiction*. Princeton.

Ferguson, J. 1972. "Seneca the Man," in D. R. Dudley, ed., *Neronians and Flavians: Silver Latin 1*, 1–23. London.

Fillion-Lahille, J. 1984. *Le de ira de Sénèque et la philosophie stoïcienne des passions*. Paris.

Fischer, S. E. 2008. *Seneca als Theologe: Studien zum Verhältnis von Philosophie und Tragödiendichtung*. Beiträge zur Altertumskunde. Berlin.

Fitch, J. G. 1981. Sense Pause and Relative Dating in Seneca, Sophocles and Shakespeare, *American Journal of Philology* 102: 289–307.

1987. *Seneca's* Hercules Furens. New York.

2000. "Playing Seneca?" in G. W. M. Harrison, ed., *Seneca in Performance*, 1–12. London.

Fitch, J. G. and S. McElduff. 2002. "Construction of the Self in Senecan Drama," *Mnemosyne* 55: 18–40.

ed. 2008. *Seneca* (Oxford Readings in Classical Studies). Oxford.

Fleury, P. 2000. "De la virulence d'un idéal rhétorique: la vitupération de Sénèque par Fronton," *Revue de Philologie* 74: 43–59.

Fohlen, J. 2000. "La tradition manuscrite des *Epistulae ad Lucilium* (ixe s. – xvie s.)," *Giornale italiano di filologia* 52: 113–62.

2002. "Biographies de Sénèque et commentaires des *Epistulae ad Lucilium* v^e – xve siècles," *Italia medievale e umanistica* 43: 1–90.

Fothergill-Payne, L. 1988. *Seneca and "Celestina."* Cambridge.

Foucault, M. 1986. *The Care of the Self* (*The History of Sexuality*: Volume 3), tr. R. Hurley. New York.

1988. *Technologies of the Self*, eds. L. H. Martin et al. Amherst, Mass.

1997. "Self Writing," in *Ethics: Subjectivity and Truth*, 207–21. New York.

2005. *The Hermeneutics of the Subject (Lectures at the Collège de France 1981–1982)*, tr. G. Burchell. New York and London.

Foulon, A. 1987. "Sur un vers de Tibulle faussement attribué à Ovide," *Bulletin de la faculté des Lettres de Mulhouse* 15: 113–8.

Fournier, M. 2009. "Seneca on Platonic *Apatheia*," *Classica et Mediaevalia* 60: 211–36.

Fowler, D. P. 1987. "Virgil on Killing Virgins," in M. Whitby, P. R. Hardie, and M. Whitby, eds., Homo Viator, *Classical Essays for John Bramble*, 185–98. Bristol.

Frede, M. 2011. *A Free Will: Origins of the Notion in Ancient Thought*. Berkeley.

Fredouille, J. C. 1991. "*Seneca saepe noster*," in R. Chevallier, and R. Poignault, eds., *Présence de Sénèque*, 127–42. Paris.

Freise, H. 1989. "Die Bedeutung der Epikur-Zitate in den Schriften Senecas," *Gymnasium* 96: 532–56.

Freudenburg, K. 2013. "The Afterlife of Varro in Horace's *Sermones*. Generic Issues in Roman Satire," in T. D. Papanghelis, S. J. Harrison, and S. Frangoulidis, eds., *Generic Interfaces in Latin Literature: Encounters, Interactions and Transformations*, 301–40. Berlin.

Friedländer, L., ed. 1921–3. *Dellungen aus der Sittengeschichte Roms* (9th and 10th edns). Leipzig.

Friedrich, H. 1991. *Montaigne*, tr. D. Eng, Berkeley. Original edition Berne, 1949.

Friedrich, W. H. 1967. "Medeas Rache," in *Vorbild und Neugestaltung. Sechs Kapitel zur Geschichte der Tragödie*, 7–54. Göttingen.

Frings, I. 1992. Odia fraterna *als manieristisches Motiv – Betrachtungen zu Senecas* "Thyest" *und Statius* "Thebais." Mainz and Stuttgart.

Furley, D. J. 1966. "Lucretius and the Stoics," *Bulletin of the Institute of Classical Studies* 13: 13–33. Reprinted in *Cosmic Problems: Essays on Greek and Roman Philosophy of Nature*, 183–205. Cambridge, 1989.

Fürst, A., T. Fuhrer, F. Siegert, and P. Walter, eds. 2006. *Der apokryphe Briefwechsel zwischen Seneca und Paulus: zusammen mit dem Brief des Mordechai an Alexander und dem Brief des Seneca über Hochmut und Götterbilder*. Sapere vol. 11. Tübingen.

Gagliardi, D. 1998. *Il tempo in Seneca filosofo*. Naples.

Gale, M. 1994. *Myth and Poetry in Lucretius*. Cambridge.

Gasti, F. 1993. "La 'Passione' di Ippolito: Seneca e Prudenzio," *Quaderni di cultura e di tradizione classica* 11: 215–29.

Gauly, B. M. 2004. Senecas *Naturales Quaestiones. Naturphilosophie für die römische Kaiserzeit*. Munich.

2012. "*Aliquid veritati et posteri conferant*. Seneca und die Kometentheorie der frühen Neuzeit," in M. Beretta, F. Citti, and L. Pasetti, eds., *Seneca e le scienze naturali*, 143–59. Florence.

Gerald of Wales. 2000. *The Topography of Ireland*, tr. Thomas Forester. Cambridge, Ont.

Gercke, A., ed. 1907. *L. Annaei Senecae Naturalium Quaestionum libros octo*. Leipzig.

Gill, C. 1988. "Personhood and Personality: The Four-*Personae* Theory in Cicero *De Officiis* 1," *Oxford Studies in Ancient Philosophy* 6: 169–99.

2006. *The Structured Self in Hellenistic and Roman Thought*. Oxford.

2009. "Seneca and Selfhood: Integration and Disintegration," in S. Bartsch and D. Wray, eds., *Seneca and the Self*, 65–83. Cambridge.

Goffman, E. 1969. *Strategic Interaction*. Philadelphia.

Goldberg, S. 1996. "The Fall and Rise of Roman Tragedy," *Transactions of the American Philological Association* 126: 265–86.

Goldschmidt, V. 1969. *Le Système Stoïcien et l'Idée de Temps*. Paris.

Gottschalk, H. B. 1982. "Diatribe Again," *Liverpool Classical Monthly* 7.6: 91–2.

1983. "More on ΔΙΑΤΡΙΒΑΙ," *Liverpool Classical Monthly* 8.6: 91–2.

Gowers, E. 1994. "Persius and the Decoction of Nero," in J. Elsner and J. Masters, eds., *Reflections of Nero*, 131–50. London.

Gowing, A. 2005. *Empire and Memory: The Representation of the Roman Republic in Imperial Culture*. Cambridge.

Graf, F. 2005. "Satire in a Ritual Context," in K. Freudenburg, ed., *The Cambridge Companion to Roman Satire*, 192–206. Cambridge.

Gratwick, A. S. 1982. "The Satires of Ennius and Lucilius," in E. J. Kenney and W. V. Clausen, eds., *The Cambridge History of Classical Literature vol. II, part I, The Early Republic*, 156–71. Cambridge.

Graver, M. 1998. "The Manhandling of Maecenas: Senecan Abstractions of Masculinity," *American Journal of Philology* 119: 607–32.

2007. *Stoicism and Emotion*. Chicago and London.

Greenblatt, S. 1980. *Renaissance Self-Fashioning: From More to Shakespeare*. Chicago.

Griffin, M. T. 1974. "*Imago Vitae Suae*," in C. D. N. Costa, ed., *Seneca*, 1–38. London. Reprinted in J. G. Fitch, ed., *Seneca* (Oxford Readings in Classical Studies), 23–58. Oxford.

1976. *Seneca: A Philosopher in Politics*. Oxford. Reprinted with postscript, 1992.

1984. *Nero: The End of a Dynasty*. New Haven.

1996. "When Is Thought Political?" *Apeiron* 29: 269–82.

2000. "Seneca and Pliny," in C. J. Rowe and M. Schofield, eds., *The Cambridge History of Greek and Roman Thought*, 532–58. Cambridge.

2002. "Political Thought in the Age of Nero," in J.-M. Croiselle and Y. Perrin, eds., *Neronia VI: Rome à l'époque néronienne*, 325–37. Brussels.

2003. "Clementia after Caesar: From Politics to Philosophy," in F. Cairns and E. Fantham, eds., *Caesar against Liberty? Perspectives on His Autocracy*, 157–82. Cambridge.

2013. *Seneca on Society: A Guide to De Beneficiis*. Oxford.

Griffith, M. ed., 1999. *Sophocles: Antigone*. Cambridge.

Grimal, P. 1970. "Nature et limites de l'éclectisme philosophique chez Sénèque," *Les Études Classiques* 38: 3–17.

1978. *Sénèque, ou la conscience de l'empire*. Paris.

1986. "La composition dans les 'dialogues' de Sénèque," in *Rome, la littérature et l'histoire*, 515–49. Rome.

ed., 1991. *Sénèque et la prose latine* (Entretiens Hardt 36). Vandœuvres-Geneva.

Gross, N. 1989. *Senecas Naturales Quaestiones. Komposition, Naturphilosphische Aussagen und ihre Quellen*. Wiesbaden.

Grotius, H. 2005. *The Rights of War and Peace*, vol. I., ed. R. Tuck. Indianapolis.

2006. *Commentary on the Law of Prize and Booty*, ed. M. J. van Ittersum. Indianapolis.

Grund, G. R., ed., tr. 2011. *Humanist Tragedies*. Cambridge, Mass.

Gualandri, I., and G. Mazzoli, eds. 2003. *Gli Annei. Una famiglia nella storia e nella cultura di Roma imperiale*. Como.

Guidorizzi, G., and S. Beta. eds. 2000. *La Metafora*. Pisa.

Gunderson, E. 1996. "The Ideology of the Arena," *Classical Antiquity* 15.1: 113–51.

Gummere, R. M. 1910. *Seneca the Philosopher and His Modern Message*. Boston.

Habinek, T. 2000. "Senecan's Renown: '*Gloria*,' '*Claritudo*' and the Replication of the Roman Elite," *Classical Antiquity* 19: 264–303.

Hachmann, E. 1995. *Die Führung des Lesers in Senecas Epistulae morales*. Münster.

Hadot, I. 1968. "Épicure et l'enseignement philosophique hellénistique et romain," in *Actes du VIII Congrès de l'Association G. Budé*, 347–53. Paris.

 1969. *Seneca und die griechisch-römische Tradition der Seelenleitung*. Berlin.

Hadot, P. 1995. *Philosophy as a Way of Life: Spiritual Exercises from Socrates to Foucault*, ed. Arnold Davidson, tr. M. Chase. Oxford.

 2002. *What Is Ancient Philosophy?*, tr. M. Chase. Cambridge, Mass.

Hahm, D. E. 2000. "Kingship and Constitutions: Hellenistic Theories," in C. J. Rowe and M. Schofield, eds., *The Cambridge History of Greek and Roman Political Thought*, 457–76. Cambridge.

Hardie, P. R. 1986. *Virgil's Aeneid: Cosmos and Imperium*. Oxford.

 1992. "Augustan Poets and the *Mutability of Rome*," in A. Powell, ed., *Roman Poetry and Propaganda in the Age of Augustus*, 59–82. London.

 1993. *The Epic Successors of Virgil: A Study in the Dynamics of a Tradition*. Cambridge.

 1995. "The Speech of Pythagoras in Ovid *Metamorphoses* 15: Empedoclean Epos," *Classical Quarterly* 45: 204–14.

 2002. *Ovid's Poetics of Illusion*. Cambridge.

Harris, W. V. 2001. *Restraining Rage: The Ideology of Anger Control in Classical Antiquity*. Cambridge.

Harrison, G. W. M., ed. 2000. *Seneca in Performance*. London.

Harrison, S. J. 2009. "Some Modern Versions of Senecan Tragedy," *Trends in Classics* 1: 148–70.

Haß, K. 2007. *Lucilius und der Beginn der Persönlichkeitsdichtung in Rom*. Stuttgart.

Hay, C. H. 1938. *Montaigne lecteur et imitateur de Sénèque*. Poitiers.

Henderson, C. 1955. "Cato's Pine Cones and Seneca's Plums: Fronto p. 149 vdH," *Transactions of the American Philological Association* 86: 256–67.

Henderson, John. 2004. *Morals and Villas in Seneca's Letters*. Cambridge.

 2006. "Journey of a Lifetime: Seneca, *Epistle* 57 in Book VI in *EM*," in K. Volk and G. D. Williams, eds., *Seeing Seneca Whole*, 123–45. Leiden.

Henke, R. 1985. "Die Nutzung von Senecas Tragoedien im Romanus-Hymnus des Prudentius," *Würzburger Jahrbücher für die Altertumswissenschaft* 11: 135–50.

Herington, C. J. 1966. "Senecan Tragedy," *Arion* 5: 422–71.

Hermann, Leo. 1979. *Sénèque et les premiers chrétiens*. Collection Latomus 167. Brussels.

Hess, G. 2009. *Der Tod des Seneca. Studien zur Kunst der Imagination in Texten und Bildern des 17. und 18. Jahrhunderts*. Rome.

Hijmans, B. L. 1966. "Drama in Seneca's Stoicism," *Transactions of the American Philological Association* 97: 237–51.

Hill, T. 2004. *Ambitiosa Mors: Suicide and Self in Roman Thought and Literature.* New York and London.

Hinds, S. 1999. "After Exile: Time and Teleology from *Metamorphoses* to *Ibis*," in Ph. Hardie, A. Barchiesi, and S. Hinds, eds., *Ovidian Transformations: Essays on Ovid's Metamorphoses and Its Reception,* 48–67. Cambridge.

2004. "Petrarch, Cicero, Virgil: Virtual Commentary in Familiares 24.4," *Materiali e Discussioni* 52: 157–75.

2011. "Seneca's Ovidian *Loci*," *Studi Italiani di Filologia Classica* 9: 5–63.

H. M. 1980. "The Manuscript Tradition of Seneca's *Natural Questions*," *Classical Quarterly* 30: 183–217.

1981. *An Edition with Commentary of Seneca's Natural Questions, Book Two.* New York.

1983. "The Younger Seneca: *Natural Questions*," in L. M. Reynolds, ed., *Texts and Transmission. A Survey of the Latin Classics,* 377–78. Oxford.

1984. "The Date of the Campanian Earthquake: A.D. 62 or A.D. 63, or both?" *Antiquité Classique* 53: 266–69.

1992. "The Manuscript Tradition of Seneca's *Natural Questions*: Addenda," *Classical Quarterly* 42: 558–62.

ed. 1996. *L. Annaei Senecae Naturalium Quaestionum libros.* Stutgardiae et Lipsiae.

2004. "*Interpretatio Stoica* of Senecan Tragedy," in M. Billerbeck and E. A. Schmidt, eds., Sénèque le tragique, Vandoeuvres-Geneva. 173–220.

2005. "Poetic Influence on Prose: The Case of the Younger Seneca," in T. Reinhardt, M. Lapidge, and J. N. Adams, eds., *Aspects of the Language of Latin Prose. Proceedings of the British Academy* 129: 211–37. Oxford.

2006. "Rome, the Cosmos and the Emperor in Seneca's *Natural Questions*," *Journal of Roman Studies* 96: 42–72.

2009. "Seneca's *Naturales Quaestiones* 1960–2005 (Part 1)," *Lustrum* 51: 253–329.

2010a. "Seneca's *Naturales Quaestiones* 1960–2005 (Part 2), with *Addenda* covering 2006," *Lustrum* 52: 7–160.

2010b. *Lucius Annaeus Seneca: Natural Questions.* Chicago and London.

2012. "Originality and Independence in Seneca, *Natural Questions* Book 2," in M. Beretta, F. Citti, and L. Pasetti, eds. *Seneca e le scienze naturali,* 31–47. Florence.

Hirai H. 2012. "Seneca's *Naturales Quaestiones* in Justus Lipsius' *Physiologia Stoicorum*: The World-Soul, Providence and Eschatology," in M. Beretta, F. Citti, and L. Pasetti, eds. *Seneca e le scienze naturali,* 119–42. Florence.

Horstkotte, H. 1985. "Die politische Zielsetzung von Senecas *Apocolocyntosis*," *Athenaeum* n.s. 63: 337–58.

Hoyos, D. 1991. "Gourd God! The Meaning of *Apocolocyntosis*," *Liverpool Classical Monthly* 16: 68–70.

Hunter, R. 2006. *The Shadow of Callimachus. Studies in the Reception of Hellenistic Poetry at Rome.* Cambridge.

Innocenti, P. 1972. "Per una storia dell'epicureismo nei primi secoli dell'era volgare: temi e problemi," *Rivista critica di storia della filosofia* 27: 123–47.

Inwood, B. 1985. *Ethics and Human Action in Early Stoicism.* Oxford.

1991. "Review of T. Rosenmeyer, *Senecan Drama and Stoic Cosmology*," *Classical Philology* 86: 248–52.

1995. "Seneca in His Philosophical Milieu," *Harvard Studies in Classical Philology* 97: 63–76.

1999a. "Rules and Reasoning in Stoic Ethics," in K. Ierodiakonou, ed., *Topics in Stoic Philosophy*, 95–127. Oxford.

1999b. "God and Human Knowledge in Seneca's *Natural Questions*," *Boston Area Colloquium in Classical Philosophy* 15: 23–43.

ed. 2003. *The Cambridge Companion to the Stoics*. Cambridge.

2005. *Reading Seneca: Stoic Philosophy at Rome*. Oxford.

2007a. "The Importance of Form in Seneca's Philosophical Letters," in R. Morello and A. D. Morrison, eds., *Ancient Letters: Classical and Late Antique Epistolography*, 133–48. Oxford.

2007b. "Moral Causes: The Role of Physical Explanation in Ancient Ethics," in P. Machamer and G. Wolters, eds., *Thinking about Causes: From Greek Philosophy to Modern Physics*, 14–36. Pittsburgh.

ed., 2007c. *Seneca: Selected Philosophical Letters*. Oxford.

2009a. "Why Physics?" in R. Salles, ed., *God and Cosmos in Stoicism*, 201–23. Oxford.

2009b. "Seneca and Self Assertion," in S. Bartsch and D. Wray, eds., *Seneca and the Self*, 39–64. Cambridge.

Jal, P. 1957. "Images d'Auguste chez Sénèque," *Revue des études latines* 37: 242–64.

Jocelyn, H. D. 1982. "Diatribes and Sermons," *Liverpool Classical Monthly* 7.1: 3–7.

1983. "'Diatribe' and the Greek Book-Title Διατριβαί," *Liverpool Classical Monthly* 8.6: 89–91.

John of Salisbury. 1990. *Policraticus*, ed. and tr. Cary J. Nederman. Cambridge.

Kamtekar, R. 1998. "*Aidôs* in Epictetus," *Classical Philology* 93: 136–60.

Kantorowicz, E. 1957. *The King's Two Bodies*. Princeton.

Kaster, R. 2002. "The Taxonomy of Patience, or When Is *Patientia* Not a Virtue?" *Classical Philology* 97: 133–44.

2005. *Emotion, Restraint, and Community in Ancient Rome*. London and New York.

2010. "Translator's Introduction," in R. Kaster and M. Nussbaum, eds., *Lucius Annaeus Seneca: Anger, Mercy, Revenge*, 133–45. Chicago.

Kennedy, D. F. 1993. *The Arts of Love: Five Studies in the Discourse of Roman Love Elegy*. Cambridge.

Kennedy, G. A. 1972. *The Art of Rhetoric in the Roman World 300 B.C.–A.D. 300*. Princeton.

Ker, J. 2004. "Nocturnal Writers in Imperial Rome: The Culture of *Lucubratio*," *Classical Philology* 99: 209–42.

2006. "Seneca, Man of Many Genres," in K. Volk and G. Williams, eds., *Seeing Seneca Whole*, 19–41. Leiden.

2009a. *The Deaths of Seneca*. Oxford.

2009b. "Outside and Inside: Senecan Strategies," in J. Dominik, J. Garthwaite, and P. A. Roche, eds., *Writing Politics in Imperial Rome*, 249–72. Leiden and Boston.

2009c. "Seneca on Self-Examination: Rereading *On Anger* 3.36," in S. Bartsch and D. Wray, eds., *Seneca and the Self*, 160–87. Cambridge.

King James VI and I. 1994. *Political Writings*, ed. Johann P. Sommerville. Cambridge.

Knuuttila, J. S. 2004. *Emotions in Ancient and Medieval Philosophy*. Oxford.

Koeler, G. D. 1819. "Disquisitio de Senecae Naturalibus Quaestionibus," in L. *Annaei Senecae Naturalium Quaestionum libri septem*, 217–59. Göttingen.

Kohn, T. D. 2012. *The Dramaturgy of Senecan Tragedy*. Ann Arbor.

Konstan, D. 1997. *Friendship in the Classical World*. Cambridge.

Korzeniewski, D. 1982. "Senecas Kunst der dramatischen Komposition in seiner *Apocolocyntosis*," *Mnemosyne* 35: 103–14.

Kraft, K. 1966. "Der politische Hintergrund von Senecas Apocolocyntosis," *Historia: Zeitschrift für alte Geschichte* 15.1: 96–122.

Kragelund, P. 1999. "Senecan Tragedy: Back on Stage?" *Classica et Mediaevalia* 50: 235–47.

Kraye, J. 1988. "Moral Philosophy," in Q. Skinner and E. Kessler, eds., *The Cambridge History of Renaissance Philosophy*, 303–86. Cambridge.

2001/2002. "Stoicism in the Renaissance from Petrarch to Justus Lipsius," *Grotiana* n.s. 22/23: 21–46.

2005. "The Humanist as Moral Philosopher: Marc-Antoine Muret's 1585 Edition of Seneca," in J. Kraye and R. Saaarin, eds., *Moral Philosophy on the Threshold of Modernity*, 307–30. Dordrecht.

2007. "Senecanismus," in G. Ueding, ed., *Historisches Wörterbuch der Rhetorik*, 826–41. Tübingen.

Krenkel, W., ed. 1970. *Lucilius, Satiren*, 2 vols. Brill. Leiden.

2002. *Marcus Terentius Varro Saturae Menippeae*, 4 vols. St. Katharinen.

Kuttner, A. 1999. "Hellenistic Images of Spectacle, from Alexander to Augustus," in B. Bergmann and C. Kondoleon, eds., *The Art of Ancient Spectacle*, 97–124. New Haven.

Laarmann, M. 2014. "Seneca the Philosor," in G. Damschen and A. Heil, eds., *Brill's Companion to Seneca*, 53–71. Leiden.

Lagrée, J. 1994. *Juste Lipse et la restauration du Stoïcisme*. Paris.

Lana, I. 1955. *Lucio Anneo Seneca*. Turin. Reprinted Bologna, 2010.

1991. "Le 'Lettere a Lucilio' nella letteratura epistolare," in P. Grimal, ed., *Sénèque et la prose latine*, 252–311 (with "Appendix" by M. Lana, 290–305). (Entretiens Hardt 36). Vandoeuvres-Geneva.

Lanzarone, N. ed. 2008. *L. Annaei Senecae Dialogorum Liber I: De Providentia*. Florence.

Lapidge, M. 1988. "The Stoic Inheritance," in P. Dronke, ed., *A History of Twelfth-Century Western Philosophy*, 81–112. Cambridge.

Lau, D. 2006. *Metapherntheorien des Antike und ihre philosophischen Prinzipien*. Frankfurt am Main, Berlin and Bern.

Laureys, M. 1991. "Quintilian's Judgement of Seneca and the Scope and Purpose of *Inst.*, 10, 1," *Antike und Abendland* 37: 100–25.

Lausberg, M. 1970. *Untersuchungen zu Senecas Fragmenten*. Berlin.

1989. "*Senecae Operum Fragmenta*: Überblick und Forschungsbericht," in W. Haase, ed., *Aufstieg und Niedergang der römischen Welt* II.36.3: 1879–1961. *Philosophie, Wissenschaften, Technik: Philosophie (Stoizismus)*. Berlin and New York.

Leach, E. W. 1989. "The Implied Reader and the Political Argument in Seneca's *Apocolocyntosis* and *De Clementia*," *Arethusa* 22: 197–230.

1993. "Absence and Desire in Cicero's *De amicitia*," *Classical World* 87: 3–20.

Lebek, W. D. 1985. "Senecas *Agamemnon* in Pompeji *CIL* IV 6698," *Zeitschrift für Papyrologie und Epigraphik* 59: 1–6.

Leeman, A. D. 1963. *Orationis Ratio: The Stylistic Theories and Practice of the Roman Orators, Historians and Philosophers*. 2 vols. Amsterdam.

Lefèvre, E 1969. "*Quid ratio possit?* Senecas *Phaedra* als Stoisches Drama," *Wiener Studien*, n.s. 3: 131–60.

ed. 1978. *Der Einfluß Senecas auf das europäische Drama*. Darmstadt.

2003. "Anneo Sereno e il dialogo *De tranquillitate animi* di Seneca," in I. Gualandri and G. Mazzoli, eds., *Gli Annei. Una famiglia nella storia e nella cultura di Roma imperiale*, 153–65. Como.

Leigh, M. 1996. "Varius Rufus, Thyestes and the Appetites of Antony," *Proceedings of the Cambridge Philological Society* 42: 171–97.

1997. *Lucan: Spectacle and Engagement*. Oxford.

Leo, F. 1878. *L. Annaei Senecae Tragoediae: Volume 1: Observationes Criticas Continens*. Cambridge.

Lethem, J. 2011. *The Ecstasy of Influence: Nonfictions, Etc.* Doubleday.

Letta, C. 1999. "Attualità e riflessione politica nelle ultime opere di Seneca: dalle Naturales Quaestiones alle *Lettere a Lucilio*," *Journal for the Promotion of Classical Studies, Seoul, Korea* 7: 93–139.

Lightfoot, J. B., ed. 1881. *The Epistles of St Paul: Philippians*. London.

Littlewood, C. 2004. *Self-Representation and Illusion in Senecan Tragedy*. Oxford and New York.

Lo Cicero, C. 1991. "*Omnium Stoicorum acutissimus*," in *Studi di filologia classica in onore di Giusto Monaco*, III, 1237–61. Palermo.

Lo Moro, F. 1976. "Seneca ed Epicuro: Memoria e Religione nel *De Beneficiis*," *Studi Urbinati* 50: 257–80.

Logan, G. M., R. M. Adams, and C. H. Miller, eds. 1995. *Thomas More, Utopia*. Cambridge.

Long, A., and D. Sedley. 1987. *The Hellenistic Philosophers*. Cambridge.

Long, A. A. 1988. "Socrates in Hellenistic Philosophy," *Classical Quarterly* 38: 150–71. Reprinted in Long 1996 in *Stoic Studies*, 1–34. Berkeley, 1996.

1991. "Representation and the Self in Stoicism," in S. Everson, ed., *Psychology: Companions to Ancient Thought II*, 102–20. Cambridge.

1996. *Stoic Studies*. Berkeley.

1999. "The Socratic Legacy," in K. Algra, J. Barnes, J. Mansfeld, and M. Schofield, eds., *The Cambridge History of Hellenistic Philosophy*, 617–41. Cambridge.

2002. *Epictetus: A Stoic and Socratic Guide to Life*. Oxford.

2003. "Stoicism in the Philosophical Tradition: Spinoza, Lipsius, Butler," in B. Inwood, ed., *The Cambridge Companion to the Stoics*, 365–92. Cambridge.

2009. "Seneca on the Self: Why Now?" in S. Bartsch and D. Wray, eds., *Seneca and the Self*, 20–36. Cambridge.

Lotito, G. 2001. *Suum esse. Forme dell'interiorità senecana*. Bologna.

Lowrie, M. 1997. *Horace's Narrative Odes*. Oxford.

Lucas, F. L. 1922. *Seneca and Elizabethan Tragedy*. Cambridge.

Lund, A., ed. 1994. *L. Annaeus Seneca Apocolocyntosis Divi Claudii*. Heidelberg.

Lyne, R. O. A. M. 1987. *Further Voices in Vergil's Aeneid*. Oxford.

Machiavelli, N. 1971. *Tutte le opere*, ed. Mario Martelli. Florence.

1988. *The Prince*, ed. and tr. R. Price and Q. Skinner. Cambridge.

Machielsen, J. 2014. "The Rise and Fall of Seneca Tragicus, c. 1365–1593," *The Journal of the Warburg and Courtauld Institutes* 77: 61–85.

Magnien, M. 2004. "Lipse, Juste," in P. Desan, ed., *Dictionnaire de Michel de Montaigne*, 595–6. Paris.

Maguiness, W. S. 1956. "Seneca and the Poets," *Hermathena* 88: 81–98.

Malaspina, E. ed. 2002. *L. Annaei Senecae De clementia libri duo*. Alessandria.

Manuwald, G. 2003. "The Concepts of Tyranny in Seneca's *Thyestes* and in *Octavia*," in M. Wilson, ed., *The Tragedy of Nero's Wife: Studies on the Octavia Praetexta*, 37–59. Auckland.

    2005. "Der Stoiker Seneca in Monteverdis *L'incoronazione di Poppea*," in Th. Baier, G. Manuwald, and B. Zimmermann, eds., *Seneca: philosophus et magister*, 149–85. Freiburg im Br.

    2009. "*Concilia deorum*: Ein episches Motiv in der römischen Satire," in F. Felgentreu, F. Mundt, and N. Rücker, eds., *Per attentam Caesaris aurem: Satire – die unpolitische Gattung?*, 46–61. Tübingen.

    2013. *Nero in Opera. Librettos as Transformations of Ancient Sources*. Berlin and Boston.

Mara, M. G. 2001. "L'epistolario apocrifo di Seneca e San Paolo," in A. P. Martina, ed. *Seneca e i Cristiani. Atti del Convegno Internazionale.*, 41–54. Milan.

Marchesi, C. 1994. *Seneca*. Milan-Messina (1st ed. 1934).

Marino, R. 1996. "Il secondo coro delle *Troades* e il destino dell'anima dopo la morte," in L. Castagna, ed., *Nove studi sui cori tragici di Seneca*, 57–73. Milan.

Markus, D., and G. Schwendner. 1997. "Seneca's *Medea* in Egypt 663–704," *Zeitschrift für Papyrologie und Epigraphik* 117: 73–80.

Martellotti, G. 1972. "La questione dei due Seneca da Petrarca a Benvenuto da Imola," *Italia medioevale e umanistica* 15: 149–69.

Marti, B. 1945. "Seneca's Tragedies: A New Interpretation," *Transactions of the American Philological Association* 76, 216–45.

Martina, A. P., ed. 2001. *Seneca e i Cristiani. Atti del Convegno Internazionale.* Milan.

Marx, F. 1904–1905. *C. Lucili Carminum Reliquiae*, 2 vols. Leipzig.

Maso, S. 1999. *Lo sguardo della verità: cinque studi su Seneca*. Padua.

Mastandrea, P. 1988. *Lettori cristiani di Seneca filosofo*. Brescia.

Mastronarde, D. J. 1970. "Seneca's *Oedipus*: The Drama in the Word," *Transactions of the American Philological Association* 101: 291–315. Reprinted in J. G. Fitch, ed. *Seneca (Oxford Readings in Classical Studies)*, 221–43. Oxford, 2008.

Maurach, G. 1970. *Der Bau von Senecas Epistulae morales*. Heidelberg.

Mayer, R. G. 1982. "Neronian Classicism," *American Journal of Philology* 103: 305–18.

    1990. "*Doctus* Seneca," *Mnemosyne* 43: 395–407.

    1991. "Roman Historical *exempla* in Seneca," in P. Grimal, ed. *Sénèque et la prose latine*, 141–69. Vandoeuvres-Geneva. Reprinted in J. G. Fitch, ed. *Seneca (Oxford Readings in Classical Studies)*, 299–315. Oxford, 2008.

    1994. "Personata Stoa: Neostoicism and Senecan Tragedy," *Journal of the Warburg and Courtauld Institutes* 57: 151–74.

    ed. 2001. *Tacitus: Dialogus de oratoribus*. Cambridge.

ed. 2002. *Seneca: Phaedra.* London.

Mazzoli, G. 1970. *Seneca e la poesia.* Milan.

1977. "Sul protrettico perduto di Seneca. Le *Exhortationes,*" *Memorie dell'Istituto Lombardo. Accademia di Scienze e Lettere. Classe di lettere, scienze morali e storiche* 36: 7–47.

1978. "Ricerche sulla tradizione medievale del 'De beneficiis' e del 'De Clementia' di Seneca, 1," *Bollettino dei classici* 26: 85–109.

1982. "Ricerche sulla tradizione medievale del 'De beneficiis' e del 'De Clementia' di Seneca, 3," *Bollettino dei classici* 3: 165–223.

1989. "Le *Epistulae morales ad Lucilium* di Seneca. Valore letterario e filosofico," *Aufstieg und Niedergang der Römischen Welt* II.36.3: 1823–77.

1990. "Seneca e il sublime," in T. Kemeny and E. Cotta Ramusino, *Dicibilità del sublime,* 89–97. Udine.

1991. "Seneca e la poesia," in P. Grimal, ed., *Sénèque et la prose latine* (Entretiens Hardt 36), 177–210. Vandoeuvres-Geneva.

1997. "Seneca, *Dialogi*: la 'forma' della crisi," in M. Rodríguez Pantoja, ed., *Séneca, dos mil años después,* 343–53. Córdoba.

2000. "Le 'voci' dei dialoghi di Seneca," in P. Parroni, ed., *Seneca e il suo tempo,* 249–60. Rome.

2003. "Seneca *de ira* e *de clementia*: la politica negli specchi della morale," in A. De Vivo and E. Lo Cascio, eds., *Seneca uomo politico e l'età di Claudio e di Nerone,* 123–38. Bari.

2005. "La retorica del destino: la *demonstratio diluvii* in Seneca, *Nat. Quaest.* III 27–30," *Pallas* 69: 167–78.

2006. "*SE-* in Seneca: il preverbio del distacco e della liberazione," in C. Santini, L. Zurli, and L. Cardinali, eds. *Concentus ex dissonis: Scritti in onore di Aldo Setaioli,* 457–67. Naples.

2008. "Paolo e Seneca: virtualità e aporie di un incontro," *Sandalion* 31: 49–64.

2010. "Boezio e Seneca: icone tragiche nei *metra* della *Consolatio philosophiae,*" in C. Burini De Lorenzi and M. De Gaetano, eds., *La poesia tardoantica e medioevale. IV Convegno internazionale di studi, Perugia, 15–17 novembre 2007,* 253–70. Alessandria

Meerseman, G. G. 1973. "Seneca maestro di spiritualita' nei suoi opuscoli apocrifi dal XII al XV secolo," *Italia medioevale e umanistica* 16: 43–135.

Megas, A. C. 1969. *Albertini Mussati argumenta tragoediarum Senecae; commentarii in L. A. Senecae tragoedias fragmenta nuper reperta.* Thessalonica.

Merchant, F. I. 1905. "Seneca the philosopher and his theory of style," *American Journal of Philology* 26: 44–59.

Meyer, M. 2006. "Einleitung," in *Zur Geschichte des Dialogs: philosophische Positionen von Sokrates bis Habermas,* 8–14. Darmstadt.

Mezzadroli, G. 1990. *Seneca in Dante.* Florence.

Miola, R. 1992. *Shakespeare and Classical Tragedy: The Influence of Seneca.* Oxford.

Momigliano, A. 1955. "Note sulla leggenda del Cristianesimo di Seneca," in *Contributo alla storia degli studi classici,* 13–32. Roma.

Monti, C. M. 2008. "La fortuna di Seneca nell'umanesimo italiano," in J. Solana Pujalte, ed. *La obra de Séneca y su pervivencia. Cinco estudios,* 107–32. Córdoba.

Moreau, P.-F., ed. 1999. *Le stoïcisme au XVIe et au XVIIe siècle*. Paris.
Morello, ed. 2007. *Seneca: Selected Philosophical Letters*. Oxford.
Moreschini, C. 2013. *Storia del pensiero cristiano tardo-antico*. Milano.
Morford, M. P. O. 1967. *The Poet Lucan: Studies in Rhetorical Epic*. Oxford.
  1973. "The Neronian Literary Revolution," *The Classical Journal* 68: 210–15.
  1991. *Stoics and Neostoics: Rubens and the Circle of Lipsius*. Princeton.
  2002. *The Roman Philosophers*. London.
Morgan, L. 1999. *Patterns of Redemption in Virgil's Georgics*. Cambridge.
  2003. "Child's Play: Ovid and His Critics," *Journal of Roman Studies* 93: 66–91.
Mortureux, B. 1989. "Les idéaux stoïciens et les premières responsabilités politiques: le 'De clementia'," *Aufstieg und Niedergang der Römischen Welt* vol. II.36.3: 1639–85.
Most, G. W. 1992. "*Disiecti membra poetae*: the rhetoric of dismemberment in Neronian poetry," in R. Hexter and D. Selden, eds., *Innovations of Antiquity*, 391–419. New York and London.
Motto, A. L. and J. R. Clark. 1968. "Paradoxum Senecae: The Epicurean Stoic," *Classical World* 62: 37–42
  1975. "*Ingenium facile et copiosum*: Point and Counterpoint in Senecan Style," *Classical Bulletin* 52: 1–4. Reprinted in *Essays on Seneca*, Frankfurt am Main and New York, 13–20. 1993.
  1987. "Time in Seneca: Past, Present, Future," *Emerita* 55: 31–41. Reprinted in *Essays on Seneca*, Frankfurt am Main and New York, 31–41. 1993.
Mouchel, C. 1990. *Cicéron et Sénèque dans la rhétorique de la Renaissance*. Marburg.
Mouchel, C., ed. 1996. *Juste Lipse 1547–1606 en son temps. Actes du colloque de Strasbourg, 1994*. Paris and Geneva.
Mowbray, C. 2012. "Captive Audience? The Aesthetics of *Nefas* in Senecan Drama," in I. Sluiter and R. Rosen, eds., *Aesthetic Value in Classical Antiquity*, 393–420. Leiden.
Müller, H. J., ed. 1887. *L. Annaei Senecae oratorum et rhetorum sententiae divisiones colores*. Vienna.
Munk Olsen, B. 2000. "Les florilèges et les abrégés de Sénèque au moyen age," *Giornale Italiano di Filologia* 52: 163–83.
Murray, O. 1965. "The 'Quinquennium Neronis' and the Stoics," *Historia* 14: 41–61.
  2007. "Philosophy and Monarchy in the Hellenistic world," in T. Rajak, S. Pearce, J. K. Aitken, and J. Dines, eds., *Jewish Perspectives on Hellenistic Rulers*. 13–28. Berkeley and London.
Mutschler, F. H. 1995. "*Dialogi* and *Epistulae*: Observations on Seneca's Development as a Philosophical Writer," *Journal of Ancient Civilizations* 10: 85–100.
Mutschmann, H. 1915. "Seneca und Epikur." *Hermes* 50: 321–56.
Nanni, F. and D. Pellacani. 2012. "Per una rassegna sulla fortuna delle *Naturales Quaestiones*," in M. F. Beretta, F. Citti, and L. Pasetti, eds. *Seneca e le scienze naturali*, 141–60. Florence.
Narducci, E. 2002. *Lucano: un'epica contro l'impero*. Roma-Bari.
Newman, R. J. 1989. "*Cotidie meditare*: Theory and Practice of the *meditatio* in Imperial Stoicism," *Aufstieg und Niedergang der Römischen Welt* II.36.3: 1473–517.
Nisard, D. 1834. *Études de mœurs et de critique sur les poètes latins de la décadence*, vol. 1. Brussels.

Nisbet, R. G. M. 1990. "The Dating of Seneca's Tragedies with Special Reference to *Thyestes,*" *Papers of the Leeds International Latin Seminar* 6: 95–114.

Niutta, F., and Santucci, C., eds. 1999. *Seneca: mostra bibliografica e iconografica.* Rome.

Norden, E. 1958. *Die antike Kunstprosa vom VI. Jahrhundert v. Chr. bis in die Zeit der Renaissance.* 2 vols. 3rd edn reprinted. Leipzig.

Nothdurft, K.-D. 1963. *Studien zum Einfluss Senecas auf die Philosophie und Theologie des zwölften Jahrhunderts.* Leiden and Cologne.

Nussbaum, M. 1993. "Poetry and the Passions: Two Stoic Views," in J. Brunschwig, J., and M. Nussbaum, eds., *Passions and Perceptions: Studies in Hellenistic Philosophy of the Mind,* 97–149. Cambridge.

1994. *The Therapy of Desire: Theory and Practice in Hellenistic Ethics.* Princeton.

1995. "Eros and the Wise: The Stoic Response to a Cultural Dilemma," *Oxford Studies in Ancient Philosophy* 13: 231–67.

2004. *Hiding from Humanity: Disgust, Shame, and the Law.* Princeton and Oxford.

O'Gorman, E. 2005. "Citation and Authority in Seneca's *Apocolocyntosis,*" in K. Freudenburg, ed., *The Cambridge Companion to Roman Satire,* 95–108. Cambridge.

Oltramare, André. 1926. *Les origines de la diatribe romaine.* Lausanne.

Osgood, J. 2007. "The Vox and Verba of an Emperor: Claudius, Seneca and Le Prince Ideal," *CJ* 102: 329–53.

2011. *Claudius Caesar: Image and Power in the Early Roman Empire.* Cambridge.

Paduano, G. 2008. *Edipo. Storia di un mito.* Rome.

Panizza, L. A. 1976. "The St. Paul–Seneca Correspondence: Its Significance for Stoic Thought from Petrarch to Erasmus," Ph.D. diss. University of London.

1977. "Gasparino Barzizza's Commentaries on Seneca's Letters," *Traditio* 33: 297–358.

1983. "Textual Interpretation in Italy, 1350–1450: Seneca's Letter I to Lucilius," *Journal of the Warburg and Courtauld Institutes* 46: 40–62.

1984. "Biography in Italy from the Middle Ages to the Renaissance: Seneca, Pagan or Christian?" *Nouvelles de la Republique des Lettres* 2: 47–98.

1987. "Erasmus' 1515 and 1529 Editions of Seneca, and Gasparino Barzizza," *Classical and Modern literature* 7: 319–32.

1991. "Stoic Psychotherapy in the Middle Ages and Renaissance: Petrarch's *De remediis,*" in Margaret J. Osler, ed., *Atoms, Pneuma and Tranquillity,* 39–65. Cambridge.

Papy, J. 1999. "Lipsius and His Dogs: Humanist Tradition, Iconography and Rubens's *Four Philosophers,*" *Journal of the Warburg and Courtauld Institutes* 62: 167–98.

2002. "Erasmus's and Lipsius's Editions of Seneca: A 'Complementary Project'?" *Erasmus of Rotterdam Society Yearbook* 22: 10–36.

Paratore, E. 2011. *Seneca tragico. Senso e ricezione di un teatro,* eds., C. Questa and A. Torino. Urbino.

Parker, H. N. 1999. "The Observed of All Observers: Spectacle Applause and Cultural Poetics in the Roman Theater Audience," in B. Bergmann and C. Kondoleon, eds., *The Art of Ancient Spectacle,* 163–80. New Haven.

Parrish, J. M. 1997. "A New Source for More's 'Utopia,'" *The Historical Journal* 40.2: 493–98.

Parroni, P., ed. 2000. *Seneca e il suo tempo*. Rome.

ed., 2002. Seneca, *Ricerche sulla natura*. Milan.

2012. "Il linguaggio 'drammatico' di Seneca scienziato," in M. F. Beretta, F. Citti, and L. Pasetti, eds., *Seneca e le scienze naturali*, 19–29. Florence.

Pellacani, D. 2012. "Le piene del Nilo. Nota bibliografica," in M. Beretta, F. Citti, and L. Pasetti, eds., *Seneca e le scienze naturali*, 81–92. Florence.

Perelli, L. 1994. "Seneca e Heidegger," *Bollettino di Studi Latini* 24: 45–61.

Peterson, W. 1891. ed., *M. Fabi Quintiliani Institutionis Oratoriae liber decimus*. Oxford.

Petrarca, F. 1978. *Epistole*, ed. Ugo Dotti. Turin.

Petrarcha [*sic*], F. 1975. *De remediis utriusque fortunae*, eds. Rudolf Schottlaender and Eckhard Kessler. Munich.

Phillips, M. M. 1970. "Erasmus and the Classics," in T. A. Dorey, ed., *Erasmus*, 1–30. London.

Pizan, C. de. 1994. *The Book of the Body Politic*, ed. K. Langdom Forhan. Cambridge.

Pohlenz, M. 1941. "Philosophie und Erlebnis in Senecas Dialogen," *Nachrichten von der Akademie der Wissenschaften in Göttingen, philol.-hist. Kl.* 6: 55–118. Reprinted in *Kleine Schriften*, Hildesheim, 1965, vol. I, 384–447.

1948. *Die Stoa*. Göttingen.

Powell, J. G. F., ed. 1988. *Cicero: Cato Maior De Senectute*. Cambridge.

Pratt, N. 1983. *Seneca's Drama*. Chapel Hill and London.

Puchner, M. 2005. *Poetry of the Revolution: Marx, Manifestos, and the Avant-Gardes*. Princeton.

Purcell, N. 1999. "Does Caesar Mime?" in B. Bergmann and C. Kondoleon, eds., The Art of Ancient Spectacle, 181–94. New Haven.

Pusch, Anna Maria. 1942. *Der dialogische Charakter von Senecas Dialogi*. Diss. Vienna.

Putnam, M. C. J. 1995. *Virgil's Aeneid: Interpretation and Influence*. Chapel Hill.

Questa, C. 1999. "Il modello senecano nel teatro gesuitico," *Musica e storia* 7: 141–81.

Quinn, K. 1979. *Texts and Contexts. The Roman Writers and Their Audience*. London, Boston, and Henley.

Quint, D. 1993. *Epic and Empire: Politics and Generic Form from Virgil to Milton*. Princeton.

Rabbow, P. 1954. *Seelenführung. Methodik der Exerzitien in der Antike*. Munich.

Reed, J. D. 2007. *Virgil's Gaze: Nation and Poetry in the Aeneid*. Princeton.

Reeve, M. D. 1984. "Apotheosis ... per saturam," *Classical Philology* 79: 305–7.

Regenbogen, O. 1927–8. "Schmerz und Tod in den Tragödien Seneca," *Vorträge der Bibliothek Warburg* 7: 176–218.

Relihan, J. 1993. *Ancient Menippean Satire*. Baltimore.

Reydams-Schils, G. 2005. *The Roman Stoics: Self, Responsibility, and Affection*. Chicago.

Reynolds, L. D. 1965. *The Medieval Tradition of Seneca's Letters*. Oxford.

ed. 1977. *L. Annaei Seneca dialogorum libri duodecim*. Oxford.

ed. 1983. *Texts and Transmission: A Survey of the Latin Classics*. Oxford.

Richardson-Hay, C. 2006. *First Lessons: Book 1 of Seneca's Epistulae Morales – A Commentary*. Bern.

Rimell, V. 2013. "The Best a Man Can Get: Grooming Scipio in Seneca Epistle 86," *Classical Philology* 108: 1–20.

Rist, J. M. 1989. "Seneca and Stoic Orthodoxy," *Aufstieg und Niedergang der Römischen Welt* II.36.3: 1993–2012.

Robinson, P. J. 2005. "In the Court of Time: The Reckoning of a Monster in the *Apocolocyntosis* of Seneca," *Arethusa* 38: 223–57.

Rodríguez Pantoja M., ed. 1997. *Séneca, dos mil años después*. Córdoba.

Roller, M. 2001. *Constructing Autocracy: Aristocrats and Emperors in Julio-Claudian Rome*. Princeton.

Roncali, R., ed. 1990. *L. Annaei Senecae Diui Claudii ΑΠΟΚΟΛΟΚΥΝΤΩΣΙΣ*. Leipzig.

Roncali, R. 2008. "Seneca, Apocolocyntosis 1980–2000," *Lustrum* 50: 303–66.

Rorty, A. 1981. *Essays on Aristotle's Ethics*. Berkeley.

Rosand, E. 1985. "Seneca and the Interpretation of *L'incoronazione di Poppea*," *Journal of the American Musicological Society* 38: 34–71.

Rosati, G. 1981. "Seneca sulla lettera filosofica. Un genere letterario sul cammino verso la saggezza," *Maia* 33: 3–15.

Rose, K. F. C. 1971. *The Date and Author of the Satyricon*. With an Introduction by J. P. Sullivan. Leiden.

Roskam, G. 2007. *Lathe Biōsas: On the Vicissitudes of an Epicurean Idea*. Leiden.

Rosenmeyer, Thomas G. 1989. *Senecan Drama and Stoic Cosmology*. Berkeley and Los Angeles.

Ross, G. M. 1974. "Seneca's Philosophical Influence," in C. D. N. Costa, ed., *Seneca*, 116–65. London.

1984. "Stoicism in Medieval Thought (review of Verbeke 1983)," *Classical Review* 34: 224–6.

Rossi, P. 2012. "Le piene del Nilo nelle *Naturales Quaestiones* di Seneca," in M. F. Beretta, F. Citti, and L. Pasetti, eds., *Seneca e le scienze naturali*, 69–80. Florence.

Rowe, C. J. 2000. "Introduction," in C. J. Rowe and M. Schofield, eds., *The Cambridge History of Greek and Roman Political Thought*, 1–6. Cambridge.

Rudd, Niall. 1990. *Horace: Epistles Book II and Ars Poetica*. Cambridge.

Rudich, V. 1997. *Dissidence and Literature under Nero*. New York.

Russell, D. A., and M. Winterbottom, eds. 1972. *Ancient Literary Criticism*. Oxford.

Russell, D. C. 2004. "Virtue as 'Likeness to God' in Plato and Seneca," *Journal of the History of Philosophy* 42: 241–60.

Russo, C. F., ed. 1965 *L. Annaei Senecae Diui Claudii ΑΠΟΚΟΛΟΚΥΝΤΩΣΙΣ*. Florence.

Russo, E. 2009. "Slander and Glory in the Republic of Letters: Diderot and Seneca Confront Rousseau," *Republics of Letters: A Journal for the Study of Knowledge, Politics, and the Arts* 1.1: http://rofl.stanford.edu/node/40.

Rutherford, D. 2004 "On the Happy Life: Descartes vis-à-vis Seneca," in S. K. Strange and J. Zupko, eds., *Stoicism. Traditions and Transformations*, 177–97. Cambridge.

Rutherford, R. B. 1995. *The Art of Plato*. Cambridge, Mass.

Salmon, J. H. M. 1991. "Seneca and Tacitus in Jacobean England," in L. Levy Peck, ed., *The Mental World of the Jacobean Court*, 169–88. Cambridge.

Santini, C., Zurli, L. and Cardinali, L. eds., *Concentus ex dissonis: scritti in onore di Aldo Setaioli*. Naples.

Santoro L'Hoir, F. 2006. *Tragedy, Rhetoric and the Historiography of Tacitus' Annales*. Ann Arbor.

Schafer, J. 2009. *Ars Didactica: Seneca's 94th and 95th Letters*. Göttingen.

    2011. "Seneca's *Epistulae Morales* as Dramatized Education," *Classical Philology* 106: 32–52.

Schiesaro, A. 2003. *The Passions in Play: Thyestes and the Dynamics of Senecan Drama*. Cambridge and New York.

    2009. "Seneca and the Denial of Self," in S. Bartsch and D. Wray, eds. *Seneca and the Self*, 221–36. Cambridge.

Schlegel, A. W. 1846. *A Course of Lectures on Dramatic Art and Literature*. London.

Schmal, S. 2008. "Held oder Harlequin? Der sterbende Seneca bei Tacitus," *Klio* 90: 105–23.

Schmeling, G. 2011. *A Commentary on the Satyrica of Petronius*. With the collaboration of A. Setaioli. Oxford.

Schmidt, E. G. 1961. "Die Anordnung der Dialoge Senecas," *Helikon* 1: 245–63.

Schofield, M. 1991. *The Stoic Idea of the City*. Cambridge. 2nd ed. Chicago 1999.

    1999. "Social and Political Thought," in K. Algra, J. Barnes, J. Mansfeld, and M. Schofield, eds., *The Cambridge History of Hellenistic Philosophy*, 739–70. Cambridge.

    2008. "Ciceronian dialogue," in S. Goldhill, ed., *The End of Dialogue in Antiquity*, 63–84. Cambridge.

    2009. "Republican Virtues," in R. K. Balot, ed., *A Companion to Greek and Roman Political Thought*, 199–213. Oxford.

Schottlaender, R. 1955. "Epikureisches bei Seneca: Ein Ringen um den Sinn von Freude und Freundschaft," *Philologus* 99: 113–48.

Schubert, W. 2004. "Seneca in der Musik der Neuzeit," in M. Billerbeck and E. A. Schmidt, eds., *Sénèque le tragique* (Entretiens Hardt 50), 369–412. Vandoeuvres-Geneva.

    2014. "Seneca the Tragedian," in G. Damschen and A. Heil, eds., *Brill's Companion to Seneca*, 75–82. Leiden.

Sedgwick, E., and A. Frank, eds. 1995. *Shame and Its Sisters: A Silvan Tomkins Reader*. Durham.

Segal, C. 2001. "Intertextuality and Immortality: Ovid, Pythagoras and Lucretius in *Metamorphoses* 15," *Materiali e Discussioni* 46: 63–101.

Sellars, J. 2003. *The Art of Living: The Stoics on the Nature and Function of Philosophy*, 2nd ed. London.

Seneca, L. A. 1554. *De' benefizii, tradotto in uolgar fiorentino da B. Varchi*. Florence.

Seo, J. M. 2013. *Exemplary Traits. Reading Characterization in Roman Poetry*. Oxford.

Setaioli, A. 1965. "Esegesi virgiliana in Seneca," *Studi Italiani di Filologia Classica* 37: 133–56.

    1980. "Elementi di *sermo cotidianus* nella lingua di Seneca prosatore, I," *Studi Italiani di Filologia Classica* 52: 5–47. Reprinted, with Setaioli 1981, in *Facundus Seneca. Aspetti della lingua e dell'ideologia senecana*, 9–95. Bologna, 2000.

1981. "Elementi di *sermo cotidianus* nella lingua di Seneca prosatore, II," *Studi Italiani di Filologia Classica* 53: 5–49. Reprinted, with Setaioli 1980, in *Facundus Seneca. Aspetti della lingua e dell'ideologia senecana*, 9–95. Bologna, 2000.

1985. "Seneca e lo stile," *Aufstieg und Niedergang der Römischen Welt* II.32.2: 776–858. Reprinted in *Facundus Seneca. Aspetti della lingua e dell'ideologia senecana*, 111–217. Bologna, 2000.

1988. *Seneca e i Greci. Citazioni e traduzioni nelle opere filosofiche.* Bologna.

2000. *Facundus Seneca. Aspetti della lingua e dell'ideologia senecana.* Bologna.

2011. Arbitri Nugae. *Petronius' Short Poems in the Satyrica.* Frankfurt am M. and Berlin.

Shelton, J. A. 1995. "Persuasion and Paradigm in Seneca's *Consolatio ad Marciam* 1–6," *Classica and Mediaevalia* 46: 157–88.

Shklar, J. N. 1990. "Montesquieu and the new republicanism," in Gisela Bock *et al.*, eds., *Machiavelli and Republicanism*, 265–79. Cambridge.

Shumate, N. 1997. "Compulsory Pretense and the 'Theatricalization of Experience' in Tacitus," in C. Deroux, ed., *Studies in Latin Literature and Roman History VIII*, 364–403. Brussels.

Sierhuis, F. 2013. "Autonomy and Inner Freedom: Lipsius and Stoicism," in Q. Skinner and M. van Geldern, eds., *Freedom and the Construction of Europe*, vol. II, 46–54. Cambridge.

Sihvola, Juha, and Troels Engberg-Pedersen. 1998. *The Emotions in Hellenistic Philosophy.* Dortrecht.

Simone, F. 1968. *Umanesimo, Rinascimento, Barocco in Francia.* Milan.

Skinner, Q. 1981. *Machiavelli.* Oxford.

2002. *Visions of Politics*, vol. I. Cambridge.

Skutsch, O. 1985. *The Annales of Q. Ennius.* Oxford.

Smiley, C. N. 1919. "Seneca and the Stoic Theory of Literary Style," *Wisconsin University Studies in Language and Literature* 3: 50–61.

Smiraglia, P. 2000. "Presenza di Seneca nella cultura del XII secolo," in A. P. Martina, ed., *Seneca e i Cristiani. Atti del Convegno Internazionale*, 265–81. Milan.

Smith, C. S. 1910. *Metaphor and Comparison in the Epistulae Ad Lucilium of L. Annaeus Seneca.* Berkeley and Los Angeles.

Smith, S. M., ed. 1975. *Petronii Cena Trimalchionis.* Oxford.

Soen, V. 2011. "The *Clementia Lipsiana*: Political Analysis, Autobiography and Panegyric," in E. de Bom et al., eds., *(Un)Masking the Realities of Power. Justus Lipsius and the Dynamics of Political Writing in Early Modern Europe*, 207–31. Leiden.

Sorabji, R. 2000. *Emotion and Peace of Mind: From Stoic Agitation to Christian Temptation.* Oxford.

Sørensen, V. 1984. *The Humanist at the Court of Nero*, tr. W. Glyn Jones. Edinburgh.

Spanneut, M. 1973. *Permanence du Stoïcisme. De Zénon à Malraux.* Gembloux.

1980. "Permanence de Sénèque le philosophe," *Bulletin de l'Association G. Budé* 39: 361–407.

1990. "Sénèque," in *Dictionnaire de spiritualité* 14: 570–98. Paris.

Stacey, P. 2007. *Roman Monarchy and the Renaissance Prince.* Cambridge.

2011a. "*Hispania* and Royal Humanism in Alfonsine Naples," *Mediterranean Historical Review* 26.1: 51–65.

2011b. "The Sovereign Person in Senecan Political Theory," *Republics of Letters: A Journal for the Study of Knowledge, Politics, and the Arts* 2.2: http://rofl. stanford.edu/node/98.

2014. "The Princely Republic," *Journal of Roman Studies* 104: 133–54.

Star, C. 2012. *The Empire of the Self: Self-Command and Political Speech in Seneca and Petronius*. Baltimore.

Stewart, J. 1997. "Challenging Prescriptions for Discourse: Seneca's Use of Paradox and Oxymoron," *Mosaic* 30: 1–17.

Steyns, D. 1907. *Étude sur les métaphores et les comparaisons dans les oeuvres en prose de Sénèque le philosophe*. Ghent.

Stok, F. 2000. "La discreta fortuna delle *Naturales Quaestiones*," *Giornale italiano di filologia* 52: 349–73.

Striker, G. 1996a. "Plato's Socrates and the Stoics," in P. Vander Waerdt, ed., *The Socratic Movement*, 241–51. Ithaca. Reprinted in *Essays on Hellenistic Epistemology and Ethics*, 316–24. Cambridge.

1996b. *Essays on Hellenistic Epistemology and Ethics*. Cambridge.

Sullivan, J. P. 1968. *The Satyricon of Petronius. A Literary Study*. Bloomington and London.

1985. *Literature and Politics in the Age of Nero*. Ithaca.

Summers, W. C. 1910. *Select Letters of Seneca*. London.

Sutton, D. F. 1986. *Seneca on the Stage*. Leiden.

Syme, R. 1958. *Tacitus*. Oxford.

Taoka, Y. 2011. "Quintilian, Seneca, *imitatio*: Re-Reading *Institutio oratoria* 10.1.125–31," *Arethusa* 44: 123–37.

Tarrant, R. J. 1978. "Senecan Drama and Its Antecedents," *Harvard Studies in Classical Philology* 82: 213–63.

1983. "The Younger Seneca: *Tragedies*," in L. D. Reynolds, ed., *Texts and Transmission: A Survey of the Latin Classics*, 378–81. Oxford.

ed. 1985. *Seneca's Thyestes*. Atlanta.

1995. "Greek and Roman in Seneca's Tragedies," *Harvard Studies in Classical Philology* 97: 215–30.

2006. "Seeing Seneca Whole?" in K. Volk and G. D. Williams, eds., *Seeing Seneca Whole*, 1–18. Leiden and Boston.

Tarrète, A. 2004. "Sénèque (Lucius Annaeus Seneca)," in P. Desan, *Dictionnaire de Michel de Montaigne*, 904–8. Paris.

Thévenaz, P. 1944. "L'intériorité chez Sénèque," in *Mélanges offerts à M. Max Niedermann à l'occasion de son soixante-dixième anniversaire*, 189–94. Paris. Reprinted in A. Traina, ed., *Seneca: letture critiche*, 91–6. Milan, 1976.

1976. *Seneca: letture critiche*, 91–6. Milan.

Tilmouth, C. 2009. "Shakespeare's Open Consciences," *Renaissance Studies* 23.4: 501–15.

Too, Y. L. 1994. "Educating Nero: A Reading of Seneca's *Epistles*," in J. Elsner and J. Masters, eds., *Reflections of Nero*, 211–24. London.

Torre, C. 2000. Il matrimonio del sapiens. *Ricerche sul De matrimonio di Seneca*. Genoa.

Torre, C., ed. 2008. Martini Bracarensis De ira. *Introduzione, testo, traduzione e commento*. Rome.

Traina, A. 1987. *Lo stile 'drammatico' del filosofo Seneca* (4ᵗʰ ed). Bologna.

2006. "*Obseruatio sui*: sul linguaggio dell'interiorità nel *De tranquillitate animi* di Seneca," in C. Santini, L. Zurli, and L. Cardinali, Concentus ex dissonis: *Scritti in onore di Aldo Setaioli*, 29–49. Naples.

Trapp, M., ed. 2003. *Greek and Latin Letters, an Anthology*. Cambridge.

Trillitzsch, W. 1962. *Senecas Beweisführung*. Berlin.

1965. "Erasmus und Seneca," *Philologus* 109: 270–93.

1967. "Seneca im literarischen Urteil der Antike." Thesis. Amsterdam.

1971. *Seneca im literarischen Urteil der Antike*. I. Darstellung; II. *Quellensammlung (Testimonien)*. Amsterdam.

1978. "Seneca Tragicus – Nachleben und Beurteiling im lateinischen Mittelalter von der Spätantike bis zum Renaissancehumanismus," *Philologus* 122: 120–36.

1981. "Der Agamemnonstoff bei Aischylos, Seneca und in der *Orestis tragoedia* des Dracontius," in G. Allegri, M. Bellincioni, G. Pisi, and G. Scarpat, eds., *Quattro studi latini (a Vittore Pisani per il suo 82° compleanno)*, 268–75. Parma.

Trinacty, C. 2014. *Senecan Tragedy and the Reception of Augustan Poetry*. Oxford and New York.

Twain, M. 1898. *Following the Equator: A Journey around the World*. Hartford.

Ueding, G., ed. 2007. *Historisches Wörterbuch der Rhetorik*, vol. 8. Tübingen.

Verbeke, G. 1983. *The Presence of Stoicism in Medieval Thought*. Washington.

Vernant, J.-P., and P. Vidal-Naquet. 1990. *Myth and Tragedy in Ancient Greece*, tr. J. Lloyd. New York.

Versnel, H. 1993. "Two Carnivalesque Princes: Augustus and Claudius and the Ambiguity of Saturnalian Imagery," in S. Döpp, ed., *Karnevaleske Phänomene in antiken und nachantiken Kulturen und Literaturen, Bochumer Altertumswissenschaftliches Colloquium* 13, 99–122. Trier.

Veyne, P. 2003. *Seneca. The Life of a Stoic*, tr. David Sullivan. New York and London.

Villa, C. 2000. "Le tragedie di Seneca nel Trecento," in P. Parroni, *Seneca e il suo tempo*, 469–80. Rome.

Villari, P. 1895–97. *Niccolò Machiavelli e i suoi tempi, illustrati con nuovi documenti*, 3 vols. Milan.

Villey, P. 1933. *Les sources et l'évolution des Essais de Montaigne* (2nd ed.). 2 vols. Paris.

Viparelli, V. 2000. *Il senso e non-senso del tempo in Seneca*. Naples.

Voelke, A.-J. 1973. *L'Idée de volonté dans le stoicisme*. Paris.

Vogel, M. 2006. *Commentatio mortis: 2Kor 5,1–10 auf dem Hintergrund antiker ars moriendi*. Göttingen.

Vogt, K. 2008. *Law, Reason, and the Cosmic City: Political Philosophy in the Early Stoa*. Oxford.

Volk, K. 2006. "Cosmic Disruption in Seneca's *Thyestes*: Two Ways of Looking at an Eclipse," in K. Volk and G. D. Williams, eds., *Seeing Seneca Whole*, 183–200. Leiden.

Volk, K., and G. Williams, eds. 2006. *Seeing Seneca Whole: Perspectives on Philosophy, Poetry and Politics*. Leiden.

Von Albrecht, M. 1999. "Momenti della presenza di Seneca nella letteratura tedesca," in I. Dionigi, ed., *Seneca nella coscienza dell'Europa*, 262–98. Milan.

2000. "Sulla lingua e lo stile de Seneca," in P. Parroni, ed., *Seneca e il suo tempo*, 227–47. Rome.

2004. *Wort und Wandlung: Senecas Lebenskunst.* Leiden and Boston.
Von Hesberg, H. 1999. "The King on Stage," in B. Bergmann and C. Kondoleon, eds., *The Art of Ancient Spectacle,* 65–76. New Haven.
Vottero, D., ed. 1990. Seneca, *Questioni naturali.* I classici greci e latini. Milan.
Vottero, D., ed. 1998. L. Anneo Seneca, *I frammenti.* Pubblicazioni del Dipartimento di Filologia, Linguistica e Tradizione Classica 10. Bologna.
Wanke, C. 1978. "Die französische Literatur," in E. Lefèvre, ed., *Der Einfluß Senecas auf das europäische Drama,* 211–20. Darmstadt.
Weber, H. 1895. *De Senecae philosophi dicendi genere Bioneo.* Diss. Marburg.
Weber, S. 2004. *Theatricality as Medium.* New York.
Weinreich, O. 1923. Senecas Apocolocyntosis. *Die Satire auf Tod, Himmel- und Höllenfahrt des Kaesers Claudius.* Berlin.
Westman, R. 1961. *Das Futurpartizip als Ausdrucksmittel bei Seneca.* Helsinki.
White, P. 2010. *Cicero in Letters.* Oxford.
Whitehorne, J. E. G. 1969. "The Elder Seneca: A Review of Past Work," *Prudentia* 1: 14–27.
Whitton, C. L. 2010. "Pliny, *Epistles* 8.14: Senate, Slavery, and the *Agricola*," *Journal of Roman Studies* 100: 118–39.
   2013. "Seneca, *Apocolocyntosis*," in E. Buckley and M. Dinter, eds., *A Companion to the Neronian Age,* 151–69. Chichester, UK and Malden, MA.
Wildberger, J. 2014. "The Epicurus Trope and the Construction of a 'Letter Writer' in Seneca's Epistulae morales," in J. Wildberger and M. Colish, eds., *Seneca Philosophus,* 431–65. Berlin and Boston.
Williams, B. 1993. *Shame and Necessity.* Berkeley.
Williams, G. D. 1994. "Nero, Seneca and Stoicism in the *Octavia*," in J. Elsner and J. Masters, eds., *Reflections of Nero,* 178–95. London.
   ed. 2003. *Seneca: De Otio, De Brevitate Vitae.* Cambridge.
   2012. *The Cosmic Viewpoint: A Study of Seneca's Natural Questions.* Oxford.
   2014. "Double Vision and Cross-Reading in Seneca's *Epistuale Morales* and *Naturales Quaestiones*," in J. Wildberger and M. Colish, eds., *Seneca Philosophus,* 135–65. Berlin and New York.
Williams, G. 1978. *Change and Decline: Roman Literature in the Early Empire.* Berkeley and Los Angeles.
Williamson, G. 1951. *The Senecan Amble.* London.
Wilson, M. 1983. "The Tragic Mode of Seneca's *Troades*," in A. J. Boyle, ed., *Seneca Tragicus,* 27–60. Berwick.
   1987. "Seneca's Epistles to Lucilius: A Revaluation," *Ramus* 16: 102–21. Reprinted in J. G. Fitch, ed. *Seneca* (Oxford Readings in Classical Studies), 59–83. Oxford, 2008.
   2001. "Seneca's *Epistles* reclassified," in S. J. Harrison, ed., *Texts, Ideas, and the Classics: Scholarship, Theory, and Classical Literature,* 164–87. Oxford.
Wiseman, T. P. 2009. *Remembering the Roman People: Essays on Late-Republican Politics and Literature.* Oxford.
   2012. "Cicero and the Body Politic," *Politica antica* 2: 133–40.
Woodman, A. J. 1993. "Amateur Dramatics at the Court of Nero: *Annals* 15.48–74," in T. J. Luce and A. J. Woodman, eds., *Tacitus and the Tacitean Tradition,* 104–28. Princeton.

Wright, J. R. G. 1974. "Form and Content in the *Moral Essays*," in C. D. N. Costa, ed., *Seneca*, 39–69. London.

Young, R. V. 2011. *Justus Lipsius' Concerning Constancy*. Medieval and Renaissance texts and studies 389. Tempe.

Zanker, P. 1988. *The Power of Images in the Age of Augustus*. Ann Arbor.

Zanobi, A. 2008. "The Influence of Pantomime on Seneca's Tragedies," in E. Hall and R. Wyles, eds., *New Directions in Ancient Pantomime*, 227–57. Oxford.

Zimmerman, D. 2000. "Making Do: Troubling Stoic Tendencies in an Otherwise Compelling Theory of Autonomy," *Canadian Journal of Philosophy* 30: 25–53.

Ziolkowski, T. 2004. "Seneca: A New German Icon?" *International Journal of the Classical Tradition* 11: 47–77.

Zissos, A. 2008. "Shades of Virgil: Seneca's *Troades*," *Materiali e Discussioni* 61: 191–210.

Zissos, A., and I. Gildenhard. 1999. "Problems of Time in *Metamorphoses* 2," in P. Hardie, A. Barchiesi, and S. Hinds, eds., *Ovidian Transformations: Essays on Ovid's Metamorphoses and Its Reception*, 31–47. Cambridge.

Zwierlein, O. 1966. *Die Rezitationsdramen Senecas*. Meisenheim am Glan.

INDEX

Aalders, G. J. D., 71n8, 74n19
Abbott, K. M., 276
Abel, K., 58n18, 58n19, 63n32, 173
Accius, 30
Achilles, 35, 38, 168, 169, 170, 172, 199n2, 210
Actium, 126
Adams, R. M., 161n3
addressees
  in Seneca's prose works, 54, 55, 56, 59, 61, 64, 65, 219
adfectus, 174, 177, 183, 193, 228, 229, 231
Aebutius Liberalis, 59, 59n23
Aedui, 101, 104
Aeschylus, *Oresteia*, 166n37
aetiology, 85, 157
Aetna, 260
affectus. See adfectus
Agrippina, 17, 20, 20n11, 22, 23, 26, 93, 97, 97n20, 97n21, 102, 103, 128, 187, 195, 263, 312, 316
Ahl, F., 31, 31n8, 32n10, 33n15
aidos, 199, 200, 206
Albanese, G., 279n15, 283n49
Alexander, W. H., 138, 138n16, 138n18, 138n19, 167n46
Allen, P. S., 284n55, 284n56, 284n57
altercatio, 58, 58n15
Althoff, J., 248n46, 248n47, 251
Altman, J., 46, 46n29
Ambrosius, 268, 274n21
amicitia. See Seneca, view of friendship
André, J. M., 251, 305n9
Andrew, E., 289n1
anger, 27, 31, 36, 72, 73, 103, 110, 143, 148, 157, 175, 176, 177, 178, 179, 180, 181, 182, 183, 230, 231, 231n34, 232n35, 247, 296. *See also* Seneca, *On anger*

apatheia, 178, 184, 199, 200, 206, 270, 271
Appius Claudius Caecus, 101
Appius Claudius Pulcher, 100
Apuleius, 55n2, 55n5, 55n6
Aquinas, 291, 291n10
Arce, J., 101n33
Areus, 62, 111, 115, 163
Ariston of Chios, 213, 214
Aristotle, 9, 64n37, 74, 76, 77, 154, 174, 176, 177, 179, 181, 202, 203, 204, 207, 209, 211, 213, 214, 215, 226, 229, 230, 237, 243, 272, 279, 280
  Meteorologica, 84
  Nicomachean Ethics, 44, 44n19, 49, 176, 203, 209
  on anger, 176
  on emotions, 178
  on shame, 203, 204
  on the mean, 179
  Politics, 71
  Rhetoric, 150, 151, 176
Armisen-Marchetti, M., 7, 43n10, 43n14, 52, 90n21, 124n5, 125n8, 133, 134, 146n50, 149, 152n6, 153n7, 160, 165n26, 189n4, 192n12, 193n15, 194n19, 265
Arnobius, 270, 271
Artaud, A., 29, 308
Ascanius, 116, 117, 118
askesis. See meditatio
Asmis, E., 2, 9, 44n25, 193, 214n1, 224, 240n3, 240n9
assent, in Seneca, 225, 230, 232
Astyanax, 35, 36, 116, 117, 118, 170n64, 171
Athenodorus of Tarsus, 78, 79, 80
Atreus, 30, 33, 34, 37, 38, 38n32, 111, 167, 167n44, 168n49, 182, 260

Thomas More, 161
Thrasea Paetus, 1, 165, 195, 197, 198
Tiberius, 24, 26, 26n20, 97n20,
    115, 130
Tillich, Paul, 11, 307
Tilmouth, C., 302
Timagenes, 110
time
    inversions of, under Nero, 124
    reversed, 125, 130, 131, 133
    treatment in Seneca, 122
Tiridates, 166
Too, Y. L., 133
Traina, A., 43n13, 137n8, 143, 144n37,
    145, 145n45, 145n46, 145n48, 146n49,
    147, 147n56, 149, 160, 162n9, 189n6,
    191n11, 243n24, 244n27, 266n2
translation
    of Stoic terminology, 155
Trapp, M., 41n1, 43n18, 47n32,
    47n33
Trevet, N., 281
Trillitzsch, W., 265, 266, 266n1, 276,
    280n29, 284n54
Trimalchio, 124, 259, 261
Trinacty, C., 116, 121, 164n19, 169n54
Tubero, 225
Twain, M., 176

unity of the self, in Stoicism, 190

Valerius Maximus, 99
Varchi, Benedetto, 291
Varius Rufus, 31, 112
Varro, 96, 96n14, 96n17, 104, 104n41, 105,
    260, 269, 275
Varro Atacinus, 112
velle, 224, 236, See voluntas
Velleius Paterculus, 97n20
Verbeke, G., 279n20
verecundia, 207
Vergil, 33n13, 40, 43, 61, 90, 111, 113, 114,
    115, 117, 118, 119, 121, 132, 172, 248,
    258, 262, 264
    Aeneid, 31, 39, 40, 100, 100n29, 112,
        113, 114, 115, 116, 117, 118, 119,
        121, 167, 167n46, 169, 169n56, 172,
        172n75
    Eclogues, 113
    Georgics, 71n9, 90, 113, 167, 169n56,
        169n57
Vernant, J.-P., 31n9

Versnel, H., 96n18
Vespasian, 95n10
Veyne, P., 21, 25n17, 26n20, 28, 46n26,
    46n28, 80n42, 189, 198
Vidal-Naquet, P., 31n9
view from above, 88
vigilance, Stoic, 136
Villa, C., 302
Villari, P., 290n2
Villey, P., 286n70
Vincent of Beauvais, 17
Viparelli, V., 124n5, 134
virtus, 234, 242, 280
Viterbo, Giovanni da, 290
Voelke, A. J., 229n29, 236n70
Vogel, M., 95n10
Vogt, K., 76n29
Volk, K., 168n49
voluntas, 176, 177, 231, 236, 237
voluptas, 50, 182, 241, 242, 243, 249
von Albrecht, M., 137n8, 396n11,
    316n26, 317
von Hesberg, H., 167n39
von Kleist, Ewald Christian, 17, 315
Vottero, D., 49n37, 57n11, 57n14, 58n18,
    62n30, 82n2, 82n3, 82n4, 84, 84n12,
    91, 118, 121, 269, 270n10, 270n11,
    270n12, 270n7, 272n16, 273, 273n18,
    274, 274n19, 275

Walter of Burley, 279
Walter, P., 276
Wanke, C, 310n19
Weber, H., 139n23, 162n11
Weinreich, O., 94n5, 96n16, 98n25
White, P., 47n32
Whitton, C. L., 59n23, 105
William of Conches, 280
William of Saint-Thierry, 280
Williams, B., 199n3
Williams, G., 2, 3, 6, 7, 8, 43n13, 51n45,
    52n48, 54, 59n20, 59n21, 59n23,
    60n24, 61n26, 63n32, 63n33, 79n36,
    79n38, 80n41, 83, 84n12, 86n16,
    91, 120, 121, 133, 162n9, 173, 223,
    227n19, 245n31, 246n35, 247n40,
    248n44, 250n49, 251, 267n5
Williamson, G., 286n67, 287n74, 288
willing. See voluntas
Wilson, M., 42n4, 43n17, 52, 65, 66, 66n41,
    67, 135n1, 136, 136n4, 137n8, 144n42,
    149, 169n53

Cambridge Companions to...

TOPICS